THE APPEALS OF COMMUNISM

THE APPEALS

OF COMMUNISM

BY GABRIEL A. ALMOND

PRINCIPAL COLLABORATORS:

HERBERT E. KRUGMAN

ELSBETH LEWIN

HOWARD WRIGGINS

PRINCETON UNIVERSITY PRESS,
PRINCETON, NEW JERSEY

To D. K. A.

". . . and let her own works praise her in the gates."

FOREWORD

THIS absorbing study of the appeals and vulnerabilities of Communism by Professor Almond and his collaborators is the first in the new series of books to be published under the auspices of the Center of International Studies of Princeton University. It is a most appropriate introduction for the series since it exemplifies in generous degree the characteristics of the research operations which the Center seeks to promote. The author has brought to bear on a crucial political problem the best of current knowledge and techniques of investigation. He has examined a huge amount of evidence and has drawn from it a number of propositions which are directly relevant to the understanding of this extraordinary phenomenon and to the appraisal of various policy alternatives in dealing with it. While he is careful to avoid any overclaiming as to the significance of his findings, he has nevertheless demonstrated quite clearly how the insights of the scholar can throw fresh light on one of the paramount issues of the age.

In the main body of the study Professor Almond lays the groundwork for a set of hypotheses about the reliability of different types of Communist party members and the conditions which are likely to put their loyalty to the party under strain. In deference to the canons of objective inquiry, he withheld until the end of his inquiry any appraisal of the ethical and political implications of his material. The reader will find these carefully analyzed in the final chapter.

To arrive at a trustworthy account of the Communist movement it is necessary to see it in its many different manifestations. As the present study shows, Communist parties tend to take on the character of the societies and cultures in which they operate. This volume deals with two of the main types of Communism—the small deviational movements of the United States and England, and the mass working-class parties of France and Italy. The recent spread of Communism in the non-Western areas represents so menacing a development that it is deserving of special attention. A study of the Communist movement in Malaya has been undertaken by Dr. Lucian W. Pye, of the Center staff, and is planned for this series in the near future.

The Center of International Studies was established at Princeton University in 1951. Its basic purpose is to bring to bear on the elucidation of foreign policy problems the full resources of available knowledge and modern methods of analysis. To this end it engages in and publishes research directed toward the development of systematic, disciplined, and comprehensive appraisals of the varied aspects of international relations, with special emphasis on the foreign policy of the United States. The members of the Center work at all times in close association, but each member is free to formulate his research projects in his own way and each published study represents an individual analysis of a problem.

FREDERICK S. DUNN
Director

Center of International Studies
Princeton University
June 15, 1954

PREFACE AND ACKNOWLEDGMENTS

THIS is a study of why people join the Communist movement and why they leave it. The findings of such a study may serve two useful purposes. First, if we can throw light on the kinds of social situations and attitudes which contribute to susceptibility to Communism, we may increase our understanding of the vulnerability of the free world to Communist penetration. Second, if we can discover those aspects of the Communist experience which create dissatisfaction among party members and contribute to defection, we may be in a position to suggest the kinds of weaknesses and vulnerabilities which are to be found within the Communist movement. Both of these contributions may provide useful leads in appraising the various policy approaches to the Communist problem.

We began this study with the assumption that the Communist movement is not the homogeneous community of professional revolutionaries celebrated in the Leninist and Stalinist classics. It was our expectation, rather, that the various national parties, social class groups, ranks, and generations of party members would all differ from one another in the ways in which they perceive and experience the movement, in the kinds of problems of assimilation that confront them, in their reasons for defection, and in their patterns of defection and readjustment. This study will therefore make a contribution to the understanding of types of Communists, and may serve to correct popular and oversimplified impressions.

Since the structure of this study is somewhat complex, a brief explanation of the purposes of the various parts of the book and of the ways in which they relate to one another may be in order. It is hardly a novel contribution to the understanding of the Communist movement to point out that there are significant differences between the experienced and "steeled" inner core of the party and the mass of the rank and file. But no systematic studies have been made of the ways in which these strata of the party differ. Part I is intended to provide formal "models" of these levels of the party—the *esoteric* and the *exoteric*, as we have come to call them. They are formal models, since they are not based upon direct observation of the party at its various levels, but on an analysis of the Communist system of communication. Thus in Part I we first analyze the ideal qualities of the fully indoctrinated and assimilated Communist as these qualities appear in the works of Lenin and Stalin. We then compare the qualities attributed to Communists in the doctrinal classics with the patterns described in the contemporary esoteric and mass media of the party. These comparisons tell us something about the problems of assimilation into the Communist movement as derived from authoritative Communist sources. It may be assumed, by way of hypothesis, that what *is* said in the inner media of the movement and *not* said at the mass level of Communist communication is what has to be learned by the Communist neophyte if he is to move into the inner party.

Though these formal models are not to be taken as the "operating reality" of the movement, they proved to be useful as analytical tools again and again in the remainder of the study. Thus the ideal properties attributed to the inner Communist suggested hypotheses as to the kinds of persons who would be likely to assimilate rapidly into the inner party. The discrepancies between the inner and outer models of the party suggested hypotheses as to the causes of dissatisfaction with and defection from the Communist movement.

Part II is an analysis of how the party is perceived and experienced by persons who have been "through it," so to speak. This is based on our collection of depth interviews with former party members. Here we are concerned with two central problems. Scholars have long been interested in the question of the role of Communist ideology in influencing Communist practice and behavior. By comparing the ways in which the movement is perceived and experienced with the ways in which the movement is represented in Communist ideology and propaganda, we are in a position to suggest those aspects of Communist doctrine relating to the proper behavior of party members which survive in the present-day Communist movement, and those aspects which have ceased to have meaning in the actual conduct of party affairs. In addition, we are in a position to contrast the ways in which the party was perceived and experienced by former party members from different countries, generations, social classes, and official ranks. Thus we are not only able to compare doctrine and practice in general terms, but also to discuss the discrepancies between doctrine and practice characteristic of different kinds of party members.

Part I of the study therefore establishes the formal dimensions of the Communist movement and Part II locates a number of different types of party members within these dimensions. Parts III and IV are concerned with the actual processes of assimilation into and defection from the Communist movement, and with describing how these processes vary from one national context to the next, from one class to the next, from one generation to the next, and among the various ranks of the party. These parts of the study generalize from the career profiles of the various types of Communists represented in our sample, describing the kinds of economic, social, and religious backgrounds from which they come, the different patterns of susceptibility to Communism which they manifest, their typical patterns of dissatisfaction with the party, and their peculiar styles of defection from the party and readjustment to the outside society. Since emotional conflict and maladjustment appear to be especially significant factors affecting susceptibility among middle-class Americans and Englishmen, an intensive analysis of the ways in which neurotic needs enter into decisions to join the party is given in Chapter 10.

A final chapter draws the significant findings of the study together and attempts to appraise the various policy approaches to the Communist problem. Because of the richness of the data on which the findings of the study are based, this critique of policy toward the Communist movement may suggest new emphases and more discriminating approaches than have previously been possible.

The findings of this study are based on two types of data which have long had widespread use in interpretations of Communism. Much of our information about the Communist movement is based on Communist doctrine and propaganda on the one hand, and on the confessions and exposés of former party members on the other. Since dependence on these kinds of data is to some extent inescapable, we sought to make a more systematic and painstaking use of them than had previously been made. Thus, rather than limit ourselves to the Communist classics for a formal picture of the desired qualities and attributes of Communists, we also sampled the various levels of Communist communication, the mass media, and the theoretical journals. And, rather than accept the published writings of former party members, which are relatively few in number and primarily representative of the experiences of Communist intellectuals, we selected a sample of former Communists which included Frenchmen, Italians, Englishmen, and Americans; workers and middle-class; those who had joined in the period before the Popular Front, and those who had joined after; and those who had served in the various echelons of the party, the high, the low, and the rank and file.

The numbers included in the sample are small, but the difficulties in locating suitable informants were great. The total number of respondents was 221. Of these, 64 were American, 50 were British, 56 were French, and 51 Italian. One hundred and fifteen had joined the party before 1935, and 106 in later years; 111 were working-class and 110 were middle-class (primarily intellectuals) in occupational background; 51 had held top party posts, 73 middle and low positions, and 97 were rank and filers. The great majority were persons who left in the 1940's and later.

In general, an effort was made to include among our respondents a large proportion of persons who had had a long tenure in the party, who had held middle- and high-ranking positions in the party hierarchy, and who had left in more recent years. This type of defector therefore probably appears among our respondents with greater frequency than would be the case in a random sample of former party members. Most of the persons approached by our interviewers agreed to be interviewed. Thus, in respects other than those indicated, this is not a special selection of ex-Communists.

The question of the particular ways in which defectors differ from persons still remaining in the party is far more complex. Part IV, which deals with the process of defection, provides the data from which a more precise answer to this question can be given. Here the point may be made that in most of our cases the reason for defection was some internal party controversy, or some impingement of party policy on the interests and values of an individual defector or group of defectors. An example of the latter was the imposition of the party line in genetics on British scientists, which created a crisis in the scientific sector of the British party. Most of the scientists were troubled by the controversy, but only some of them defected. Similarly, the Russian campaign against "cosmopolitanism" created conflicts among Jewish party members everywhere, but only some of them left the party in consequence. During general party crises such as the Nazi-Soviet Pact, party members experienced some demoralization, but only some of them defected. This sort of evidence suggests that in general defectors differ in degree, rather than in kind, from those who remain in the party, and that it is not an unsound procedure to formulate hypotheses about the attractions and repulsions of the party from data derived from defectors.

In addition to these interviews with former party members, biographical data were gathered on the present members of the Central Committees of the Communist parties of France, Italy, and the United States. Thus, for such questions as class origin, occupation, education, and age at time of joining the party, it was possible to introduce data on the present Communist leadership and thereby check the validity of findings based on our sample of ex-Communist respondents.

In order to gain insight into the kinds of psychological problems which may lead to joining the party, we interviewed a group of American psychoanalysts who had had Communists as patients. These analysts provided us with thirty-five clinical case histories of Communists. These case histories suggested hypotheses as to the ways in which emotional disorders of one kind or another may contribute to susceptibility.

It is quite clear from the foregoing that the data used in this study fail to fulfill the canons of scientific method. But the scholar who wishes to make a contribution to the understanding of a significant social problem is free to adapt scientific methodology to what is possible, so long as he avoids overstating his case. It can be said of this study that while it makes no claims to statistical validity, it is based on the largest and most carefully selected body of empirical data so far collected on these aspects of the Communist problem.

Not only are the findings based on substantial evidence, but the individual findings have a logical consistency and build up into a coherent theory of assimilation into the Communist movement. When a large body of individual findings cohere in a meaningful system, another kind of test of validity is satisfied. Thus this study is based upon evidence, and the individual items of evidence fit together into a meaningful explanation of the phenomena with which we are concerned.

There is an unhappy tendency for the various disciplines in the social sciences and humanities to make exaggerated claims for their several approaches and methods. In our efforts to gain understanding of a problem as grave as the one with which we are here concerned, there is an obligation to try all methods and to listen with patience to all responsible voices. The approaches and methods used in this study are not represented as better than other methods and approaches. The methods of this study cannot take the place of historical or institutional methods, or of ethical and logical appraisals based on philosophical methods. Its findings can provide grist for these other mills, just as our findings and the interpretations based upon them have been influenced by historical knowledge and philosophical insights.

Since we relied so heavily on the recollections of former

party members as a means of deriving hypotheses about the attitudes and characteristics of persons still in the party, something ought to be said about the methodological implications of this procedure. When we say that our middle-class respondents perceived the party in one way while the working-class respondents perceived it in another way, we are simply suggesting the hypothesis that similar tendencies would be discovered among contemporary middle-class and working-class party members if it were possible to get such information from a statistically valid sample of such party members. It is not out of the question that some of the hypotheses suggested by this study can be tested by direct surveys among certain party groupings in certain areas. Indeed, some of our findings have been confirmed by public opinion surveys in France and Italy.

The former Communist is hardly an unbiased reporter of his own experience. To point out that the faithful Communist would also be a prejudiced informant, although in another direction, does not eliminate the problem, but merely underlines the difficulties of getting reliable firsthand information about the party. Some observations about the characteristics of the ex-Communist population may give us a clearer grasp of the problem of bias. First, it must be kept in mind that the former party members who have written about and published their experiences in the party are not representative of the ex-Communist population as a whole. Their very acts of public confession differentiate them from the great mass of former party members, who from motives of fear, or from particular conceptions of personal dignity, or from lack of skill in expression, remain silent about their experiences. Most of the well-known ex-Communists are intellectuals, and at the very best their analyses of their motives in joining the party or their reasons for leaving it will reflect motives current among their class. They may hardly be taken as representative of working-class or peasant Communists. And since they are so few in number, as compared with the total population of former Communist intellectuals, they may not even be safely viewed as representative of their own groupings.

Several steps were taken in our interviewing program in an effort to limit the impact of bias. First, we sought as many interviews as our resources permitted, and we sought to distribute them regionally and occupationally. Secondly, we avoided those party members who had discussed their experiences publicly and therefore might be viewed as having a commitment to a particular interpretation of their party membership. There were a few exceptions, but an overwhelming majority of our respondents were leading quiet lives. Finally, the type of questions asked deliberately avoided any moral judgment of their behavior or of the movement. The questions drew the respondent into recollecting particular experiences, magnitudes, processes, and atmospheres.

Quite aside from the special element of bias in a group of respondents such as this, the validity of the data is subject to the general limitations of life history and interviewing material. Recollections of the past are unavoidably colored by subsequent experiences, and when these experiences involve disenchantment, shock, and personal suffering, the coloring of the past may be strong indeed. Nevertheless, it is suggested here that the validity of the responses varies with the particular aspect of experience in the party which is being recalled. A respondent who was asked how many evenings out of a week were spent in party activities would probably not be under any great pressure to slant or misrepresent. This would be less true of questions regarding his original motives for joining or his reasons for leaving. In these cases, a respondent's current image of himself may have required that he offer an interpretation of the past consistent with this present image.

A number of further points have to be made about the interviewing situation and its relation to bias. In a number of cases, particularly in France and Italy, respondents were in fear of physical retaliation by the party. This may have inhibited the honesty and spontaneity of some of their responses. In the United States, the high state of public feeling about Communism may have led former party members to overstate their ignorance of the nature of the party at the time of joining and to exaggerate their opposition to party strategy and tactics while in the party and during and after defection. All respondents were promised anonymity, and the private and academic auspices of the study were made clear in every case. In general, the scientific and confidential auspices of the interviewing situation encouraged a rather free flow of self-analysis and recollection. The respondent generally felt free to say favorable things about the party and his experience in it and to reject the current stereotypes.

All of these considerations suggest that any judgments as to the degree and kind of bias would have to discriminate between respondents, the political conditions obtaining at the time of the interviews, and the content of the questions or probes. It would be as indefensible, however, to reject this method of getting data on the party as it would be to accept it without qualification. Obviously, defectors are the most direct and best source of information on the processes of defection from the party and reassimilation into society. Their reliability on other aspects of their experience would vary with the opportunities they had had to observe the particular phenomena in question, the recency of their experiences, their capacity for discriminating observation and detachment, and the like.

The results of this study represent the combined efforts of a group of collaborators. Those mentioned on the title page were associated with the study at its inception and made contributions to the basic theory and research design of the project. Howard Wriggins made the basic study of the model of the Communist militant based upon the Leninist and Stalinist writings. His work appears in full in the form of a doctoral dissertation entitled *The Ideal Image of the Bolshevik Militant* (Department of International Relations, Yale University, 1952). Chapters 1 and 2 of the present book specifically summarize his findings, but the model which he developed was of use throughout the study.

Herbert E. Krugman carried out the interviewing of former party members in the United States, as well as the interviewing of psychoanalysts. He made a major contribution to the development of the interviewing schedules and the training of our foreign interviewers. He also was identified with the project from its inception and made a fundamental contribution to the theory and research design of the study. His analysis of the American data was accepted by the Department of Sociology of Columbia University as a doctoral dissertation under the title, *The Interplay of Social and Psychological Factors in Political Deviance* (Faculty of Political Science, Columbia University, 1952). Part III of the present book was substantially influenced by his prior work.

Elsbeth Lewin carried a major role in the planning and execution of the content analysis of the Communist media, and in the coding, tabulating, and interpretation of the interviewing material.

There were a number of other collaborators whose association with the project was of a more limited duration and of a more specialized character. Violet Cook Lynch began the content analysis of the Communist media and completed the actual coding of the *Daily Worker* editorials. She also prepared a memorandum summarizing the literature of social psychology dealing with radicalism. Louise Tompkins helped in the later stages of coding and tabulating the interviews. Professor Charles Micaud of the University of Virginia did part of the French interviewing and made a study of the organization of the French Communist Party. Robert Holt of Princeton University carried out the biographical study of the Central Committees of the French, Italian, and American Communist parties. The work of Howard Wriggins, Herbert Krugman, Charles Micaud, and Robert Holt has resulted in separate publications.

To the many psychoanalysts who cooperated with the study and who must remain anonymous, a special note of gratitude. I should also like to express my warm thanks to Elmo Wilson and his associates, Mark Abrams and Ernesto Norbedo, for their help in arranging and carrying out the interviewing programs in England and Italy.

My colleagues at Princeton University, Frederick S. Dunn, Hadley Cantril, Hans H. Toch, Marion J. Levy, Jr., Bernard C. Cohen, Lucian W. Pye, Elliott Mishler, and Roger Hilsman, read the manuscript in first draft and gave me invaluable help in matters of organization, substantive interpretation, and style. Professors David Truman of Columbia University and Jerome Bruner of Harvard also gave me the benefit of their thoughtful criticism. Dr. Alexander L. George of the RAND Corporation made a most useful and penetrating criticism of Parts I and II of the study. Jean MacLachlan provided constant editorial advice as the book was being completed, carried out the final editing, and prepared the index.

It is a special pleasure to record again my obligation to Harold D. Lasswell. It was under his direction years ago in the depth of the depression that I first did research on the characteristics of Communist leaders and rank and filers. In addition, the content analyses reported in this study owe much to his pioneering experimentation with this method of studying communications and communications systems. More recently, Nathan Leites' highly original analyses of Lenin's and Stalin's writings contributed to the methods and hypotheses of this study, in particular to the construction of the model of the Communist militant carried out by Howard Wriggins.

This study was made possible by funds granted by Carnegie Corporation of New York. That Corporation is not, however, the author, owner, publisher, or proprietor of this publication, and is not to be understood as approving by virtue of its grant any of the statements made or views expressed herein.

GABRIEL A. ALMOND

CONTENTS

PART I

THE STRUCTURE OF COMMUNIST COMMUNICATION

CHAPTER 1

THE COMMUNIST MILITANT: ENDS AND MEANS

POLITICAL MOVEMENTS, like other social groupings, place certain standards of conduct before their memberships. A civic organization such as the League of Women Voters confronts its members with a partly explicit, partly implicit model of an active and alert female citizen who employs her political influence intelligently with regard to the whole range of political issues, from the simple to the complex and from the immediate to the remote. Affiliation with the League implies an acceptance in some degree of these ideals, and a will to conform to them. The coalitions of groupings which make up the major American parties similarly confront their participants with ideals of behavior and aspiration. But these models are as various as are the constituent elements within the larger movements. They are in conflict with one another, and they are in constant process of change. Affiliation with one of the major parties involves a commitment of only a part of the individual, and furthermore it is only a tentative commitment to a set of standards which are vague and largely implicit. In most cases the commitment may be withdrawn without suffering heavy sanctions.

Most Americans find themselves involved in a variety of associations, each one setting forth its ideals, and each one making its claims for loyalty. A workman may be a parent and in this capacity be exposed to a variety of parental images transmitted to him through such organizations as the school, the church, and the various groups of which he is a member, as well as through the media of communication. Thus, even as parent, he has a good measure of leeway and may fashion an ideal of parenthood from among a number of competing ideal-images, and may indeed alter this image in response to shifting pressures or growing insight. He may be a Catholic and endeavor to conform in varying degree to the Catholic image of man. But even in relation to this most homogeneous and compelling of religious associations, he may without great risk engage in a certain amount of picking and choosing without provoking the admittedly severe sanctions which the Catholic Church has at its disposal. In his occupational capacity he is exposed to the ideals set by his trade, his management, and his trade union, and here again he has a range of discretion in selecting his patterns. Similarly, in his political affiliations, his social relations, and his recreational life, he is not required to make binding commitments to exclusive ideals and obligations. Because the various associations and groupings compete with one another for his loyalty and adherence, there is a very real sense in which he is master and can make choices, as well as fulfill demands which are made of him in a spirit and degree which are in good part a matter of his own decision. Furthermore, the images confronting him conflict with one another, leave certain problems of conduct unresolved, or specifically invite him to participate in the ideal-setting process. Thus, to make a whole man out of the various roles, associations, and ideals which confront him, he cannot avoid a certain measure of creativity and invention. A man, however aesthetically unimpressive his job may be, undoubtedly makes something out of himself which is greater than his social parts.

This is not intended to minimize the compulsive elements which are obviously present in American society, but rather to suggest that its real content of freedom derives from a pluralism of compulsions, a system which limits the impact of any particular compulsion, which offers escape and refuge, and which ensures a range of choice. While the doctrines of the free competition of ideas and ideals and freedom of association are as illusory as is the doctrine of the free market, the pluralism of ideals and of association is real indeed, and is the very flesh and blood of the Western heritage.

In contrast to the multiplicity of models confronting men in Western societies, and in contrast to the vague and largely implicit character of most of them, the Communist movement confronts its membership with an exclusive and explicit model. This model may not be and, in most cases, is not visible at the point of first recruitment. On the contrary, at the point of entrance into the movement, the party is all things to all men. It tempts the workman with an image of the alert and militant trade unionist, concerned with the pragmatic and immediate needs of the working class. It confronts the peasant with the ideal of the militant defender of the rights of the small farmer and farm laborer. It offers the intellectual the tempting model of the artist or writer employing his talents effectively in the cause of social justice. It offers the native colonial the image of the militant patriot driving the imperialists before him, wiping out the indignities of centuries of exploitation and humiliation. And before all potential party recruits and supporters, it holds up the generalized image of the militant and effective reformer locked in battle with injustice.

These images are the public or exoteric images of the Communist movement; they are the tools of agitation especially fashioned to suit the susceptibilities of particular audiences. Once drawn into the movement, the neophyte is exposed in varying degrees to the esoteric model of the Communist militant. Perhaps for most of the rank and file of the Communist movement—and this is particularly true in the mass parties—this exposure to the esoteric model is quite superficial, and in this sense they are not true Communist militants. They have incorporated the agitational or tactical conceptions of the party; they are not the "cadres."

The process of recruitment in the Communist movement has at least two stages. The first is that of attraction to one of the many agitational representations. The second stage, that of training and testing in action, screens out those recruits who have suitable qualities and potentialities. It is these elements which are effectively exposed to the esoteric model of the Communist militant.

This esoteric model is related to the set of qualities and characteristics attributed to "good Communists" to be found in the Communist classics, but it is by no means identical with it. While this doctrinal model may be inferred from the Communist classics and theoretical literature, the real or operational model is not fully explained or elaborated any-where. As in other organizations, it is assimilated from the environment through experience with party processes and activities. It is the set of rules which is learned the hard way as the recruit moves up the party hierarchy and discovers how to win approval and avoid alienating the powerful.

Part II, based on interviews with former Communist party members, will attempt to describe certain aspects of this operational model of the Communist militant. The present and following chapter present certain aspects of the doctrinal model which have been inferred from the classical writings. An examination of the picture of the Communist militant which emerges from an analysis of the Communist theoretical literature is valuable for two reasons. First, selected works from this literature are used within the party in its training schools. The standards of conduct emphasized in these docu-ments are constantly brought to bear upon young recruits, so that they may be said to constitute an explicit set of ideals to which Communist aspirants are exposed. Second, the Com-munist classics and theoretical literature present the model of the Communist militant in its most ideal and favorable ver-sion from "unimpeachable sources." Communists cannot quarrel with the pattern which emerges save insofar as they can demonstrate a manipulation or misrepresentation of the sources.

The Emergence of the Model of the Communist Militant

The ideal image of the Communist militant bears the im-pression of both Western European and Russian influences. The anarchism of the Marxist utopia represented an extreme case of the rational humanism of the Enlightenment and the eighteenth-century revolutions. Man, through his reason, would emancipate himself from oppressive institutions, and release his great potentialities for humane achievement. But, unlike the utopian liberals and socialists who believed in the self-transformation of mankind through the appeal of reason, Marxist doctrine was preeminently concerned with effective means. Marx rejected the naive optimism of the nineteenth-century utopian conception of man and the extreme voluntarism of its view of the historical process. In place of the abstract conception of man as a free agent capable of remaking his attitudes in accordance with the dictates of his reason, Marx developed the concept of men as grouped in social classes which set the premises of their attitudes, and restricted the role of reason to that of discovering and advancing the interests of their particular class. Men acted inescapably as members of economic functional groups, and these groups rose and fell as material technologies changed. The social class brought into being by the new technology had the future on its side and would inevitably supplant the masters of the old. Instead of a naive optimism, Marx developed, in the guise of a new realism, a kind of optimism that stressed conflict and costs. Instead of a simple and unequivocal faith in progress, he offered a dialectic of progress that emphasized the persistent conflict between progress and reaction, in which progress triumphed but only with costs. This did not in any sense diminish the brightness of the vision of the socialist utopia. On the contrary, it acquired a kind of special apocalyptic shine by virtue of the very catastrophe which had to precede it. It was a significant element of the strong appeal of the Marxist millennium that it was an earned utopia, which, like goods that are scarce and have costs, perhaps provides more satisfaction than one that is free. At any rate, Marxist utopianism appeared to rest on a more realistic appraisal of the social and historical process and fitted the mood of the second half of the nineteenth century, which, assimilating the lessons of the past, had begun to despair of rational voluntarism as a way out of evils and oppressions. Marxism offered the promise of human emancipation in a setting of "realism" and with a heavy stress on effectiveness. In order to be effective pursuers of the ultimate human good, men needed a science of the social and historical process. This Marxism proceeded to offer in the form of the materialistic conception of history, the doctrine of class struggle, and the doctrine of the culmination of this process in the dictatorship of the proletariat, the last class dictatorship before man's final emancipation.

The image of the socialist or Communist militant in Marx was of a leader, guide, and organizer of the proletariat, of an individual who educated the working class in its function of conquering political power. The conception of the revolutionary militant which emerged in the writing of Marx and Engels had much in common with the later Leninist and Stalinist doctrinal conceptions, but also differed in very fundamental ways.[1] Revolutionary militants in Marxism were conceived as "scientific socialists" acting in full knowledge of the laws of history and the social process. They were above all rational calculators of the effectiveness of the various means available to achieve the dictatorship of the proletariat. They were the vanguard of the working class; they were good organizers and tacticians. Their allegiance was to the international proletariat and not to their own nations. And they were the builders of the new, the humane society. All of these elements are to be found in the Marxist image of the revolutionary, as well as in the Leninist-Stalinist model.

The most significant general similarity between the images was the great emphasis on means and tactics. The scientific revolutionary differed from his utopian predecessors in avoiding all "pointless" discussion of the ultimate ends of his actions. These would be taken care of by the historical process itself. He turned away from daydreaming about the future and devoted himself to the hard task of analyzing the political situation and determining his tactics accordingly. This great emphasis on the rational or scientific tactician was already present in Marx. The legitimate goal was the establishment of the dictatorship of the working class, and the qualities required in a good member of the vanguard had to do with clarifying, preparing, and leading the working class from

[1] Rudolf Heberle, *Social Movements* (New York: Appleton-Century-Crofts, 1951), pp. 335 ff. Nathan Leites' *A Study of Bolshevism* (Glencoe, Ill.: The Free Press, 1953) was not available until the present study was completed, but his thinking and research in this general field greatly influenced the model of the Communist militant developed by Howard Wriggins which appears in this book.

its condition at any given time and place to the seizure of political power.

But the two models differ in crucial ways. In Marx the emphasis on the inevitability of the historical process resulted in a conception of the party which was not sharply differentiated from the conception of the proletariat. Expectations of the rapid rise to class consciousness of the proletariat limited the role of the vanguard to that of clarifier and guider. At the time of the seizure of power, the whole proletariat would be conscious of its goals, and would be formed in close echelons around its leadership. The leadership would differ in degree, not in kind, from the rest of the proletariat.

In Lenin, on the other hand, the Communist militant was viewed as a very special kind of person, a member of a kind of aristocracy, sharing in an esoteric knowledge not assimilable by the average proletarian during the era of the bourgeois dictatorship. This conception was implicit in the distinction between propaganda and agitation. Only the full initiates, the militants, could be effectively exposed to the complex appraisal of situations and the applications of Marxist-Leninist analysis to them. The simple proletarian could only be effectively told what the next step was. He had to be directed to specific actions through agitation.

This concept of an exclusive society of party militants carries through most of the other significant themes of the Leninist image of the Communist militant. Certainly, in Marx as in Lenin, the quality of dedication was possible only for and to be required only of the revolutionary elite. Both Marx and Lenin placed emphasis on revolutionary activism, but in Marx a generalized activism among the proletariat was assumed, with the revolutionary leadership differentiated by a more correct sense of direction and a greater degree of activism. In Lenin purposive activism was the monopoly of the party, and furthermore the activism of this purposive minority was total. The Communist militant was a full-time revolutionary, dedicated to a professional revolutionary calling.

Perhaps the most important difference between the Marxist and Leninist models of the Communist militant had to do with organization. In Marx the leaders were organizers, but they were organizers of large proletarian formations, such as trade unions and broad labor parties, leaders of study circles, editors of newspapers, and the like. The kind of organizing activity engaged in was ambiguous and vague. In Lenin, organization was perhaps the most explicit and fully elaborated category with both passive and active components. The militant was organized in a highly disciplined and centralized party, and it was through this tightly knit organization that the proletariat and other social formations were to be organized in dependent, manipulatable, "transmission-belt" formations.

These special features of the Leninist image of the militant were very largely the product of specifically Russian influences. Lenin's conception of the party met strong opposition among the more Westernized moderate Russian socialists, and within the international socialist movement. The opposition took different forms. The Western European Social Democrats, at the time of the elaboration of Lenin's conception of the party, were already the chiefs of large trade unions and mass socialist parties. These were loose and heterogeneous formations with a relatively thin lacquer of Marxist doctrine. The ultimate ends of socialism were left up to the historical process. The leaders of Western social democracy confined their efforts to improving the conditions of the working class and winning political rights for it. Their parties were open to all comers who had a general interest in social and political reforms. Even the left-wing socialists in Western Europe who fought these moderate reformist trends tended to reject Lenin's conception of the party. The idea of the party as a closed elite was strongly and specifically rejected, for example, by Rosa Luxemburg, who pointed to the grave dangers of such a manipulative conception. While she shared with Lenin his emphasis on the importance of revolutionary activism and leadership, she differed from him sharply in her faith in the revolutionary potentialities of the working class. Only a self-liberation by the proletariat could really bring about a genuine humane emancipation. She believed the closed Leninist party could achieve a party dictatorship, but not a proletarian dictatorship.[2]

There were, however, a few Western European forerunners of Lenin's conception of the revolutionary party. A number of conspiratorial socialist societies had been formed in Western Europe in the first half of the nineteenth century. The Blanquist movement in France came closest to the later Leninist conception.[3] It was a conspiratorial, armed formation dedicated to the seizure of power by *coup d'état*. But with the achievement of constitutional reforms in Western Europe and with the emergence of trade unions and mass socialist parties as effective instruments of the working class, these movements either ceased to exist or dwindled into insignificance.

Despite these Western European forerunners, the Leninist conception of the party and of the party militant was primarily a product of specifically Russian influences. The Russian intelligentsia which supplied most of the early revolutionaries was an extremely marginal social formation. Their exposure to Western European culture unfitted them for adjustment to the traditional and backward Russian society. In the words of Bertram Wolfe, they "lived precariously suspended as in a void, between an uncomprehending autocratic monarchy above and an uncomprehending unenlightened mass below. Their mission as independent thinkers was to be critics of the world in which they had no place and prophets of a world that had not yet come into being, and might have no place for them either."[4] Lacking the discipline which might have resulted from broad social and political participation and involvement, the Russian intelligentsia was given to extreme and fanatical views. Among many of them the rational criticism of oppressive traditional institutions took the form of nihilism, an advocacy of the total destruction of tradition. Within this formation of rootless intellectuals

[2] Rosa Luxemburg, *The Russian Revolution* (New York: Workers' Age Publishers, 1940).

[3] Heberle, *op.cit.*, p. 335.

[4] Bertram Wolfe, *Three Who Made a Revolution* (New York: Dial Press, 1948), p. 33.

with a taste for integral transformations there had already emerged, before Lenin, most of the essential components of his conception of effective political organization and leadership. The Russian anarchist Bakunin had developed the plan of an international conspiratorial society consisting of fully dedicated militants, highly centralized in organization, inspiring and leading the masses by revolutionary deeds and example. Sergei Nechaev, the Russian revolutionary portrayed in Dostoevsky's *The Possessed*, is perhaps the most extreme example of the nihilistic revolutionary terrorist of the 1860's and 1870's. In the Catechism of *The Revolutionist*, the authorship of which has been attributed to Nechaev or Bakunin, the revolutionary is described as a man with ". . . no personal interests . . . , sentiments, attachments, property, not even a name of his own. Everything in him is absorbed by the one exclusive interest, one thought, one passion—the revolution. . . . In the very depth of his being, not merely in word but in deed, he has broken every connection with the social order . . . with all the laws, appearances, and generally accepted conventions and moralities of that world which he considers his ruthless foe. Should he continue to live in it, it will be solely for the purpose of destroying it the more surely."[5]

The social revolutionary Peter Tkachev was one of the most immediate forerunners of Lenin. Tkachev's conception of the revolutionary party was of a highly centralized, disciplined, fighting formation, organized for the purpose of seizing power from established authority. Like Lenin, he had no faith in the spontaneous revolutionary potentialities of the masses.[6] But while Tkachev's party would seize power in the name of the "people" whenever a favorable opportunity presented itself, Lenin's party was to seize power in the name of the proletariat, and at least paid lip service to the Marxist timetable.

[5] Max Nomad, *Apostles of Revolution* (Boston: Little, Brown and Co., 1939), p. 228.
[6] M. Karpovich, "A Forerunner of Lenin: P. N. Tkachev," *The Review of Politics*, Vol. VI, 1944, p. 340.

Leninism may, therefore, be understood as a marriage of Marxism with this extreme Russian revolutionary current. It is the Russian component which is essentially responsible for the explicitness, the exclusiveness, and the extraordinary emphasis on tactics which is to be found in the image of the Communist militant.

In the analysis which follows, the portrait of the Communist militant has been constructed from the Communist classics. As has already been pointed out, the classics portray the Communist in the most favorable light from the party's point of view. Later analyses will show in what ways the classical portrait deviates from other representations of the attributes of the movement. Both qualitative and quantitative methods of analysis have been used. Three of the party classics, Lenin's *What Is To Be Done* (1902) and *Left-Wing Communism* (1920) and Stalin's *History of the Communist Party of the Soviet Union (Bolshevik)* (1938), were quantitatively analyzed.[7] The main themes associated with the Communist Party or its members were first established tentatively through an intensive study of the texts. The frequencies with which these themes occurred were established through the methods and reliability checks of content analysis. Although the limitations of applying quantitative methods to the analysis of doctrine are recognized, the frequencies thereby established have nevertheless proved to be suggestive. In addition, the component elements of the ideal image have been subjected to logical analysis, and the premises and implications and interdependence of the various themes have been explored.

In addition to the three texts which were analyzed both qualitatively and quantitatively, a number of other classics were examined in order to check on validity, or for the purpose of clearing up problems raised by the findings of the intensive analysis. These included Lenin's *State and Revolution* and *Imperialism*, and Stalin's *Foundations of*

[7] All of Lenin's *Left-wing Communism* was analyzed quantitatively. In Lenin's *What Is To Be Done* and Stalin's *History*, a sample of every other page was used.

Leninism and *Problems of Leninism*. The persistence of these same themes and their frequent expression in the Communist periodical and pamphlet literature was explored through analyzing such sources as the Cominform periodical *For a Lasting Peace, For a People's Democracy*, the American party theoretical journal *The Communist* (later *Political Affairs*), the French *Cahiers du Bolshèvisme* (later *Cahiers du Communisme*), the obituaries of party heroes appearing in various sources, and selected items from the Communist pamphlet literature.

The selection of the three classics for intensive analysis was intended to give representation to both the Leninist and Stalinist versions, as well as to the early and late doctrinal versions of the Communist militant. Since one hypothesis had been that the image of the militant in "popular-front" periods would differ from that of integral Communist periods, Lenin's popular-front classic, *Left-wing Communism*, was compared with his integral "organizational" classic, *What Is To Be Done*. The exposition of the doctrinal model which follows is based upon these sources and methods of analysis.

General Characteristics of the Communist Model

The general characteristics of the model of the Communist militant which have been commented on in the present chapter are (1) its explicitness, (2) its exclusiveness, and (3) its special approach to the problem of values and means. The explicitness of the Communist image results inescapably from Lenin's whole approach to the problem of political organization. If the revolution is to be made by a specially selected, trained, and indoctrinated elite, it follows that the characteristics of this elite must be elaborated. It is hardly necessary to demonstrate this particular point. Even a casual reading of the Communist theoretical literature makes clear the extraordinary emphasis placed upon the schooling of the party member in specific attitudes and skills. In this respect the party differs from most political movements and may best be compared to certain kinds of religious orders with

elaborately codified rules of conduct and with intensive training programs intended to ensure the assimilation of the code.
The very elaborateness and explicitness of the code is an
element in the appeal of Communism. It opens the way for
becoming "something very definite" which is quite attractive
to individuals confused and uncertain about their own iden-
tities. In addition, the explicitness of the ideal image is a
factor making for stability among Communist Party militants. Once this self-image is incorporated, it establishes certain set ways of viewing the self and others, of appraising
situations, and of organizing behavior, from which escape
is costly and difficult. The painfulness of this process of
escape, however, is to be attributed not only to the fact that
an individual has assimilated a highly elaborated code of
conduct and now has to reject it, but also to the fact that
this has become his only code and that now in a very real
sense he has to destroy this self and find a new one. The
Communist Party demands the submission of the whole man
to the movement. He must hold nothing back, not even life
itself. All other values, ties, and associations are instrumental.
They may be maintained to the extent that they contribute to
the movement. They must be cut to the extent that they compete. This is true not only for associations and ties such as
the family, profession, community, and the like. It is also
true for feelings, attitudes, values, and ideas which are in
conflict with, or even blur the sharpness of, the movement's
imperatives.

Perhaps the most distinctive feature of the model of the
Communist militant which emerges from an analysis of Communist theoretical sources is the extraordinary emphasis
upon, and elaborateness of, those qualities and characteristics
which have to do with power tactics. The militant is almost
always portrayed as an individual who is effective in protecting and expanding the power position of the party.

Professional politicians in the United States have a similar
concern for the power and prosperity of "the party," and it
may be useful in developing the image of the Communist
militant to bring out these similarities as well as the contrasts.

Professional politicians in the major American parties fall into at least three significant groupings from this point of view. The simple party workers who make up the larger part of the "cadres" of the major parties are typically involved in party work as a means of making a living. As a reward for effective canvassing, a precinct worker may attain a minor government post. Anyone who has ever attended a ward or district club meeting is aware of the fact that there is a kind of tactical code which good party workers assimilate. But the requirements of the code are not extreme. They can hardly be said to demand the whole man. So that even while in his political action he is predominantly concerned with tactics, this is only one among a number of codes of conduct to which he, unlike the Communist, is exposed. In the Communist model, party activity is his whole life, and in this sense the ideal of the skillful power tactician tends to be the ideal image of the whole man.

A second class of professional politicians are the political bosses. For these, too, politics has a primarily tactical meaning. The difference between the ward boss and his precinct captain is one of power and influence. The boss makes a better living out of politics than a ward heeler, but politics is not his whole life. It is viewed as a kind of entrepreneurial status, or as a means of attaining entrepreneurial status and most of the middle-class values and associations which are related to it. And even though the political boss and the Communist militant view themselves as political tacticians, the content of their tactical images differs sharply. The boss of a machine views himself as a broker who maintains his position in a constantly changing political and social situation. His striving for power has geographic and functional limits, and he is seeking for a kind of power which can for the most part be exchanged for other values. Tactics for him means buying and selling services, exchanging, compromising, adjusting, making combinations. The Communist militant, on the other hand, seeks total power by whatever means necessary, including the ultimate and final elimination of all competition at the first favorable opportunity. And he seeks it as a member of a corporate group to which he subordinates himself entirely.

A third group of professional politicians are the elected political officeholders who also typically make their living from politics, but whose approach to politics is more complex than that of the patronage politicians. The image which elected executives and legislators have of themselves is hardly one of simple feeders at the public trough. They view themselves as users of power to achieve specific, morally desirable goals. A conservative Senator may see himself as a guardian of public honesty and efficiency and a protector of traditional virtues and institutions. Certainly part of his image of himself includes tactical skills in campaigning and organizing, and in the legislative process itself. But this tactical image is in some kind of balance with a value image of a quite concrete nature. He has a specific record as a voter in the legislative body, and as an advocate or even floor manager of certain pieces of legislation. He can say of himself: "I am a smart politician. I know how to operate in a campaign in my home state and in the Congress." But he also says of himself: "I saved the taxpayers x million dollars through my actions in such and such appropriation measures." Or, "I was partly responsible for the enactment of legislation which makes possible the more effective utilization of water resources in my home state." In his image of himself, tactics and ends are in some kind of balance.

For the Communist militant, tactics are concrete and elaborate, while goals other than power are suspended into the remote future and are abstract and simplified. This is not to say that the Communist militant does not carry on campaigns for specific ends. This is his most effective agitational stock in trade. But the achievement of specific concrete ends is viewed in the simple light of tactics. According to Lenin, to view the struggle for the eight-hour day as anything other than a tactical maneuver to improve the power position of the party was the most vulgar reformism. Indeed, the good militant in the Communist view must not only regard concrete gains won for specific groupings as instrumental to the improvement of the power position of the party, but must also be prepared at any time to sacrifice group gains if this will enhance the power of the party. Thus the long history of Communist attacks on the moderate trade union movements reflects this purely instrumental view of immediate objectives and gains. This is so much the case and is brought out so clearly in Communist doctrine—as well as in practice —that immediate gains (other than power gains) can hardly be said to be ends of action in the Communist system. The "good" Communist is quite capable of striving for immediate and tangible losses for the working class or for any other group. The real end is therefore not the gain at all; it is the power of the party.

The legitimate ends of action in the Communist image of the militant are the seizure of power by the party and the ultimate values to which this seizure is supposed to lead. From the very beginning the treatment of the ultimate ends of Communist action was formulated in highly abstract terms. The democratic politician tends to appraise his power by the criterion of tangible accomplishments, i.e., "I employed a given power position to attain such and such non-power objectives." The Communist politician according to his own doctrine appraises his power by the criterion of power, i.e., "I employed a given power position to attain such and such power objectives."

Thus, to summarize the value orientation of the ideal Communist militant, it should be pointed out that all values save power have been squeezed out. It is all a matter of power tactics. The world as at present constituted is incapable of realizing humane values. All the values advocated by groups (including the Communists) in the world here and now are false values used by power groups to conceal the sordid power reality. The only meaningful ethical orientation in the here and now is one which turns away from all short-run and false humanitarianism and strives for a monopoly of power which will then lead to the era in which genuine values may be achieved. All non-power ends are suspended in the ideal image of the Communist militant.

This is brought out very clearly in the analysis of the Communist classics. In Lenin's first organizational text, *What Is To Be Done*, published in 1902, only 6 out of a total of 801 references to the traits and actions of militants and the revolutionary party deal with the ultimate constructive aims of the movement. In Lenin's *Left-wing Communism, An Infantile Disorder* (1920), less than 4 per cent of a total of 764 references to the party and its members have to do with the ultimate objectives of the Communist movement. Thus, at one point in this post-revolutionary work, he says, "We in Russia . . . are taking the first steps in the transition from capitalism to Socialism, or the lowest stage of Communism."[8] More explicitly in this same publication, he says that the task of the party is ". . . to assist the revolutionary class in its struggle for the emancipation of toiling humanity from the exploiters,"[9] that Communists must be prepared ". . . for the impending Communist reorganization of the whole of social life after the victory. . . ,"[10] and that it is the party's ". . . mission . . . to overthrow the bourgeoisie and transform the whole of society."[11] This small group of very general statements about the ultimate non-power objectives of the movement stands in sharp contrast to the vast number of references to the tactics of the party and the tactical prerequisites for "good militant" status.

But it would be misleading to rest this general characterization of the Communist value system on these two essentially organizational and tactical works of Lenin. If we were to generalize from these sources alone, we would have to conclude that non-power values and ends have practically no place at all in the code of the Communist militant, a position which would be quite incorrect. Non-power values play an important role in the ideal image of the Communist. It is just that they are viewed as the automatic consequences of the total seizure of power. While there is a remarkably full elaboration of what qualities the party and its members must

[8] Lenin, *Left-wing Communism* (New York: International Publishers, 1940), p. 28.
[9] *Ibid.*, p. 53.   [10] *Ibid.*, p. 80.   [11] *Ibid.*, p. 11.

have and what activities they must undertake in order to achieve this seizure of power, there is no elaboration at all of the means which are necessary to make a party dictatorship into a proletarian dictatorship, and to make the proletarian dictatorship into the promised Communist society. This is brought out quite clearly in an analysis of Lenin's eschatological classic, *State and Revolution* (1917).

In this pamphlet, written on the very eve of the Bolshevik Revolution, Lenin's stated purpose was that ". . . of elucidating to the masses what they will have to do for their liberation from the yoke of capitalism in the very near future."[12] In describing the goals and stages of the Communist revolution, he relies entirely on an exegesis of the Marx-Engels texts, particularly Engels' *Origins of the Family, Private Property and the State, Anti-Dühring*, and *The Housing Question*, and Marx's *Poverty of Philosophy, The Eighteenth Brumaire*, and the *Manifesto of the Communist Party*. By citations from these texts Lenin develops the following familiar theses. Before the Communist revolution, the state is to be understood as a simple apparatus for the suppression of the proletariat by the bourgeoisie. The function of the dictatorship of the proletariat is to smash the oppressive state apparatus of the bourgeoisie; that is to say, the state will continue to exist as a repressive force against the oppressors. Having fulfilled this function, it will cease to exist. Lenin in effect equates the dictatorship of the proletariat with the dictatorship of the party, ". . . the dictatorship of the proletariat—i.e., the organization of the vanguard of the oppressed as the ruling class for the purpose of crushing the oppressors. . . ." There is literally no elaboration of the means required to move from a party *coup d'état* to the broadly shared "democratic" proletarian dictatorship. Nor is there any elaboration of the means required to move from the proletarian dictatorship to the ultimate equalitarian and libertarian society. In other words, the Communist moves from an era in which he is totally concentrated on power tactics,

[12] Lenin, *State and Revolution* (New York: International Publishers, 1932), author's preface, p. 6.

to an era in which ultimate values are achieved without any tactics whatever.

Building from the texts of Marx and Engels, Lenin lays down a few specifications as to the content of this ultimate society. During the dictatorship of the proletariat, the officials of the state will be paid at the rate of workmen's wages. There will be no distinction between bureaucratic officials and the simple workmen. Similarly, the deliberative agencies of the dictatorship of the proletariat will not be parliamentary bodies, i.e., talking bodies. There will be no need for controversy and discussion since there will be no policy problems. Policy problems belong to the era of class struggle. The deliberative bodies will be "working bodies" making simple technical decisions and carrying them out. And as the dictatorship of the proletariat "withers away," there will be the ". . . gradual creation of a new order, an order without quotation marks, an order which has nothing to do with wage slavery, an order in which the more and more simplified functions of control and accounting will be performed by each in turn, will then become a habit, and will finally die out as *special* functions of a special stratum of the population."[13] This future society will be characterized not only by an absence of policing agencies and professional bureaucracy but by a swift improvement in mass living conditions. There will be "real" freedom and equality and a regime of value abundance in which the needs of individuals will be supplied without regard to social distinctions of any kind.

In Stalin's *Foundations of Leninism* (1924) many of these same themes are reiterated, but with even less content for the ultimate stage than is to be found in Lenin. The terms "withering away of the state" and the "future stateless Communist society" are simply used without specification.

Stalin's *History of the Communist Party of the Soviet Union (Bolshevik)* was the most important training text used in the schools of the Communist movement at the time this study was conducted. Every militant was still required to read and study it. Furthermore, unlike the two Leninist

[13] *Ibid.*, p. 43.

texts which were analyzed quantitatively, the *History* covers not only the period of the struggle for power, but a substantial part of the period during which the party has held power in the Soviet Union. It is interesting to note, therefore, that more than 94 per cent of the references to the traits and actions of the party and its militants are references to tactical qualities and actions associated with seizing, manipulating, or consolidating power. Only 6 per cent of a total of more than 2,000 references to the party and its activities describe it as achieving non-power goals. In the majority of cases these are esoteric socialist goals achieved after the seizure of power by the Bolsheviks in 1917. They refer to the transformations of the Russian economy and society which are described in the language of Marxism-Leninism. In that part of the *History* which describes the pre-revolutionary struggle for power, there are a number of references to party goals which are not in the specific context of socialism. At one point the party is represented as advocating "freedom of the press, freedom of speech, freedom of association for the workers, the convocation of a Constituent Assembly for the purpose of changing the political system of Russia, equality of all before the law, separation of church from the state, termination of the war, an 8-hour working day, and the handing over of land to the peasants."[14] But it is quite clear in the general context that the advocacy of these aims by the Bolsheviks was simply a tactical maneuver. In planning the January 9, 1905, procession and presentation of the petition at the Winter Palace, a number of meetings were held by the striking St. Petersburg workers. Bolshevik agitators were detailed to speak at these meetings ". . . without openly announcing themselves as such,"[15] in order to broaden the scope of the petition to include the bourgeois revolutionary aims listed above. The general context in the *History* where these aims are expressed makes it unambiguously clear that a bourgeois revolution must precede the proletarian dictator-

[14] Stalin, *History of the Communist Party of the Soviet Union* (*Bolshevik*) (New York: International Publishers, 1939), p. 57.
[15] *Ibid.*

ship, and that the Bolsheviks must take the initiative in the first revolution in order to make possible the second.

In general, the treatment of party goals throughout the *History* is extraordinarily consistent in avoiding the slightest implication of "vulgar reformism." The tactical significance of moderate reformist objectives is made clear wherever such goals are referred to, either in the specific context, or in the general context. Thus, in the discussion of the program of the Second Congress, democratic revolutionary objectives are referred to as the minimum program which deals ". . . with the immediate aims of the Party, aims to be achieved before the overthrow of the capitalist system and the establishment of the dictatorship of the proletariat, namely, the overthrow of the tsarist autocracy, the establishment of a democratic republic, the introduction of an 8-hour working day, the abolition of all survivals of serfdom in the countryside. . . ."[16]

Of the 133 references to party goals tallied in the *History*, only 40 represent the party as advocating or achieving short-run or minimum goals of a democratic and non-socialist variety. And in all these cases it is clear, either from the immediate or the general context, that such goal advocacy or achievement was simply instrumental to the power aims of the party and the ultimate socialist aims of the movement.

In that part of the *History* which describes Bolshevik accomplishments after the revolution, most of the references to non-power goals take the form of sweeping generalizations that a socialist society is in process of being achieved or has already been attained. Thus, "the effect of the First Five-Year Plan was to lay an unshakable foundation of a Socialist economic system in our country in the shape of a first-class Socialist heavy industry and collective mechanized agriculture, to put an end to unemployment, to abolish the exploitation of man by man, and to create the conditions for the steady improvement of the material and cultural standards of our working people."[17]

The *History* points out, "Our revolution differs from all

[16] *Ibid.*, p. 41.   [17] *Ibid.*, p. 330.

other revolutions in that it not only freed the people from tsardom and capitalism, but also brought about a radical improvement in the welfare and cultural condition of the people."[18] By 1936 ". . . in the new Socialist Society . . . the exploitation of man by man had been abolished forever . . . crises, poverty, unemployment, and destitution had disappeared forever. The conditions had been created for a prosperous and cultured life for all members of Soviet society."[19] The three constituent elements of Soviet society—the proletariat, the peasantry, and the intelligentsia—were no longer exploited.

"The proletariat of the U.S.S.R., possessing the state power, had been transformed into an entirely new class. It had become a working class emancipated from exploitation . . . a working class the like of which the history of mankind had never known before."[20] An entirely new peasantry had grown up in the U.S.S.R. "There were no longer any landlords, kulaks, merchants, and usurers to exploit the peasants. The overwhelming majority of the peasant households had joined the collective farms, which were based not on private ownership, but on collective ownership of the means of production . . . which had grown from collective labor. This was a new type of peasantry, a peasantry emancipated from all exploitation. It was a peasantry the like of which the history of mankind had never known before."[21]

The intelligentsia had also been transformed. "It had for the most part become an entirely new intelligentsia. The majority of its members came from the rank of the workers and peasants. It no longer served capitalism. . . . It had become an equal member of the Socialist society. . . . This was a new type of intelligentsia, which served the people and was emancipated from all exploitation. It was an intelligentsia the like of which the history of mankind had never known before."[22]

Thus the non-power achievements of the party in Stalin's *History* are either represented as instrumental to the attain-

---

[18] *Ibid.*, p. 341.   [19] *Ibid.*, p. 343.   [20] *Ibid.*
[21] *Ibid.*, pp. 343-344.   [22] *Ibid.*, p. 344.

ment of power or take the form of simple assertions that certain socialist goals have been attained. There are no detailed specifications as to how these socialist goals were attained, and no elaboration of their content, a situation quite in contrast with the elaborate discussions of means and tactics in the attainment and consolidation of power. The evidence, then, would seem to be overwhelming that the image of the Communist militant which may be constructed from the Leninist-Stalinist classics is essentially that of a totally absorbed power tactician, elaborately schooled in a set of skills and placed in an organizational framework which is to lead to a monopoly of power. Non-power ends are certainly meaningful, but they are present in the form of an unelaborated faith that total concentration on power tactics will automatically lead to the negation of all power and the achievement of a state of integral humaneness.

CHAPTER 2

THE POWER-ORIENTED TACTICIAN

THE EVIDENCE in the most authoritative Communist sources leaves little doubt that the doctrinal model of the Communist is one of a skilled tactician wholly engaged in the struggle for power. His involvement with power goals and his reduction of short-run social gains to power tactics clearly distinguish him from the familiar types of democratic politicians. The content of his tactics similarly places him in sharp contrast with these democratic models. The democratic models are essentially secular and civilian, secular in the sense that there is comparative freedom in the choice of ends and means. While there are limits in the democratic model as to the kinds of ends which may be sought and the kinds of means which may be employed, on the whole the model permits a good measure of eclecticism. There are expectations of flexibility, change, adjustment, and compromise with regard to both ends and means. In the Communist model, as we have already seen, all ends acquire their legitimacy through their relation to the seizure of total power. For the fully committed Communist, political objectives can have no other meaning. Similarly, certain of the means which are to be used in seizing power have a sacred character, at least verbally. In practice, this Communist doctrine as to means may amount to little more than the humble acceptance of party directives and the energetic conduct of the party's business. In the doctrinal model the approved pattern involves a more complicated organization of means. Certainly, the "party of a new type," the party of professional revolutionaries, is the central instrumentality. The party is said to have a monopoly of the only valid science of the social process. It derives its policies from this science, and in this sense the doctrinal model portrays a scientific professional revolutionary whose actions are based upon something comparable to the precise calculations and readings of the pilot or navigator. The party carries on its action in certain hallowed ways. The militant imputes special virtues to the proletariat, and has a quasi-sacred obligation to it. Similarly, the infiltration and manipulation of mass organizations through the party is an inescapable duty, as is the employment of illegal and coercive means in the seizing of power. This sacred tactical doctrine has in part never been an operational reality, and in the course of time certain other elements have become obsolete. Some of its principles, however, are still binding, and even those which are not binding are continually reasserted. The discrepancies between the doctrinal model of Communist behavior and the operational model are dealt with by a scrupulous description of all Communist action in the language of the system. Not one of these tactical principles has ever been explicitly set aside, and the sources to which militant Communists are exposed, and which constitute their holy books and commentaries, continually affirm their validity.

The democratic politician is essentially a civilian. He does not distinguish between himself and his antagonists in the military categories of "friend" and "enemy." He does business with his antagonists, and acts on the premise that he will always share power with competitors. Both he and his antagonists operate under a shared set of rules which limit the modes of competition. In contrast, the Communist model is deployed in military units on a field of battle. He is at war with established society, or when he has conquered power he is at war with vestiges of the old order, material circumstances, or encircling enemies. His only legitimate aim is total victory over and the destruction of the old society, external enemies, and the complete mastery of material forces. Occasional combinations and coalitions with antagonists are viewed as simple military ruses, or as psychological warfare measures.

The Qualities of the Communist Militant

Analysis of Lenin's *What Is To Be Done* and *Left-wing Communism* and Stalin's *History of the Communist Party of the Soviet Union* (*Bolshevik*) brings out some eleven themes which are present in all the texts but with different emphases. Three themes which are quite minor in a quantitative sense may be grouped together as relevant to goals rather than to tactics: they describe the ideal Communist in a non-power value context as a bearer of man's socialist salvation, as an achiever of short-run objectives (such as the eight-hour day), and as a member of an "international movement." From a quantitative point of view there are four dominant tactical themes. The Communist is described as militant, rational, organized and disciplined, and as a leader of the masses. Less heavily stressed themes portray him as activistic, dedicated, unique, and confident (see Table I).

Militance. The attribute of militance is heavily emphasized in all three texts (22 per cent of all references to the qualities of the party and its members in *What Is To Be Done*, 24 per cent in *Left-wing Communism*, and 28 per cent in the *History*) and the combativeness of the party and its members is viewed as beneficent and constructive. It is in this combat that the Communist is steeled and tested and acquires the skills necessary to carry on his tasks. In his *State and Revolu-*

TABLE I

Percentage Distribution of Qualities Attributed to the Ideal Communist in Three Communist Classics
(in per cent)

	What Is To Be Done	Left-wing Communism	History of CPSU(B)
Goal qualities	1	4	6
Tactical qualities			
Militance	22	24	28
Rationality	34	35	23
Organization and discipline	12	7	16
Leadership of the masses	16	14	13
Activism	5	3	3
Dedication	3	5	3
Uniqueness	5	3	3
Confidence	2	5	5
Total per cent	100	100	100
Total tallies	801	764	2208

tion, Lenin quotes approvingly from Engels on the constructiveness of force: ". . . it is the midwife of every old society which is pregnant with the new . . . it is the instrument with whose aid social movement forces its way through and shatters the dead, fossilized political forms."[1] In the early days of the struggle between the Bolsheviks and their competitors, Lenin represented intra-party struggles in the same light: "The battle over the slaughter of the organizations was bound to be terribly fierce. The fresh breeze of free and open struggle blew into a gale."[2] This theme of the beneficence of struggle and combat was repeated in Lenin's address to the Communist youth: "In order to bring such a society into being we need a generation of youth capable of becoming the persons able to cope with a situation of disciplined, desperate struggle with the bourgeoisie. Such a struggle develops real Communists; to that struggle, and with it, the youth must subordinate and connect every phase of its study, education, and upbringing."[3]

The Communist engages in all modes of combat, from verbal polemics to actual military operations. But whether the means consists of words or bullets, it is always combat. This is so much the case that, regardless of what kind of arena the Communist finds himself in, he thinks and speaks in military symbols. Thus Lenin constantly refers to the party as the "vanguard fighters" "marching at the head of the movement," and as "systematically organizing troops." The party is "the general staff" of the working class and includes "detachments of specially trained working-class revolutionists . . . 'of all arms' . . . ."[4] The use of military metaphor increases substantially in the language of Stalinism. Stalin's *History* identifies the party as "the principal *weapon* of the proletariat, without which the struggle for the dictatorship of the proletariat cannot be won."[5] In his description of the

[1] Cited in *State and Revolution*, p. 19.

[2] Lenin, *One Step Forward, Two Steps Back* (London: Lawrence and Wishart, 1941), p. 275.

[3] Quoted in *The Communist*, October 1933, p. 1004.

[4] Lenin, *What Is To Be Done* (New York: International Publishers, 1929), p. 124.

[5] *History*, p. 51.

events before the outbreak of World War I, Stalin refers to the Bolsheviks as starting ". . . an energetic struggle to convert the legally existing societies into strongholds of our Party."[6] In Stalin's speech on the death of Lenin, he refers to the party as ". . . the army of the great proletarian strategist, the army of Comrade Lenin."[7]

From Lenin on, the actions of the Communist movement are represented in the light of strategy and tactics. Stalin in his *Foundations of Leninism* refers to the party leadership as "strategic and tactical leadership." He defines the function of strategic leadership as ". . . the concentration of the main forces of the revolution at the enemy's most vulnerable spot at the decisive moment, when the revolution is already ripe. . . . The selection of the moment for the decisive blow, of the moment for starting the insurrection, so timed as to coincide with the moment when the crisis has reached its climax, when it is fully apparent that the vanguard is prepared to fight to the end, the reserves are prepared to support the vanguard, and maximum consternation reigns in the ranks of the enemy."[8]

Movements of the party are treated in the military language of attack, offensive, retreat, and counterattack. Thus Lenin, in discussing his polemic technique, stated that it was his ". . . habit to reply to attacks, not by defense, but by counterattacks."[9] In Stalin's *History* the party is described as launching a ". . . determined offensive against the Kulaks."[10] When the occasion requires, as ". . . in the period of the Brest-Litovsk peace, Lenin taught the Party how to retreat in good order when the forces of the enemy are obviously superior to our own, in order to prepare with the utmost energy for a new offensive."[11] And in *Left-wing Communism*, Lenin refers to the party as having learned to attack: "Now they have to realize that this knowledge must be supplemented by the knowledge of how to retreat prop-

[6] *Ibid.*, p. 156.   [7] *Ibid.*, p. 268.
[8] Stalin, *Foundations of Leninism* (New York: International Publishers, 1939), pp. 95-96.
[9] *What Is To Be Done*, p. 86.   [10] *History*, p. 292.
[11] *Ibid.*, p. 219.

erly. They have to realize—and the revolutionary class is taught to realize by its own bitter experience—that victory is impossible unless they have learned both how to attack and how to retreat properly."[12] These same themes are repeated in Stalin: "Manoeuvering the reserves with a view of effecting a proper retreat when the enemy is strong, when retreat is inevitable, when to accept battle forced upon us by the enemy is obviously disadvantageous, when, with the given alignment of forces, retreat becomes the only way to ward off a blow against the vanguard and to keep the reserves intact."[13]

The immediate aims of the party are similarly represented in military terms. The party is to exploit weaknesses in the line of the bourgeoisie. "The more powerful enemy can be conquered only by exerting the utmost effort, and by *necessarily*, thoroughly, carefully, attentively and skillfully taking advantage of every, even the smallest, 'rift' among the enemies, of every antagonism of interest among the bourgeoisie of the various countries. . . ."[14] The party has as its purpose the smashing and destruction of its antagonists, their liquidation as effective fighting forces. From the very earliest Bolshevik writings up until the present time, this aim of destruction and liquidation of antagonists has perhaps been more often directed against other revolutionary groupings or "deviationists" within the party than against the bourgeoisie. The latter objective tends to be taken for granted. Thus Lenin, after the breach between the Bolsheviks and Mensheviks, frankly avowed his intention of destroying the "splitters" and "seceders." Stalin's *History* is full of references to the "rout of the bloc of Trotskyites and Zinovievites," the destruction of the "Bukharin-Rykov Anti-Party group," and the "liquidation of the remnants of the Bukharin-Trotsky gang of spies."

The Communist views the means which he employs in military terms. His organization is a steeled and hardened

---

[12] *Left-wing Communism*, pp. 13-14.
[13] *Foundations of Leninism*, p. 97.
[14] Lenin, *Left-wing Communism*, p. 53.

weapon, the vanguard of an army. The party is not led in its lower echelons by civilian officials but by "cadres." Like a military unit it must be vigilant, ready to spring into action at a moment's notice, and is ever preoccupied with internal "security," for "the easiest way to capture a fortress is from within."[15] Lenin wrote, "We must put our party into readiness to spring to its post and fulfill its duty at the very first, even unexpected, call."[16] And Stalin, years later, "We must not lull the party, but sharpen its vigilance; we must not lull it to sleep, but keep it ready for action; not disarm it, but arm it; not demobilize it, but hold it in a state of mobilization for the fulfillment of the Second Five-Year Plan."[17]

In his employment of the written and spoken word the Communist is a polemicist. Language is a weapon. In his conflict with the moderate Social Democrats in the early 1900's Lenin stressed the value of verbal attack on party enemies. The extraordinary brutality of the language in the *History*, particularly when it refers to party opponents, reflects the accentuation of this pattern of verbal violence. Lenin approved violence in the party's mass communications, justifying the spreading among the masses of hatred toward deviationists and party opponents. He favored the use of the ". . . most offensive and contemptuous mode of expression" against such deviationists.[18] The persistence in the contemporary Communist media of communication of this pattern of verbal militance, of annihilating opponents through language, will be brought out in detail in the following chapter.

Rationality. The theme of the rationality of the Communist receives even more emphasis in the classic writings than does that of militance (see Table 1). The Communist model of rationality is one in which a single goal, that of seizure of power, is given as an absolute end, and the problem of knowledge and analysis is reduced to that of appraising the appropriateness of means within this very simple framework. Its

---

[15] *History*, p. 360.   [16] *What Is To Be Done*, p. 163.
[17] *History*, p. 323.
[18] Lenin, *Selected Works* (New York: International Publishers, n.d.), Vol. III, p. 495.

simplicity arises from the elimination from its system of the two most difficult intellectual and moral problems of political action. First, the conflict between power and non-power values which troubles the consciences and inhibits the action of democratic politicians is no problem for the Communist. One of the essential postulates of his system is the rejection in principle of the validity of non-power values in the epoch of capitalist domination. From this point of view his goal is clear, unmuddied with sentimentality, untroubled by the problem of value costs. Second, the Communist system simplifies the problem of the choice of means. No means which have a possible power increment are excluded in principle from the system. This flexibility in the employment of means ranges all the way from favoring coalitions with mortal enemies likely to produce a power increment, to the integral liquidation of entire classes of actual or potential antagonists when a substantial power gain is anticipated. This attitude is not to be confused with simple bloodthirstiness or sadism. The doctrine is explicitly opposed to spontaneous and joyous liquidation. It is always dispassionate liquidation, calculated in terms of gains and losses of power.

A number of significant sub-themes of the category of rationality call for comment. The doctrinal model of the Communist portrays him as a man of systematic knowledge, i.e., he has a theory. His theory is scientific, realistic, complete, and gives unequivocal answers to practical problems of decision. Because of his training in this theory, and his experience in applying it in action, he makes correct judgments, can forecast the future, never loses sight of his goals, and never gives way to irrelevant feelings.

The stress on the importance of theory in the writings of Lenin and Stalin is impressive. In *What Is To Be Done* Lenin asserts, "Without a revolutionary theory there can be no revolutionary movement. This cannot be insisted on too strongly."[19] And again in the same text, "A man who is weak and vacillating on theoretical questions . . . such a man is not a revolutionist but a hopeless amateur."[20] Stalin in the

[19] *What Is To Be Done*, p. 28.   [20] *Ibid.*, p. 118.

final chapter of the *History* points out, "The history of the Party further teaches us that a party of the working class cannot perform the role of leader of its class, cannot perform the role of organizer and leader of the proletarian revolution, unless it has mastered the advanced theory of the working-class movement, the Marxist-Leninist theory."[21] Stalin elaborates on the values and uses of theory, stressing its predictive value, its value for guiding action. "The power of the Marxist-Leninist theory lies in the fact that it enables the Party to find the right orientation in any situation, to understand the inner connection of events, to foresee their course, and to perceive not only how and in what direction they are developing in the present, but how and in what direction they are bound to develop in the future."[22] This insistence on the relationship of theory to action is constantly reiterated in the writings of Lenin and Stalin and other lesser figures. The general theme is that theory divorced from action becomes sterile and rigid; while action divorced from theory is opportunism.

Because it is always being tested in action the theory is constantly being amplified. Communist theory does not change, it is "enriched." None of the propositions of Marx are ever represented as having been wrong: new elaborations are made as the theory is applied. ". . . In restoring these Marxian ideas, Lenin did not—and could not—confine himself to merely repeating them, but developed them further and moulded them into a harmonious theory of Socialist revolution by introducing a new factor . . . an alliance of the proletariat with the semi-proletariat."[23] But the number of those having competence to enrich Marxist theory is limited: "It may be said without fear of exaggeration that since the death of Engels, the master theoretician Lenin, and after Lenin, Stalin and other disciples of Lenin, have been the only Marxists who have advanced the Marxist theory and who have enriched it with new experience in the new conditions of the class struggle of the proletariat."[24]

[21] *History*, p. 355.   [22] *Ibid.*   [23] *Ibid.*, p. 75.
[24] *Ibid.*, p. 358.

This proposition of course gives a certain freedom of action to the leadership of the party, which has a monopoly on the enrichment of Marxism. This flexibility is enhanced by the companion principle of avoiding literalism in the interpretation of the theory: ". . . to master Marxist-Leninist theory we must first of all learn to distinguish between its letter and substance."[25] The discretion of the party leadership is further expanded by the emphasis on the flexibility of tactics. The net effect of these themes, which on the one hand emphasize the stability and continuity of the theory, and on the other the avoidance of literalism and the creative theoretical role of the party leadership, is to have one's cake while eating it. The psychological advantage of asserting the stability of knowledge and principle is retained, while at the same time no insurmountable barriers are raised to action in changing circumstances.

The theory which is represented as governing the action of the party is "scientific"; in fact, it is the only true science of society. In reality, the approach of the Communist to his science is quite similar to the approach of the priest to his theology. The basic postulates are given; they never change. They have only been enriched and interpreted by those who are in the direct line of succession. The various propositions of Marxism-Leninism-Stalinism should not be confused with hypotheses. They have been fully validated and are now laws of historical development. Thus Lenin, ". . . since the appearance of *Capital*, the materialist conception of history is no longer hypothesis, but a scientifically demonstrated proposition."[26]

The science of Communism consists of fully validated propositions—in other words, "laws of society." They provide the party with unambiguous guides to historical development, and hence to political action. Stalin observes, "But in order that it may be really the vanguard, the Party must be armed with revolutionary theory, with a knowledge of

[25] *Ibid.*, p. 355.
[26] Lenin, "What the 'Friends of the People' Are and How They Fight the Social Democrats," *Selected Works*, Vol. 1, p. 84.

the laws of the revolution."[27] And again, in the *History*, Stalin emphasizes that because such a scientific theory makes it possible to predict the course of historical development, it is bound to provide the correct guidance, the successful "line"; ". . . such a social theory, such a social idea as correctly reflects the needs of development of the material life of society . . . is therefore capable of setting into motion broad masses of the people. . . ."[28] Because of their careful study of this true and complete science of society, Communists always have a clear and precise policy. The party leaders, and in particular Lenin and Stalin, are portrayed in the doctrine as being "clear and definite," as showing the correct policy with the "utmost clarity."

This conception of the Communist theory as fully validated science providing the movement with precise directives, coupled with the principle that interpretation and enrichment of the theory is a monopoly of the "apostolic" succession— Marx-Engels-Lenin-Stalin—implies a quite limited role for intra-party discussion and debate of policy. The theory provides the "one right answer" to meet any given situation, and competence to derive this answer from the theory is vested in those who have attained the rank of "creative theorists." Thus, for a fully indoctrinated Communist the absence of democratic discussion in the party is not a serious problem, despite the principle of "democratic centralism." If the theory is scientifically true and complete, the directives derived from it clear and precise, and capacity to interpret the theory specifically located in Stalin and the other "disciples of Lenin," a doctrinal justification exists for the delineation and direction of discussion by the party leadership.

The existence of a Communist theory constantly being applied and tested in action implies that the Communist must be constantly studying and learning. He studies the theory and learns from experience. And since this experience consists in part in the application of theoretical principles to action, learning from theory and experience are parts of the same process. The Communist is both an intellectual and a

[27] *Foundations of Leninism*, p. 109.   [28] *History*, p. 117.

man of action, a philosopher-politician who avoids the sterility of professional intellectuals and the opportunism of ordinary politicians. This great emphasis on studying and training and learning from experience is reflected not only in the Communist classics and in the theoretical journals of the various national Communist parties, but in the substantial allocation of resources for training programs and schools in all of the Communist parties.

The theme of the rationality of the ideal Communist is not developed in the explicit context of theory alone. In his political action he is portrayed as planful, calculating, flexible in his tactics, and unmoved by irrelevant emotions. In *What Is To Be Done*, Lenin said, ". . . a man is not a revolutionist but a hopeless amateur . . . if he is unable to conceive of a broad and bold plan that would command the respect even of opponents."[29] And in the *History*, Lenin is credited with working out the plan for the October Revolution: "In his articles and letters to the Central Committee and the Bolshevik organizations, Lenin outlined a detailed plan for the uprising, showing how the army units, the navy and the Red Guards should be used, what key positions in Petrograd should be seized in order to ensure the success of the uprising, and so forth."[30] Planfulness in every phase of party activity is stressed in the classic writings and in the later party theoretical and tactical literature. The training of the cadres must be planned. Careful plans have to be laid for underground operations. The infiltration and manipulation of mass organizations and parliaments must be done according to a plan. If "plan" and "planning" are highly valued terms, "haphazardness" and "improvisation" are universally condemned.

Calculating, analyzing, judging, gauging, and estimating are represented as significant components of Communist behavior. Thus Lenin criticizes the utopian socialists ". . . because they are accustomed to build up their programs and plans of activity . . . not on the basis of an exact calculation of the real classes operating in the country and placed by

[29] *What Is To Be Done*, p. 118.
[30] *History*, pp. 204-205.

history in certain relationships."[31] And again, "It is not sufficient to refer to our program to determine the slogan of the struggle that is *now* impending, in the summer and autumn of 1906. For this purpose the *concrete* historical situation must be examined, the whole development and the whole consecutive march of the revolution must be traced; our tasks must be deduced not only from the principles of the program, but also from the *preceding* steps and stages of the movement. Only such an analysis will be a truly historical analysis, binding for a dialectical materialist."[32]

While the goal of the movement is represented as stable and unchanging and is never lost sight of by the Communist militant, great emphasis is placed on flexibility of tactics. In 1902 in *What Is To Be Done*, Lenin described his plan of party organization as designed to attain ". . . the necessary flexibility," i.e., "an ability to adapt itself immediately to the most diverse and rapidly changing conditions of struggle, an ability to 'renounce an open fight against overwhelming and concentrated forces, and yet capable of taking advantage of the awkwardness and immobility of the enemy and attack at a time and place where he least expects attack!' "[33] And in 1920 in *Left-wing Communism* Lenin placed even greater weight on flexibility: "Only one thing is lacking to enable us to march forward more surely and more firmly towards victory, namely, the full and completely thought-out conviction on the part of all Communists in all countries of the necessity of displaying maximum flexibility in their attacks."[34] A classic formulation of the stability of goals and the flexibility of tactics is to be found in *Left-wing Communism*, the "party manual" for popular-front periods. "The strictest loyalty to the ideas of Communism must be combined with the ability to make all the necessary practical compromises, to manoeuvre, to make agreements, zigzags, retreats, and so

[31] Lenin, "Tasks of the Russian Social-Democrats," *Selected Works in Two Volumes* (Moscow: Foreign Languages Publishing House, 1946), Vol. I, p. 139.
[32] Lenin, *Selected Works*, Vol. III, pp. 370-371.
[33] *What Is To Be Done*, p. 162.
[34] *Left-wing Communism*, p. 82.

on. . . ."[35] And in much the same terms this theme is found in Stalin: "Tactics change according to flow and ebb. While the strategic plan remained unchanged during the first stage of the revolution, tactics changed several times during that period. . . . The same must be said of the second and third stages of the revolution, during which tactics changed dozens of times, whereas the strategical plans remained unchanged."[36]

The avoidance of irrelevant feelings is another component of Communist rationality. The principle may be put in simple terms: Communists use moods but don't give way to them themselves. Lenin makes this point in *Left-wing Communism*: ". . . without a revolutionary mood among the masses, and without conditions favoring the growth of this mood, revolutionary tactics would never be converted into action; but we in Russia have been convinced by long, painful, and bloody experience of the truth that revolutionary tactics cannot be built on revolutionary moods alone. Tactics must be based on sober and strictly objective estimation of *all* the class forces."[37]

Lenin stresses the importance of coolness and impersonality even in relationships within the party, citing as an illustration his famous quarrel with Plekhanov. He describes the lesson he derived from this experience, ". . . an enamored youth receives from the object of his love a bitter lesson: To regard all persons 'without sentiment'; to keep a stone in one's sling. . . . Blinded by our love, we had actually behaved like *slaves*."[38] The emotions of pity and compassion are admissions of bankruptcy, of "philistinism." Lenin, referring to complaints that persons removed from the editorial board of *Iskra* might have their feelings hurt, remarked, ". . . such arguments simply put the whole question on the plane of *pity and injured feelings*, and were a direct admission of

[35] *Ibid.*, p. 76.
[36] *Foundations of Leninism*, pp. 92-93.
[37] *Left-wing Communism*, p. 46.
[38] Lenin, *Collected Works* (New York: International Publishers, 1929), Vol. IV, Book I, p. 31.

bankruptcy as regards real arguments of principle, real political arguments. . . ."[39]

In general, the doctrinal model portrays the Communist as subordinating the self to the party. True Communist courage is defined as this capacity to subordinate the self. Thus, in Stalin, ". . . for without the manhood, without the ability to overcome, if you like, one's self-esteem, and subordinate one's will to the will of the collective, without these qualities, there can be no collective, no collective leadership, no Communism."[40]

From these and other comments, and from the fact that in the classic doctrine there is no elaboration of the concept of Communist friendship or comradeship, one may infer that the model of interpersonal relationships within the party stresses coolness, impersonality. Warmth and compassion to the extent that they stand in the way of the efficient employment of the party are viewed as philistinism.

The obligation in the doctrinal model to avoid moods is elaborated in two ways. Communists avoid panic in moments of difficulty, and overenthusiasm in periods of success. Thus, in the *History*, the ideal of conduct placed before Communists is to be free ". . . from all panic, from any semblance of panic, when things begin to get complicated and some danger or other looms on the horizon . . . they should be as free from all semblance of panic as Lenin was."[41]

At the same time, Communists avoid getting overconfident. Thus, in the *History*, "The Fifth Congress [1907] was a big victory for the Bolsheviks in the working-class movement. But the Bolsheviks did not allow this to turn their heads; nor did they rest on their laurels. That was not what Lenin taught them. . . ."[42] Stalin's "Dizzy with Success" speech at the time of the collectivization campaign is the most elaborate development of this theme. "Comrade Stalin warned the Party that although Socialism had achieved great successes, successes of which we could be justly proud, we

[39] *One Step Forward, Two Steps Back,* p. 154.
[40] Central Committee, C.P.U.S.A., *Stalin's Speeches on the American Communist Party,* May 1929, p. 37.
[41] *History,* pp. 351-352.   [42] *Ibid.,* p. 91.

must not allow ourselves to be carried away, to get 'swelled head,' to be lulled by success."[43] There is to be no resting on laurels, no conceit, since this means loss of vigilance, failure to correct mistakes, failure to exploit opportunities.

Another theme portrays the Communist as combating spontaneity. This is closely associated with the themes of planfulness and calculation. The Communist is represented as being in intellectual control of situations, in contrast to the spontaneity of the rank-and-file members of the proletariat and the trade union movement. "The more spontaneously the masses rise, the more widespread the movement becomes, so much the more rapidly grows the demand for greater consciousness in the theoretical, political, and organizational work of Social Democracy."[44]

Organization and Discipline. The themes of militance and rationality taken together constitute around half of all the references to the party and its members in the three classics. While less heavily stressed than the first two sets of characteristics, those themes which describe the Communist as a disciplined member of a special kind of organization, and as a mobilizer and manipulator of other groups, are of great importance in the doctrinal model of the militant and his party (see Table 1). The internal logic of this theme is that by virtue of the kind of organization which he has, the Communist is able to mobilize other groups and to influence the masses.

Lenin's stress on the importance of "effective organization" was, of course, the basis of the original split between the Mensheviks and Bolsheviks. He pointed out, "If we are properly welded and fully organized, if we remove all the faint-hearted and deserters from our midst, our solid core, small as it is, will lead the whole horde of 'organizational amorphousness.' And unless we have a core, the Mensheviks, having disorganized themselves, will disorganize us as well."[45] The central importance of organization did not cease after the Bolshevik Revolution, and not even after the tri-

[43] *Ibid.*, pp. 322-323.   [44] Lenin, *What Is To Be Done*, p. 52.
[45] *Selected Works*, Vol. III, p. 455.

umph of the first Five-Year Plan. "The question of organization had acquired even greater importance now that the general line of the Party had won and the Party policy had been tried and tested by the experience of millions of workers and peasants."[46]

Through the existence of such an organization Communists are enabled to mobilize the masses, set up new organizations, and seize control of existing ones such as trade unions and and military formations. The unified disciplined party is the primary instrumentality which makes Communists effective. In *What Is To Be Done* Lenin wrote, "We must have 'our own men,' Social Democrats, everywhere, among all social strata and in all positions from which we can learn the inner springs of our state mechanism. Such men are required for propaganda and agitation, but in a still larger measure for organization."[47] And in 1920, "Therefore, to be a Communist means to organize and unite the entire generation, to give an example of devotion and discipline in this struggle. Then you will be able to begin and lead to a finish the construction of a Communist society."[48] The Communist classics develop in great detail the kind of organization which is capable of playing this role of mobilizing the masses, carrying through a successful revolution, and organizing the revolutionary victory.

The outstanding attribute of the party organization is its centralized, monolithic, unified character. The *History*, discussing the famous Social Democratic Congress of 1903 in which Lenin's organizational principles won out, concludes, ". . . and so it was that, instead of a monolithic and militant party with a clearly defined organization, for which Lenin and the Leninists fought at the congress, the Martovites wanted a heterogeneous and loose, amorphous party."[49]

The theme of the centralized character of the party is reiterated in all of Lenin's writings. "Only a centralized,

[46] *History*, p. 323.   [47] *What Is To Be Done*, p. 83.
[48] Lenin, "Speech to the Communist Youth," quoted in *The Communist*, October 1933, pp. 1004-1005.
[49] *History*, p. 42.

militant organization . . . can safeguard the movement against making thoughtless attacks and prepare it for attacks that hold out the promise of success."[50] In *Left-wing Communism* Lenin argued that ". . . the experience of the victorious dictatorship of the proletariat in Russia has clearly shown . . . that absolute centralization and the strictest discipline of the proletariat constitute one of the fundamental conditions for victory over the bourgeoisie."[51] Radek's obituary for Lenin points to this dominant theme of centralization in Lenin's work. "Forms have changed, but through all these changing forms, Lenin pursued one idea : that the proletariat needs a revolutionary organization to assure its victory. This organization must be united and centralized, for the enemy is ten times more powerful."[52]

Another term closely related to the theme of centralization is unity. Stalin in his speech on the death of Lenin said, "Departing from us, Comrade Lenin adjured us to guard the unity of the party as the apple of our eye. We vow to you, Comrade Lenin, that this behest, too, we will fulfill with honor!"[53] Other terms which develop this same general theme are "solidarity," "unanimity of will," "cohesion of the ranks." The main threat to unity of the party is the "existence of factions" which ". . . leads to the existence of a number of centers, and the existence of a number of centers connotes the absence of one common center in the Party, the breaking up of the unity of will, the weakening and disintegration of discipline, the weakening and disintegration of the dictatorship . . . the Party represents unity of will, which precludes all factionalism and division of authority."[54] The sinfulness of factions receives extraordinary stress in the classics, and in particular in the *History*, much of which is taken up with discussions of intra-party struggles in which the "deviations" are described in the most violent language. This "anti-factional," "unity and discipline" theme takes on far more im-

[50] *What Is To Be Done*, p. 128.
[51] *Left-wing Communism*, p. 10.
[52] *International Press Correspondence*, Vol. IV, 1924, No. 18.
[53] *History*, p. 269.
[54] Stalin, *Foundations of Leninism*, p. 121.

pressive proportions than is indicated by quantitative frequency.

The distribution of authority within this unified, centralized organization is treated with some ambiguity. On the one hand, the principle of democratic centralism implies the free election of higher party echelons by the lower ones and the free discussion of issues until a majority decision has been arrived at in the top governing organ of the party, the Central Committee. These formal principles are explicitly described as non-operative at times during which the party is underground and under threat. And even when the party may function freely, the term "democracy" seems to be employed with tongue in cheek. Thus Lenin, "Is it possible for all the revolutionists to elect one of their number to any particular office when, in the very interests of the work, he *must conceal his identity* from nine out of ten of these 'all'? Ponder a little . . . and you will realize that 'broad democracy' in party organization, amidst the gloom of autocracy and the domination of the gendarmes, is nothing more than a *useless and harmful toy.* . . . Only abroad, where very often people who have no opportunity of doing real live work gather together, can the 'game of democracy' be played here and there, especially in small groups."[55]

Similarly, the democratic content of the doctrine of democratic centralism is undercut by the principle that minorities must submit to the majority. The meaning of the Communist version of majority rule, as elaborated during the struggle between Trotsky and Stalin, is that, once a position becomes a minority position in the Central Committee, the members of the minority may no longer agitate and propagandize for this position. To do this is to create a faction, which is a violation of basic party principles. "The principle of the minority submitting to the majority, the principle of directing Party work from a center, not infrequently gives rise to attacks on the part of wavering elements, to accusations of 'bureaucracy,' 'formalism,' etc. It need hardly be proved that systematic work by the Party, as one whole, and the directing

[55] *What Is To Be Done*, p. 130.

of the struggle of the working class would have been impossible if these principles had not been adhered to. Leninism in the organizational questions means unswerving applications of these principles."[56] If one adds to these principles of centralization and the submission of the minority to the majority, the location of the authority to interpret Marxism-Leninism in "Stalin and the other disciples of Lenin," one recognizes that the democratic component of "democratic centralism" is a very minor doctrinal theme indeed. Nevertheless, the doctrine of democratic centralism continues to be affirmed in the theoretical and tactical literature, and the forms of democratic election are insisted upon in situations in which the party is a legal organization.

The party operates both legally and illegally, has both a legal and illegal apparatus. In its illegal phases and manifestations, the doctrine stresses the importance of conspiratorial skills and the tactics of concealment. Even in periods of legality, the party must retain its illegal apparatus, since suppressive action by the bourgeoisie is inevitable. When the entire party is illegal it must employ its secret apparatus in such a way as to maintain control of legal non-party organizations. "The centralization of the more secret functions in an organization of revolutionists will not diminish, but rather increase the extent and the quality of the activity of a large number of other organizations intended for wide membership and which, therefore, can be as loose and as public as possible, for example, trade unions, workers' circles for self-education, and the reading of illegal literature, etc."[57]

After the Revolution of 1905, when it became possible for the party to operate in the open, Lenin urged that the party preserve its illegal apparatus and develop a special apparatus to engage in open activity.[58] Stalin in the *History* also stresses the importance of this double role for the successes of the Bolsheviks. "The preservation of the illegal Party organiza-

---

[56] Stalin, *Foundations of Leninism*, p. 114.
[57] Lenin, *What Is To Be Done*, p. 118.
[58] Lenin, "Two Tactics of Social Democracy in the Democratic Revolution," *Selected Works in Two Volumes*, Vol. 1, p. 407.

tion, and the direction of all other forms of political work through this organization, enabled the Party to pursue a correct line and to muster forces in preparation for a new rise in the tide of revolution."[59]

Item 12 of the Statutes of the Communist International made it obligatory for all parties adhering to it to form illegal Communist organizations. "The general state of things in the whole of Europe and of America makes necessary for the Communists of the whole world an obligatory formation of illegal Communist organizations along with those existing legally. The Executive Committee shall be bound to see that this shall be carried out everywhere."[60] The obligation to maintain an illegal organization even in democratic countries would appear to be clear. But the relative emphasis on legal and illegal activity varies with the conditions in any country and with party tactics. Thus the doctrinal model includes the conspiratorial theme. Militants must be good conspirators, must be skilled in concealment, and must be able to manipulate legal, mass organizations from camouflaged positions.

The doctrinal model of the Communist militant elaborates a number of characteristics of good party members which are closely related to the structure and distribution of authority within the party. If the party is centralized, monolithic, and unified, party members are represented primarily as disciplined and loyal. Communist discipline is "iron discipline." Party discipline is like military discipline. Lenin eulogized military organization and discipline and implied quite clearly that the military pattern of organization was his ideal for the party. "Take the modern army. It is one of the good examples of organization. This organization is good only because it is *flexible* and is able at the same time to give millions of people *a single will*. Today these millions are living in their homes in various parts of the country; tomorrow a call for mobilization is issued, and they gather at the appointed centers. Today they lie in the trenches, sometimes for months at a stretch;

[59] *History*, p. 134.
[60] *Blueprint for World Conquest* (Washington-Chicago: Human Events Press, 1946), p. 39.

tomorrow they are led to attack in another formation. Today they perform miracles hiding from bullets and shrapnel; tomorrow they perform miracles in open combat. . . . When, in the pursuit of one aim, animated by one will, millions change the forms of their intercourse and their actions, change the place and the method of their activities, change their tools and weapons in accordance with changing conditions and the requirements of the struggle—this is organization."[61] "Iron discipline" must be maintained even after the party seizes power. Thus Stalin, "The achievement and maintenance of the dictatorship of the proletariat is impossible without a party which is strong by reason of its solidarity and iron discipline. But iron discipline in the Party is inconceivable without unity of will, without complete and absolute unity of action on the part of all members of the Party."[62]

Discipline is linked with loyalty. Stalin in his speech to the American party asked, "Can you picture a Communist, not a paper Communist, but a real Communist, avowing loyalty to the Comintern, and at the same time refusing to accept responsibility for carrying out the decisions of the Comintern? What sort of loyalty is this?"[63] The party purge is the sanction employed to maintain party discipline and loyalty. "Purging and consolidating its ranks, destroying the enemies of the Party, and relentlessly combating distortions of the Party line, the Bolshevik Party rallied closer than ever around its Central Committee, under whose leadership the Party and the Soviet land now passed to a new stage—the completion of the construction of a classless, Socialist society."[64]

Leadership of the Masses. The militant is described in the classics as being in the leadership of the working class or of the masses. The Marxist phrase "vanguard of the working class" is often used. But generally when this phrase occurs, a qualification is added which identifies the vanguard of the working

[61] Lenin, "Collapse of the Second International," *Selected Works*, Vol. V, pp. 214-215.
[62] *Foundations of Leninism*, pp. 119-120.
[63] Central Committee, C.P.U.S.A., *Stalin's Speeches on the American Party*, p. 23.
[64] *History*, p. 329.

class with the party. Two purposes are served by this identification: it stresses the continuity of Marxism-Leninism-
Stalinism, and at the same time, in effect, it supplants the
looser and more ambiguous Marxist concept by the Leninist-
Stalinist "party." The vanguard of the working class *is* the
party, and the party leads the working class and the masses.
While the party must be constantly related to the working
class, know its moods, needs, and aspirations, it must never
submerge itself in it, or lose its identity. Lenin observed, "To
forget the distinction between the vanguard and the whole
of the masses which gravitate towards it, to forget the constant duty of the vanguard to *raise* ever wider strata to this
most advanced level, means merely to deceive oneself, to shut
one's eyes to the immensity of our tasks, and to narrow
down these tasks."[65] At the same time there is constant re-
iteration of the obligation to maintain the closest connections
with the masses. To lose contact with them is to become ineffective. "The history of the party teaches us that unless it
has wide connections with the masses, unless it constantly
strengthens these connections, unless it knows how to harken
to the voice of the masses and understand their urgent needs,
unless it is prepared not only to teach the masses, but to learn
from the masses, a party of the working class cannot be a
real mass party capable of leading the working class millions
and all the laboring people."[66] The weight placed upon maintaining relationship with the masses is reflected in the fact
that the concluding paragraphs of the *History* quote from a
speech of Stalin's on this very theme. The Bolsheviks, ". . .
like Antaeus, are strong because they maintain connection
with their mother, the masses, who gave birth to them,
suckled them and reared them. And as long as they maintain
connection with their mother, with the people, they have
every chance of remaining invincible. That is the key to the
invincibility of Bolshevik leadership."[67]

The leading role of the party and the party militants is
elaborated in a number of sub-themes. Leadership is described

---

[65] Quoted in Stalin, *Foundations of Leninism*, p. 111.
[66] *History*, p. 362.　　　　　　　[67] *Ibid.*, p. 363.

as an art. Communist leadership must always be in advance of all other groups. Communists take the initiative, and are the "driving force." The Communist leader is a teacher, a clarifier, a man who trains others, who inspires and arouses enthusiasm.

This mass leadership theme is an important one in the Communist classics (see Table 1). Communist leadership is described as a science or an art which the great Bolsheviks have learned and have taught to their successors. Stalin defined Leninism as a ". . . science of leadership in the class struggle of the proletariat."[68] And again, Stalin refers to the "art of leadership." Practitioners of this Communist art of leadership avoid lagging behind popular movements, just as they avoid getting too far ahead. "He who wishes to lead a movement and at the same time keep touch with the vast masses, must conduct a fight on two fronts, against those who lag behind and against those who rush ahead."[69]

Communist leadership involves being ahead of the masses, seeing farther than they do. Communists always take the initiative, and are the driving force of political action. In other Communist writings, mechanical metaphors are used. The party is the "transmission belt" or the "dynamo."

The Communist leader is a charismatic teacher. Lenin argued that without constant education the masses would never develop socialist consciousness. It is the task of the party "actively to take up the political education of the working class and the development of its political consciousness."[70] The party and its members are constantly portrayed in the *History* as explaining and clarifying things to the working class. They are also constantly engaged in schooling and training themselves and the working class. Thus Lenin, ". . . the masses will never learn to conduct the political struggle until we help to *train* leaders for this struggle."[71] The *History* proudly describes the results of Communist training: ". . .

[68] *Foundations of Leninism*, p. 88.

[69] Stalin, *Leninism* (London: Modern Books, Ltd., 1933), Vol. II, pp. 285-286.

[70] *What Is To Be Done*, p. 57.   [71] *Ibid.*, p. 150.

the Petrograd workers of those days showed what a splendid schooling they had received under the guidance of the Bolshevik Party."[72]

But the leading role of the party is not simply didactic; it is also inspiring. Lenin wrote in 1902, "We can thereby . . . stimulate our people to march untiringly along all the innumerable paths which lead to revolution."[73] In the later texts and theoretical writings these themes of rousing, exhorting, stimulating, and inspiring are frequently reiterated. "Inspired by the Bolsheviks, the workers and peasants mustered all their forces to smash the enemy."[74] "The Bolshevik Party roused the workers for a war *for the fatherland*."[75]

Activism. The Communist is represented as an activist. He is both active himself, and activates others. He lives in a constant state of tension. He is constantly pressed for time, and is confronted by ever-mounting demands. Lenin in *What Is To Be Done* referred to the "seething energy" of the revolutionary,[76] and to the ". . . miracles that the energy, not only of circles, but even of individual persons is able to perform in the revolutionary cause."[77] The *History* reports a Central Committee resolution of 1923 which urged, ". . . What was now required was that everybody should join in the common effort, roll up his sleeves, and set to work with gusto. That is the way all who were loyal to the Party thought and acted."[78] The energetic action of the Communist is described as "Bolshevik tempo." The Sixteenth Party Congress, meeting in 1930, ". . . instructed the Central Committee of the Party to 'ensure that the *spirited Bolshevik tempo* of Socialist construction be maintained, and that the *Five-Year Plan be actually fulfilled in four years*."[79] And the Stalin Constitution of 1936 defined Communists as ". . . the most active and politically conscious citizens in the ranks of the working class. . . ."[80]

The activism of the Communist involves thoroughness,

[72] *History*, p. 208.
[73] *What Is To Be Done*, p. 156.
[74] *History*, p. 238.
[75] *Ibid.*, p. 247.
[76] *What Is To Be Done*, p. 100.
[77] *Ibid.*, p. 101.
[78] *History*, p. 265.
[79] *Ibid.*, p. 311.
[80] *Ibid.*, p. 346.

scrupulous attention to detail, and versatility. Lenin portrays the party leaders as ". . . able to react to every manifestation of tyranny and oppression, no matter where it takes place, no matter what stratum or class of the people it affects."[81] And again, ". . . we must . . . set to work to 'stir up' all and sundry, even the oldest, mustiest and seemingly hopeless spheres, for otherwise we shall not be able to cope with our tasks."[82] And in his advice to the British Communist Party Lenin urged, "The Communists in Great Britain should constantly, unremittingly, and undeviatingly utilize parliamentary elections and all the vicissitudes of the Irish, colonial, and world imperialist policy of the British government, and all other spheres and sides of public life."[83]

The party must be versatile. It ". . . must be able to master all forms or sides of social activity without exception. . . . Everyone will agree that an army which does not train itself to wield all arms, all the means and methods of warfare that the enemy possesses, or may possess, behaves in an unwise or even in a criminal manner. But this applies to politics even more than it does to war. . . . Unless we master all means of warfare, we may suffer grave and decisive defeat."[84]

Not one grievance or potential grievance is to be overlooked by the party in its efforts to mobilize the masses. "We would be . . . Social Democrats only in name (as very often happens) if we failed to realize that our task is to utilize every manifestation of discontent and to collect and utilize every grain of even rudimentary protest."[85] And in Stalin, ". . . the task of tactical leadership is to master all forms of struggle and organization of the proletariat and to ensure that they are used properly so as to achieve, with the given alignment of forces, the maximum results necessary to prepare for strategic success."[86]

Communist activism is not spontaneous; it is consistently goal-oriented, and it admits of no obstacles which may not be

[81] *What Is To Be Done*, p. 77. [82] *Left-wing Communism*, p. 80.
[83] *Ibid.*, p. 78. [84] *Ibid.*, pp. 76-77.
[85] Lenin, *What Is To Be Done*, pp. 83-84.
[86] *Foundations of Leninism*, p. 99.

overcome. Strategic leadership means ". . . undeviating pursuit of the course adopted, no matter what difficulties and complications are encountered on the road towards the goal; this is necessary in order that the vanguard may not lose sight of the main goal."[87] Stalin recommends a combination of "American efficiency"and "Russian revolutionary sweep." He attributes American accomplishments to ". . . that indomitable force which neither knows nor recognizes obstacles; which with its business-like perseverance brushes aside all obstacles; which continues at a task once started until it is finished, even if it is a minor task; and without which serious constructive work is inconceivable."[88]

The Communist is never finished with his tasks. Each achievement imposes the obligation for further achievements. "It is sometimes asked, whether it is not possible to slow down the tempo a bit, to put a check on the movement. No, Comrades, it is not possible! The tempo must not be reduced! . . . To slacken the tempo would mean falling behind. And those who fall behind get beaten."[89]

Dedication. The Communist is absolutely devoted to the revolutionary cause. No part of him is held back. He accepts any sacrifice or cost, undergoes persecution, imprisonment, exile, without weakening in his loyalty and determination. To be a Communist means to have accepted inescapable obligations. Tasks given by the party to its members, however difficult and distasteful, are "obligatory," and "must be carried out." In describing the qualifications of professional revolutionaries Lenin exhorted, "We must train people who shall devote to the revolution not only their spare evenings, but the whole of their lives."[90] The Bolshevik Party was ". . . strong in its revolutionary spirit and readiness for any sacrifice in the common cause."[91] The cause to which the Communist is ready to sacrifice everything is the "revolution," and the "party of the revolution." Since the party is the only vehicle of the revolution, dedication and readiness

---

[87] *Ibid.*, p. 97. [88] *Ibid.*, p. 126. [89] *History*, p. 314.

[90] Lenin, "Urgent Tasks of Our Movement," *Collected Works*, Vol. IV, Book I, p. 57.

[91] *History*, p. 245.

to sacrifice all for the revolution is synonymous with dedication to the party.

To be dedicated to the party means to accept danger and risk. "We are marching in a compact group along a precipitous and difficult path, firmly holding each other by the hand. We are surrounded on all sides by enemies, and are under their almost constant fire."[92] The *History* portrays Lenin as accepting great risks in directing the revolutionary uprising of 1917, and as continuing his work even in his last illness. ". . . When already a very sick man, he wrote a number of highly important articles."[93] Good Communists die at their posts.

Uniqueness. The Communist is different from all other men, and the Communist Party is "a party of a new type" and is different from all other parties. Communists are professionals, a selected group, they are capable of tremendous deeds, and what they accomplish is unbelievable. The Communist movement has prestige, it has a glorious past. All other movements pale before it in its brilliant accomplishments.

Many of these themes are affirmed in Stalin's vow at the bier of Lenin. "We Communists are people of a special mold. We are made of a special stuff. We are those who form the army of the great proletarian strategist, the army of Comrade Lenin. There is nothing higher than the honor of belonging to this army. There is nothing higher than the title of member of the Party whose founder and leader is Comrade Lenin. . . ."[94]

The theme of professionalism is a dominant one in *What Is To Be Done*. Communists are made only as a result of long schooling and training. Those wishing to merit the calling of professional revolutionary face ". . . the serious and imperative task of training themselves."[95] Selection of recruits must be strict. "The only serious organizational principle the active workers of our movement can accept is:

[92] Lenin, *What Is To Be Done*, p. 15.
[93] *History*, p. 261. [94] *Ibid.*, p. 268.
[95] Lenin, *What Is To Be Done*, p. 130.

strict secrecy, strict selection of members, and the training of professional revolutionists."[96]

Only superior candidates are admitted to the party. "The Party must absorb all the best elements of the working class, their experience, their revolutionary spirit, their selfless devotion to the cause of the proletariat."[97] And in the *History* the point is made that only ". . . people really advanced and really devoted to the cause of the working class, the finest people of our country . . . ,"[98] should be admitted.

This theme of the strict selection of party membership, of admission of only the best elements, tends to be played down in popular-front periods of mass recruitment when the party "opens its doors wide." But all such periods of mass recruitment are followed by purges when the less reliable members are expelled, only the worthy retained, and the theme of special selection is reaffirmed.

The uniqueness of the Communist is also related to his heroism. The party engages in "heroic exertions." The party has a "heroic past." Stalin's *History* opens with this heroic theme, "The Communist Party of the Soviet Union (Bolshevik) has traversed a long and glorious road. . . ."[99]

The Communist Party is a unique institution. It is ". . . fundamentally different from the Social-Democratic parties of the Second International. . . ."[100] The Bolshevik Party was "unsurpassed in its ability to organize millions and to lead them properly in complex situations."[101] The party is the ". . . highest of all forms of organization."[102]

Assertions about the unique characteristics of the party and its members seem to take up little space in the three classics (see Table 1), but actually the theme of uniqueness receives far greater emphasis than the table indicates since the themes of militance, rationality, leadership, dedication, and activism also carry the implication of special qualities, of attainments of the highest order, and of membership in the community of the elect.

---

[96] *Ibid.*, p. 131.   [97] Stalin, *Foundations of Leninism*, p. 109.
[98] *History*, p. 239.   [99] *Ibid.*, p. 1.   [100] *Ibid.*, p. 142.
[101] *Ibid.*, p. 245.   [102] *Ibid.*, p. 48.

Confidence. Finally, the Communist is represented as a man of confidence, whose claim upon the future is unequivocal. It is unthinkable for a Communist to doubt his inevitable triumph. "It would be criminal cowardice to doubt even for a moment the inevitable and complete triumph of the principles of revolutionary Social Democracy, of proletarian organization and Party discipline."[103]

Communist confidence rests on two pillars. First, the Communist's theory, which is the only true theory of the historical process, promises him inevitable victory. Secondly, the success of the party in the Soviet Union is proof of the validity of the theory, and tangible evidence that the future is his. The theme of "theoretical confidence" is perhaps most clearly stated in Lenin's "Speech to the Communist Youth": "Marx based himself on the lasting foundations of human knowledge gained under capitalism; having studied the laws of development of human society, Marx understood the inevitability of capitalist development which leads to Communism, and, what is more important, he proved this, on the basis of the most exact, most detailed and deepest study of capitalist society."[104] The *History* places emphasis on the party's record as a basis of confidence in the future. ". . . the study of the history of the CPSU (B) strengthens our certainty of the ultimate victory of the great cause of the Party of Lenin-Stalin, the victory of Communism throughout the world."[105]

Even though he makes mistakes, the Communist will triumph in the end. ". . . our people may commit stupidities (provided, of course, that they are not too serious and are rectified in time) and yet in the long run come out the victors."[106]

The successful accomplishments of the party of the Soviet Union are, of course, proof of ultimate victory. Indeed, in the classics which appeared after the Russian Revolution, confidence is made to rest more on tangible successes and

[103] Lenin, *One Step Forward, Two Steps Back*, p. 276.
[104] Quoted in *The Communist*, October 1933, p. 997.
[105] *History*, p. 2.
[106] Lenin, *Left-wing Communism*, p. 64.

accomplishments than on theoretical validity. "In the period 1930-34 the Bolshevik Party solved, what was, after the winning of power, the most difficult historical problem of the proletarian revolution, namely, to get the millions of small peasant owners to adopt the path of collective farming, the path of Socialism."[107] It goes without saying that in the contemporary literature the spread of Communism into China and Eastern Europe is celebrated as further proof of the inevitable world-wide triumph of the movement. While the proportion of explicit references to the movement and its members describing them as confident is 5 per cent and under in the three classics, confidence is implied in a number of other themes, particularly those which stress the complete validity of Communist theory, the precision and correctness of Communist calculations, and the effectiveness of Communist organization.

The Logical Consistency of the Model

What emerges from this analysis of the doctrinal model is an extremely complex combination of roles. It is inconceivable that such a combination could be pursued by the same individual or within the framework of a loose organization. Thus, on the one hand, the Communist is represented as a philosopher-theologian possessed of a set of axiomatic principles, and on the other he is portrayed as a scientific empiricist constantly testing principles in action. Without some built-in corrective mechanism, the roles of empirical scientist and theologian would inevitably conflict, since empirical evidence would raise questions as to the validity of his axioms. Similarly, the role of combative, disciplined soldier would exist in a state of tension with the role of the clarifying, explaining teacher. Here, too, a mechanism is required to give signals as to how far to pursue each role, and when the one and when the other. Again, the roles of nihilist and saint, the pitiless destroyer of historical culture and the midwife of a new and humane society, are difficult to combine in the same person. Without the strongest of pressures, most

[107] *History*, p. 329.

persons professing to such a combination of roles could not escape the question of how much one may legitimately destroy and coerce in order to eliminate destructiveness and coerciveness.

There are two corrective mechanisms which prevent these combinations of roles from springing apart through internal contradictions of the strongest sort. On the one hand, Communist theory implies a division of labor and a timetable of roles. Even though there is emphasis on versatility, all Communists are not required to play all the roles. The party has its military specialists, its agitators, its organizers, its teachers and theorists—"its units of all arms." Furthermore, tensions between the coercive and educative roles, between the theologian and scientist roles, between the destructive and constructive roles, tend to be resolved through the Communist timetable and rules of "target selection." There is a time to destroy, and a time to build; a time to hide, and a time to act openly; a time to fight, and a time to be peaceful; a time to attack, and a time to retreat; a time to tolerate, and a time to repress; a time to preach, and a time to teach; a time to recruit, and a time to expel. Similarly, roles are differentiated according to a Communist "target plan." There are groups to love, and groups to hate; groups to crush, and groups to foster; groups to be taught, and groups to be roused. But even if the theory recognizes that roles are to be adapted to skills, targets, times, and situations, the problem of role contradiction is still not solved since, given such an elaborate array of role choices, only the most rigid type of discipline would make it possible for the party members to be deployed from one role or set of roles to another.

The solution to the problem of role conflict in both the doctrinal and the operational models, then, is centralized organization and rigid discipline. In effect, the movement offers its members a flattering self-image of versatility and high attainment of a variety of skills and honors in exchange for obedience. One must practice any given role only to specified limits, and one must turn roles on and off in response to changes in party tactics. In this respect, the doctrine is quite explicit.

It may even be said that in the doctrinal model itself, if its implications are logically elaborated, the effect of the principles of centralization and discipline is such that many of the other roles become inoperative or possible only in a very special sense. Communists "play at" being scientists, since they must turn science on and off in response to directives. Even as theological explicators of the theory, the location of the creative theoretical role in the "apostolic succession" of the party leaves practically all Communists, whether leaders or rank and file, the simple function of apologetics. The role of leader of the masses (except in the most limited military sense) is fraudulent in a setting in which the content of leadership is the simple execution of commands. The role of builder of a new and humane socialist society is fraudulent if the individual Communist turns over to the movement all rights to appraise action in the light of goals. Once these roles are logically elaborated, only the most unambiguously tactical ones survive in some kind of compatible and consistent system. Thus, one can be a disciplined member of a highly centralized organization, and at the same time be militant, dedicated, activistic, and confident. Once we have subjected the doctrinal model to the test of logic, this is all that seems to survive.

But for the Communist no such logical analysis of the doctrine is possible, for the "good books" of the Communist movement are sacred possessions. He must somehow believe in the reality of the doctrinal image of the Communist, and the compatibility of its component elements. For this reason the party member who has read and registered the doctrine before or at the time of joining cannot escape a certain disillusionment as he becomes exposed to the reality of party life. But there are ways of minimizing this disillusionment. As a new recruit he may feel that the more humble and instrumental attitudes of discipline, militance, dedication, activism, and confidence are appropriate to his rank, while the role of leader, theorist, teacher, and a full initiate into the mysteries of the eschatology are qualities of the adepts. If through time the continued existence of these discrepancies troubles him, the party makes convenient formulae available to him, and presses him away from sensitive areas. At any given time the party member is confronted by authoritative directives which specify his roles, and provide him with the supporting logic and language. He is even confronted with different classics at different times and places which provide him with a version of the ideal image suitable to party tactics.

Variations in the Communist Model

While the main themes of the Communist model carry through from the earlier to the later classics, there are a number of variations in emphasis which call for comment. *What Is To Be Done* is the basic organizational classic which first portrayed the party and the militant in full scope, while *Left-wing Communism* is essentially the popular-front classic typically introduced in party curricula at times when the party tends to de-emphasize its peculiar characteristics in the interest of fostering alliances with other political groups. The *History of the Communist Party of the Soviet Union (Bolshevik)*, which at the time of writing was the basic text in all Communist Party training courses, was written by Stalin after the great purge. Consequently, two different comparisons are possible; first between Lenin's "left" and "popular-front" models; and second, between the Leninist and the Stalinist models.

The comparison of the two Leninist classics brings out a number of differences. In the popular-front classic there is less emphasis on the leading and vanguard role of the party, and more emphasis on the relatedness of the party to the working class. In other words, the leading activity of the party and the passivity of the working class are less heavily stressed. The party, in a sense, conceals itself in the working class. There is nobody there but the proletarian chickens. A more detailed breakdown of these themes into sub-categories shows that while 13 per cent of the references in *What Is To Be Done* refer to the leading role of the party, only 8 per cent in *Left-wing Communism* portray the party in this light. The term "professional revolutionary" is used 11 times in *What Is To Be Done* and does not appear at all in *Left-wing Communism*. While the over-all references to the rationality of Communists is approximately the same for the two texts, there are significant differences in sub-themes. In *Left-wing Communism* the tactic of working with other movements is heavily stressed, while in *What Is To Be Done* the theme hardly appears at all. Finally, the themes of organization, centralization, and discipline are more significant in *What Is To Be Done* than in the popular-front Leninist text, 12 per cent in the first, 7 per cent in the second.

The differences which emerge from a comparison of the Leninist models with the Stalinist are of interest since they show how the doctrinal models have been adapted to changes in practice. Perhaps the most striking difference between the Stalinist representation of the Communist and that of Lenin is the *History's* heavy emphasis on organization, and particularly on centralized direction, discipline, and loyalty (see Table 1). Thus 16 per cent of the references to the Communist movement in the *History* develop organizational themes, as compared to 7 per cent in *Left-wing Communism*, and 12 per cent in *What Is To Be Done*. Almost 8 per cent of the references in the *History* stress loyalty and discipline, party unity, and centralized control, to under 2 per cent in *What Is To Be Done* and less than 4 per cent in *Left-wing Communism*.

The Leninist classics emphasize the themes of rational calculating behavior to a greater extent than Stalin's *History*. Thus 34 per cent of the self-references in *What Is To Be Done* and 35 per cent in *Left-wing Communism*, as compared with 23 per cent in the *History*, portray the Communist as having a science and a theory and as engaging in calculating and analytical behavior. Similarly, more of the references to rationality in the *History* are simple affirmations that Communists have a theory, while in the two Leninist texts rational, calculating behavior is elaborated more frequently in specific ways.

It is of course not surprising that the Stalinist transformation of the Communist movement into an even more highly centralized, disciplined apparatus than it had been under Lenin should be reflected in the doctrine by greater stress on the themes of organization and discipline. It was also to be expected that the intensified restrictions on freedom of party discussion and glorification of the party leadership under Stalin should be reflected in a decline of emphasis on rational, calculating behavior.

The analytical model of the Communist militant which we have constructed from Communist doctrine will be of use in a number of ways in later parts of the study. Thus, in the analysis of the structure of Communist communication, the degree to which and the ways in which the pictures of the Communist found in the movement's mass and elite media conform to the doctrinal model will constitute a formal description of the problem of assimilation in the Communist movement. In other words, those traits in the doctrinal model which are not to be found in the Communist mass media or other levels of Communist communication may be assumed, hypothetically, to be the ones which may have to be learned after joining the party. These traits, concealed in the mass media, may also be assumed hypothetically to be the ones which create difficulties in assimilation, which set the standards for admission into the cadres on the one hand, or the requirements which cause defection on the other.

The model will also be of use in the analysis of the ways in which the movement is perceived and experienced by different kinds of former party members. Thus it will be possible to offer generalizations about the degree to which the membership of the various national parties, the various ranks of the movement, the party members joining at different chronological periods and from different social classes, incorporate or fail to incorporate the esoteric image of the party—a kind of index of "Bolshevik purity." This in turn will be of use in developing hypotheses about the weaknesses and susceptibilities of different kinds of party members.

CHAPTER 3

ESOTERIC AND EXOTERIC
COMMUNICATION

IDEOLOGICAL GROUPINGS differ from one another in the ways in which they portray the world of politics. An ideology imputes a particular structure to political action. It defines who or what the main initiators of action are, whether they be individuals, status groups, classes, nations, magical forces, or deities. It attributes specific roles to these actors, describes their relationships with one another, and defines the arena in which actions occur.

If we compare the Communist and liberal democratic ideologies from the point of view of these categories of types of actors, roles, modes of interaction, and arena, we will arrive at something like the following. The Communist doctrine presents a dualistic model of political action. That is, there are really only two significant political actors—first, the various political manifestations of the bourgeoisie; and, second, the Communist movement, behind which are ranged actually or potentially all of the non-bourgeois elements of the world society. In the Communist ideology, the problem of the multiplicity of political actors (i.e., the multiplicity of nations and of political groupings within nations) is solved by defining all political actors by reference to a particular conception of historic mission. There are, on the one hand, those political actors whose inescapable and futile mission it is to preserve a historically outmoded political-social structure, and, on the other, those whose role it is to establish a new and historically appropriate political-social structure. Within this massive dualistic system there are indeed a variety of sub-actors and sub-roles, but these may perhaps be best described as "nominal" rather than "real" actors, surface manifestations of the "real forces."

The Communist doctrinal model of political action also imputes particular modes of interaction to these actors and sub-actors. These modes of interaction are *integral associa-*

tion and *integral antagonism.*[1] The various sub-actors related to the Communist movement (e.g., the working class, peasantry, intelligentsia, colonial peoples, etc.) are integrally associated with it. They have no other legitimate and historically meaningful association. Actors which are not integrally associated with it are integrally antagonistic to it. The problem of passive actors is again resolved by the distinction between the nominal and the real. At any given point in time, a given actor such as the "proletariat," or the "masses," may appear to be passive, neutral, or even antagonistic to the Communist movement. But this is always attributable to the temporary and tactical failures and successes of the main actors—to bourgeois measures of repression and propaganda, or to the shortcomings in communication and organization of the Communist movement. In the "real" (i.e., dialectical) sense, the main as well as the sub-actors have inescapable roles which involve final commitments and a final accounting, an ultimate antagonism in which the Communist actor destroys its antagonist and, having fulfilled its purpose, ceases to exist itself.

The Communist doctrinal representation of political action also defines the arena of political action in certain special ways. In a geographic sense it is a world-wide arena, in which particular areas are treated as sectors or "fronts." And in a social functional sense, it views every type of action—economic, religious, convivial, aesthetic, and intellectual—as political, and employs the same kinds of terms—"fronts" and "sectors"—to refer to the struggle for the control of these functions. Hence the Communist model of the political arena is world-wide and functionally total.

In contrast, the liberal-democratic representation of political action (1) presents a pluralistic system of political actors; (2) the modes of interaction involve limited association and limited antagonism; and (3) the arena of political action tends to be limited in area and restricted to certain functions.

[1] See Nathan Leites, *Operational Code of the Politburo* (New York: McGraw-Hill, 1951), pp. 53 ff.; and his *A Study of Bolshevism, op.cit.*, pp. 379 ff.

In the liberal-democratic ideology the individual is viewed as the basic unit of political action, and political movements as well as nations are looked upon as functional associations intended to realize the ends of individuals. While these group-actors may have stability, it is a basic premise that they may and do change, divide, combine, cease to exist, and new ones come into being. No actor is more or less real than the others. This premise of change and transiency of political association applies even to nations, which are denied any organic or metaphysical properties and which may come into being and pass away as do other political associations.

The political relations between individuals and groups in the liberal-democratic ideology take the form of coalitions, functional associations, or alliances, whether these be between individuals, groups, or nations. It is of course true that individuals, groups, and nations may form binding associations, but the liberal-democratic pattern generally requires some maintenance of group and individual autonomy, and at least formally holds open the possibility of disestablishing even the most stable of associations.

If association is thus limited, so is antagonism. Within the nation-state, political struggle is limited to the means of persuasion and economic rewards and punishments, and political controversy is resolved by some form of majority rule within the electorate and the legislative agencies. While antagonism between states may take the form of war, war is not assumed to be the necessary and permanent mode of interaction between states. The liberal-democratic view of political struggle is that conflicts of interest may be limited and harmonized through the use of reason.

The liberal-democratic ideology does not view the world as a single political arena. Its conception of arenas is pluralistic; it has tended to view the world as divided into many more or less autonomous arenas, each with its political actors, resolving their political controversies according to their own modes of political action. The doctrines of the right of self-determination and of non-intervention in the internal affairs of other states imply this limited and pluralistic conception of the political arena, which is in sharp contrast to the integral and world-wide arena presented in the Communist ideology. Similarly, the liberal-democratic ideology sets a functionally limited scope to politics. Certain activities are beyond the range of political action, and may not be controlled by political decision, while in the Communist ideology all action is political and is subject to political control.

In briefest summary, if the principles of the liberal-democratic representation of political action are *pluralism*, and the *limitation* and *localization* of *politics*, the Communist system rests on the principles of *dualism, integral antagonism*, and *total politicization*.

An analysis of the appeals of Communism may begin with descriptions of how the movement is portrayed, the image it communicates of itself and its antagonists. A description of how the movement portrays itself is hardly a simple task. The doctrinal model of Communism and the ideal Communist is rarely perceived by persons at the point of admission into the movement. Ordinarily, the Communist is exposed to this esoteric picture of the movement only after he has been a member of the party for some time and has manifested leadership potentialities.

The Communist system of communication may be viewed as having four components: (1) the classical writings of Marx-Engels-Lenin-Stalin; (2) the leadership media such as the theoretical journals of the individual national parties, and the over-all leadership organs of the party such as the Comintern and Cominform periodicals; (3) the specialized audience media directed at functional groups such as the peasantry, the workers, the intellectuals, and particular geographic regions; (4) the general mass media such as the American and the British *Daily Worker, L'Humanité, L'Unita*, and the like. In this analysis of Communist communication we will not concern ourselves with the specialized audience media, but will concentrate on a comparison of the inner or esoteric media with the external or mass media.

From the very formation of the Bolshevik movement, it has been recognized that in the era of capitalism the greater part of the working class and of other Communist audiences are unable to assimilate the Marxist-Leninist dialectic. This is attributable to the repressions of capitalism and to its monopoly of educational and propaganda agencies, which make it difficult, if not impossible, for most of the working class to recognize its own "true interests." The masses are only capable of registering their grievances; they cannot grasp the shape and form of the historical process in which those grievances are mere necessary incidents. Hence, at the level of mass appeals, the Communist movement portrays itself in ways which are adapted to specific social and political settings. Persons attracted to these external representations may later be systematically exposed to the esoteric or internal doctrine in the training schools and in the higher echelons of the movement.

These external representations of Communism and of the world in which it operates may be constructed from the mass periodicals and newspapers of the Communist movements in the various countries. They differ sharply from one another in the kinds of actors and modes of action represented, since they are adapted to the value and grievance patterns of particular countries and social groupings. Communist newspapers directed to an Asiatic, a British, a French, or an American audience, or to audiences which are primarily peasant or industrial in composition, represent the movement as involving different objectives and characteristics. These external representations are a part of what it is that an individual is exposed to at the point of admission into the movement.

While the mass media of the party vary with the audience characteristics of the various areas in which the party operates, the internal or esoteric representation of the movement tends to be the same in all Communist movements. Thus, some of the writings of Marx, Engels, Lenin, and Stalin, and especially Stalin's *History of the Communist Party of the Soviet Union (Bolshevik)*, are used in all the training schools and courses of the Communist movement. This should not be construed to mean that the patterns of behavior and the "interior atmosphere" of all party organizations are the same, but only that one of the influences on these patterns of behavior—the formal doctrine—is very much the same the world over.

One of the primary purposes of comparing the internal and external representations of the Communist movement is to place the problem of assimilation of members into the party in a systematic framework. The great majority of Communist party members at the point of admission have only accepted one or more of the many propaganda representations of the party. And perhaps a very large percentage, if not the great majority, of party members are never fully assimilated to the esoteric doctrine and practice of the party. In this sense they are unstable party elements, who may defect under circumstances in which party practice impinges on non-party loyalties and values. The fully assimilated Communist, as we have already seen, has no non-party loyalties and values.

In the present chapter we shall compare a selection of internal and external representations of the party. For the internal representation of the movement we have selected Stalin's *History of the Communist Party of the Soviet Union* (*Bolshevik*) and the Cominform periodical, *For a Lasting Peace, For a People's Democracy*. The leading editorials of this latter publication for the year 1948 were selected for analysis. These editorials typically offered authoritative appraisals of the political situation and laid down the Communist strategy and tactics. It is quite evident that *For a Lasting Peace* is directed at the professional Communist audience. It reproduces in full the official reports of the various Communist parties and contains lengthy articles and speeches by party leaders on the political situations in individual countries and regions. It contains no features, no general news, no concessions to a lay audience. While it is formally directed to the members of the Cominform—Russia, the Eastern European satellites, France, and Italy—it is the closest thing to an organ of the international Communist movement.

The American *Daily Worker* was taken as an example of an external Communist source, a source directed to the mass membership of the party and non-party sympathizers or potential sympathizers. Furthermore, as the organ of one of the weakest Communist parties, it was anticipated that the contrast between it and the esoteric media would be striking and hence analytically useful. Every fourth editorial was analyzed for the year 1948, a total of more than 180 editorials. The comparison of the *Daily Worker* with the Cominform periodical and Stalin's *History* should not be viewed as fully valid evidence of the differences between the internal and external representations of the Communist movement. Hypotheses drawn from these comparisons may be tested by studies of other examples of party literature, such as the various national party theoretical journals and the mass party newspapers of countries in which the party is either in power or has a mass base.

Esoteric and Exoteric Communication: General Characteristics

Perhaps the most striking characteristic of the party mass media (insofar as the American *Daily Worker* reflects the general pattern) is the enormous emphasis on the action of antagonistic actors such as the American government, capitalism, and the like, and the comparatively slight emphasis on the actions of the Communist movement or related groupings (see Table 1). In contrast, the Communist movement, its leaders, associated groupings, and ideological formations (referred to as the "self" in Table 1) appear as the actor in more than half the action propositions in the editorials of the Cominform periodical. In other words, Communism and the persons and groups identified with it emerge in full outline and with great frequency in an inner party periodical such as *For a Lasting Peace, For a People's Democracy*. In the *Daily Worker* such self-actors appear in only 11 per cent of the action propositions, while "enemy" or antagonist actors appear more than 80 per cent of the time. Object actors such as "workers," "peasants," "masses," "peoples," and the like appeared relatively infrequently in both media.

The great spread in these figures suggests that in its mass

TABLE I

*Frequency of References to Self, Object, and Antagonist
in the Cominform Periodical and* DAILY WORKER *Editorials
for the Calendar Year 1948*
(in per cent)

	Cominform	Daily Worker
Self	52.1	11.1
Object	18.9	8.6
Antagonist	29.0	80.3

propaganda in areas not controlled by the Communist movement, the main objective of the Communist movement is to
portray the evil characteristics of the actors of the established
order, while the actions of the self are soft-pedalled. The self
tends to be concealed, while the antagonists emerge in a
veritable riot of color and detail. This would seem to imply
that at the level of mass recruitment the potential or low-
echelon Communist is simply required to accept an essentially negative and evil picture of the existing political setting.
The good alternative (i.e., the Communist Party, the Soviet
Union, the People's Democracies, the Progressive Party)
appears only in very vague outline. This tendency may vary
with objective conditions and the tactics of the party in particular settings. In other words, in "left revolutionary" periods, or in areas where the party is large and powerful, the
action of the Communist movement may appear with a much
higher frequency than was the case with the *Daily Worker*
in 1948. The general hypothesis advanced here is that regardless of tactics, objective circumstances, or the power of the
party, the mass periodicals of the party tend to underplay the
self and conceal its properties and magnify and elaborate the
evil properties of the antagonist.

These points are brought out in greater detail in Tables
2, 3, and 4 where self, object, and antagonist actors are
listed in sub-categories. The "self" as defined in this analysis
includes the "primary self" such as Communism, Communists, the Soviet Union, and the like. In the Cominform
periodical the primary self appears in almost 40 per cent of
the actions, while in the *Daily Worker* it appears in only

6 per cent. In another category of self-actors are the propaganda versions of the self—"democratic" and "peace-loving forces," "anti-imperialists," "anti-Fascists," and the like. These self-actors portray the movement in terms of its popular propaganda goals. While in actual practice these propa-

TABLE 2

Frequency of References to Self-actors in the Cominform Periodical and DAILY WORKER *Editorials for the Calendar Year 1948*
(in per cent)

	Cominform	Daily Worker
Primary self (Communism, Communists, Soviet Union, etc.)	39.6	6.1
Propaganda versions of the self (democratic and progressive forces, freedom-loving and patriotic forces, peace-loving forces, anti-imperialists, anti-Fascists)	7.3	1.0
The New Democracies	4.3	.3
The Progressive Party—U.S.	—	3.6
The unsatisfactory self	.9	—
Total	52.1	11.

ganda versions of the self are either defined as Communist or as affiliated with and sympathetic to the Communist movement, for propaganda purposes they tend to portray the movement as identified with all the broad and morally desirable forces of mankind—the "peace-lovers," the "freedom-lovers," the "progressives," the "fighters for independence," and the like. These propaganda versions of the self appear as actors in more than 7 per cent of the action propositions in the Cominform periodical and in only 1 per cent of the cases in the *Daily Worker*. The frequent appearance of the "New Democracies" (the Communist-dominated governments of Eastern Europe) in the Cominform periodical and the Progressive Party in the *Daily Worker* are obvious consequences of the audiences served by these publications. *For a Lasting Peace,*

For a People's Democracy is primarily a European and East-ern European publication, while the *Daily Worker* is the organ of the American Communist Party. The "unsatis-factory self," which appears only in the Cominform publica-tion, includes those actors who are failing in their duties but are still considered salvageable and viewed as part of the self. They appear in the form of vague propositions such as "The party leadership in France is not taking advantage of its revolutionary opportunities," or "*x* party has failed to make a proper calculation of the balance of forces." The "unsatisfactory self" must be sharply distinguished from the "renegade antagonist" and the "right-wing socialists," who have gone over to the enemy and are even more reprehensible than the enemy, since they divide the ranks of the working class and have violated their historic mission.

Both in the Cominform periodical and the *Daily Worker*, "object-actors" appear rather infrequently and in the form of very general "mass" concepts such as the "working class," the "masses" or "peoples," or the "intelligentsia" and "peas-antry." They are generally portrayed as following the self-actors, as sympathetic to them, and as similar to them in a variety of ways. The object-actors are represented as victim-ized by the antagonists and as responding positively to the constructive leadership of the protagonists. At times some of the self-actors, such as the "progressive" and "peace-loving forces" (in other words, the propaganda versions of the self), are represented as having the same qualities as the "working classes," the "masses," or the "peoples." At other times, the propaganda versions of the self are represented as though they were identical with the Communist movement. Some-times they are portrayed as sharing leadership with the self. From the point of view of Communist propaganda tactics, these propaganda selves perform the function of integrating the active self with the object-masses around acceptable moral goals. Thus the Communist movement and the working class and oppressed peoples, taken together, constitute the "demo-cratic," "peace-loving," "anti-Fascist," and "anti-imperialist" forces.

TABLE 3

Frequency of Editorial References to Object-actors in the Cominform Periodical and DAILY WORKER *for the Calendar Year 1948*
(in per cent)

	Cominform	Daily Worker
Working class	10.5	4.9
Peoples	4.8	2.8
Masses-peasantry	2.2	—
Intelligentsia	1.4	.2
Colonial and dependent nations, minority groups	—	.7
Total	18.9	8.6

From this point of view, the "masses," the "working class," the "peasantry," and the "peoples" are not really object-actors in the sense that they are separable from the self. They are the *potential* parts of the self which are being repelled by the antagonists and assimilated by the self. They are in process of becoming the self and hence are really elements of an essentially dualistic action system.

The representation of antagonists in the editorials of the Cominform periodical is markedly different from that in the *Daily Worker*. First, as to frequency, it is clearly the action of the antagonist which dominates the field of action represented in the *Daily Worker*, while in the Cominform periodical it is the action of the self. But, in addition, the antagonists of the *Daily Worker* tend more frequently to be local rather than generally ideological. As pointed out in Table 4, more than 44 per cent of all the actors in the sample of *Worker* editorials were the American or other governments or governmental agencies—national, state, and local, executive, legislative, and judicial. This compares with under 6 per cent in the editorials of the Cominform periodical. On the other hand, generalized ideological antagonists—such as "capitalism," "imperialism," "war-mongers"—formed a larger proportion of total references to antagonistic actors in the Cominform periodical than in the *Daily Worker*. As will later be brought out, these particular differences suggest that the arena of action of such an esoteric publication as the Cominform periodical tends to be world-wide, with universal antagonists pitted against one another, while in a "popular" newspaper such as the *Daily Worker* the stage tends to be more local. These are, of course, only tendencies. The evi-

TABLE 4

Frequency of References to Antagonist Actors in the Cominform Periodical and DAILY WORKER *for the Calendar Year 1948* (in per cent)

	Cominform	Daily Worker
U.S.A. (executive, legislative, judicial, local, political parties, American imperialists)	3.0	39.0
Other countries and regions (Western countries, Anglo-America, Arab states, Nationalist China)	2.7	5.3
Ideological antagonists (imperialists, reaction, capitalism, Fascism, ruling cliques, capitalist press, war-mongers, anti-Communists, lackeys, kulaks)	16.1	25.7
Renegade antagonists (right-wing Socialists, labor leaders, "liberals," traitors)	4.7	10.3
Tito	2.5	—
Total	29.0	80.3

dence makes it clear that local actors appear in the Cominform publication, and general ideological actors are to be found in the *Daily Worker*.

If we take these data describing the frequencies with which different types of actors appear in these two Communist publications, a number of general points may be made as to the process of assimilation into the Communist movement. At the first stage of recruitment—the level of the readership of the *Daily Worker*—the neophyte is asked to accept a representation of politics which is dominated by evil local antagonists which are associated with generalized ideological antagonists such as "capitalism," "imperialism," "Fascism," and the like. But the focus is predominantly on antagonists and on local antagonists. The representation of the self is pallid and definitely played down. In the Cominform periodical the self dominates the arena, the arena tends to be world-wide, and the antagonists are predominantly the generalized ideological antagonists well known in the Communist demonology. Put in other terms, the first phase of assimilation involves the corrosion of loyalty to local authorities and institutions; the second phase involves the establishment of a new loyalty to a Communist movement which is world-wide in scope and the acceptance of the esoteric Communist hagiology and demonology.

Esoteric and Exoteric Styles

It is impossible to read the editorials of the Cominform periodical and the *Daily Worker* without being struck by differences in style and sentence structure. Thus, in *For a Lasting Peace*, actors typically appear with strings of cliché modifiers or modifying clauses. Social Democrats are never represented simply as Social Democrats but as the "right-wing Socialist provocateurs," the "corrupt lackeys of imperialism," the "despicable hirelings of American imperialism," the "petty bourgeois and treacherous Social Democratic parties of the Second International." Similarly, the kinds of action of which Social Democrats are capable are limited and stylized. They "toady" to the American imperialists, commit "treason" against the working class; they are the "hired men" of capitalism, and the like. This same stereotyping of actors and of action applies to all the actors in the Cominform periodical. Actually, the Cominform editorials have very little "news" or "event" content. They convey the impression of a series of puppet performances, with a limited number of plots, and with the same actors continuing from performance to performance, going through a limited number of stylized motions.

Two stylistic patterns contribute to this over-all effect. The actors in the Cominform periodical are almost always group actors—"capitalists," "working class," "peoples," the "New Democracies"—or "force" actors—the "peace-loving forces," the "imperialist camp," the "Anglo-American imperialists." Secondly, these "groups" and "forces" always appear with the same or similar modifiers or attributes— "stooges," "lackeys," "toadies," "hirelings," "reactionary," "imperialist," "Fascist," and the like.

These stylistic devices appear with far less frequency in the *Daily Worker*. The actors are local or individual, as in the following: "Truman's appointees in the NLRB are smashing strikes," "Washington bought the Italian election," "Stalin stripped the plans of the war-mongers before the eyes of the world." And the *Daily Worker* is much more spare in its use of cliché modifiers. It does not say, "The Anglo-American war-mongers are whipping up a frenzy for a new war," but "The Soviet Union wants to negotiate a settlement, and the Truman-Marshall planners are deadset against any such settlement."

In summary, in the Cominform periodical the properties of the actors are stable, explicit, and fully elaborated. In the *Daily Worker*, on the other hand, the properties of the actors may be inferred only from a constant sequence of recurring actions. In other words, if, through time, the American courts are represented again and again as victimizing the working class, the reader may draw the inference that working-class victimization is a stable property of the American courts. Nevertheless, this form of representation of action involves a concealment of stable ideological properties as compared with such Cominform delineations as the "imperialistic, war-mongering ruling circles of the United States," or the "Fascist and reactionary press." In the latter examples, certain kinds of evil action are represented as stable properties of the actor (i.e., the U.S. is intrinsically imperialistic, and the specific act of imperialism described is simply another illustration of the general pattern).

Thus it appears that the picture of politics in the *Daily Worker* places great emphasis on the action of the antagonist and soft-pedals the Communist movement; the arena of politics tends to be local and not world-wide; and the properties of the actors are largely left to inference. Some parts of the inner Communist doctrine—in particular, the demonology—may be inferred from the *Daily Worker*, but is not explicitly communicated. In contrast, *For a Lasting Peace* stresses the actions of the Communist movement, places the actors in a world-wide arena, and portrays the attributes of the actors in explicit terms.

Portrait of the Self

While the general outlines of Communist esoteric and exoteric communication have been brought out in the preceding material, the specific contents of the roles of the various actors have been left blank, so to speak. What kind of image of the Communist does the neophyte see in the mass media of the party, and what does he see when the curtain rises and he is exposed to the inner media? How is the enemy portrayed at the mass level, and how have his features been transformed in the inner communication of the party? What is the posture of the combatants at the periphery and at the center of Communist communication?

In the analysis of the qualities attributed to the Communist movement and allied groups in the *Daily Worker* and *For a Lasting Peace*, the same categories were used as in analyzing the classics. Hence it is possible to compare these two contemporary periodicals with the authoritative representations of the qualities of Communism and the Communist movement (see Table 5).

A number of points emerge from this comparison. The relative frequency of explicit goal qualities versus tactical qualities is roughly the same in Stalin's *History of the Communist Party* and the Cominform periodical, but these publications differ in two significant respects. In the first place, while there is relatively little explicit stress on the goals of the self, *For a Lasting Peace* represents the Communist movement and other related actors as striving almost exclusively for exoteric or popular goals such as democracy, peace, freedom, humanitarianism, and national independence for their own sake, rather than for the doctrinally appropriate goals of the dictatorship of the proletariat and the establishment of socialism. A second and perhaps equally significant difference calls for comment.

There is a type of self-actor which appears in the Cominform periodical which does not appear in the Communist

TABLE 5

Qualities Attributed to the Self in Stalin's HISTORY, *the Cominform Periodical, and the* DAILY WORKER

(in per cent)

	History		Cominform		Daily Worker
Goal qualities	6		8		26
Esoteric		4		0.5	
Exoteric		2		7.5	26
Tactical qualities	94		92		74
Militance		28		25	35
Rationality		23		10	2
Organization		16		9	3
Leadership		13		19	11
Activism		3		7	6
Uniqueness		3		6	1
Dedication		3		7	13
Confidence		5		9	3
Total per cent	100		100		100

classics at all. This we have called the "propaganda self." It includes a variety of "forces" and groups—the "peace-loving forces," the "progressive forces," the "anti-Fascist forces," the "anti-imperialist forces," and the like. The goals of these actors are, so to speak, built into the actor himself. And the goals which are built in are always popular mass goals. It would therefore be inaccurate to say that the distribution of emphasis between goals and tactics is the same for Stalin's *History* and the Cominform periodical, and that the sole difference lies in the stress on popular goals in the second. There is a far greater emphasis on goals in the Cominform periodical if one includes the references to the popular goal-oriented "forces." It would be similarly inaccurate to say that goals receive greater stress in the *Daily Worker* than in

For a Lasting Peace. For if one were to group together the propaganda actors with the explicit references to goals, the percentage of references to goals would be about the same for both publications. The significant difference would be that in the *Daily Worker* the popular goals are attributed to the Communist movement proper, while in *For a Lasting Peace* a separate class of self-actors has been contrived which has the special function of striving for "innocent" goals and which lacks the manipulative and hence morally problematic attributes of the primary self.

The difference may be put in these terms. In the *Daily Worker* the Communist Party is represented as peace-loving, freedom-loving, democratic, and the like, and it is not represented as having the distinctive goal characteristics which were brought out in the analysis of the classics. In *For a Lasting Peace*, the Communist movement is relatively infrequently represented as striving for these popular goals, but a number of innocent alternate actors have been invented who do. The advantage which results from this role differentiation in the Cominform periodical is that the party is enabled to have its cake and eat it, too. It can on the one hand preserve the integrity of the "inner" self, and on the other present an innocent self from which the disturbing features have been removed. This is unnecessary in the *Daily Worker*, since the qualities of the Communist movement simply do not appear in that medium at all.

In other words, both the Cominform periodical and the *Daily Worker* place a heavy stress on popular goals but in different ways, quite in contrast to Stalin's *History*. The latter, as we have already seen, rarely represents the party as achieving any goals other than the power of the party, the revolution, the dictatorship of the proletariat, and the realization of socialism. It is hardly surprising that this stress on popular goals should characterize the *Daily Worker*, the organ of a small movement which, if it is to recruit at all, has to adapt itself to the prevailing moral climate. The stress on popular goals in the Cominform periodical can hardly be explained in these terms. In most of the countries served by the Cominform periodical, the party is in power. And in France and Italy, where it is not, there are powerful mass parties. It is not the weakness of the movement in these areas which accounts for the pattern described above, but perhaps the newly won strength and power of the movement. The audience which is exposed to the Cominform periodical, despite its level in the Communist hierarchy, is after all a somewhat heterogeneous group. In the satellite countries of Eastern Europe the Communist parties have expanded rapidly in the last seven or eight years, as have the parties of France and Italy. As a consequence of this expansion, the lower leadership echelons are probably populated by new and only partly assimilated cadres. Thus even the "cadre audience" is diluted and may in large part be incapable of accepting the reduction of all goals to party power goals. It may be necessary in even so esoteric a medium as the Cominform periodical to lay claim not only to the ultimate humanitarian goals of the Communist movement, but to the popular goals of the world outside, such as simple reformism, pacifism, patriotism, and the like. Then, too, the Cominform periodical is available to the rank-and-file Communist audience and to non-Communists as well. By identifying the movement with the simple goals of the market place, it avoids confronting the rank and filers and party sympathizers with difficult ethical problems. For example, it does not tell a simple trade unionist who has joined the party for trade union objectives that actually the trade union is to be used to enhance the position of the party. A periodical such as *For a Lasting Peace* portrays the party as striving for trade union objectives and revolutionary objectives as well. The "true doctrine" of which comes first, which is means and which is end, is to be found only in the classics. The identification of the party with the popular goals of peace, democracy, and moderate reforms in such periodicals as *For a Lasting Peace* makes it possible to avoid the confrontation of the partly assimilated cadres, the rank and filers, and the sympathizers with this difficult doctrine of ends.

That the Communist movement speaks with more than

one tongue is hardly a new discovery. From its origin, it has had one word for the party elite and another for the philistines. The authoritative portrait of the party is to be found in the Communist classics and, at any given time and place, in the particular classics which the party direction emphasizes. Since its appearance after the purge trials, Stalin's *History* has been *the* authoritative text in the Communist training schools, so that it is legitimate to refer to the representation of Communism in that source as the authoritative one. The Communist movement, however, is confronted by the problem of communicating to a mass and unassimilated audience which might be repelled by the starkness and absolutism of the esoteric representation. Hence, from its very beginning the party has made a practice of maintaining two systems of communication, one adapted to inner party circles and the other to external communication. What is of interest in the present comparison is that an inner party publication such as the Cominform periodical departs from the esoteric pattern and lays claim to such goals as the maintenance of national sovereignty, individual freedom, and simple reforms, and represents itself as always favoring peace—goals which fly in the face of Communist ideology.

On the whole, the tactical qualities attributed to the self in Stalin's *History* and the Cominform periodical are similar both in content and proportions. The major themes of militance, rationality, organization and discipline, and mass leadership appear in both sources and with similar frequencies (see Table 5). It is of interest, however, that the themes of "rational calculating behavior" and of "organization and discipline" appear with substantially less frequency in the Cominform periodical than in Stalin's *History*. It is also of interest that the theme of "confidence" appears more frequently in the Cominform periodical. This last difference, however, may be accounted for by the fact that one of the functions of the editorials in *For a Lasting Peace* is to list the successes and advances of the Communist movement in the Eastern European satellite countries. In a later detailed analysis it will become clear that, despite these over-all differences in thematic emphasis, roughly the same sub-themes are involved. Hence it will be possible to conclude that the Communist movement as represented in the *History* and the Cominform periodical have the same tactical qualities, but differ in their goal qualities. The Cominform self is exoteric in its goals, but esoteric in its tactics, while the Stalin *History* self is esoteric both in its goals and tactics.

The self represented in the *Daily Worker* is esoteric neither in its goals nor in its tactics. It is, taken all in all, an ingenuously virtuous self both in means and ends. Its goals are peace and liberty. The significant tactical characteristics of the self as represented in the *Daily Worker* are "militance" and "dedication." But, as we shall see below, the militance of the self as represented in the *Daily Worker* is a moral and defensive militance. It exposes and fights evil and defends the masses from their antagonists. Communist militance, as described in the authoritative doctrine, involves "taking the offensive," "smashing," "demolishing," "leading revolutions." These themes do not appear in the representation of militance in the *Daily Worker*. Communist dedication as represented in the *History* and in the Cominform periodical consists of "steadiness," "thoroughness," "faithfulness," and "unremitting struggle" for Communist goals. In the *Daily Worker* dedication consists almost entirely of "martyrdom." The *Daily Worker* self hence bears little resemblance to the esoteric model.

The Communist Thesaurus: The Self

The formal categories employed in the preceding analysis, while essential for the purpose of making systematic quantitative comparisons, have tended to obscure the differences in mood and tone of the two Communist publications. We have sought to remedy this by comparing the actual language each employs.

Militance. Thus the terms used to convey the impression of militance are far more vigorous and aggressive in the Cominform periodical than in the *Daily Worker*. The self portrayed in the Cominform periodical "mobilizes," "sounds a clarion call," "closes its ranks," "battles," "wages struggles," "launches campaigns," "takes the offensive," "hits out," "strikes," "deals blows," "seizes strategic bases," "defeats," "routs," "smashes," "exterminates," "liquidates," "crushes," "overthrows," "tramples underfoot," "uproots," "disarms," "foments revolutions." The self of the *Daily Worker*, while overlapping in some of these qualities, does not share the more aggressive ones and does not manifest any of them with anything approximating the frequency of the Cominform periodical self. The *Daily Worker* self is more characteristically defensive, e.g., "defending," "safeguarding," and "protecting," or indignantly "protesting" and "exposing" the aggressiveness of the antagonist, e.g., "condemning," "defying," "asserting rights," "revealing," "disclosing," "drawing attention to," "denouncing," "branding," and "charging."

Rationality. The rational, calculating, manipulative qualities of the self in *For a Lasting Peace* also emerge in clarity and detail. The self "analyzes," "expounds," "draws conclusions," "gains by experience," "estimates," "cautions against haste," "recognizes mistakes," is "clear-sighted," "conscious," "logical," "scientific," "methodical," "systematic," "concrete," "profound," "wise," "brilliant," "foresighted," "armed with revolutionary theory." In the *Daily Worker* these essential esoteric properties of the self simply do not appear at all.

Organization and Discipline. The categories of organization and discipline are similarly represented in rich detail in the Cominform periodical. The self "forms," "builds," "constructs," "creates," "establishes," is "merged," "welded," "linked," "fused," "cemented," "consolidated," "centralized," and "disciplined." The self of the *Daily Worker*, to the extent that it appears at all in this aspect, is represented as having to overcome "indiscipline."

Leadership. In the leadership dimension, the Cominform periodical representation of the self has the full initiative and appears with the specifically Communist type of leadership. It "heads," "spearheads," "guides," "directs," "paves the way"; it consists of the "foremost units," the "forward

units"; it is the "backbone," the "heart and soul," the "cor-
ner-stone," the "pivot"; it "educates," "teaches," "trains,"
"shows the example"; it "has ties with the working class,"
"promotes the growth of the working class," "steels the will
of the working class." The *Daily Worker* self, on the other
hand, is represented more often as "inspiring" and "supporting," and, interestingly enough, never in the specifically
Marxist aspect as a vanguard and never as a "clarifier."
Among the leadership qualities, "clarification" overlaps with
the rational categories, and it is noteworthy that this term
did not appear in the *Daily Worker* editorials as an attribute
of the self.

Activism. The same general points may be made with
regard to the activism of the self. The self of *For a Lasting
Peace* is "forging ahead," "gaining momentum," "going all
out," "reaches and surpasses its goals," "fulfills its tasks," is
"dynamic," has "stamina," "vitality," is "tireless," "untir-
ing," "inexhaustible," does not "rest on its laurels." These
properties appear in the *Daily Worker* rarely, if at all.

Uniqueness. The self of the *Daily Worker* makes almost
no claim at all to being unique, while the Cominform periodical self is represented as being "superior," "supreme," "outstanding," "exceptional," "unprecedented"; it "towers above
the world," is "superior above all organizations," is "un-
paralleled," consists of "the best, the finest people," "purifies
its ranks," is "the highest form of organization," is "a party
of a new type," is "proud," has "an inescapable historic mission"; it is "majestic," "glorious," "mature," "tempered,"
"tested," and "tried."

Dedication. The dedication of the self in the Cominform
periodical consists of remaining "faithful," being "selfless,"
and "enthusiastic." The self is "persistent," "resolute," "re-
lentless," "unwavering"; its efforts are "unremitting"; it is
"devoted," "sincere," "solid," "staunch"; it is "whole-heart-
ed," and "always in readiness." The *Daily Worker* self, on
the other hand, is "hard-pressed," "hounded," "bullied,"
"slandered," "expelled," "barred," "insulted," and "denied
a livelihood."

Confidence. Finally, the Cominform periodical self appears as successful and confident, while the *Daily Worker* representation of the self is almost silent in this respect. In *For a Lasting Peace* Communists and related groupings are characterized as "invincible," "irresistible," "indomitable," "nothing can stop them"; they "score successes," "come into their own," "win the fruits," "get results," "advance toward victory," and "constantly increase in strength."

Portrait of the Antagonist

The antagonist as portrayed in the editorials of the *Daily Worker* so dominates the field of action that the over-all impression which is conveyed is one of a world of unmitigated and aggressive evil surrounding a small and victimized self. This "atmosphere" is in sharp contrast with that of the Cominform periodical, in which the self dominates the field of action and is successfully engaged with powerful enemies. The *Daily Worker* editorials not only concentrate on the antagonist in a quantitative sense but constantly stress and elaborate his evil properties. The tone of the *Daily Worker* editorials is shrilly moral, while the tone of the editorials of *For a Lasting Peace* tends to be tactical. Table 6 demonstrates that the evil goal qualities of the antagonist appear almost four times as frequently in the *Daily Worker* editorials as in the Cominform periodical. The latter publication presents the antagonist in tactical aspects proportionately more frequently than goal aspects. Aggressiveness, domination, and lack of confidence are the primary tactical attributes of the antagonist in both publications, but there is far more emphasis on these properties in the *Daily Worker*.

Some explanation is necessary of the distinction between goal and tactical properties. If one goes beyond explicit propositions, it is clear that the representation of self and object in both the Cominform periodical and the *Daily Worker* is almost totally moral. That is to say, it is implied that the tactics of the Communist movement, the working class, *et al.*, are moral since they are employed for moral goals, just as it is implied that the tactics of the antagonist

TABLE 6

Qualities Attributed to the Antagonist in the Cominform
Periodical and the DAILY WORKER *for the Year 1948*
(in per cent of references to all actors)

	Cominform		Daily Worker	
Goal qualities	11.5		42.8	
Tactical qualities	17.7		37.5	
Militance-aggressiveness		4.2		14.7
Rationality		.2		.4
Irrationality		.7		2.0
Organization		.5		.2
Disorganization		.8		1.1
Domination		5.0		9.3
Dominated		1.6		4.9
Activism		.6		.1
Uniqueness		—		—
Dedication		.2		—
Confidence		.1		.2
Non-confidence		3.8		4.6
Total	29.2		80.3	

are immoral since they are employed for immoral goals. This is not only clear by implication, but also comes out in the quality of the language employed to describe the tactics of the self and antagonist. The self is militant; the antagonist is aggressive. The self leads; the antagonist dominates. The self is organized and disciplined; the antagonist is bureaucratic. Nevertheless, the distinction between goal and tactical qualities is a useful one, since self and antagonist never share goals, but frequently share tactics. The tone of the Cominform periodical editorials approximates the neutral tactical language of the military communiqué in which a maneuver is a maneuver, an attack is an attack, a tactical error is a tactical error, whether it is made by the self or the antagonist. The figures in Table 6 suggest that the representation of the antagonist in the Cominform periodical comes closer to this neutral tactical mode than does the *Daily Worker*. Thus about 43 per cent of the references to the antagonist in the *Daily Worker* stress his evil goals, as compared with under 12 per cent in the Cominform periodical. In the editorials of

For a Lasting Peace self and antagonist are pitted against one another in a struggle for power, and the actions of both are essentially described in the form of tactical maneuvers directed toward the maximization of power. On the side of the self is ranged the Communist movement, which is a combination of general staff and over-all cadres; and in serried formation behind the primary self are the shock troops of the New Democracies, the auxiliary light infantry of the peace-loving, democratic, and progressive forces, and the militia of the working class, the peoples of the world, the masses, the peasants, and the like. On the side of the antagonist are capitalism and imperialism, which are also represented as a general staff and cadres—with Wall Street and American capitalism playing the dominant role—the compulsory levies in countries such as the United States and Great Britain and the other countries dominated by them, and the mercenary and renegade formations of the "false" labor leaders, the "phony" liberals, and the like.

If one examines the attributes of the antagonist in general in comparison with the qualities of the self (see Tables 5, 6, and 7), it is apparent that there are substantial differences both in properties and in proportions. Militance appears in comparable proportions, but the militance of the antagonists has a definite flavor of aggression. Different terms are used to describe this behavior. Properties in the rational dimension appear hardly at all for the antagonist and, when they do, they are almost always irrational properties. Organizational themes are not frequently associated with the antagonist and, when they are so associated, they are primarily attributions of lack of discipline and effective organization. Leadership becomes domination in the antagonist, and instead of followership we have certain of the antagonist actors represented as "dominated." Activism, uniqueness, and dedication hardly appear at all as properties of the antagonist. And instead of confidence, we have a number of themes which develop the hopelessness of the cause of the antagonist. As far as goals are concerned, the separation is complete. The self and object share all the appropriate and acceptable goals, while the antagonist has a monopoly of evil.

TABLE 7

Qualities Attributed to the Antagonist in the Cominform Periodical and the DAILY WORKER *for the Year 1948*
(in per cent of references to antagonist actors)

	Cominform	Daily Worker
Goal qualities	39.6	53.4
Tactical qualities	60.5	46.6
Militance-aggressiveness	14.4	16.8
Rationality	.4	.4
Irrationality	2.4	2.6
Organization	1.8	.2
Disorganization	2.5	1.4
Domination	17.6	13.2
Dominated	5.5	6.1
Activism	2.0	.1
Uniqueness	—	—
Dedication	.6	—
Confidence	.3	.2
Non-confidence	13.0	5.7
Total	100.1	100.0

In Table 7, the properties of the antagonist are computed in percentages of references to the enemy actors, rather than in percentages of references to all actors. This brings out a number of differences between the esoteric and exoteric representation of the antagonist which did not emerge clearly in Table 6. Weakness and despair as attributes of the antagonist appear in *For a Lasting Peace* more than two times as often in percentage as in the *Daily Worker*. This suggests that the mood of the Cominform periodical is one of comparatively greater confidence. While organization-disorganization is not a significant theme pertaining to the antagonist in either publication, it occurs far more frequently in *For a Lasting Peace*, mainly in the form of assertions that the antagonist actors are disorganized and lacking in discipline. In other words, the Cominform periodical stresses the discipline of the self and the indiscipline of the antagonist, while this theme does not appear significantly in the *Daily Worker* as an attribute of the self or the antagonist.

The Communist Thesaurus: The Antagonist

Goals. While the goals of the enemy in the *Daily Worker* are similar to those attributed to it in the Cominform periodical, there are a number of exceptions; for example, the antagonist is described as "nationalist" in *For a Lasting Peace* in just under 2 per cent of antagonist references, while there are no such references in the *Daily Worker*. Capitalist-exploitative goals are attributed to the *Daily Worker* antagonist more frequently than is the case in the Cominform periodical. But in the *Daily Worker* the specific terms used are those which have been made familiar in the anti-"Wall Street" and anti-"Big Business" themes of American populism and agrarian radicalism. In the Cominform periodical, on the other hand, the capitalistic goals of the antagonist have a very definite Marxist flavor. Just as nationalist goals appear entirely in the Cominform periodical, "imperialism" similarly is a goal of the esoteric antagonist. There are 36 references to imperialist goals in *For a Lasting Peace* and only 3 in the *Daily Worker*. At the same time, Fascist goals appear frequently in the *Daily Worker* and quite infrequently in *For a Lasting Peace*. "Imperialism" is the generic goal of the antagonist, and Fascism is merely one of the species. The predominance of "imperialism" in *For a Lasting Peace* and "Fascism" in the *Daily Worker* reflects one of the differences between the inner and popular demonologies.

Perhaps most interesting of all, however, is the fact that the most frequent types of goals in both publications are not the doctrinally appropriate ones, but essentially the accepted evils of the market place such as dishonesty, deceit, corruption, and the like. In this respect, the representation of the antagonist follows the pattern of the self. The self in both publications pursues popular moral goals, and the antagonist pursues primarily popular evil goals. And this is as true for the Cominform periodical as it is of the *Daily Worker*. Twenty per cent of the references to the antagonist in *For a Lasting Peace* and just under 22 per cent in the *Daily Worker* are attributions of simple evil such as dishonesty and corruption. These attributions of evil in terms which have general moral currency make up the greater part of the content of the Communist demonology. And the largest category of generally immoral attributes are those having to do with dishonesty. The antagonist is "treacherous"; he "deceives," "covers up," "misleads," "falsifies," "distorts," "spreads legends," "cloaks," "camouflages," "conceals," "veils purposes," "tricks," "betrays," "lies," "fakes," "misleads," "fools," "sidetracks," "pretends," "poses," "defrauds," "double-crosses," "confuses," "engages in 'double talk,'" "ballyhoos," offers "phony bait," and "talks out of both sides of his mouth." Certain of these terms are specific to the Cominform periodical, and certain others to the *Daily Worker*. The *Daily Worker* uses Americanisms such as "fake," "phony," "double-cross," "double-talk," and "ballyhoo," while *For a Lasting Peace* uses terms more familiar in the European and Russian Communist settings such as "humbug," "troubador," "divert," "cloak," and "camouflage."

Another large category attributes criminality and corruption to the antagonist. He is "criminal," "inspires crime," or "plots vile crimes." He undertakes "bandit actions," "illegal activities." He "robs," "loots," "plunders," "gouges," "gyps," "picks pockets," "raids," "kidnaps," "assaults," uses "strong-arm measures," "murders," "terrorizes," "assassinates," "bribes," "buys elections." He enacts measures which are "monstrous," "brutal," "draconic." The antagonist is corrupt in a great variety of ways. He is "vicious," "mean," "vindictive," "dirty," "verminous," "disgusting," "pornographic," "rotten," "foul," "putrid," "base," "venal." The dominating antagonist actors are "boastful" and "insolent," "unceremonious," "sneering," "impudent," "smug," "arrogant," "haughty," "notorious," "arrant." The dominated antagonists, on the other hand, are "ignoble," "despicable," and are compelled to do things which are "disgraceful," "degrading," "humiliating," "shameful," "ignominious," and "miserable."

Aggressiveness. The patterns of aggressiveness attributed to the antagonist in the Cominform periodical and the *Daily Worker* differ in a number of significant respects. The antagonist is described as "fighting" and "attacking" with much greater frequency in *For a Lasting Peace,* just as the self was represented as "fighting" and "attacking" with greater frequency in the Cominform periodical. Both self and antagonist are represented as "destroying" in *For a Lasting Peace.* In the *Daily Worker,* on the other hand, the antagonist is represented as "destroying" the self and objects, but the self is never represented as destructive of anything. This pattern tends to confirm the general proposition that the esoteric mode of communication approximates that of a military communiqué in which self and enemy fight, attack, and destroy. In the *Daily Worker* only the antagonist destroys, and the self fights infrequently and never mobilizes or attacks. The antagonist destroys, and the objects and self are victimized.

It is also of considerable interest that the antagonist in the *Daily Worker* is frequently represented as "conspiring," while in *For a Lasting Peace* conspiracy never appears as an attribute of the enemy. This may be due to the fact that conspiracy is an acceptable but hidden tactic of the esoteric self and hence may be an inappropriate quality to attribute to the antagonist. But since the *Daily Worker* self is represented as non-manipulative and as fulfilling all virtues, conspiracy may be attributed to the antagonist without embarrassment.

While the self and antagonist in the Cominform periodical fight, attack, and destroy, the specific quality of the language used is often quite different. The self does not "instigate war," "murder," or "violate," nor is it "predatory" or "provocative." But it is of interest that the destructive properties are often shared by the esoteric self and antagonist. They both "smash," "exterminate," "liquidate," "crush," "trample underfoot," "uproot," "shake," "cripple," and "wipe out."

Irrationality. As has already been pointed out, the rational properties of the antagonist are almost entirely on the irra-

ESOTERIC AND EXOTERIC COMMUNICATION

tional end of the continuum. But there are striking differences between the Cominform periodical and *Daily Worker* in this respect. The largest single rational category in *For a Lasting Peace* is "miscalculate." In the *Daily Worker* the largest category is "cold-blooded," a quality which is completely lacking in the Cominform periodical. The reason for this seems to be clear. Cold-bloodedness (in other terms, of course) is a virtue of the esoteric self and cannot, therefore, be a sin of the esoteric antagonist. But where the rational and "unemotional" properties of the self are concealed, as in the *Daily Worker*, "cold-bloodedness" may be safely attributed to the antagonist.

Organization-Disorganization. Organizational properties are more frequently attributed to the antagonist in the Cominform periodical than in the *Daily Worker*. The antagonists in the Cominform periodical are described as organized and united on the one hand, and as lacking in organization and discipline on the other. The indiscipline of the antagonist consists of "impetuosity," "unbridledness," and "haste," qualities which are closely related to the "emotionalism" of the antagonist in the rational category. The antagonist is "enraged," "feverish," "delirious," "frenzied," "frantic," "rabid," "ferocious," and "violent." Being moved by emotions of this kind, he is unable to maintain discipline. The antagonists "scramble" toward their objectives, and "evade the consequences." They attempt to "escape," "shift responsibility," "place the burden of their mistakes on the working class"; they "deny," "take refuge," "justify," "ignore," "sit on the fence," "duck the issue," and "leave the masses to their fate." The pattern in the *Daily Worker* is similar to the above, except that positive organizational properties are not attributed to the antagonist.

Domination. The patterns of domination attributed to the antagonist in the Cominform periodical and the *Daily Worker* are quite similar. In both publications the antagonist is described as "enslaving," and "colonizing." He "imposes regimes," "holds the reins of power," "harnesses," "enthralls," "transforms into protectorates," "tightens his hold," "calls the shots," turns areas into "jumping-off grounds." The antagonist "manipulates" and "engineers." He "intrigues," "makes tools" of people, "plants stooges," "bribes," "subverts," "steamrolls," "railroads," "makes decisions behind the scenes," "pulls wires," "frames." He victimizes the objects and the self. He "threatens," "intimidates," "frightens," "uses terror," "witch-hunts," "blackmails," "bullies," "torments," "cracks the whip," "hounds," "slugs," "clubs." The dominated antagonists are described as "acting under orders," as "servants," "tools," "agents," "salesmen." They "cringe," "kow-tow," "sell their souls," "sell out." They are "hired men," "servile," "slavishly devoted," "cowardly," and "yellow."

Activism, Uniqueness, Dedication. In *For a Lasting Peace* the enemy shares some of the qualities of dedication and activism attributed to self and object. Thus the antagonist is described as "exerting effort," as "putting on pressure," as "going all out." He is also described as "steady" and "assiduous" in his efforts. These themes hardly appear at all in the *Daily Worker*. This reflects the more neutral, tactical orientation of the Cominform periodical.

Confidence—Despair. Analysis of the elements of confidence attributed to the antagonist in the two publications makes it clear that the Cominform periodical represents the antagonist as suffering more serious setbacks and defeats than does the *Daily Worker*. The *Worker* pictures the antagonists as "disconcerted" and "afraid." They are "frightened," "panicky," "anxious," "alarmed," "worried," and "dismayed." *For a Lasting Peace*, on the other hand, describes the enemy more frequently as "collapsing," "declining," "crumbling," "weakening," "shrinking," "losing ground," "suffering fiascos," "meeting with defeat," "floundering," "scurrying about," "slipping into crisis," "suffering from impending crisis," "facing disaster," "wavering," and "tottering."

The enemy in the Cominform periodical is more often represented as being "frustrated," "checked," "prevented," "stopped," "unable to reverse history," and as having his "cards upset." He is also represented as being on the defensive, as being "forced" into actions, as having to "make concessions," "retreat," "admit defeat." This greater tone of confidence in the Cominform periodical may in large measure be attributable to the world-wide scope of the arena characteristic of *For a Lasting Peace*. The *Daily Worker* editorials deal very largely with developments within the United States, where it would be quite a strain on reality to attribute defeat and collapse to the antagonist. The Cominform periodical, on the other hand, describes the collapse of "capitalism" and "reaction" in the "New Democracies," the "crumbling-away" of the Kuomintang, the economic and political "bankruptcy" and "crisis" of the "Wall Street-dominated ruling circles" of France, England, and other countries. Furthermore, the mode of interaction in the Cominform periodical is one of unequivocal antagonism in which a militant self is engaged with the enemy on all fronts, "frustrating" him, "imposing defeats" upon him, and "upsetting his plans."

General Conclusions

A review of the main findings as to the ways in which the Communist movement represents political action may furnish a useful bridge to the later analysis of the appeals of Communism. Perhaps the most important finding is the sharp contrast between the internal and external representations. This would suggest that the great problem of learning in the Communist movement is not posed at the point of admission to the movement but only after admission, as recruits are exposed to the inner doctrine and practice of the party. A person who has simply assimilated the pattern of political action represented in the American *Daily Worker* has no conception whatever of what the Communist movement really is. He has identified himself with a rather pallid champion of generalized virtue and has accepted a somewhat watered-down version of the Communist demonology.

If we were to think of Communist ideology and propaganda in terms of religious theology, we would have to say that it is the hagiology—the doctrine of the "saints"—which is the essentially esoteric doctrine. It is the "true lives" of the saints, from which one can infer the principles of "true saintliness," which are completely concealed in the popular materials of the party. This hagiology is not even fully communicated in such an esoteric publication as the Cominform periodical. The tactical virtues of the Communist saints are fully represented in *For a Lasting Peace*, but not the "true doctrine of ends." The special burden of Communist "sainthood" is concealed even in a medium such as this, and only properly appears in the sacred books. This "true doctrine of ends" is the denial of the validity of all goals save power in the period prior to the revolution, and the complete subordination of all aspects of the person to the instrumentality of power, the party.

The roles of the actors in the Communist system of communication are fully elaborated in the Leninist-Stalinist classics and, to a considerable degree, in its "inner" periodicals. The party emerges with all its tactical properties—its vigor and militance, its fully valid tactical and strategic doctrine, its centralized organization and discipline, its special form of leadership—rooted in the working class—its unrelenting activism, its true eliteness, its unwavering dedication, and its unequivocal claim upon the future. In the popular representation of political action, roles are unclear and indistinct. The party is not differentiated from its "front" organizations or from the working class and the masses.

While the representation of the self differs sharply in the inner and mass media, the representation of the antagonist is more similar. Nevertheless, there is a small learning problem here as well. The popular antagonists tend to be local instrumentalities such as the police, the courts, local "big business," or institutions such as the press. They are not fully assimilated to the dialectical antagonists such as capitalism and imperialism, although these actors sometimes appear. Similarly, in the popular media the evil of the antagonist is not the dialectical evil of being on the wrong side of history, so to speak, but the simple evils of the market place—deceit, corruption, and crime.

The claim in the inner party periodical, *For a Lasting Peace*, as well as in the *Daily Worker*, that the Communist movement has a monopoly on the simple as well as the dialectical virtues may not present the difficulties which an outside observer might anticipate. It is certainly clear that any devotee of Marxism-Leninism-Stalinism must eschew the vulgar reformism implied in such goals as peace, freedom, and democracy. A fully indoctrinated Communist knows that he is at war with the established order—and in a military sense when violence is appropriate. Since all of his energies are devoted to the monopoly of power by his party, he knows that he does not believe in freedom and democracy, not even within the party itself, since the party must be so disciplined as to constitute a weapon, and a weapon cannot be free and democratic. And yet he may claim to be all these things in a dialectical sense, for, viewing the problem from within his system, he may say there is no peace, there is no freedom, there is no democracy, save through the power of the party. From his point of view, his claim on the exoteric goals of freedom and democracy are the white lies that one is permitted to tell children, since they are not "developed" enough to hear the truth.

The mode of interaction between the self and antagonist actors in the Cominform periodical tends to be military-tactical in quality. The self and antagonist are integrally and universally engaged. Actions are parts of battles, battles of campaigns, and campaigns of the war. In the short run, the fortunes of war change and the instruments of conflict shift. Here it is diplomatic, there is military. In one place, the main objective is organization; in another, it is production; in still another, cadres are being tested by maneuvers. In the *Daily Worker* the action is not represented as integral, nor is the self represented as being actively and aggressively engaged. The antagonist is the aggressor, the self is victimized and oppressed. Actions are represented individually and discretely. Here a group of workers are suppressed in their efforts to organize; there Negroes are denied housing or education; in still another place, a corrupt and Fascist government is propped up through the pressure of American "big business." The interdependence of the arena, the assimilation of all discrete actions to dialectical and "real" action, were not to be found in the *Daily Worker* and may also be absent in all Communist mass communication.

This sharp break between the inner and popular representations of political reality provides a clue to the main vulnerability of the Communist movement. The capacity to move from an acceptance of a plausible, concrete, and immediate demonology to a conception of politics in which power is the only meaningful goal, total destruction of the antagonist the only legitimate outcome, and the reduction of the individual to a tactically proficient instrumentality the only criterion of virtue, is the test of the true, the inner Communist. How difficult this test is, the kinds of conflicts which it imposes on Communist neophytes, the kind of conditions under which the test may be delayed and evaded, as well as those which tend to force it upon the party membership, the types of individual characteristics which facilitate successful passage of the test, as well as those which contribute to failure, are themes which will be developed in later parts of this study.

PART II

HOW THE MOVEMENT IS PERCEIVED AND EXPERIENCED

CHAPTER 4

THE PERCEPTION OF GOALS
AND THEORY

IN THE PRECEDING CHAPTERS we have examined the ways in which the Communist movement portrays itself and the world of politics in which it operates. This analysis has suggested that there are stages in the representation of the goals and tactics of the party and, therefore, that first impressions of the party based upon exposure to the Communist mass media would be strikingly different from later impressions based on exposure to the inner or esoteric party publications.

It cannot, of course, be assumed that the perceptions of the party by its members necessarily coincide with the published representations of the party. It is indeed probable that for most individuals publications constitute only a secondary source of information about the party, while direct, firsthand experience of those aspects of the party with which individuals come in contact constitutes their primary source of information. In this respect, the Communist movement may differ only in degree from most other associations in which publications and formal doctrine are far less important than communication in intimate groups and information from trusted associates. One is led, however, to attribute a greater importance to formal doctrine and the formal media in the case of the Communist Party. The movement has always stressed intellectual mastery of the doctrine through the reading of certain selected classics, and has always been lavish in the production of published materials and the proliferation of media directed at various audiences. But, even given this stress on publications in the Communist movement, conclusions based upon firsthand data on the ways in which the party is perceived and experienced by its members will be more reliable than conclusions which are inferred from the content of party publications. At the same time, two purposes have been served by the analysis of the published media. First, it has established authoritative models of the movement at various levels of ideological indoctrination; and, second, it has suggested hypotheses about the ideological and political stratification of the movement which may be tested by an examination of other more direct sources of information.

Perception of Party Goals at Time of Joining

In the analysis of the party media of communication, it was pointed out that the appeals of the Communist movement in its mass media differed sharply from the appeals to be found in its theoretical literature. The greatest stress at the mass level was on the evils of the outside world, and the party appeared as a generalized symbol of virtue. This pattern suggested the hypothesis that relatively few individuals at the point of recruitment to the party perceive the doctrinal pattern as it has been described in the analysis of the classics and the Cominform periodical. This point is clearly made in Table 1, where it appears that only 27 per cent of the respondents had been exposed to the classical writings of Communism before or at the time of joining. Twenty-seven per cent is an outside figure, since any reference to having read or having been otherwise exposed to

TABLE I

Perception of Goals of Party at Time of Joining by Country
(in per cent)

	U.S.	U.K.	France	Italy	All respondents
Number of respondents	*64*	*50*	*56*	*51*	*221*
Exposure to esoteric goals	. 28	16	46	14	27
Perception of agitational goals	95	100	98	92	96
Non-political perceptions	73	54	45	55	58

"Marxism-Leninism-Stalinism" was recorded. No effort was made to separate out those who had been exposed to the esoteric doctrine but had not registered its significance, or those who registered it and rejected it in whole or in part.

A comment of an American party member may illustrate the kind of exposure which is not really registered by the new recruit: "While I was trying to get in . . . the members were looking me over. Finally X started giving me pamphlets to read. The first was against Trotsky, of whom I had never heard. It was eighty pages long. The most dreary thing; I couldn't understand it. Later they gave me Stalin's *Foundations of Leninism* and some Marx."[1] This type of exposure is not very different from the many cases of individuals who deliberately avoided exposure to the doctrinal complexities of the party: "I didn't worry through the thick books on Marx. I joined the party when it moved a widow's evicted furniture back into her house. I thought it was right. That's why I joined."

Some of the respondents had been exposed to the doctrine through reading the classics, but were not especially impressed by this experience. A former French party member commented, "I read Marx, Lenin, and even Stalin. I was seduced by the thorough analysis of politics that I found there. But my readings did not determine a change of outlook as much as did human contacts. In Toulouse I lived in a working-class section and met workers in the restaurant and was much attracted toward them. They were simple people, more honest, more alive, than the *petits-bourgeois* I had known. For a young man they held the attraction of life."

Also among those exposed to the party doctrine were some who registered its content but explicitly rejected it in whole or in part. A French respondent remarked, "I entered the Communist student organization early in 1939, without adhering to the philosophy of Marx. I did not believe in materialism any more than in deism or idealism. I was interested in Kierkegaard and the German existentialist philosophy as early as 1936 and 1937." Similarly, a British former party member registered but partly rejected the party doctrine: "A political outlook based on a Marxist and dialectical materialist approach appealed to me as an attempt at

---

[1] All quotations, unless otherwise identified, are taken from interviews.

a scientific approach to politics. But I never fully accepted the CP's dogmatic interpretation of events. . . . I was prepared to tolerate the interpretation at the time because I felt the party was moving in the right direction. I was young and restless and wanted to be positive about something, and one can't be positive about anything in the Labor Party."

At the same time, there were some exposed to the doctrine who registered its content and fully accepted it. The comment of a French respondent may illustrate this pattern: "I was not a Marxist at first, but rather an anarchist. I read Sorel, Pelloutier, and Proudhon and then joined the Syndicalist Youth. This anarcho-syndicalist period was a temporary one, sentimental in character. In Lyons, socialism was too parliamentary and municipal, left-wing elements were automatically anarchistic. I was thirsty for logic and clarity. It was only after reading Lenin, Radek, and Bukharin that I understood that authentic socialism was being renovated by Bolshevism. They acted as powerful searchlights for young men who had a taste for systematic thinking and were seeking the absolute."

An Italian former party member, referring to his first exposure to doctrinal materials while a member of a group of anti-Fascist university students in Rome in the middle 1930's, recalled, "I received and read, printed on very thin paper, the *Foundations of Leninism*. On reading the text I found myself to be in agreement. No information in my possession from a credible source could contest, so far as regards history, the reasoned account which was offered me. A certain dryness and inhumanity of style was unpleasing, but it was a political document, edited in such a way as to be within the reach and understanding of everyone, and designed to give them the impulse to act."

However, among the small proportion of the respondents who were exposed to the esoteric doctrine at the time of joining the party, there were very few who had registered and accepted it. Far more typical of the respondents at the time of their affiliation was the perception of the movement as a means of attaining certain non-specifically party goals.

Almost all the respondents perceived the party at the point of joining in terms of one or a combination of its agitational goals, as a means of combating and destroying Fascism, racial, ethnic, and religious discrimination, or imperialism; or positively as a means of attaining trade union objectives, peace, general social improvement, or humanitarian socialist goals. If these findings are an accurate reflection of the general pattern of perception of the movement, then it can be said that the typical party member does not perceive the esoteric properties of the party at the time of joining, but is attracted to one or more of the agitational goals. In this respect, there is a significant correspondence between the representation of the party in the mass media and the perception of the party by new recruits.

But the party is not only perceived politically in terms of its agitational or esoteric properties; it is also quite frequently perceived as a means of attaining personal and non-political objectives. More than half of the respondents (58 per cent) saw the party at the time of joining as a way of solving personal problems or attaining personal ends. At the same time, only the rare case perceived the party entirely in personal, non-political terms. The typical perception involved a combination of one or more agitational goals with some conscious personal need and expectation. Thus, the party was often viewed as a means of gratifying general anti-authoritarian and anti-conventional impulses, as a way out of personal isolation, as a means of understanding the world around one, or quite simply as an avenue to a career.

But, as Table 1 shows, and as subsequent tables will support, the perceptions of the party varied from country to country and from group to group. Substantially more of the American respondents (73 per cent) perceived the party as a means of satisfying non-political needs. More than 30 per cent of the American cases saw the party as an anti-authoritarian organization, and thereby as a means of gratifying their own desire for rebellion, and 39 per cent viewed it as a way of relating themselves to a congenial group, thereby solving the problem of loneliness or isolation. Thirty-three per cent viewed the party as a means to an intellectual mastery of the world around them.

The French respondents provide a striking contrast to the American. Almost half (46 per cent) had been exposed to Marxist-Leninist-Stalinist doctrine at the time of joining, and only 45 per cent viewed the party as a means of satisfying personal non-political needs. The French cases thus would appear to conform most closely to the early Bolshevik principle that recruits be indoctrinated before being accorded membership in the revolutionary elite. However, the French group included a disproportionately large number of former high-echelon Communists and persons who had joined in the early years of the movement. It may be that these differences are related more to echelon and period of joining than to the national factor.

There is considerable variation from country to country in the political perceptions of the party. In both England and the United States, the party was seen as a means of achieving trade union objectives more often than was the case in France and Italy. In France and Italy, on the other hand, the goals of the party were more often viewed as coinciding with the socialist-humanitarian aspirations which were deeply rooted in those countries before the advent of Communism. In the United States and England, the political goals of the party were more often perceived as general social improvement and bettering of conditions than as specifically socialist aims. These differences may have two causes. In the first place, the party shapes its agitational goals to coincide with the already existing goal aspirations of the groups to which they appeal. And second, the new recruits at the point of joining tend to see the party in a relationship of continuity with their prior goal aspirations.

There are a number of interesting differences in non-political perceptions of the party among the groups of national respondents. Common to all four groups is the identification of the party as anti-authoritarian, as a means of rebelling and rejecting, and as an "exciting" and unconventional thing to join. But the perception of the party as a means of solving problems of loneliness and isolation was far more frequent among the American and British cases than among the French and Italian. Thirty-nine per cent of the Americans and 38 per cent of the British described their early perceptions of the party in these terms, as opposed to only 20 per cent of the French cases and 10 per cent of the Italians. An obvious hypothesis to account for this extraordinary disparity is that among the American and British cases (and in the American and British parties as well) there is a relatively high proportion of foreign-born and first-generation native-born individuals of Eastern European origin. Members of minority groups are confronted with a serious problem of conformity and assimilation to the dominant society. Feelings of vulnerability and of isolation are often associated with this social status, particularly among the more socially mobile elements. Similarly, many of the group memberships available to those of the dominant ethnic group are not equally available to them. It is not surprising, therefore, that minority group members who are about to affiliate with the party should perceive it as a way of coping with feelings of vulnerability and of isolation. In contrast, France and Italy have had relatively few immigrants in the last decades. The Communist movements in these countries are made up almost entirely of the native stock, for whom the problem of social relatedness does not bulk as large. Such perceptions of the party as a means of solving problems of social relatedness as have occurred among our French and Italian cases were almost entirely limited to intellectuals.

In Table 2 a comparison is made of the perceptions of the

TABLE 2

Perception of Goals of Party at Time of Joining by Social Class
(in per cent)

	Intellectual and middle class	*Working class*	*All respondents*
Number of respondents	110	111	221
Exposure to esoteric goals	32	21	27
Perception of agitational goals	94	99	96
Non-political perceptions	71	44	58

goals of the party by intellectuals and middle-class recruits as against working-class recruits. The intellectual and middle-class respondents were exposed to the classics more often than the working-class selection (32 per cent to 21 per cent). In addition, personal and non-political perceptions occurred more frequently among the middle-class respondents than among the working class (71 per cent to 44 per cent). These findings suggest the plausibility of the general hypothesis that working-class party recruits more often perceive the party in pragmatic and immediately functional terms. For the working-class respondents, the most common perceptions of the party associated it with trade union objectives, socialist humanitarian objectives, or general improvement of conditions. Nevertheless, it is important to keep in mind that these are differences in degree. Many of the working-class recruits were ideologically indoctrinated, and many of the intellectuals were not.

There are also differences in non-political perceptions as between the middle-class and working-class respondents. The ratio of middle-class to working-class respondents who perceived the party as a means of rebelling against authority was almost 2 to 1, as a means of gratifying bohemian impulses almost 3 to 1, as a means of relating themselves to a group almost 2 to 1, as a means to intellectual mastery more than 3 to 1.

The respondents were also divided into those who had joined the party before the advent of the Popular Front era, and those who had joined later (see Table 3). Here again the differences are striking and suggest a deterioration through time in the ideological "purity" of the recruitment practices of the party from the point of view of the Leninist model. Only 15 per cent of the post-Popular Front recruits had been exposed to the doctrine before affiliation, while 37 per cent of the early recruits had been so exposed. Similarly, 68 per cent of the late recruits perceived the party as a means to personal, non-political ends as opposed to 48 per cent of the early recruits. Among those who joined in the 1920's, the party was perceived most frequently in terms of pacifism, socialist humanitarian aims, and romantic expectations of the Soviet Revolution. For the later recruits, anti-Fascism and the general betterment of conditions were the most common goal perceptions. There does not appear to have

TABLE 3

*Perception of Goals of Party at Time of Joining
by Period of Joining**
(in per cent)

	Early joiners	Late joiners	All respondents
Number of respondents	115	106	221
Esposure to esoteric goals	37	15	27
Perception of agitational goals	97	96	96
Non-political perceptions	48	68	58

* For three of the four countries, "early joiners" included those joining before 1935. "Late joiners" were those who joined in 1935 or later. Since the Italian party was underground until 1943, this was the year taken to divide the Italian respondents on the basis of period of joining.

been a significant shift in the non-political perceptions of the party between the earlier and later periods, except insofar as might have been accounted for by the increase in middle-class and intellectual party members during the post-Popular Front era. Thus, intellectual mastery and social relatedness appear more frequently among the late recruits.

There is a significant correspondence between rank attained later in the party and the early perception of the party (see Table 4). Respondents who had been exposed to the doctrine at the time of joining more often entered the cadres of the party or became high-echelon officials. There is also an inverse relationship between non-political perceptions of the party and later rank. Only 37 per cent of the high-echelon respondents had perceived the party as a means to personal, non-political ends, while 67 per cent of those who never emerged from the rank and file had perceived it in these terms. The reasons for these marked distinctions would appear to be clear. In the first place, a prior exposure to the doctrine suggests a greater commitment to the party at the time of joining. Presumably, such individuals would join the party with a certain momentum, would know more of the party cues, and hence would move into positions of leadership. Secondly, exposure to the classics and particularly to the writings of Lenin and Stalin might minimize conflict in

TABLE 4

Perceptions of Goals of Party at Time of Joining by Echelon*
(in per cent)

	Rank and file	Low echelon	High echelon	All respondents
Number of respondents	97	73	51	221
Exposure to esoteric goals	17	30	41	27
Perception of agitational goals	99	96	92	96
Non-political perceptions	67	59	37	58

* "Rank and file" was defined as holding no party office whatever. "Low echelon" was defined as including persons holding the rank of cell secretary up to, but not including, the level of the most inclusive regional offices. "High echelon" was defined as including persons holding offices in the "regional," "federation," or national organs of the party.

the process of assimilation within the party. The learning problem would be less serious.

It is also suggested that those coming to the party with expectations which could be satisfied as well or better in other relationships or activities are more likely to remain rank and filers and have a short tenure of membership. Thus perceiving the party as a means of attaining social relatedness, intellectual mastery, or a career was more characteristic of the rank and file than of the low- and high-echelon respondents. The perception of the party as a means to rebellion was the only non-political perception characteristic of the party leaders among our respondents. This would suggest that of all the non-political expectations of the party, rebellion is the least in conflict with full assimilation into the party. The problem of forms and degrees of rebellion and resentment and the particular ways in which they may be assimilated and transformed in the party will be dealt with in detail at a later point.

These general findings as to the lack of indoctrination of the great mass of the rank and file of the Communist movement are confirmed by other studies. Thus recent public opinion surveys in France and Italy show that adherence to, or sympathy for, the party are typically based on the party's agitational themes and not on knowledge of the doctrine or esoteric party practice. Seventy-six per cent of the French Communist respondents in a survey conducted in the spring of 1952 reported that their membership in the party was due to their living conditions; only a small minority reported doctrinal reasons for party membership. Sixty-five per cent of the Communist respondents thought that France should remain neutral in a war between the United States and Russia.[2] The same survey also showed that most of the Communist respondents perceived the party in its local setting, in relation to their own problems and grievances, rather than in its international ramifications. Similar findings were reported recently in a series of surveys made in Italy by the Italian public-opinion polling organization *Doxa*.[3]

Thus the great bulk of party members would appear to be unaware of the esoteric properties of the party at the time they join. They have not read the classic Communist writings from which these properties might be inferred, and they have had no experience with the actual operating code of the party. But there is a sense in which these findings may be seriously misleading, particularly if one should draw the inference that most persons joining the party are "innocent dupes." There are certainly many such, and it is probably true that whole sectors of the party—for example, among the peasants—consist of persons of this type. However, a great many of those who have not been exposed to the esoteric doctrine of the party nevertheless register the fact that there is an esoteric discipline in the party which is deviant, iconoclastic, and antagonistic to the dominant society. Thus many

[2] *Realités*, May 1952, pp. 37-44.
[3] Unpublished report.

of the middle-class intellectuals perceived the party at the time they joined it as something bohemian, exciting, dangerous, and the like. They were not aware of the specific esoteric properties of the party, but they registered its negative and antagonistic tone, and were positively attracted to it in these terms.

Theoretical Indoctrination While in the Party

Although relatively few of the respondents had been exposed to the party doctrine at or before the time of joining, most of them experienced some theoretical indoctrination while in the party. Only 37 per cent had no formal training whatever, and even among these there were quite a few who picked up party doctrine informally. The most characteristic mode of training was through self-teaching, i.e., reading and informal discussion. More than 30 per cent of the respondents received their indoctrination by this means. Only a small number were tutored by some senior party member, but this kind of training experience was often quite effective. A British party member was tutored by a leading British Communist who had served as a representative to the Comintern. He described his tutor as ". . . one of the iron Bolsheviks who knew all the phrases, could adjust to any situation or remodel the situation to suit the party's requirements. Through him I learned what a marvellous instrument of knowledge dialectical materialism was." Eighteen per cent of the respondents had participated in local party study groups of one kind or another. Seven per cent had attended national or regional schools for three- or six-month periods, and only 2 per cent had attended the Lenin School in Moscow.

Differences from one group of national respondents to the next reflected either the special selection of the respondents or the special experience of the party in the particular country. While the Italian party has established an elaborate network of training schools since the end of the war, these schools have been in existence only for a short period of time. Thus, only 21 per cent of the Italian respondents had been trained in local, regional, or national schools, in contrast to

39 per cent for the American group, and 30 per cent for the British. Most of the Italians exposed to some form of indoctrination had been self-taught.

As might be anticipated, more of the working-class respondents (45 per cent) had had no formal training than the middle-class respondents (29 per cent) (see Table 5).

TABLE 5

Theoretical Indoctrination While in Party by Social Class
(in per cent)

Kind of indoctrination	Middle class	Working class	All respondents
Russian party schools	1	3	2
National or regional schools	7	7	7
Local training activity	17	19	18
Individual tutoring	5	5	5
Self-taught	41	21	31
No formal training	29	45	37
Total	100	100	100

This is hardly a consequence of oversight on the part of the party leadership. Special efforts are made to recruit working-class members for the party schools, but working-class party members, unless they become functionaries, are less free to leave their work, and because of lack of formal education are often frightened or repelled when exposed to an intellectual experience. A fairly large proportion of the working-class respondents might be described as simple activists capable of grasping only one objective at a time, and more than ready to leave doctrine to the others. While this would appear to be the dominant pattern among working-class members, there is a relatively small but significant group of self-educated workers who made a real effort to better themselves intellectually, and for whom the party was a means of transforming their orientation to life from a simple passive acceptance of their surroundings to the excitements of intellectual mastery.

Differences in the mode of indoctrination as between those who joined in the periods before and after the Popular Front policy are of some interest. The national party schools began to function on a large scale only in the 1930's. As a consequence, proportionately more of the late recruits had had some formal training experience. Thus 35 per cent of the late recruits had attended national, regional, or local party schools, as compared with 20 per cent for the early recruits (see Table 6). More of the early recruits had been trained by tutors, were self-taught, or had reported no formal training experience.

TABLE 6

Theoretical Indoctrination While in Party by Period of Joining
(in per cent)

Kind of indoctrination	Early joiners	Late joiners	All respondents
Russian party schools	4	—	2
National or regional schools	4	10	7
Local training activity	12	25	18
Individual tutoring	8	2	5
Self-taught	37	24	31
No formal training	35	39	37
Total	100	100	100

There are a number of differences in indoctrination as between the three echelons into which the respondents were divided. As might be anticipated, more of the high-echelon respondents attended the Lenin School in Moscow. More of the low-echelon respondents attended the national or regional party schools, while almost all the rank and filers who had undergone formal training were exposed only to local and part-time study groups (see Table 7). That so large a percentage of the high-echelon respondents were either self-taught or had no formal training is attributable to the fact that most of them joined the movement in the 1920's—in other words, before the establishment of the Communist training school system. Either they had been self-taught before joining, or they picked up the doctrine informally after joining the party. The fact that so few of the rank and file had formal training is hardly surprising, since one of the

TABLE 7

Theoretical Indoctrination While in Party by Echelon
(in per cent)

Kind of indoctrination	Rank and file	Low echelon	High echelon	All respondents
Russian party schools	1	1	6	2
National or regional schools	2	15	4	7
Local training activity	24	18	8	18
Individual tutoring	1	7	10	5
Self-taught	27	32	39	31
No formal training	45	27	33	37
Total	100	100	100	100

qualifications for selection for the central party schools is the manifestation of a capacity for leadership. One of the most important functions of the party schools is to select potential cadres and shape them into trustworthy party militants to be used to staff the middle echelons of the party bureaucracy.

How the Training Experience Is Perceived

At an earlier point, it was found that the theme of rational calculating behavior is heavily stressed in the Communist classics as a property of the Communist militant. The militant possesses the only true theory of society and of the laws governing its transformation. He constantly uses this theory in comprehending political reality, and tests it in concrete actions and situations. But it was also found, particularly in the writings of Stalin, that only certain Communists have played an active and creative theoretical role, i.e., the apostolic succession from Marx to Stalin. It was discovered that the theoretical, rational calculating role is overshadowed by the great emphasis on organizational discipline and the strict centralization of authority in the doctrinal portrayal of the party. It was suggested that a careful reader of the Leninist and Stalinist classics might conclude that while the party has a theory, the right to be "theoretical" (i.e., draw inferences from the theory, and apply it to reality) is carefully located in the central organs of the party, and all that is left to the echelons below is the power to expound, and perhaps, within limits, to explain.

The material from our interviews which has so far been presented shows how this rational, theoretical component of the party is perceived by persons within the movement. We have seen that very few of our respondents were exposed to the authoritative doctrine of the party before or at the time of joining. However, most of our respondents were exposed during the course of their membership either through self-teaching or through some formal training experience. While the rational component of the party impinges on the member in many other ways, the training experience is in a sense a "concentrated dose of indoctrination," and the perception of this experience may be representative of the general perception of the theoretical aspect of the party by our respondents.

It may therefore be useful to refer to some of the comments of our respondents about their experience as students in these schools. And since some of our respondents were teachers in or directors of party schools, or high-echelon officials who lectured in them, we may cite their observations on the aims and techniques of instruction in these institutions.

A British cell leader recalled, "I went to study groups, but got out of them whenever I could. It was a most banal business, especially the *History of the C.P.S.U. (B)*, by question and answer." An American Negro who was sent to Moscow to study at the Lenin School referred to this experience as the "thing that weaned me away from the CP. The dogmatic attitude with regard to mental discipline didn't seem in keeping with Marxism. It was indoctrination training in leadership, a training in the acceptance of upper-echelon dictates. . . . In quizzes they would make statements which they would word trickily in order to get you to pick the wrong interpretation. Then you would be jumped on by the rest of the class and the instructor. One by one, those who erred would weasel over to the other point of view, and the last one would be the one who originally made the mistake."

An Italian working-class respondent was utterly bored by the proceedings and commented, "I can only tell you that an instructor talked for hours together, repeating the same things time after time to the point of boredom, and that no one was allowed to interrupt him unless he had previously studied the subject of the lecture for days and days. Only then were we allowed to offer some objections, which were immediately rejected and denied." An Italian party functionary, summarizing the effects of this experience on himself and his fellow students, concluded, "It may be said that people enter these schools as individuals, but they leave as cogs of a machine." Another Italian who went through the schools observed, in speculating about their techniques and objectives, "In this way the individual loses, little by little, the faculty of judging facts and situations objectively, and begins to reason not by virtue of his own intelligence but by rote, using from time to time those key reasonings with which he has been indoctrinated, and which for him have now assumed the value of an axiom. To obtain these results is neither simple nor easy. It requires, above all, strong will power or, more precisely, a certain volition, in order to overcome the fatigue and the monotony which this surgical operation requires. This act of volition, which is really an act of renunciation, is facilitated by the skillful technique manifested in the conduct of the discussions."

Comments from those respondents who had been indoctrinated in the 1920's described a strikingly different atmosphere. Doctrinal discussions were lively. Conflicting points of view were tolerated. Discipline was relatively loose and easy. Party leaders were in a position to indoctrinate others by virtue of their dedication, their intellectual ability and moral prestige. Nowhere is this more marked than in the recollections of some of the Italians whose schooling took place during *confino*, in the prisons. An Italian intellectual who left the party at the time of the Nazi-Soviet Pact said, "Amongst those confined were some of the chief exponents of the clandestine movement who transfused into us their strength and their unshakable faith. There was Gramsci, whom the Fascists had decided to allow to die of his incurable disease, and who in his solitude elaborated the study of the purest socialist ideology. . . . There were Terracini and Scoccimarro, two leaders of exceptional intelligence and great communicativeness, and many others around whom we young ones gathered with confidence. . . . That could really be considered the school of the party, where we studied in the real sense of the word, on pure philosophical bases, a school with bars at the windows, but where there was freedom of thought."

But even in the prisons the Stalinization of the party resulted in a change in the pattern of indoctrination. After describing the early prison atmosphere of "free discussion," one former political prisoner stated that the spirit changed during the later years of his confinement. "In this later period the conception of the Russian 'idol' . . . began to insinuate itself. . . . Indoctrination became a rigid unyielding weapon which the party used for the purpose of creating . . . a definite species of man. In brief, if in the prewar period, the period of the persecutions, the indoctrination gave to the party real Communists, during the war the party's objective was to train cadres, and today, only automatons."

A former high regional official commented on the changes in the Italian party schools from the immediate prewar period to the present: "As soon as they took on the Muscovite physiognomy the schools completely abandoned every interest in culture. True history is banished. . . . They want to obtain men who accept the dogma, men who know how to defend the version of the events which is considered useful. . . . There is perhaps no more profound break with the Italian and European humanist tradition than that which is going on in the courses and in the schools of the party. To take simple comrades . . . and to exploit their eagerness to learn, which does them honor, and to create in them the conviction that they are in the possession of the truth about philosophy, history, and politics . . . is one of the gravest crimes against culture. The party aims in these schools to banish the process of critical thought. I have heard one of the high functionaries of the party say that persons are sent to the schools in order to break their independence of judgment, not to learn doctrine. Working-class comrades sent to the schools often suffer a physical and nervous collapse which is accepted as a part of the process of adaptation to the mental mechanism of passive obedience, to the suppression of personality. Some can't hold out and abandon the courses; others become simple fanatics; others accustom themselves to hypocrisy."

From a quite different quarter, the United States, and from a respondent who was himself in charge of a regional training school comes a confirmation of this aim of breaking down those aspects of the personality which resist discipline. Commenting on the technique of "Pop" Mindel, the director of the National Training School, our respondent stated: "He was a good teacher, but used to enrage and attack people, then suddenly lighten up with a joke—then suddenly attack again. The object was to break down independence of judgment and character. Pop Mindel was a destroyer of individuality. . . . He broke one man completely one day—and then sat up all night speaking softly and 'inspirationally' to him. Mindel's techniques came from the Lenin School." Remarking on the criteria for selection of persons to be admitted to the schools, this informant said, "You were always looking for incompatibles, people who were completely loyal, but who had initiative and ability—conformity in the larger sphere, initiative in a very limited sphere."

From other comments as to the ways in which cell meetings are conducted, and the ways in which directives are imposed and enforced on the lower leadership echelons by the higher, it is apparent that the dogmatic and authoritarian pattern of the party schools is typical of the intellectual processes in the party. As one American respondent put it, "If there are ten party members in a room, regardless of whether it is a party meeting or a social affair, it is taken for granted that some one member has the authority. Others may ask for 'clarification,' a favorite term, but only the highest ranking 'insider' has the power to 'clarify.' Ninety per cent of the party membership are simply asking for clarification in the humblest sort of way."

Is there a conflict between the representation of the rational-theoretical aspect of the party in the classics, and its perception by persons who have experienced party membership? The answer is not a simple one. A careful, critical reading of the classics, and particularly the writings of Stalin, might prepare the party initiate for a rather severely circumscribed form of intellectual participation. After all, the rational function is to be carried on in a highly centralized, disciplined organizational setting, a readily manipulated army. This is hardly the kind of setting in which free discussion and creative rationality can long survive. But it is apparent that the small proportion of party members who are exposed to the doctrine at or before the time of joining do not subject the classics to a critical analysis. More often than not, they read like eager candidates for discipleship; and as a consequence they may not be prepared for the intellectual authoritarianism of the party. It often comes as something of a shock. For those who have not been exposed to the doctrine at the time of joining but who perceive the theoretical and rational claims of the party and are attracted to them, the same kind of shock is experienced when they undergo indoctrination. This type of shock or repulsion is more characteristic of the party intellectuals than of other groups. For this group, it is one of the most important tests of capacity for survival and leadership in the party. If they can give up their own intellectual "illusions" and accept the status of an intellectual tactician, then their prospects for long tenure and preferment are good.

Interpersonal Relations in the Party

The theme of Communist rationality as developed in the classics rejects spontaneity, moods, irrelevant feelings. The Communist is in full rational control of himself and of situations. It would appear that the model of interpersonal relations that emerges from the classical doctrine is impersonality and functional solidarity. Loyalty is to the party, and not to friends or other persons with other common interests. Clustering on the basis of other than party interests reduces the maneuverability of the party membership, and introduces extraneous and often corrupting elements. The dangers and threats which confront the party both because of the hostility of the external world, and because of the internal possibilities of relaxation of effort and yielding to moods, require a constant "vigilance" in one's personal relations inside as well as outside the party. The institution of the purge, the dramatic expulsions and exemplary punishments of defectors, the existence of control commissions, the maintenance of dossiers on individual party members, all create and maintain an atmosphere of vigilance and distrust. The requirement that party members sever all ties with defectors and hate and revile them also contributes to this inhibition of impulses toward openness and warmth in personal relations. It stresses by implication that the enjoyment of solidarity is strictly conditioned upon full and implicit loyalty to the party. The model Communist gives up his right to friendship in exchange for "comradeship."

Less than 30 per cent of the respondents saw little or no difference between the pattern of interpersonal relations in the party and outside it. Among this minority, some even viewed friendship in the party as closer and more intense than relationships in the outside community. An American woman defector remarked, "The friendship was closer. There was a stronger bond. There was so much that you shared together that you understood, and didn't have to argue about. . . . Then again, friendships were deeper because you were aware of the hostility of the outside world." "Yet," this respondent added, as an afterthought, "those friendships which you thought were so deep and personal evaporated when you left the party." A French woman, a former leading party member, spoke almost in the same terms: "There was great comradeship and mutual confidence. We were like a real family. In the committees we were glad to see each other again and talk about our work. There is a very peculiar atmosphere there; if one stays in line one feels comfortable; if not, it's most uncomfortable."

But these comments definitely represented a minority view. The more common responses described personal relationships as "detached and functional" (20 per cent), or characterized them as colored by "suspicion and distrust" (15 per cent). A smaller proportion (8 per cent) described personal relations as warm in the rank and file of the party, but not in the higher echelons. Another 8 per cent described them as warm in the earlier years of the party's existence, but as having changed after the Stalinization of the Communist movement in the late 1920's and early 1930's.

A former member of the British Politburo described his party friendships as having been strictly functional: "We'd been in politics together since we were lads. Nearly all my friendships grow out of political association. Most of my friends were inside the party, though I had a few outside. In general, my friendships not only grew out of political activity, but were held together by it." An Italian remarked, "Party discipline does not admit of friendship. So human a sentiment would bind together individuals who must be Communists above all, rather than normal men. Friendship would also interfere with the careful reciprocal surveillance among the comrades. The Communist therefore has a tendency to retire within himself, isolating himself to defend his thoughts, and his intimate opinions." An American Communist stated, "The amount of trust and confidence between two people is in direct proportion to the confidence people have in the person's trust and loyalty to the party as such. Outside the party one can tell things to friends, even with misgivings, knowing it will be honored. Confidences in the party are more guarded, even with one's best friends."

Perception of personal relations in the party as clouded by suspicion and fear was also a common response. A British former party member put it in these terms: "I think that in any warm human friendship inside the party there would eventually come a political rift. For that reason there were very few human friendships and it became a cold callous business. Since I've left the CP my wife says I've become human." An Italian commented, "The Communist Party has created an atmosphere of merely formal fraternal spirit, with relations limited to a cordiality which excludes any form of intimacy. On the contrary, under this apparent cordiality each one is looked upon with suspicion by the others, because it is notorious that particularly tried and faithful elements mix with the members for the purpose of listening to and then reporting speeches and opinions—really spy work." An Italian, a former high party official, remarked about personal relations at the top level of the Italian party, "The relations between party chiefs which the romantic imagination of the crowd thinks are fraternal are remarkable for their strict reciprocal surveillance, for the extreme reserve in judging every little question, for the fear that one's own words might be used at a later time to prove heresy." An American former party member observed, "I made a very good friend within the party, and he left the party at the same time as I did. We had been as close as friends can be, yet it was only after we left the party that the full humanness of the friendship appeared." And the institutionalization of surveillance was also perceived in the American party: "Then there was the control commission—watching every tiny thought or remark. You couldn't trust yourself with anyone. They keep a record of every remark and I'm a guy who likes to open his mouth." A Frenchman felt that distrust was more characteristic of the intellectual sectors of the party: "There is a subterranean mistrust on the part of all those who think. Suspicion is a political reflex that they insist upon. But it must not be paralyzing; they want to hit a balance. The word is *vigilance*."

Others viewed friendship and warm personal relations as more characteristic of the party rank and file. As a Britisher put it, "At the lowest level there is implicit trust, but the higher you get the less there is." This view was confirmed by a high-echelon American woman, "I don't think in the 'Apparatus' anyone ever trusted anybody else. There was constant watching, and God help you if you ever made a misstep. But I believe the rank and file trusted one another." And another American: "I would have to differentiate between two groups. Among the rank and file there was a considerable amount of trust. Up above there was probably very little. That was one of the things that shocked me and made me want to leave. . . . The CP is a wonderful outlet for hostile and contemptuous feelings. You can be hostile without guilt because it's for something bigger than yourself—and not for personal reasons."

Those who had been in the party in its earlier days or who joined it during the resistance felt that the atmosphere of the party had greatly changed from this early romantic period. As an Englishman put it, "At the beginning the British party was a party of friends—through all the levels. There was constant criticism from the Russians to break it up. People had to be politicians, not friends." Or an Italian, "During the clandestine period the comrades felt like brothers in the struggle. The postwar Communists were altogether different. A new generation had developed, superficial, corrupt, distrustful of one another. Even the older generation was unrecognizable." An American who had served the party for a long period and reached a high position argued that there were few real friendships in the party. He pointed out that ". . . in the Communist Party emotional affect is associated with mass meetings, or with situations. There were very few warm people in the top leadership of the American party, in contrast to the British. . . . If you had cold tendencies, the party reinforced them. Browder had warm tendencies but they were crushed." At another point the same respondent remarked, "While I was in the party I could pass beggars in the street, but now I am uneasy."

It is of interest that the observation of this last respondent about the differences between the British and American party leaderships should be so strikingly confirmed in Table 8. Fifty-two per cent of the British respondents characterized the pattern of interpersonal relations in the party as no different from that which obtains outside. This compares with 22 per cent for the American, 28 per cent for the French, and 18 per cent for the Italian. As we shall see below, this finding is but one of a number which, taken together, suggest the hypothesis that, of all those studied, the British party deviates most sharply from the model elaborated in the party doctrine.

TABLE 8

Quality of Friendships in Party by Country
(in per cent)

	U.S.	England	France	Italy	All re-spondents
No special party pattern	22	52	28	18	29
Detached, functional	11	10	27	31	20
Suspicion and distrust	27	6	4	19	15
Warm in rank and file, not in higher echelon	14	4	7	6	8
Warm at beginning, not later	3	8	5	16	8
Other	11	6	2	2	5
No answer	12	14	27	8	15
Total	100	100	100	100	100

It is also of interest that a larger proportion of the Italian respondents described personal relations in the Italian party as detached and functional or as characterized by fear, suspicion, and distrust. This may be due to two factors. Most of the Italian respondents joined the party during or immediately after the resistance. They had been exposed to the partisan "mystique," or to the revolutionary romanticism of the immediate postwar period. The imposition of bureaucratic controls and of a system for supervising and observing individual conduct perhaps came as a shock to a great many of these new recruits. Secondly, most of the respondents (and most of the Italian party) joined the party as a protest against Fascist militarism and suppression of freedom. The rather sudden imposition of a similar pattern in the party would then come as a sharp disillusionment.

There do not appear to be any significant differences in the perceptions of personal relations in the party as between middle-class and working-class respondents. On the other hand, those who had joined the party in the pre-Popular Front era more often described personal relations in this earlier period as warm and friendly in contrast to the later period.

There are a number of interesting differences related to rank in the party. As one might expect, fewer of the high-echelon respondents perceived no differences between personal relations in the party and outside—only 19 per cent of the high-ranking respondents as compared with 33 per cent of the low echelon, and 32 per cent of the rank and file (see Table 9). The high-echelon respondents described personal

TABLE 9
Quality of Friendships in Party by Echelon
(in per cent)

	Rank and file	Low echelon	High echelon	All respondents
No special party pattern	32	33	19	29
Detached, functional	14	21	28	20
Suspicion and distrust	16	16	10	15
Warm in rank and file, not in higher echelon	6	10	10	8
Warm at beginning, not later	5	8	12	8
Other	8	3	4	5
No answer	19	9	17	15
Total	100	100	100	100

relations more frequently in the doctrinally appropriate terms of detachment and vigilance than in moral terms of suspicion and distrust. This is another bit of evidence which suggests that the party model is perceived and described more correctly among the high-echelon party members.

If we compare the perceptions of interpersonal relations in the party with the model stressed in the party doctrine, a number of points are suggested. The model stresses impersonality and rationality, and warns against spontaneity and sentiment. It calls for comradely solidarity rather than "philistine compassion," and rules out the cultivation of any other loyalty than to the party. Personal relations in the party were perceived in these terms only by a minority of our respondents, and a high proportion of these were among the "inner core" party leaders. Perceptions of interpersonal relations in the party deviated from the model in two ways. On the one hand, many of the lower-echelon party members described personal relations as being quite like those in the outside society. On the other hand, a sizable group viewed the relations of party members as marred by suspicion and distrust, fear of denunciation, and power-striving. On the whole, the evidence suggests that the atmosphere of party life does not conform to the model of impersonal loyalty and a purely rational focusing of energies on the objectives of the party. For many party members and within many sectors of the movement, the party has failed to destroy "sentimental compassion" and the multiplicity of interests and involvements typical of personal relations in the general society. And when it has accomplished these objectives, rather than producing rational impersonality and unambiguous devotion, it has created an atmosphere of hostility and fear.

These general points are supported by other data on the emotional tone of party life. Both Lenin and Stalin warned strongly against giving way to moods, either of elation or of depression. Successes are to be met by sober planning for the next step; defeats are to be viewed as the temporary consequences of tactical misjudgments, which in most cases are blamed on specific individuals. No momentum is to be lost through giving way to emotions. While the party leadership constantly seeks to control emotional reactions to defeats and victories, the typical pattern of response to victory and defeat would appear to be strongly emotional. One American respondent described the celebrations after the elections of Davis and Cacchione to the New York City Council as marked by "wild enthusiasm." An American trade union leader commented, "Failure to win an election in an industry produced a funereal atmosphere. Two of the party leaders in the union had heart attacks, and one girl had to be taken out with hysterics. . . . They really say some wild things to us at a time like that. It took them three weeks to recover." Another American respondent remarked that party reactions were fanatical and hysterical: "I remember when Browder was let out of jail. I was at Penn Station and saw a good cross-section of the party weeping and carrying on for joy." A

British trade union leader also reported, "They reacted to failure by 'self-criticism.' Somebody's head was on the charger, not always the right head. They were extremely unbalanced, liable to get dizzy with success and rend themselves over failure. Some party members were miserably happy in failure. They enjoyed crucifying themselves."

Nevertheless, a large proportion of the respondents were aware of the fact that emotionalism was in conflict with the party ideal. Almost all of them had participated in sessions of "socialist self-criticism," in which the reasons for particular defeats were discussed by the party membership. But many of those who described their experience with "self-criticism" felt that its main function was to find scapegoats, or provide opportunities for breast-beating to cope with feelings of guilt, anxiety, and resentment.

In other words, the evidence suggests that while the party model of impersonality and rationality is widely perceived in the movement, the emotional atmosphere of the party is not experienced in these terms. Apparently, singleness of devotion to party goals cannot be attained save through extensive internal espionage and pressure and exemplary punishment of offenders. And the introduction of these practices has not produced impersonality and rationality, as conceived in the model, but rather a suppression of feeling and a widespread underlying fear and distrust. The presence of these attitudes on a large scale in the movement may create a constant need for outside targets upon which hatred can be discharged, and for mass meetings and demonstrations at which party members may give vent to their feelings. As one former student party leader put it, "We called five thousand students out for a mass meeting. It was terribly impressive, and I was limp with elation and fatigue."

CHAPTER 5

THE PERCEPTION OF
TACTICAL ASPECTS

IN THE ANALYSIS of the self-portrait of the Communist movement in the classics and in the other media of communication of the party, it was pointed out that the most heavily stressed theme was that of militance. The party is aggressive, effective, "means business." This aspect of the party is almost always perceived by recruits at the time of joining, and constitutes one of the most important appeals. As one American respondent put it, "You have to consider the difference between a quiet Socialist office with nothing going on and a CP office where people, including workers, were coming and going, where there was a strike tomorrow and many activities. You had to decide whether you really wanted to do something." Or, in the words of an Italian, "The organization of the Communist Party was powerful and strong, the men who animated it had given proof of courage and sacrifice, while a magnificent spirit of solidarity united all the elements, heads and members."

Militance

Since the respondents were not asked directly whether they had perceived the militance of the party when they joined, their spontaneous description of it in these terms is impressive. Sixty-nine per cent voluntarily gave the militance and aggressiveness of the party as one of their reasons for joining it. The proportion referring to it in these terms was highest among the Italian respondents (86 per cent). This may be accounted for by the fact that most of the Italian respondents had joined during the resistance when the party was carrying on military action against the Fascists. This response was also relatively more frequent among the high-echelon respondents than among the rank and file. Fifty-eight per cent of those who had held no party offices referred to the militance of the party, as compared with 80 per cent for the high-echelon respondents.

In the analysis of the *Daily Worker* it was suggested that the main stress in Communist mass communication was on the evil attributes of the party's antagonists, and that relatively little was said about the aims and characteristics of the party itself. In our interviews with former party members, we sought to determine if the emotional tone of party life corresponded to this pattern, if the main emphasis was negative, hostile, antagonistic. An American respondent attributed crucial importance to this primarily negative emphasis of the party: "In my opinion, the reason the appeal of the Communist movement is so strong, pervasive, and justifiable, is that 99 per cent of its appeal has nothing to do with Communism. In many ways their weakest link is Communism, hence they don't advance it. Communist propaganda is 99 per cent aggressive, critical, and there is so much to criticize in the *status quo* that the propaganda is bound to be effective. . . . To the extent that Communist propaganda emphasizes the defects of the *status quo*, they can win over people with all types of real grievances. They are against something, not for something. It is only later that some people leave the party because their need to be against something has been satisfied, but their need to be for something has not."

The American and British respondents were specifically asked whether hatred played a significant role in party life (see Table 1). Only a very small number of the respondents attributed little or no importance to hatred of the antagonist

TABLE I

Perception of Hatred in the Emotional Tone of Party Life among American and British Respondents
(in per cent)

	United States	England	All respondents
Hatred of no importance	5	8	6
Hatred of some importance	23	36	29
Hatred of great importance	41	28	35
Other	3	6	4
No answer	28	22	26
Total	100	100	100

in the emotional tone of party life. Forty-one per cent of the American respondents and 28 per cent of the British attributed great or crucial importance to hatred, and referred to it as deliberately cultivated in order to keep the party in a constant state of tension. This tendency was noted more frequently by those who had held party offices—in other words, those who were more familiar with party tactics, and who had shared in the inner party atmosphere. Many of the French and Italian respondents also referred to this aspect of the party, even though the question had not been asked of them. As one Italian put it, "The struggle against these enemies must be carried on, according to the party, with the greatest violence, based on fanaticism and hate—above all, hate." In the words of a Frenchman, "Hatred of the enemy is essential. . . . The Stalinists always looked for a symbol to canalize hatred. *Figaro* is a demon, or it may be *Le Dauphin Libéré*. Other papers are not mentioned. They concentrate on a few symbols. There is the myth of Truman, an evil man who wants war." A British respondent commented, "Hatred was essential. As soon as one begins to see any good points in the enemy, one begins to drift away from the party." An American remarked, "There's a premium put on hatred. You are deliberately encouraged to hate. Adjectives of obscenity are always linked to the enemy. You can't fight unless you hate."

While this kind of response was the more typical, there were a number of interesting deviations from the pattern. Some former party members commented that, rather than encouraging you to hate, the party created an atmosphere of threat. It was the outside world which was hating you. As one American respondent put it, "I wouldn't call it hatred. But the feeling of being different and of being an object of hostility is perhaps fostered." A British former party member referred to the same pattern: "Hatred of the enemy was of quite considerable importance. You maintained your devotion by being a persecuted minority with all the world against you." Hating or feeling one's self as being hated, threatening or being threatened, are closely related, perhaps interdependent, feelings. It is of interest that some of the respondents perceived the passive, rather than the active, aspect of this antagonistic theme in the emotional atmosphere of party life.

In some cases, hatred of the antagonist was not perceived as an important aspect of party life. This was especially marked among the British respondents who had been affiliated with the party as university students. One British intellectual reported, "In the student party, hatred was not very important, in the sense that people in private discussion spent very little time talking about the horrors of Fascism. That was left for the public meetings. The approach was mainly a rational one, and the aim was to remove lack of understanding." Another former British university party member said, "A speech expressing only hatred left an air of embarrassment, whereas no one was out of sympathy when the benefits of socialism were stressed." Another British respondent claimed that it was almost impossible to get Communist trade union members to ". . . hate other members of his trade union just because they are members of the Labor Party. It is hard for new members coming from the Labor Party to heckle or break up a labor meeting. It is much easier to get bourgeois recruits to see the necessity for this policy because they come at it intellectually, and have no close or emotional ties with the labor movement. . . . Certainly the party has not succeeded in instilling opposition to the Labor Party to anything like the extent it would like."

In other words, there were party units where the typical pattern of hatred of the antagonist was not stressed, or was not effective. But the party members reporting these deviant patterns were rarely fully assimilated Communists themselves. They were rank and filers and often belonged to party units which were physically remote from the points of concentration of the party in the large urban centers, or served in "mass" organizations, controlled or influenced by the party but not within the party itself. This point is supported by the finding that the perception of hatred was more characteristic of the higher-echelon respondents.

The kinds of antagonists against which the hatred of the party was directed vary to some extent from one political setting to the next. For example, the Catholic Church appears to be a commonly perceived target of hatred in the Italian party. This is true to a lesser extent among the French respondents, and hardly appears at all among the Americans and British. There are certainly other specifically local antagonists such as the Tory Party in England, the Christian Democrats in Italy, governmental agencies such as the FBI and the Department of Justice in the United States. The objects of hostility most frequently referred to by the respondents of all four countries were the standard ideological targets of "Capitalism," "Fascism," "Right-wing Socialism," and party "renegades." These antagonists occur among all four national groups, among the intellectual and middle-class as well as the working-class respondents, and within all the echelons. The frequencies differ, however, from group to group. The English respondents referred to the Labor Party far more frequently than the French and Italian respondents did to the moderate left movements in their countries. This may be due to the fact that the moderate left is relatively weak in France and Italy and hence does not bulk as large as an antagonist as does the British Labor Party.

The moderate left was cited as an object of party hatred by working-class respondents far more frequently than by intellectual and middle-class former party members (see Table 2). Thus 28 per cent of the working-class group referred to

TABLE 2

*Objects of Party Hatred by Social Class**
(in per cent)

	Middle class	Working class	All respondents
Moderate left	15	28	21
Trade unionists	4	3	3
Renegades	15	6	11
Conservatives	8	11	10
Capitalism	26	26	29
Fascism	14	15	15
United States	5	4	4
Other	16	20	18
No answer	34	40	38

* Multiple responses.

the moderate left, as compared with 15 per cent for the intellectuals and middle-class respondents. On the other hand, defectors or renegades were more often cited by the middle-class respondents than by the laboring group (15 per cent to 6 per cent). These differences may be related to the special problems peculiar to the status of these two groups of former party members. Most of the working-class respondents were in the trade union movement, and their main competitors for the support of the workers were the moderate left trade union leaders. The rate of turnover and defection is higher among middle-class than among working-class party members, and as a consequence the dangers and threat of defection are more sharply registered by them.

TABLE 3

A Comparison of Objects of Party Hatred for Rank-and-file and High-echelon Former Party Members*
(in per cent)

	Rank-and-file	High-echelon	All respondents
Moderate left	17	41	21
Trade unionists	3	4	3
Renegades	11	14	11
Conservatives	10	8	10
Capitalism	20	28	26
Fascism	10	29	15
United States	5	4	4
Other	18	14	18
No answer	44	31	38

* Multiple responses.

A comparison of the perception of the antagonist for rank-and-file and high-echelon respondents in Table 3 shows a much higher frequency of references to the moderate left for the high-echelon respondents than among the rank and file (41 per cent for the former and 17 per cent for the latter). This suggests that the special antagonism of the party toward the "Right-wing Socialist lackeys" is more characteristic of the inner organization of the party than of the general membership.

The above analysis has merely indicated frequencies of reference to party antagonists, and has not in any way distinguished between intensities of antagonism. The qualitative evidence on this last point suggests that the intensity of the antagonism or hatred is greatest with regard to those objects which are closest to the party. As a British respondent put it, "Anyone who ratted was regarded with particular loathing." Another Britisher commented, "For a capitalist or Fascist there is respect and acceptance because he is the reason for your existence. There is no such basis for the existence of social democracy, which is claiming to do what you are claiming to do in a better way. That is why Trotsky and Tito were pursued with such venom. . . ." An American comment supports this distinction: "Hatred for capitalism was never strong enough, but hatred for ex-members was very strong." An Italian high-echelon respondent remarked, "I am certain that the Comintern hated Trotsky more than the foreign powers; that the Cominform considers Tito a worse enemy than America; and that the leadership of the Italian party fears and hates Magnani and Cucchi more than De Gasperi and the Pope." A former American Communist trade union leader made a similar point, "They hate renegades worse than others. They hate Quill more than Curran; Curran more than Green. The closer you were to the party, the greater the hatred when you leave."

Organization and Leadership

Perhaps the most distinguishing feature of the Communist movement is its stress on effective organization. It was Lenin's emphasis on an organization of professional revolutionaries that led to the original formation of the Bolshevik Party. For both Lenin and Stalin, the pattern of organization against which the party was constantly appraised was the military one. Discipline was the central theme, and a ready maneuverability of the various units of the party, a capacity to deploy them quickly from one task to another with maximum effectiveness, was the aim of all organizational effort. With such an "organizational weapon"[1] looser formations

[1] For a penetrating recent analysis of Communist organizational theory

and associations could be manipulated and infiltrated until finally all organizational alternatives would be destroyed. While the overwhelming emphasis in the doctrinal model is on strict discipline, the doctrine also describes the party as "democratic centralist" in character. What this concept seems to imply is that party decisions are to be discussed at the rank-and-file level, recommendations submitted to the higher echelons, and a final decision reached which is then completely binding on the party as a whole. Similarly, in the party electoral process, the higher organs of the party are to be elected by the lower organs. But neither with regard to decisions on policy, nor with regard to the election of leading personnel, were factions (i.e., more or less permanent oppositional groups) to be tolerated.

It has already been pointed out that the doctrinal model of organization contains contradictory elements. The great stress on discipline and the dreadful consequences of "factionalism," which are especially elaborated on in Stalin's *History*, leaves almost no scope for the democratic element in "democratic centralism." This is clearly reflected in the impressions of the Communist organizational pattern in our interviews (see Table 4).

Only 2 per cent of the respondents described party organization as democratic. Eleven per cent said it was democratic in the early years of their membership but not later. Four per cent thought that there was democracy in their own group but not in the upper echelons; and 63 per cent described the organizational pattern as authoritarian.

When asked who made decisions in his own unit, a top-echelon American official said with praiseworthy brevity, "I made them, usually." An Italian, speaking of the atmosphere of terror in the postwar Italian party, said, "Anyone who shows the least tendency toward any form of deviationism

---

and practice, see Philip Selznick, *The Organizational Weapon: A Study of Bolshevik Strategy and Tactics* (New York: McGraw-Hill, 1952). Certain similarities in the model of the party in the Selznick analysis and the present study are due in part to the fact that both have been greatly influenced by the earlier work of Nathan Leites. See his *Operational Code of the Politburo, op.cit.*

is intimidated by menacing voices which murmur phrases such as 'We'll get you some day,' 'Your kind don't live long,' 'The party doesn't want cowardly traitors.' " Another Italian commented on the rigid control of the channels of communication in the party : "If you entered the federation and heard strike x being discussed, you could be certain that the follow-

TABLE 4

Perception of Organizational Structure of Party by Country
(in per cent)

	U.S.	England	France	Italy	All respondents
Authoritarian	53	66	66	66	63
Democratic in own group, authoritarian in upper echelon	3	8	2	4	4
Democratic early, authoritarian later	10	4	13	20	11
Generally democratic	—	—	5	4	2
No explicit reference	34	22	14	6	20
Total	100	100	100	100	100

ing day at the section level the subject under discussion would be strike x, and two days later in the cell the rank and file would be talking about strike x." An Englishman observed, "Even if you were a local leader, you weren't a leader in the ordinary sense, but a mouthpiece for someone else."

Another Britisher commented on the electoral process in the party. In all of his twenty years as a party member he could not recall any open or free election for any committee or council. "It might appear free, but the political leaders would submit a panel of names which everybody voted for. There would be a list of fifty nominations sent to the panels commission, but twenty of these would be recommended by the panel, and everyone voted for the panel."

Only one or two of the respondents used the term "democratic centralism" to describe the decision-making process in the party. Some of them, however, spoke of a kind of initiative which was possible at the local level. A British trade unionist pointed out, "We had a chance to thrash out the line in industry. There was free discussion. While the line had usually been decided at the national level, we were free to make local modifications." An American commented on the function of discussion at the local level: "You knew what decisions had been made beforehand, even when discussion took place. You thought of the discussion as an opportunity to understand the decision and to practice arguments in its defense." Another American on the same point: "Of course the CP gives a semblance of having discussion on all issues, but you will be given an outline to follow and the questions raised will not involve disagreements but only requests for clarification."

One quite common response regarding the organizational structure of the party described it as having been democratic in the earlier period, but as having changed in an authoritarian direction in later years. A high-echelon Italian party leader remarked, "The life of the partisan brigades was an example of simple democracy. The commanders were elected by the men, and dismissed by them when they no longer enjoyed their confidence." Similarly, in the "prison schools" of the Italian party before World War II there was considerable ideological freedom. "Before the liberation," said one Italian old-timer, "there was no ideological surveillance in the party. Because the party was underground security measures were necessary, but ideologically speaking we studied Marxism individually or in collective reading and discussion. The most fervent studying and most audacious interpretations took place in prison, where the Communists paid the price for the ideas they held." An Englishman who had been in the party from the time of its formation described the change in tone in party discussions from the early period: "The tone then was warm and unrestrained, but by the end of the 1920's this was beginning to change with the tightening of the bureaucracy in Russia. . . . The rank and file didn't feel any restraint until 1930-31."

There were almost no significant differences in the impressions of the organizational structure of the party as between the middle-class and working-class informants. But, as one might expect, there were substantial differences as between the early and late recruits (see Table 5). Almost all of those who described the organizational structure as having changed from the early period to the later had joined the party in the

TABLE 5

Perception of Organizational Structure of Party by Period of Joining
(in per cent)

	Early recruits	Late recruits	All respondents
Authoritarian	54	72	63
Democratic in own group, authoritarian in upper echelon	2	7	4
Democratic early, authoritarian later	19	3	11
Generally democratic	3	2	2
No explicit reference	22	17	20
Total	100	100	100

1920's or during the resistance periods in World War II. Similarly, rank in the party affected the perception of the organizational pattern. Only the rank and file described their own units as democratic and the higher echelons as authoritarian (see Table 6). At the same time, it was mainly the high-echelon respondents who stressed the change in organizational pattern from the early period to the later. This may be explained by the fact that almost all the high-echelon people had joined the party early and had remained in it through and after the period of "Bolshevization" in the late 1920's and early 1930's.

This general perception of the party as authoritarian is also reflected in the specific impressions of the qualities of Communist leadership, and of the changes which take place in individuals as they enter the cadres and move into positions of leadership. The quality most frequently referred to as influential in selection for leadership was loyalty and

TABLE 6

Perception of Organizational Structure of Party by Rank
(in per cent)

	Rank and file	Low echelon	High echelon	All respondents
Authoritarian	60	66	63	63
Democratic in own group, authoritarian in upper echelon	9	—	—	4
Democratic early, authoritarian later	8	11	18	11
Generally democratic	—	5	2	2
No explicit reference	23	18	17	20
Total	100	100	100	100

discipline (see Table 7). Simple availability or willingness to work was the second most frequently given. Qualities less often mentioned were theoretical knowledge, intelligence and ability, skill in political manipulation, popularity, ambition, and seniority.

TABLE 7

Perception of Qualities of Persons Selected as Leaders by Country*
(in per cent)

	U.S.	England	France	Italy	All respondents
Loyal, obedient	56	54	32	59	50
Willing to work	38	46	29	10	31
Popular personalities	16	14	2	4	9
Intelligence and ability	14	22	11	8	14
Those trained in classics	27	12	18	22	20
Those with seniority	8	2	36	16	7
Ambitious	14	10	2	2	7
Skillful politicians	11	6	29	8	14
Other	5	8	20	10	10
No answer	13	12	30	12	17

* Multiple responses.

A former Italian inspector of the party schools recalled, "The party stated specifically that each cell leader must encourage the new recruits to attend the party schools, and that the 'best-adapted' should be sent to the central schools. It is difficult to say what was meant by the 'best-adapted.' My impression while I was inspecting the schools was that those persons were especially singled out whose personalities were more easily adjustable to the standard Communist mentality." An American respondent commented, "Loyalty was the important thing. The CP has found that brains are cheap, and dangerous. Every change in line involves a crisis of loyalty. Any person who is in the movement for a period of time must take things on faith in the crisis situation. If you have loyalty, anything else can be forgiven." In moments of doubt or indecision, a good CP leader knows how to keep quiet. A Frenchman remarked, "When I was expelled, I was called to the secretariat of the Paris region. They said to me, 'You are crazy. We too have disagreements with the party, but we do not say so.'"

But while discipline and obedience to party orders must be complete, a capacity for initiative of a special kind is also important. This initiative must be limited to the selection of ways and means of carrying out party objectives, or to the elaboration of appropriate arguments in support of party directives—a kind of capacity for the tactical initiative. As a former French party member put it, a good Communist leader needs ". . . enough intelligence to take the initiative in the carrying-out of orders, but not enough intelligence to question those orders. For there are two kinds of intelligence, and it is the secondary intelligence that is required, the ability to carry out an order that is never questioned."

Simple willingness to work was the second most frequently mentioned quality necessary for leadership. In the words of a British respondent: "Anybody can be a leader if he is prepared to work like a slave. Leaders select themselves, not for intellect, but for beaver-like qualities." Willingness to work was especially emphasized among the American and British respondents as a way of attaining leadership. This may be due to the fact that the British and American parties had relatively little to offer in patronage or opportunities for power, and in addition involved a greater risk. An English-woman remarked, "I don't think most party members are particularly anxious to get ahead or want to become leaders." An American party member observed that one of the reasons FBI agents were so successful in getting into responsible positions was that there was a constant shortage of willing workers in the American party.

A number of respondents stressed indoctrination, knowledge of the classics, and ability to use the Communist language as an avenue to leadership. But, in the words of a French respondent, this theoretical ability is of a special order: "A leader must know how to read between the lines. He must have the intuition to grasp a policy that is never expressed in black and white but which underlies everything that appears in the press or is publicly stated. . . . He is the man who knows, who explains things, makes things understandable. . . . He facilitates integration with the party by translating what comes from above. . . . He has no doubts. He stands on his own two feet. Without that, he would not fulfill his function, which is to bring certitude and appeasement. He has to incarnate certitude."

Among the other qualities relevant to leadership were class and ethnic characteristics. In all the parties, special efforts were made to recruit laborers to leading positions. Almost peculiar to the United States, however, was the special emphasis on ethnic characteristics. Many American respondents referred to the effort in the American party to push Negroes forward. Others pointed out that Jews and the foreign-born were held back from public positions wherever possible, and persons of old American stock were given public prominence. In the words of one of the American respondents, "They certainly made a fuss about Browder's Kansas background, and Foster's ancestors having come over on the *Mayflower*."

There were a number of interesting differences in the perception of leadership qualities in the various countries. It has already been pointed out that simple availability was viewed as far more important in the British and American parties than in the French and Italian. In the French party, which has had a sizable bureaucracy with attractive jobs and perquisites for a long time, seniority was viewed as an important qualification for leadership. For perhaps the same reason, skill in political manipulation, in bureaucratic "infighting," was also stressed among the French respondents.

Comparison of the perception of leadership qualities among the various party ranks brought to light only one or two significant differences (see Table 8). Twenty-four per cent of

TABLE 8

Perception of Qualities of Persons Selected as Leaders by Echelon
(in per cent)

	Rank and file	Low echelon	High echelon	All respondents
Loyal, obedient	42	59	53	50
Willing to work	32	34	24	31
Popular personalities	11	11	2	9
Intelligent	11	16	14	14
Those trained in classics	23	15	22	20
Those with seniority	8	7	6	7
Ambitious	8	7	6	7
Skilled politicians	4	19	24	14
Other	8	7	20	10
No answer	24	8	16	17

the high-echelon and 19 per cent of the low-echelon respondents referred to skill in political manipulation as a qualification for getting ahead in the party, as compared with merely 4 per cent for the rank and file. Simple availability for assignments was referred to more often among the low-echelon and rank-and-file respondents than among the former top party leaders. This may mean that simple willingness to work might get one into the low-echelon leadership, but not into the top positions.

A substantial body of evidence derived both from the self-portrayal of the party and from the perceptions of the party has shown that there is a difficult problem of assimilation from the point of admission to the party to admission into the "hard core." This would imply the necessity for a significant change in attitude and behavior as individuals move from rank-and-file status into the cadres and the party leadership. As we have already seen, most party members join because they see in the party a way of dealing with specific grievances, and they are far more aware of the evil properties of their antagonists than they are of the properties of the self. The stringent discipline of party life, the massive risks of dishonor and falling from grace, the sharp tension and fear affecting intra-party personal relations cannot fail to produce basic changes in attitude from the early years of innocent apprenticeship. The doctrine describes the "hard core" militant as "steeled," "hardened," "tested," and "tried."

Our respondents were asked to comment on the changes which took place in people as they moved into the inner party. The most common terms used to describe these changes were "hard," "ruthless," "cold," "remote," and "cynical" (see Table 9). As a former high-echelon American party member put it, "The party's goal is to develop a hard core of automa-

TABLE 9

*Perception of Changes in Leaders as They Move Up the Ladder by Country**
(in per cent)

	U.S.	England	France	Italy	All respondents
Hard, ruthless	34	26	32	22	29
Cynical	16	8	5	12	10
Remote	20	20	13	51	25
Humorless	5	—	—	—	1
Dogmatic	13	10	7	2	8
Opportunistic	17	4	5	4	8
Selfish	6	2	9	6	6
Bossy	9	6	14	10	10
More informed	2	2	5	—	3
More efficient	—	2	—	—	1
Other	16	6	4	4	8
No change	—	4	13	—	4
No answer	31	44	38	29	35

* Multiple responses.

tons who can nevertheless think, be brave, and continue to believe that they are human beings." One of the more articulate women respondents elaborated on the inner feelings of the party leaders: "They become hardened, cynical, bitter about a great many things. Bitter because in order to be a good party member you have to give up the niceties of life. You have to forget you have a family—you have no time for them. While you're supposedly a member of an organization that does things collectively, you always have to be on guard for fear your best friend may expose you for some slight deviation, even a joke. Then again, you're forced all the time to make excuses for changes in the party line. . . . You are always under strain. You find that more and more your circle of friends is confined to a smaller group in the party. The circle grows smaller because you have nothing in common with people outside the party." And another American: "A certain terrible chilliness takes over these people." Or again, "As they get higher, in practically every case their idealism is distorted and twisted into a ruthless, dehumanized thing." In the language of a former American party intellectual, "We all admired Eisler. He typified the ideal professional revolutionary. He was hard, no crap about him."

Most of these comments were made by persons who had themselves experienced "going up the ladder" in the party. For the rank and filers a more common term to describe the change in people as they rose was "remoteness." This expression is interesting, since it sometimes implied participation in a kind of esoteric mystery not accessible to the rank and file. As an Italian expressed it, "In the higher spheres of the party, the leader enters into the Olympus of the unreachables." A former American party member described this feeling of remoteness as she herself moved into the inner circle: "I became the 'doer' instead of the 'receiver.' . . . I did things to other people. I learned to do to other people what had been done to me. I acquired a 'knowing smile.' I learned to 'develop' people."

Although less common than the attribution of hardness, coldness, or remoteness, a substantial number of respondents said that party members who moved into positions of power became cynical. From the various observations of our respondents this cynicism seems to have the following sources. In the first place, one has to deal with the rank and file and with the general public in a language and according to standards quite different from that which is used in the inner circles. One is constantly under the need to manipulate, to misrepresent, to say one thing and really mean another. Thus honesty and consistency have to be viewed as expendable. But one also has to view other values than words, such as human dignity, personal relationships, and life itself, as expendable. As an American respondent explained, "After a while there is almost an effort to develop the kind of cynicism which will allow the leader to be willing to do almost anything. The combination of absolute loyalty and absolute cynicism is the final essence. People who would die for the party but had no illusions about it. . . ." And at a later point the same respondent said, "As you begin to move into the top leadership you are shocked by their cynicism. 'I'm naive,' you say to yourself, 'mustn't reveal my naïveté, therefore keep quiet about it.' There is no place for sentimentality and tender feeling. The more cynical you are, the more loyal you are to the party and the party's power." Another respondent argued that while the party leaders were cynical, some faith always remained: "The cynicism is intense, yet it must stop somewhere or they'll destroy themselves. For top people it stops at Stalin. At a lower level you could stop with Browder, or at a still lower level, V. K. Jerome." There must be some faith in someone, or in some entity. Thus a party leader may feel that much of what the party says and does is fraudulent, but still retains his faith in the upper party leadership. Somehow the top people know the answers which will justify and perhaps even ennoble the morally problematic actions in which he is required to participate.

A smaller number of respondents felt that there were no significant changes in character in persons as they moved into party leadership. A Frenchman saw the process of change as resulting from the change in political position:

"The man who becomes secretary of a cell or a section sees the events from another angle, less limited. He looks down on comrades who are shortsighted." An Italian, referring back to the underground period, also claimed that the changes which took place were simply functional: "The only change was due to the different type of assignment which a comrade ascending the ladder was supposed to fulfill." An Englishman gave a more differentiated comment: "Some people can't go wrong. Harry Pollitt and Johnny Campbell remained unspoiled. Others became harder, more given to casuistry, more suave—in fact, they take on the characters of some personalities in any career."

There were a few differences in these impressions of changes in the characteristics of leaders among sub-groups of the respondents. Thus the Italian respondents stressed remoteness. This may be due to the recent and rapid transformation of the Italian party from groups of loosely coordinated underground cells, and practically independent partisan formations, to a highly organized and centralized mass party. The sudden shift in authority from the base to the central apparatus may account for this especially widespread feeling of distance between the rank and file and the leadership. While this response was particularly marked among the Italian respondents, it tends to be the case for the later recruits of England, France, and the United States as well. Two factors may account for this. The "Stalinization" of the various parties in the late 1920's and 1930's tended to shift authority from within the national parties to Moscow. In addition, the parties increased in size after the Popular Front period and generally became more bureaucratic in their internal organization.

While Lenin very clearly stressed the difference between the fully indoctrinated professional revolutionaries in the party and the naive and shortsighted proletariat, he also emphasized that leadership in the party was not to be a status, but merely a differentiation on the basis of function. He continually inveighed against bureaucracy, against special privileges for the leadership, against losing contact with the rank and file and the masses. The leaders were to be the thoroughly indoctrinated, the completely dedicated, the specially skilled. While this leadership doctrine continues to appear in Stalin's writings, it is not as heavily emphasized as is discipline and the shaping of the cadres. And outside the doctrine there has developed a leadership cult centered around the top party leaders which has influenced the leadership pattern throughout the movement. A third of our respondents described the attitude of the rank and file toward the leadership as being one of awe, veneration, even idolization. This attitude was far more frequent among the American and Italian respondents than among the British and French (see Table 10). The explanation for this pattern in the Italian party would appear to be more obvious than in the case of the American. Certainly, the Italians of this generation were long exposed to an authoritarian and charismatic mode of leadership. The sudden influx into the party of hundreds of thousands of Italians, the majority of whom grew up in the Fascist era, may, therefore, be one of the reasons for the attitude toward leadership observed by the Italian respondents. The large

TABLE 10

Attitude of Rank and File toward Leaders by Country
(in per cent)

	U.S.	England	France	Italy	All respondents
Admiration, respect	28	64	43	26	39
Awe, adulation	55	14	16	43	33
Other	—	—	2	—	1
No answer	17	22	39	31	27
Total	100	100	100	100	100

number of American respondents reporting similar observations is more difficult to explain, since awe and adulation toward authority are hardly typical of the general American attitude. The answer appears to be related to the ethnic composition of the American party. The predominance of foreign-born and first-generation native-born persons of European origin in the American party may account for this peculiar pattern. One may expect among the foreign-born feelings of distance between leaders and led which are carried over from their experience with Eastern European patterns of government'and social structure. More particularly, persons of foreign-born, Eastern European Jewish background are characterized by a veneration for learning. And since the Communist leadership is also in part based upon a kind of theological knowledge and casuistry, it may be accorded a similar veneration by persons of that faith.

While this ethnic-religious factor may account for the attitude of awe among the foreign-born, the problem of the first-generation native-born is of another order and will be dealt with in detail at a later point. Here we may only repeat that the child of the immigrant has a general problem of adjustment to authority. In the process of adjusting to the native culture, he tends to reject the patterns of culture of his parents. At the same time, he feels unable to assimilate the native culture fully. Hence he grows up in a state of conflict about authority, with strong needs for authority and with strong impulses to reject it. For an individual of this kind the party often serves as an at least temporary solution to the problem of conformity and authority, and the leadership of the party may be clung to and adored, since belief in it serves one of his deepest needs.

Activism

In the doctrine, the Communist is pictured as living in a constant state of activism, tension. His task is never finished; he may never rest. This aspect of the party was perceived and experienced by almost all of our respondents. Even those who themselves were relatively inactive were aware that they were failing to live up to party standards. Forty-nine per cent of our respondents had been functionaries, that is, paid employees either in the party apparatus itself or in organizations controlled by the party. But these full-time functionaries are hardly comparable to ordinary employees. A British party functionary reported his time devoted to the party as ". . .

eighteen hours a day, seven days a week, a total of 80-100 hours a week." Of those who were not full-time party work-ers, 16 per cent reported that they gave all their spare time, and another 16 per cent that they were active during most of their spare time. Only 5 per cent reported spending very little spare time on party work.

The atmosphere of the American party was described as full of tension, urgency: "The party was perpetually in a fire brigade atmosphere, always an emergency. Any task is always the most critical possible task, because on this every-thing else depends." And a Frenchman said in a similar vein, "The atmosphere was severe, puritanical. There was some-thing voluptuous in those meetings, we worked with passion. It was a religious atmosphere, tense, puritanical, full of political passion."

A number of respondents suggested that the activism of the party had as one of its functions to prevent the members from thinking and from being exposed to outside influences. An Italian remarked, "They try to keep the party members constantly occupied from morning to night, and to really tire them with a load of tasks and assignments. This process of keeping people always on the alert, in continuous agita-tion, goes under the name of 'activation.' The result is that the individual becomes accustomed to thinking of the party from the moment he awakens to the moment he goes to sleep. He is so completely absorbed in the system that 'activity' becomes second nature . . . it becomes a way of life. If, for any reason, this responsibility of being an activist is taken away, he finds himself lost, and is absolutely incapable of re-adjusting his personality." An Englishman described the process of addiction to activism: "When I first joined I gave two evenings a week. After two or three years I was giving five evenings a week, and one weekend in two, organizing meetings, selling literature, canvassing, attending confer-ences, branch committees, discussion circles, etc. You soon get so that you are bored stiff if an evening is not taken up by party activity."

While intense activity is the norm of the party, it would,

of course, be a mistake to assume that every party cell lives up to these requirements. An American party journalist reported, "I gave as few evenings as I could get away with. Our unit met once a week (on Tuesdays), but we didn't begin until the radio program 'Information Please' was over." And a Frenchman pointed out, "We had cell meetings about once a month, and then even less frequently. On New Year's we had a party with wine in order to recruit people. It was quite a problem to get them to pay their dues, and to attend meetings. Generally, only the four or five members who were officers would come, unless there was a political event, or the visit of a leader." And an Italian woman Communist leader who was in charge of a woman's section in a working-class district recalled, "Out of 120 members, only from twenty to fifty came to cell meetings. They spent most of their time gossiping among themselves or quarreling. Nothing that I could say had any effect on them."

Generally speaking, those who had joined the party in the pre-Popular Front period were more active than those who joined later. Almost all the early recruits were functionaries or devoted all or most of their spare time to the party (see Table 11). These data seem to suggest that the development

TABLE 11

Proportion of Time Devoted to Party by Period of Joining
(in per cent)

	Early recruits	*Late recruits*	*All respondents*
Functionary	61	36	49
All spare time	16	16	16
Most spare time	13	19	16
Some spare time	4	17	10
Very little spare time	2	9	5
Unknown	4	3	4
Total	100	100	100

of mass parties in the decades since the Popular Front has meant a decline in the activity norm of the party. In acquiring a mass membership, the party in all likelihood loses some of its maneuverability and momentum.

To move from the rank-and-file party status to party office necessarily meant a heavier work load. While almost a third of the rank-and-file respondents gave only some or very little of their spare time to the party, this was true of only 4 per cent of the low-echelon respondents (see Table 12).

But the striking thing about these general findings is not that they show some 15 per cent who were relatively inactive, but that the great majority of our respondents were so deeply

TABLE 12

Proportion of Time Devoted to Party by Echelon
(in per cent)

	Rank and file	Low echelon	High echelon	All respondents
Functionary	26	48	94	49
All spare time	12	30	4	16
Most spare time	23	16	2	16
Some spare time	21	3	—	10
Very little spare time	11	1	—	5
Unknown	7	1	—	4
Total	100	100	100	100

committed to and engaged in party activity. If we leave out the half of our respondents who were paid officials and employees, it would appear that the norm of activity for "non-functionary" party members was the greater part of their spare time or, in terms of actual time, four or five evenings a week. This degree of activity sharply sets the party off from most, if not all, other voluntary associations. It would be difficult indeed to find another political organization which could lay claim to most of the spare time of more than half of its rank and file. These data suggest the obvious point that in calculating the political balance of forces in particular countries, comparisons of numbers of members may be highly misleading. A very substantial part of the Communist Party membership carries on a degree of activity which is to be found only among the upper echelons of other political movements. This is true not only in terms of the gross amounts of time available for party work, but in the readiness of party members to carry out any and every task which the party leadership assigns them.

Dedication

This maneuverability and availability of the party membership for the work of the party is also reflected in the way in which party members view competing interests, values, and associations. Thus, recreation according to our respondents is viewed as instrumental to the party. As a British respondent put it, "One's first duty was as a Communist and one should remember it even when relaxing. One was first and foremost a party member. This meant that unless we took recreation in company with other party members and in a party atmosphere, it was frowned on as bourgeois and escapist. Most organized games were suspect as part of the existing social fabric. Recreation was all right in small doses so long as one was doing party work at the same time." The party creates a network of recreational opportunities in order to prevent members from exposing themselves to non-party influences. Thus an Italian respondent said, "The CP is very active in the organization of pastimes for the members, so as not to give them the opportunity to wander off and have their minds diverted from the spirit of the party even during their recreation. They have created recreation clubs in the 'Casa del Popolo,' with card rooms, and libraries. Dances are organized as well as sporting events, and lectures during which the same slogans are tirelessly repeated."

Almost half the respondents described the party attitude toward recreation as requiring that it be instrumental to the party (see Table 13). Only 8 per cent (and the largest number of these were among the British respondents) were not aware of any special party attitude toward recreation. Another 6 per cent described the party attitude as encouraging relaxation in order to renew the energies of overworked party members. The remaining responses either described the party attitude as opposed to recreation and relaxation, or as giving mere lip service to the idea, but making it impossible in practice.

It is of interest that those respondents who joined in the post-Popular Front period more often described the party attitude as favoring the use of recreation for party purposes.

TABLE 13

Party Attitudes toward Recreation by Country
(in per cent)

	U.S.	England	France	Italy	All respondents
No special attitude	1	20	7	4	8
Encouraged to renew strength	5	8	11	4	6
Encouraged in theory, not in practice	6	12	2	—	5
Recreation instrumental to party	53	30	39	61	46
Opposition to outside recreation	19	6	3	2	8
Other	5	4	—	—	2
No answer	11	20	38	33	25
Total	100	100	100	100	100

This probably reflects the development of a new party tactic in the later period to relate the party to other political groupings and to broaden its recruitment base by means of an active entertainment program. Certainly, the institution in Italy in the postwar period of party-controlled clubhouses offering recreational opportunities serves as a means of attracting new members, as well as of preventing members from seeking entertainment elsewhere and thereby being exposed to other ideological influences.

The perception of the party attitude toward recreation differed substantially among the ranks of respondents. Apparently the problem varied from echelon to echelon. Among the rank-and-file and low-echelon respondents entertainment was used to recruit new members, or to strengthen the hold of the party on its newer recruits. Among the high-echelon people it would appear that the party has a real problem of fatigue, and that it encourages the taking of vacations, and other opportunities for relaxation for these persons.

High-echelon people, according to our respondents, found it difficult to relax. If ordered to take leave, leaders would view this as a rejection by the party, as the beginning of the end of one's party career. Apparently there is a "work compulsion" among party leaders. As one American respondent put it, "Though I heard many say, 'Oh, how I wish I could get away for a week!' they didn't really mean it. If they did go away, they would come back soon. They would get lonely and panicky. If they had half a day free, they would look for another Communist to spend it with. They feel the world will fall apart if they are away from their work. People who went on summer vacations tried to go to places where they knew there would be other Communists. They wanted to avoid the need for self-examination, and comparison with other types of people and styles of life."

The efforts of the party to get its high-echelon people to relax was often viewed as mere lip service to the principle, since, as one high-echelon American respondent said, "The glamour surrounded those who gave twenty-four hours a day, and therefore each one tried to outdo the other. God help the person who objected to a meeting on Sunday because he wanted to be with his family! You would be reminded that this was a revolutionary movement."

But while the high echelon rarely took vacations, they appear to have been accorded special privileges, including free clothing, cars, medical and dental care, and the like. They also had special sexual privileges. As an English respondent said, "There is a doctrine that the functioning of the party members—especially of the leaders—is of interest to everyone in the party, and therefore if anyone wants a girl, someone has to volunteer." This subordination of sexuality to the efficient functioning of the party appears to be characteristic of the movement as a whole. The sentimental approach to love is rejected as "bourgeois." It is a problem that has to be solved in the most efficient way and with the least loss to the party. Another British respondent offered an illustration. "I remember a chap who was a terrific worker for the party saying to us quite seriously one evening, 'Comrades, I'm taking tomorrow morning off in order to resolve my sex life.' So next morning he met the girl, who came from a good middle-class family, and took her for a long walk round Regent's Park. By the time they got around the Park he had persuaded her to go and live with him. After that he said he felt better able to cope with party work."

At the same time, the party attempts to control promiscuity, and positively forbids perverse relationships. This has been especially true during the later period. In the words of an Italian respondent, "They did not go in for a spartan mentality, but anyone who drank or wenched too much immediately became suspect. That applied to everyone for whom luxury, eccentric amusements, drink, or women became a necessity." An American respondent remarked to the same effect, "They told one girl who was promiscuous to stick to one man. They put a 24-hour watch on her house. . . . By and large, the party was much more puritanical than I had expected. . . . They even sent a homosexual friend of mine to a psychiatrist, because it would be bad for the reputation of the party."

If sexuality tends to be viewed as strictly functional to the party, then the family and personal relations of the Communist must be similarly subordinated. Not only is his time at the disposal of the party, but his personal ties and interests as well. This is certainly required in the doctrinal model, and on the whole it is confirmed by our respondents. Thirty-five per cent of the group as a whole reported that the party took the position that in any conflict between family and party, the party should come first. An American respondent said, "When you joined the party, your family was supposed to be like all your other connections. You could recruit from it and raise money from it. You should try to lessen your obligation to it so that you would have more time and money for the party. All this was duck soup for me, a wonderful excuse for avoiding obligations to my family."

In dealing with problems of family-party conflict, the party recommends different courses of action, depending on the circumstances. Male party members were generally urged to bring their wives into the party; and wives their husbands. As a former American party member said, "Anyone whose spouse was not a CP member was not fully trusted, and it was made clear to the person involved." And a Frenchman, to the same effect, "As a general rule the party tries to get the husband to bring his wife, if not into the party, at least into one of the para-Communist organizations. This prevents the wife from objecting to her husband's nights out. She becomes more sympathetic."

Party leaders were under special pressure to make their families conform. An Italian section head commented, "I was reproved because my wife, who is very religious, had entered my daughter in a Catholic club. They told me that while the question did not affect the party directly, it was a bad example for a party leader's family to go against the ideological line of the party. This might have an unfavorable influence on the members whom I commanded, and might even diminish my authority."

If it proved to be impossible either to incorporate a member's family in the party, or at least to neutralize it, then the individual might be encouraged to break from his family. But while a party member might be aware of the party pattern, it did not necessarily follow that he conformed to it. An Italian commented, "In case one's parents or other members of one's family were anti-Communists, the party asked us to consider them as potential enemies without hesitation. I always refused to consider my mother as an enemy, and never even tried to induce my father to leave his socialism for my Communism. I thought, they are old and have a right to think as they want, and generally speaking I am of the opinion that each one should be master of his own thoughts." An English respondent said, "I felt that my relationships with my family came between me and the party. They more or less demanded eventually that I tell my parents, in spite of my explaining about my mother's state of health. 'A party member,' they told me, 'must not lack iron.' If necessary I should leave home."

Another pattern, characteristic of periods when the party was following a popular-front tactic, was to encourage and foster good family relations in order to improve the public relations of the party. There was a real effort to eliminate the bohemian atmosphere of the party after 1935. Members were encouraged to be faithful to their wives and live wholesome existences. Students were urged not to press issues to the point of creating conflicts with their families. A British respondent referred to a problem which came up in a university branch of the British party. "A chap and his girl were going to get married. The parents wanted them married in church, but they were unwilling to do so. They referred the matter to Pollitt, who told them not to be fools and to get married in church if it pleased their parents. In the Popular Front days there was not much stress on acting in a revolutionary manner. Nobody wanted to shock people, rather the contrary." This party pattern has been generally applied to the working class. The party has always sought to create the impression that the working-class members are the elite of the proletariat. As a consequence, they encouraged sobriety and dignity among the Communist workmen. An Italian respondent observed, "In fact, in the Trastevere ward the comrades were not allowed to get drunk, to be seen with loose women, or to gamble. Severe disciplinary measures were taken against offenders; they were warned, suspended, or even expelled for moral reasons."

While the position of the party on the family varied with the circumstances and the groups involved, the most common response implied that in a conflict between party and family interests, the latter must be subordinated. There were, however, a number of significant variations among the different groups of respondents (see Table 14). The British respondents deviated most sharply from the doctrinal model. Fifty-eight per cent of the British group reported that the party expressed no position on the family, as compared with 6 per cent for the American, 25 per cent for the French, and

16 per cent for the Italian. This is simply another indication that, of the four national movements included in the study, the British party is least like the doctrinal model. The shift in the party position on the family after the Popular Front period is suggested by the fact that 12 per cent of the late recruits reported that the party encouraged good family relations, as compared with 6 per cent of the early recruits.

TABLE 14

Party Attitude toward Family by Country
(in per cent)

	U.S.	England	France	Italy	All respondents
Party comes first	44	20	27	49	35
Encouraged break from family	13	6	11	—	8
Encouraged good relations	17	8	5	4	9
No attitudes expressed	6	58	25	16	25
No answer	20	8	32	31	23
Total	100	100	100	100	100

The party attitude toward the family appears to have differed according to rank. A relatively small proportion of the rank and file reported the party position as requiring the subordination of the family, and a relatively high proportion of them reported that the party encouraged good family relations. This would appear to make the obvious point that the party requires a higher degree of dedication and readiness to sacrifice from its leaders. It also suggests, along with many other indices, that the rank and file is far from being assimilated to the party model.

The question of the relations of party members with non-party individuals and groups emerges only by implication from the doctrine. On the one hand, the doctrine charges the party to establish and maintain its roots among the working class, never to lose its contacts with the masses, never to become isolated from the masses, move too far ahead of them, or lag behind them. On the other hand, the party requires complete separation of its members from the outside society, a complete professionalism and sharing in the inner doctrine, in order that the party may not lose itself in the masses, or fall to the level of mass instability and spontaneity.

It would appear from our respondents that there were no very clear directives on the question of extra-party friendships, except for extreme cases. Friendships with renegades were strictly forbidden. To be seen with a Trotskyite would constitute a basis for expulsion. On the other hand, to be seen with fellow travelers, liberals, and even conservatives was viewed as proper since the party hoped to recruit from among these elements. Indeed, "contacting" outsiders was generally encouraged for purposes of recruitment. But this general party directive apparently came into conflict with the process of assimilation into the party. As members moved into the inner party, their capacity for friendship and communication with non-party people tended to deteriorate. And this in turn forced the leadership to depend on partly assimilated people to operate in mass organizations and with non-party groups. There would appear to be a real plane of cleavage in the party between the inner core and the members operating in trade unions, youth organizations, and similar "transmission belts." Inner-core people frequently tend to have an almost trained incapacity to be effective with non-party groups. Workers in mass organizations have to avoid full assimilation in the party, if their capacity for effective communication and mass leadership is to be maintained.

This process of impairment of personal relations outside the party is described again and again, particularly by people who were in the upper echelons. An American party leader said, "I didn't have a genuine friend, with few exceptions, who was not a Communist. I could not be completely comfortable with others. It was like being more comfortable with members of your own faith." This impairment was described by some respondents as deliberate, and by others as an inescapable consequence of being deeply committed to the party. After being in the party for a while, another American respondent pointed out, "Your opinions, gestures, mannerisms all reflect the party, and your conversation is only political and dogmatically so. After a while you can't carry on a conversation with others." Or, in another instance, "The non-member had a terra incognita with his CP friend. There was a large area of unshared experience. You could try to bring your friend into it—gradually. Otherwise, you recognize this is impossible and break off friendship because you have nothing in common, or you disguise your views— or avoid the subject." Another high-echelon respondent commented, "I had difficulty making love or even spending an evening with a non-Communist." And again, "Party members get very limited in their friends, and more so as time goes on. Many live in a fool's paradise. They talk only to each other. They also get a sense of the party being stronger than it is, a basic reason for party mistakes." Another high-echelon respondent, recently expelled from the party, cited this "full incorporation" into the inner core and its impairment of the capacity for friendship as one of the reasons why leaving the party was such a shock: "For a person who is highly political it is hard to make friends. I don't play bridge or canasta. I'm impatient at just spending hours in social intercourse. I'm used to discussing important problems, and people are either afraid to discuss them, or don't have the same level of information or understanding. In the CP we at least all had the same level of information."

This process of impairment of personal relations outside the party parallels the process of impairment of personal relations within it. The doctrine stresses impersonality and functional relatedness within the party, and manipulativeness in relations outside the party. The net effect of these processes, if they are carried to their logical conclusions, is the shaping of an individual to the point where he will betray his family, his friends, his mate, and his country, if necessary. A Frenchman recalled, "Something terrible happened on the Côte d'Azur. A member of the party, a worker and a Municipal Councillor, was excluded from the party. His mother and brother made a public declaration that they refused to have anything to do with him now that he was expelled."

TABLE 15

Effect of Party Membership on Personal Relations by Country
(in per cent)

	U.S.	England	France	Italy	All respondents
Entirely within party	14	16	20	10	15
Almost entirely within party	23	24	18	6	18
Relations outside instrumental to party	8	2	—	21	7
Retained a few friends outside	22	10	12	6	13
Retained many friends outside	19	34	39	47	34
Retained most friends outside	9	14	2	6	8
No answer	5	—	9	4	5
Total	100	100	100	100	100

Table 15 shows an almost equal distribution of respondents among those whose relations were almost entirely, or entirely, within the party, and those who retained many or most of their friends outside the party. It is of interest that the American respondents had the smallest proportion of persons who maintained their outside relationships. This may be due to the ethnic aspect of the American party. Since a very large proportion of the American respondents were foreign-born or first-generation native-born, alienated from their own cultures, and unassimilated to the native culture, they probably had fewer personal, meaningful ties to cut once they had joined the party.

It is also of interest that more than half of those who joined the party after the Popular Front period retained many or most of their friends outside the party. This difference can be readily understood as one of the consequences of the Popular Front tactic of minimizing the exclusive character of the party. Members were under pressure to broaden their contacts and associations. As they were taken in, new members were not placed under any pressure to cut their family and other personal ties. On the contrary, they were often required to retain these ties and avoid conflicts.

Table 16 brings out quite clearly the connection between rank and complete involvement in the party. Fifty-three per cent of the rank and file retained many or most of their friends outside the party as compared with 25 per cent for the upper-echelon respondents. Thirty-one per cent of the high-echelon group had their personal relations entirely within the party as compared with 6 per cent for the rank and file.

TABLE 16

Effect of Party Membership on Personal Relations by Echelon
(in per cent)

	Rank and file	Low echelon	High echelon	All respondents
Entirely within party	6	15	31	15
Almost entirely within party	18	21	16	18
Relations outside instrumental to party	8	7	8	8
Retained a few outside friends	10	15	16	13
Retained many outside friends	39	33	25	34
Retained most outside friends	14	5	—	8
No answer	5	4	4	4
Total	100	100	100	100

Uniqueness

In the doctrine, the Communist is portrayed as a hero, as a member of a special elite. No specific question was asked the respondents as to whether they viewed their party membership as giving them a special superiority, but about one-third of them spontaneously described the appeal of the movement in these terms. Such responses were substantially more frequent among the high-echelon respondents than among the rank and file (39 per cent to 21 per cent). It is also of interest that more of the intellectuals than of the working-class respondents referred to "eliteness" as one of the attractions of the movement. A few of these comments may illustrate the attitude:

"I felt vastly superior to non-Communists."

"We were the chosen few who would lead the revolution."

"Joining the party increased my contempt for non-Communists."

"There was a halo around it."

"The feeling of superiority is consciously encouraged. They are always saying, 'Comrades, we are a special breed of people.'"

It is on the whole likely that the appeal of becoming members of an elite which has an unequivocal claim on the future was far more widespread than the above figures would suggest. Eliteness is implied in the conception of Communist rationality: "We have the only true science of society." It is also implied in the Communist conceptions of militance, dedication, and activism: "We really mean business; we have no time for private lives."

Confidence in the Future

The Communist is confident of the future. The doctrinal basis of this confidence is elaborated in the theory of dialectical materialism, which maintains that history is a succession of class struggles, and that the class arising out of the newer form of production will inevitably take power and inherit the future. Only 13 per cent of the respondents reported that they had no confidence in the success of their parties at home. As one might anticipate, these non-confident responses were more frequent among the American and British respondents than among the French and Italian (see Table 17).

The most common bases for this confidence in the future reported by our respondents were that "History is on one's side," "Marxist diagnosis is accurate," and "The capitalist system is decaying." Most of the references to history stressed the element of inevitability. As a British former Communist explained it, "The emphasis on inevitability in the theory is a tremendous comfort. It counterbalances the discouragement of failure in one's own lifetime. And for the lazy-minded, getting a good strong sweep in the canvas of history absolves you from the necessity of burrowing around among the detailed facts about specific policies." In the same vein, another British respondent commented, "With this outlook, it didn't

TABLE 17

*Confidence in the Future of Communism by Country** (in per cent)

	U.S.	England	France	Italy	All respondents
Historical inevitability	14	26	25	23	22
Good cause bound to win	9	8	11	12	10
Accuracy of Marxist diagnosis	31	34	14	18	24
Decay of capitalist system	34	38	9	6	22
Example of Soviet Union	23	8	13	8	14
Continued spread of Communism	13	12	7	10	10
Solidarity and faith in organization	—	6	13	12	8
Not confident of victory at home	17	22	5	8	13
Other	5	4	4	2	4
No answer	13	4	38	41	24

* Multiple responses.

matter if the CP made mistakes—that proved it was human. It would continue to make mistakes until, at one with the forces of history, it achieved its objective. Time didn't matter. Something was going on that one just had to accept, and its eventual success was part of the general law of the universe." Belief in the accuracy of the Marxist diagnosis was closely related to a belief in the decay and rottenness of the capitalist system. As an American respondent said, "One believed in the inevitability of socialism. The non-Communist world keeps getting itself into trouble. . . . There is a feeling that no matter how many mistakes the CP makes, the capitalist world will make twice as many, that inevitably the situation will one day be 'ripe.' " Or, in the words of an Englishman, "The analysis seemed to be consistent with the situation. It was impossible to see how it could develop in any other way. One of Marxism's great claims was the prediction of the 1929 crisis by the economist Varga."

Another recurrent theme which was cited as a basis for confidence in the future was the example of the Soviet Union, the *mystique* of the October Revolution, and the subsequent growth of Russian power. This was most common among the American respondents, who included among their number the largest number of persons born in Russia, or children of Russian-born parents. A Russian-born American said, "The October Revolution was beaten into the heads of people over and over again. This was the glue, the mucilage which kept the party together. This was the objectification of everyone's fantasy, the living reality of the power. The point was emphasized that no matter how weak and small Lenin's forces were, they had the true gospel and were destined for victory. Since the American CP had the same gospel and techniques, they too would succeed." Another American respondent observed that Russia somehow gave strength and courage to people whose personal chances of success were slight. "For them the existence of the U.S.S.R., the success of the Five-Year Plan and, most important, the existence of the powerful Red Army with its parades of many tanks was very important. The Red Army was something that was going to protect us all."

A relatively large proportion of the French and Italian respondents stressed the effectiveness and power of their party organization as a basis of confidence in the future. A French respondent said, "There are no organizations powerful enough to stop the party. The Communist Party has the advantage of thirty years of organization; nothing can be created quickly to oppose it." And another Frenchman, "The war machine of the party can't be beat; the other parties are

puny by comparison." That this response should have occurred among the French and Italian respondents, and with
far less frequency among the British and not at all among
the Americans, seems to reflect the relative size and power
of the parties in these countries.

The comparison of the bases of confidence for intellectual
and middle-class respondents with those of the working class
brings out an interesting point. The intellectuals based their
confidence more often on historical materialism, while the
working class tended to be more pragmatic, relying on empirical evidence that Marxism was right in its diagnosis of
depressions and crises, and the decay and decline of capitalism.

It was found that the early recruits were more impressed
by Marxist-Leninist historical dialectics than were those of
the post-Popular Front period. The early recruits were also
more heartened by the coming to power of Communism in
the Soviet Union, while the later recruits cited the further
advances of Communism into Eastern Europe and China as a
basis for their confidence in the future.

The differences in the reasons given for confidence by
rank in the party reflect differences in the degree of indoctrination. The higher-ranking respondents cited dialectical
materialism and the Marxist analysis of the crisis of capitalism more frequently than the rank and file. In general, the
confidence of the high-echelon respondents was based on a
more elaborate intellectual structure. They were more likely
to cite interconnections between dialectical materialism, the
Marxist analysis of capitalism, and the special features of
Communist Party organization than were either the low-
echelon or the rank-and-file respondents. This is reflected in
the fact that the high-echelon respondents cited more reasons
for their optimism than did the rank and file. It is also significant that only 4 per cent of the high-echelon group had
not been confident of the future, as compared with 14 per cent
for the low echelon, and 18 per cent for the rank and file.

The preceding analysis has made possible a systematic
comparison of Communist doctrine with Communist Party

practice as it is recalled by different types of former party members. The summary of these findings in the chapter which follows may be of use in indicating the ways in which the "operating code" as derived from these sources conforms to or is different from the doctrinal code, which was analyzed at an earlier point. Since the patterns of perception of the party differed from group to group, it will also be useful to draw together the findings reflecting these differences in perception among the various national groups, generations, classes, and ranks.

CHAPTER 6

DOCTRINE AND PRACTICE

PERHAPS THE MOST significant discrepancies between Communist doctrine and practice are in the sphere of rationality and organization. These discrepancies have already been foreshadowed in the analysis of the classics. The doctrine, particularly as formulated in Lenin's writings, describes the membership of the party as a fully indoctrinated revolutionary elite. Earlier Communist recruitment practice attempted to enforce this principle by requiring a period of candidacy and a stringent screening of recruits before admission. The evidence clearly reveals that most new recruits have not even been exposed to Communist doctrine, to say nothing of registering and agreeing with it. Most of them would appear to have entered the party with rather vague political expectations based upon Communist agitational representations, and with expectations that the party would solve certain of their personal problems.

Rather than limiting admission into its ranks to indoctrinated people, the party in reality throws out a wide and coarse net, admits all comers, and relies upon internal pressures and training devices to make Communists out of this heterogeneous human material. Most of our respondents had undergone some form of indoctrination after admission into the party, but here again the evidence shows a striking discrepancy from doctrinal requirements. The Communist is supposed to have a theory and a science, and he is supposed to carry on an active intellectual life in applying the theory to reality, and in elaborating the theory on the basis of experience. In actuality, the exposure to indoctrination in the party schools and training groups takes the form of a simple inculcation of dogma, in which even the interpretation of general principles is strictly monitored by the party authorities. Rather than a training in rational calculation, Communist pedagogy has as its aim the attainment of an almost automatic conformity. There is some evidence to suggest that intellectual ingenuity of a special kind is rewarded within the Communist system. This is a capacity to accept party decisions quickly, regardless of their consistency with the basic doctrine or with previous practice, and to develop and elaborate the supporting argumentation. The skills involved are similar to those which are required in the sport of debating, except that such activity is hardly a sport in the Communist system. This skill in developing supporting arguments is the sole intellectual gratification which is tolerated in the Communist movement. Here is the intellectual reality, in contrast to the pattern described in the doctrine which implies a sharing in the intellectual processes within the movement. The doctrine as elaborated in Stalin appears to conform to reality more closely than the earlier formulations in Marx and Lenin. But even in Stalin the strict location of all "intellectual activity" in the party center is only implied, while in the actual experiencing of the party the restrictions on intellectual participation appear to be massive.

The doctrine is in conflict on the question of sharing in the decision-making process. The formula of democratic centralism appears to require a two-way process of decision-making, in which the lower echelons discuss policy issues, make recommendations, and elect representatives to the higher echelons. Once the higher organs have made their decisions on the basis of this discussion and electoral process, complete discipline is required in execution. The doctrine also requires "socialist self-criticism," which has a democratic overtone. It is mainly applicable to situations in which mistakes have been made and in which lessons are to be drawn. Our evidence suggests that there is no significant sharing of political power in the Communist movement, that "democratic centralism" as a process is hardly mentioned at all in the conduct of the party's activities, and that "socialist self-criticism" is a simple device by means of which the rectitude and propriety of higher party directives are reinforced and responsibility for failures is laid at the door of lower-echelon performance or individual or group disloyalty. This is not to suggest that the kind of discussion which takes place in the lower echelons of the Communist movement has no function. It does provide a means of reestablishing morale and of directing resentment away from the higher organs of the party. Our evidence would seem to suggest that the discrepancy between doctrine and practice in this connection is one of the most common sources of defection in the Western Communist movements.

There is another area in which there is a conflict between Communist doctrine and practice. The ideal of leadership in the Communist doctrine is a functional one. The Communist leader leads by virtue of his "doctrinal purity" and his full dedication. While intra-party relations, including relations between leadership and rank and file, are not supposed to be marred by "philistine compassion" and sentiment, they are presumed to be "comradely," even "fraternal." The evidence, however, suggests that there is a chasm between the inner and the outer party, that the principle of manipulation of the proletariat by the party has invaded the party itself. This is so much the case that, if our evidence does not mislead us, each echelon would appear to have a manipulative attitude toward the level below, until one reaches the Soviet party leadership which, at least in the eyes of the echelons below, is the "unmoved mover." The result is a feeling of remoteness and distance between levels of leadership and between the leadership and rank and file. As the leaders move up in the hierarchy, they seem to those below them to take part in an inner mystery.

The dedication demanded in the doctrine is absolute. What the party gets, however, would often appear to be a good deal less than this, and often a good deal more, but not in the sense of the doctrinal requirements. That one ought to sacrifice family, recreation, and personal relations when the party requires it is widely perceived. But there would appear to be strata in the movement not fully aware of this requirement. Many of those who are aware of it have never been called upon to live up to it. And there are indeed some who, when confronted with this obligation, have evaded it and remained in the party for long periods of time and carried on in other respects without difficulty.

There is also evidence to suggest that the party's demand for dedication often produces consequences which are quite in conflict with the other doctrinal and practical demand that the party maintain close contact with the masses. A process of isolation from the outside world appears to take place as individuals move into the inner core of the movement, impairing communication between the rank and file and the party leadership. There is communication from the top down, but not effectively and as a matter of course from the bottom up. While it is possible to remedy this failure of communication by special devices and efforts to "test" mass attitudes, it is an almost inescapable consequence of this one-way communication pattern that miscalculations will be made in the appraisal of mass moods and of the readiness of the party rank and file to carry out orders.

This party pattern of communication and of decision-making has almost inevitably produced a division in the party leadership between those who man the internal party apparatus and those who staff the mass organizations controlled or influenced by the party. The inner party leadership rules by virtue of its loyalty and conformity to the Moscow center. The mass leadership, on the other hand, is dependent on a clientele which has expectations that often conflict with the requirements of party tactics. There is a plane of cleavage between the party organization and the organizations which it controls; and the party leadership which operates at this point has a power base that often makes possible a certain amount of independence vis-à-vis the internal party leadership. Since the leadership at this point is often pulled in conflicting directions, and furthermore has an easier exit, it is more prone to defection than are the central party functionaries.

In most other respects, the discrepancies between doctrine and experience would not appear to be of great significance. The doctrine requires a degree of militance and activism far in excess of that demanded by other types of associations. The various national movements also demand this aggressiveness and activity, and most members tend to conform to it. Doctrinally, participation in the party is viewed as membership in an elite of chosen men who will inherit the future. Our evidence suggests that party membership tends to be perceived in these terms.

Taken all in all, persons moving into the party via the doctrinal classics cannot escape a number of shocks. The operating'ideal of the Communist movement, if our data do not mislead us, offers little more than an instrumental role and, since party membership tends to absorb most of the energies and interests of those who join, one must consent to subordinate the whole of one's self to this instrumental function. It is true that one can gain satisfaction from being a loyal, militant, thoroughly dedicated, and active instrument, but this is a far cry from the doctrinal portrait of the Communist as a member of a consecrated order of comradely professional revolutionaries, sharing in the doctrinal and intellectual heritage and in the decisions of the movement.

In actual fact, however, it appears that few party members are ever exposed to the doctrine in any independent way. They are exposed within the party setting itself, so that the relationship of the individual to the theory is made clear. He may have the theory in the sense of a sacred possession, but only if he consents to use it "through channels," so to speak. In the case of the unindoctrinated mass of new recruits to the party, the question of whether or not an individual will be repelled by this pattern of intellectual and organizational authoritarianism will depend on what expectations he had of the movement at the time of joining, and on the ways in which the intellectual and organizational pattern of the party impinges on him. This is by no means uniform for the various countries, classes, periods, and party ranks.

National Differences

Our analysis of the ways in which the party has been perceived by persons who have been party members has brought out a number of differences among the four national groups. It is perhaps not too risky an inference to suggest that these differences in perception may reflect differences in the national parties themselves.

The heavy predominance of the foreign-born or first-generation native-born in the American party,[1] concentrated in the leadership at all echelons and also in substantial numbers among the rank and file, is the most distinguishing characteristic of the American party. It suggests that a very large proportion of the American party members are persons caught in the processes of cultural assimilation which involve the rejection of their older cultural patterns and efforts to adapt and assimilate to the new. This process of assimilation often produces personal disorganization, role confusion, resentment, feelings of unworthiness and isolation. The data thus far presented suggest that the atmosphere of the American party is strongly affected by these patterns. A higher percentage of the American respondents than of the other nationalities viewed the party as a means of solving the personal problems of rebelliousness, isolation, and the need for certainty and security. Personal relations in the party were more often described in terms of distrust and suspicion. Hatred of the antagonist was revealed as especially intense. The leaders were more often characterized as ruthless, hard, and cynical. The leaders were said to "pull their rank," and the rank and file viewed the leadership with awe and adulation. Respondents reported more frequently that they had broken with their families and cut themselves off from earlier ties and associations.

In practically all these respects, the British respondents reported strikingly different patterns. They included a very small number of persons who were exposed to Communist doctrine at the time of joining. There was an extremely high percentage reporting that relations among party members were no different from personal relations outside the party. Hatred of the antagonist does not appear to have been as strongly stressed in the British party. The relationships between the leaders and the rank and file seem to have been more relaxed and close. Only a small proportion of the British respondents felt under pressure to subordinate their family and other personal relations to the party. The British group

[1] See Chapter 7 for an analysis of the ethnic composition of the American party.

also included the largest proportion of respondents who reported that, although they were members, they had little confidence in the party's prospects in England.

With the exception of a few thousands of survivors of the Fascist prisons and exile, the Italian Communist Party consists of an enormous mass of new, unindoctrinated, or half-indoctrinated recruits.[2] The Italian respondents included the largest proportion of persons who had not been exposed to the doctrine at the time of joining. They also included the largest contingent who had received no formal doctrinal training while in the party. The Italians also registered more frequently than others the shift in the character of the party from the days of the underground and the resistance to the post-liberation period. A substantial number felt that the democratic, warm, and fraternal atmosphere of the party in the earlier period had changed radically to a cold, bureaucratic authoritarianism in the later period. Of all the national groups, the Italian respondents retained their non-party connections and associations to the greatest extent. These findings suggest that the Italian party, while numerically the largest in Western Europe, actually may be one of the least well-integrated and indoctrinated.

The French group, which was somewhat heavily weighted with high-echelon respondents who had joined the party in the earlier years, included the largest proportion of persons who had been exposed to the doctrine at the time of joining. Other evidence seems to support the hypothesis that the French party has the largest core of fully indoctrinated and dedicated militants of any of the parties of the West. More of the cadres trained and "steeled" in the 1920's and 1930's have survived than in the case of Italy. As a consequence, the French party has a far better supply of militants within the cells and sections. But even though it is in this advantageous position, it also has a huge mass of unassimilated party members recruited in the Popular Front, resistance, and postwar

[2] See Aldo Garosci, "The Italian Communist Party," in Mario Einaudi, Jean-Marie Domenach, and Aldo Garosci, *Communism in Western Europe* (Ithaca, N.Y.: Cornell University Press, 1951), pp. 198 ff.

years.[3] Because of the fact that the French party has been a mass party for the last fifteen years, seniority and political skill appear to have been quite important in the making of party careers, far more so than has been the case in the other three countries. It is also of interest that the French respondents, like the Italians and the British, seem to retain their extra-party ties. But, unlike the Italians, the relations between leaders and rank and file appear to be relatively relaxed and close. Another finding which suggests that the French party is the most cohesive and best organized of those included in this study is that more of the French respondents attributed their confidence in the future of Communism to the organizational factor, to the effectiveness and strength of the party apparatus.

Differences Based upon Period of Joining

Before 1935 the Communist movement had been explicitly revolutionary, with the exception of occasional and localized "coalition tactics." The adoption of the Popular Front policy in 1935 represented a much more thoroughgoing change in party tactics than any that had occurred before.[4] The response of the Soviet Union to the threat of German and Italian Fascism and Japanese militarism was the adoption of a policy of alliances with the non-Fascist powers. The response of the Communist International and the various national movements was to advocate moderate anti-Fascist coalitions with the socialist and liberal parties in their respective countries.

The period from 1935 to 1939 was a moderate or "right" period, as was the period from 1941 to 1947. Most of those who joined the party in the post-1935 period joined during these Popular Front phases, while most of those who joined the party in the pre-1935 period joined while the party was in a left or revolutionary phase.

[3] Jean-Marie Domenach, "The French Communist Party," in Einaudi, et al., op.cit., p. 100.

[4] See Franz Borkenau, *World Communism* (New York: W. W. Norton & Co., 1939), pp. 386 ff.; Hugh Seton-Watson, *From Lenin to Malenkov: The History of World Communism* (New York: Frederick A. Praeger, Inc., 1953), Ch. 9.

Since the Communist parties behaved differently in the Popular Front and revolutionary periods, it is to be expected that they would be perceived and experienced differently by persons joining in these two periods. The deterioration of the party from the point of view of the doctrinal model is clearly reflected in the fact that the respondents who joined early were much more frequently indoctrinated before joining than the later group. In addition, they were more frequently self-taught, while the later recruits were exposed by means of the strictly controlled training schools. The post-1935 recruits were not only less frequently indoctrinated, but came into the party far more frequently with personal rather than political expectations.

The early recruits who had been in the movement before the parties were "Stalinized" in the late 1920's and early 1930's reflected the change in party atmosphere in their perceptions. Thus they tended to describe the pattern of personal relations in the earlier years as warm and fraternal, and as marred by distrust and suspicion in the later years. Similarly, they registered the change in the Communist organizational pattern. They described communication and participation in the early period as a two-way pattern, from the bottom up and from the top down; while in the later period the party was seen as becoming increasingly authoritarian. Relationships between leaders and rank and file were often perceived as having been close and relaxed in the early period. The late recruits, with the exception of those drawn into the party via the resistance, did not refer to changes in party pattern, but tended to describe the party atmosphere as consistently authoritarian, and the relations between leaders and rank and file as remote.

Deterioration of party practice from the point of view of the doctrinal model is also reflected in the fact that the early recruits gave more of their time to the party, and tended to subordinate their non-party relations and associations to the interests of the party more frequently and to a greater degree than those who joined later. Similarly, the optimism of the earlier recruits was more often phrased in doctrinally appropriate terms than that of the late recruits.

These findings, as well as other considerations, suggest that the problem of defection is substantially different for earlier recruits and for the later. Since the early recruits more often made an independent reading of the doctrine, it is they who are most strongly confronted by the discrepancies between doctrine and reality. In addition, they have experienced the effect of the Stalinization of the party on its atmosphere and organizational tone. It might be supposed that these individuals would be more likely to leave the party. But by virtue of their seniority and degree of commitment, the early recruits tend to occupy leadership positions. Thus the costs of leaving the party are greater for them and often counterbalance the repulsions and discontents which arise as a consequence of their early experience. But, even though they remain, and indeed constitute, the party elite, it is useful to consider that in all likelihood memories of a different (and perhaps happier) kind of party and of a greater congruence of doctrine and practice may trouble their minds. This condition of memory may perhaps lie behind the cynicism and coldness which our respondents report as attributes of the party leadership.

While the more recent recruits lack both the prior indoctrination and the memories of the pre-Stalin party, on the other hand they come to the party with both political and nonpolitical expectations which are bound to be thwarted by their later experience. And, since the later recruits are concentrated in the lower echelons, the costs of leaving the party are lower. Among the hypotheses suggested by these findings is that the later recruits tend to leave the party more quietly, less painfully, and for non-doctrinal reasons, while the early recruits support their defection with doctrinal justifications, and tend more often to join movements laying claim to the Communist doctrine, but in competition with the party.

Differences Based upon Class

The main differences between the middle-class and working-class respondents have to do with the degree of indoctrination and the scope of perception. Fewer of the working-class respondents had been exposed to the Communist classics at or before the time of joining, and a very large proportion of them remained unindoctrinated in any formal sense of the term while in the party. The approach of the working-class respondents to the party tended to be more pragmatic, concrete, reality-oriented. In contrast, the middle-class recruits were often exposed to the doctrine before joining, and more often experienced formal indoctrination while in the party. At the same time, the middle-class respondents tended to come to the party with more complex value patterns and expectations which were more likely to obstruct assimilation into the party. These differences may suggest one of the reasons for the comparative instability of middle-class party members. They are more likely to have an independent conception of the goals and tactics of the party which may conflict with party decisions and tactics, and they also have expectations of the party which may be more adequately satisfied in other relationships and activities. The working-class party member, on the other hand, is relatively untroubled by doctrinal apparatus, less exposed to the media of communication, and his imaginative and logical powers are relatively undeveloped. In many working-class settings no particular stigma (often quite the reverse) attaches to party membership. As a consequence, it is less of an act of deviation to join and the repulsions of party life are fewer.

Differences Based on Rank

The differences in the perception and experience of the party based upon rank are among the most striking brought out in the preceding analysis. The high-echelon respondents had been exposed to the doctrine before or at the time of joining far more frequently than the rank and file and lower echelons. In addition, the high-echelon respondents came to the party far less frequently with the expectation that the party would solve personal emotional problems. The high-echelon respondents more frequently perceived the leadership as becoming ruthless, hard, and cynical as it moved up the hierarchy, and they also stressed political skill as a means of rising in the party much more often than the lower echelons. The high-echelon respondents were far more active, and far more dedicated, as this is defined in the study. For them, the party attitude toward recreation was perceived as encouraging vacations and relaxation because of fatigue from overwork, and yet most of the high-echelon people reported that it was impossible to rest and relax in any genuine sense of the term. The rank-and-file respondents, on the other hand, were encouraged to take their recreation under party auspices and to use convivial occasions for recruitment purposes.

The leadership respondents more often subordinated family and personal relations to the party, and they tended to cut off all their non-party ties and associations. On the other hand, the rank and file tended to maintain their extra-party personal relations and to maintain their family ties. The leadership group also was most frequently confident of the future, and their confidence tended to be based on doctrinal considerations.

Just as the early recruits to the party had memories of an early pattern of more fluid organization, more congenial party atmosphere, and a greater consistency between doctrine and practice, so did the higher-echelon respondents. They also more frequently described the top party leadership as being cynical. These two findings may be closely related. It is the indoctrinated, veteran, high-echelon party member who has lived through many changes in party line and who therefore is most exposed to the inconsistencies between doctrine and party policy. Furthermore, it is the party leader who converses in the two languages of the party, and who cannot fail to register the manipulative attitude of the party leadership toward the rank and file and the "masses."

These differences in the ways in which the party was perceived and experienced by the various strata and groupings among our former Communist respondents are related to the different patterns of recruitment to the party characteristic of these groupings, the kinds of needs and interests which they sought to serve by joining the party, the kinds of things about the party which created dissatisfaction, and the kinds of problems which they experienced in leaving the party and reassimilating into society. These are the themes which are developed in the chapters which follow.

PART III

SOCIAL AND PSYCHOLOGICAL
CHARACTERISTICS

CHAPTER 7

SOCIAL CHARACTERISTICS

AMONG THE INTERPRETATIONS offered to account for the appeal of Communism it is possible to distinguish at least five types of emphasis. First, there are studies which stress economic considerations. Thus it has been argued that poverty without hope of betterment, negative changes in economic status resulting from depression and unemployment, occupational obsolescence owing to technological change, or striking inequalities in wealth, income, and opportunity, may create susceptibility among the groups and individuals so affected.[1] Second, there are sociological interpretations which suggest that susceptibility to Communism is related to social disorganization—that is, to the creation of situations in which established loyalties and social relationships are undermined. These situations give rise to feelings of isolation, vulnerability, and resentment which may be relieved through affiliation with the Communist movement.[2] While the sociological view often includes religious ties among the relationships whose impairment creates susceptibility, there is a third view which treats Communism as a secular or "political" religion that provides substitute satisfactions for those who have broken from traditional religious orientations, or that fulfills some deeply rooted human need.[3] A fourth approach

[1] See, among others, Harold D. Lasswell and Dorothy Blumenstock, *World Revolutionary Propaganda* (New York: Alfred A. Knopf, 1939), pp. 22 ff., 270 ff.; Franz Borkenau, *World Communism* (New York: W. W. Norton & Co., 1939), pp. 357 ff.; Eric Hoffer, *The True Believer* (New York: Harper & Brothers, 1951), pp. 42 ff.; Einaudi, Domenach, and Garosci, *Communism in Western Europe, op.cit.*, pp. 42 ff.

[2] See, among others, Lasswell and Blumenstock, *op.cit.*, Ch. 15; Borkenau, *op.cit.*, p. 420; Hoffer, *op.cit.*, pp. 23 ff.; Rudolf Heberle, *Social Movements* (New York: Appleton-Century-Crofts, 1951), pp. 126 ff.; A. Rossi, *A Communist Party in Action*, trans. by Willmoore Kendall (New Haven: Yale University Press, 1949), pp. 218 ff.; Philip Selznick, *The Organizational Weapon* (New York: McGraw-Hill, 1952), Ch. 7; Jules Monnerot, *Sociologie du communisme* (Paris: Gallimard, 1949), *passim*.

[3] Monnerot, *op.cit.*, pp. 9 ff., 276 ff.; Borkenau, *op.cit.*, p. 419; Hoffer, *op.cit.*, pp. 80 ff.; Henri Polles, *Psychoanalyse du communisme* (Paris:

emphasizes psychological factors—attitudes, feeling tones, developmental patterns—as creating susceptibility. This view is rarely elaborated in "purely" psychological terms.[4] More often it is advanced in combination with sociological factors. A fifth view, more characteristic of traditional political analysis, stresses institutional patterns and structures which facilitate the appeal of Communism. Here it is argued that certain types of political social structures—authoritarian and narrow right-wing regimes, colonial areas dominated by imperialist nations, or regimes marked by political stalemate and incapacity to arrive at urgent social decisions—build up pressures among the disadvantaged elite and other groupings which may be mobilized in support of the Communist movement.[5]

It is, of course, clear that all of these factors are related to the appeal and spread of Communism. The present study does not attack the validity of any of these interpretations, although the obvious point must be made that no one of them can account for the variety of phenomena involved in the

Henri Lefebvre, 1949), pp. 205 ff.; Nicolas Berdyaev, *The Origins of Russian Communism* (New York: Charles Scribner's Sons, 1937), pp. 191 ff.; Morris L. Ernst and David Loth, *Report on the American Communist* (New York: Henry Holt & Co., 1952), pp. 11 ff.; Erich Fromm, *Psychoanalysis and Religion* (New Haven: Yale University Press, 1950), pp. 31 ff.; Fulton J. Sheen, *Communism and the Conscience of the West* (Indianapolis: Bobbs Merrill, 1948), pp. 76-77; Waldemar Gurian, *Bolshevism* (Notre Dame, Ind.: University of Notre Dame Press, 1952), pp. 5 ff.; Ernst Kris and Nathan Leites, "Trends in Twentieth-Century Propaganda," in Geza Roheim, ed., *Psychoanalysis and the Social Sciences*, Vol. 1 (New York: International Universities Press, 1949).

[4] Lasswell and Blumenstock, *op.cit.*, Ch. 15; Ernst and Loth, *op.cit.*, pp. 4 ff., 78 ff.; Heberle, *op.cit.*, pp. 93 ff.; Hoffer, *op.cit.*, pp. 57 ff.; Rossi, *op.cit.*, pp. 229 ff.; Harold D. Lasswell, *World Politics and Personal Insecurity* (New York: Whittlesey House, 1935), pp. 264 ff.; Lasswell, "Psychopathology and Politics," in *The Political Writings of Harold D. Lasswell* (Glencoe, Ill.: The Free Press, 1951), pp. 78 ff.; J. C. Flugel, *Man, Morals, and Society* (New York: International Universities Press, 1945), p. 281; J. C. Flugel, *Men and Their Motives* (New York: International Universities Press, 1947), p. 165.

[5] Borkenau, *op.cit.*, pp. 415 ff.; Einaudi, Domenach, and Garosci, *op.cit.*, pp. 6 ff., 51 ff., 112 ff., 190 ff.; Monnerot, *op.cit.*, pp. 17 ff.; Heberle, *op.cit.*, pp. 118 ff., 341 ff.; Rossi, *op.cit.*, pp. 218 ff., 230 ff.; Charles Micaud, "Organization and Leadership of the French Communist Party," *World Politics*, Vol. IV (April 1952), pp. 318 ff.; Sigmund Neumann, *Permanent Revolution* (New York: Harper & Brothers, 1942), pp. 236 ff.

processes of recruitment to the Communist movement. Nor can they be taken together and offered as a general theory of "the appeal" of Communism, since it is quite clear that we are not dealing with a homogeneous phenomenon. Thus we have already seen that the meanings the movement has to those who join it vary substantially from place to place, group to group, and time to time. This would suggest that it is inaccurate and misleading to talk of "an appeal" of Communism, that rather we must talk of types of appeals, to various types of persons, in different kinds of situations. The present study, limited as it is to a few countries in the West, and to only a few of the possible "types," should be viewed merely as a preliminary exploration of the problem.

In the present and following chapter, we shall describe the economic, social, and political backgrounds of our respondents, showing the differences among the various national groups, generations, social classes, and ranks. In Chapters 9 and 10 we shall examine the various kinds of needs and interests which may be served by joining the party, and the different need patterns characteristic of these groups.

Class Origin

The point has often been made that susceptibility to Communism is not the simple consequence of poverty. Indeed, there are many former party members among our respondents who grew up in extreme want, but this was not the typical background. Our data suggest that by far the largest proportion of party members in the urban-industrial areas to which the study was confined came from middle- and low-income groupings, but not from poverty-stricken homes.[6] These findings are based upon personal appraisals and not on objective income indices. Thus, many working-class respondents referred to their family income situation as being in the middle range, which meant very simply that they

[6] Ernst and Loth (*op.cit.*, p. 3) report their three hundred cases of rank-and-file former American party members as having ". . . been brought up, in general, in comfort and often in luxury." Since the meaning of "comfort" and "luxury" is not made specific, it is difficult to compare these findings with those of the present study.

perceived their living conditions as average in the social setting in which they lived. Fifty-two per cent of the respondents described their families as being in the middle range, and 30 per cent reported them as having low incomes. Only 7 per cent represented their families as having high incomes, and 10 per cent claimed to come from poverty-stricken homes.

A number of points may be made with regard to the socio-economic origin of different groups of party members. The intellectual and middle-class respondents came predominantly from middle-income homes, while the working-class respondents came with equal frequency from low- and middle-income backgrounds (see Table 1).

TABLE I

Reported Income Status of Parents by Social Class
(in per cent)

	Middle class	Working class	All respondents
High	14	—	7
Middle	64	40	52
Low	19	41	30
Poverty	3	16	10
Unknown	—	3	1
Total	100	100	100

The relatively small proportion of respondents who reported high-income backgrounds were all intellectual and middle-class respondents, and the similarly small proportion who reported poverty-stricken childhood circumstances were almost all working-class respondents. Those respondents who joined the party in the period after 1935 were far more frequently from middle- and upper-income homes than were the earlier recruits (see Table 2). But the point still remains that even the earlier recruits were drawn overwhelmingly from middle- and low-income families rather than from poverty-stricken homes.

A comparison of the income backgrounds of the three ranks into which our respondents have been classified brings out

TABLE 2

Reported Income Status of Parents by Period of Joining
(in per cent)

	Early joiners	Late joiners	All respondents
High	4	10	7
Middle	41	64	52
Low	40	19	30
Poverty	13	6	10
Unknown	2	1	1
Total	100	100	100

several points. The rank-and-file respondents reported middle- and low-income families almost exclusively (see Table 3). The high-echelon respondents show a very large concentration of middle-income backgrounds, and a smaller one of poverty-stricken families. The low-echelon respondents fall in between these two tendencies. This pattern of distribution

TABLE 3

Reported Income Status of Parents by Echelon
(in per cent)

	Rank and file	Low echelon	High echelon	All respondents
High	8	10	2	7
Middle	44	46	74	52
Low	43	29	8	30
Poverty	3	14	16	10
Unknown	2	1	—	1
Total	100	100	100	100

suggests that persons of low-income background are less likely to become top party leaders than persons of middle-income families, on the one hand, and persons of poverty-stricken backgrounds, on the other. These tendencies may be more the consequence of political exposure and motivation than simply of family income level. Those persons from the lowest social strata who are exposed to the party and who are sufficiently strongly motivated to join may tend to a more complete commitment and make a career out of the party. Low income, on the other hand, may be associated with a generally low aspiration and skill level, which would effect motivation for success and chances for success in the party as in other areas. Middle income may be related to high status in the party as a consequence of two factors. In the first place, middle income is probably associated with higher aspiration and skill levels. In the second place, trade unionism and political radicalism made their greatest headway among the skilled workers during the decades when our respondents were growing up. Thus persons of middle-income background may as a rule be more aggressive and competent and more likely to have been politically exposed than persons of low-income background.

Occupation at Time of Joining

While our selection of respondents cannot be viewed as representative of the Communist population as a whole in the four countries studied, the data on occupational distribution may suggest the main types of occupational groupings to be found in the various sectors of the party. The occupations were reported as of the time of joining the party. The main groups were skilled workmen (24 per cent), members of the professions, particularly teaching and journalism (22 per cent), students (23 per cent), and unskilled workmen (13 per cent). Represented only in very small numbers were foremen and lower managerial personnel (4 per cent), and white-collar workers (6 per cent). Those respondents classified in the middle-class category consisted almost entirely of students, teachers, and journalists. In the working-class category there were almost twice as many skilled workmen as unskilled.

Just as the data on family income showed a substantial increase in the middle- and higher-income family categories for the post-1935 party recruits, so also do the data on occupation reflect an increased influx from the middle-class occupational statuses for the later period (see Table 4).

TABLE 4
Occupation at Time of Joining by Social Class
(in per cent)

	Early joiners	Late joiners	All respondents
Unskilled workmen	19	7	13
Farm labor	1	1	1
Skilled workmen	27	22	24
Foremen and lower managerial	4	4	4
White-collar	5	8	6
Small entrepreneurs	2	—	1
Students	18	27	23
Professions	19	24	22
Others	5	7	6
Total	100	100	100

The higher-echelon respondents differed in occupational composition in a number of ways from the lower-rank party officials and the rank and file. The figures reported in Table 5 suggest that students and members of the professions move into low-ranking party offices, but are less likely to climb to

TABLE 5
Occupation at Time of Joining by Echelon
(in per cent)

	Rank and file	Low echelon	High echelon	All respondents
Unskilled workmen	8	17	18	13
Farm labor	1	—	2	1
Skilled workmen	22	23	31	24
Foremen and lower managerial	4	1	8	4
White-collar	6	6	8	6
Small entrepreneurs	—	—	4	1
Students	27	26	10	23
Professions	23	23	17	22
Others	9	4	2	6
Unknown	—	—	—	—
Total	100	100	100	100

top-ranking positions than skilled and unskilled workmen. Thus, while there were only 8 per cent of unskilled workmen among the rank-and-file respondents, 18 per cent of the high-echelon respondents had been unskilled workmen at the time of joining the party. Similarly, the proportion of skilled workers was larger among the higher-echelon respondents than among the lower. At the same time, the proportions of students and the professions were smaller in the high echelon than among the rank and file. In other words, while middle-class and working-class occupations are roughly equally represented in the rank and file and the lower echelons, the middle-class category drops and the working-class category increases in the high echelon. In general, this pattern of occupational distribution shows that while the party is open to all comers, working-class party members have better prospects of success in the party than middle-class recruits. This is probably due both to party policy, which has always manifested greater confidence in the reliability of working-class recruits, and to the difficulties of assimilation into the party generally experienced by middle-class party members. These points will be dealt with at greater length below.

In order to check on the representativeness of our high-echelon respondents, a special study was made of the social characteristics of the present Central Committee members of the Communist parties of France, Italy, and the United States. The findings suggest that our high-echelon respondents are very similar to the present Central Committee members in their occupational backgrounds, as well as in other respects (see Table 6). Out of a total of 109 Central Committee members for whom these data were available, 49 per cent were workers and 31 per cent were members of the professions and students. Just as with the high-echelon respondents, teaching and journalism were the main professions represented. This comparison suggests that the selection of former party leaders is very similar in its social composition to the present leadership of the party. We shall have occasion to check the validity of this proposition in other respects at later points in the analysis.

TABLE 6

Comparison of Occupational Composition of High-echelon Respondents and Present Central Committee Members of France, Italy, and the United States*
(in per cent)

	High-echelon respondents	Members of the Central Committees
Workers	59	49
White-collar	8	14
Small entrepreneurs	4	6
Students and professions	27	31
Others	2	—
Total	100	100

* The data on the present membership of the Central Committees is adapted from a study prepared by Robert Holt of Princeton University as a part of this study. His analysis was based on biographical sketches of 123 Central Committee members of Italy, France, and the United States. Some of his findings are reported in his memorandum, *Some Characteristics of the Communist Leadership in Italy and France.*

Education

Educational opportunity is, of course, related to social origins, but the pattern varies from country to country. Thus the American respondents included the largest proportion who had some university education and the smallest proportion who had had primary school educations only. Even the American working-class respondents had had secondary educations, in contrast to those of England, France, and Italy. Taking the respondents from all four countries together, more than 70 per cent of the middle-class respondents had attended universities, while more than half of the working-class respondents had only attended primary schools.

The changing composition of the party from the period before the Popular Front to the period after is reflected in the educational data. Almost half of the later recruits had attended universities, as compared with only a third in the earlier period (see Table 7). The percentage of those having only primary educations dropped from 38 per cent in the early period to 19 per cent in the later.

TABLE 7

Education by Period of Joining
(in per cent)

	Early joiners	Late joiners	All respondents
None	2	—	1
Primary	38	19	29
Secondary	26	31	28
Higher	33	47	40
Unknown	1	3	2
Total	100	100	100

A comparison of differences in education of the various ranks shows that the largest proportion of university-educated respondents were among the rank and file, and the smallest among the high-echelon respondents. Forty-nine per cent of the high-echelon respondents had only been educated at the primary level, and had gone to work at a very early age (see Table 8).

Since advanced education generally results in better occupational and professional opportunities, the lack of such education among the high-echelon respondents may have made party careers appear to be attractive opportunities. In contrast, a far larger proportion of the rank-and-file and low-echelon respondents had more varied and more attractive occupational opportunities. For the university-educated among these groups, full-time party careers ordinarily involved

TABLE 8

Education by Echelon
(in per cent)

	Rank and file	Low echelon	High echelon	All respondents
None	1	—	2	1
Primary	25	21	49	29
Secondary	25	41	18	28
Higher	46	37	31	40
Unknown	3	1	—	2
Total	100	100	100	100

significant income and status sacrifices. Similarly, advanced education probably means a longer and more concentrated exposure to the humane intellectual and cultural tradition of the West. This would, of course, create difficulties in the process of assimilation into the Communist movement. In contrast, persons with little education or with none would tend to have less basis for intellectual resistance to the processes of indoctrination in the movement.

It would seem that the educational pattern of our high-echelon respondents is still more or less characteristic of the top leadership of the Communist movement. Table 9 makes a comparison of the high-echelon former party members with the present membership of the Central Committees of the Italian, French, and American parties. This comparison

TABLE 9

Comparison of Education of High-echelon Former Party Leaders and Present Central Committee Members
(in per cent)

	Central Committee members	High-echelon respondents
Primary or none	31	51
Secondary school	16	18
College or university	33	31
Unknown	20	—
Total	100	100

shows an almost equal representation of secondary and university-educated members in both groups. On the other hand, the group of former party leaders includes a larger percentage of persons with only primary education or none at all than does the present membership of the Central Committees. It may be that this discrepancy is attributable to the large percentage of unknowns among the Central Committee members. One would have to make the assumption that failure to report education generally reflects little or no education. While there is a certain plausibility in such an assumption, there is no need for such speculation to make the point that the educational backgrounds of our high-echelon former party leaders is on the whole similar to those of the present Central Committee membership.

Social Mobility

The point has often been made that "negative social mobility" is associated with susceptibility to revolutionary extremism. Persons whose social statuses have deteriorated, who are on the "down grade," are likely to be resentful and hence more likely to associate themselves with movements favoring rapid and thoroughgoing political and social change. Most of the studies, however, have demonstrated a connection between negative social mobility and Fascism or right-wing extremism[7] or potentially Fascist attitudes such as ethnocentrism and anti-Semitism. There may be some value therefore in examining the careers of our former Communist respondents from this point of view.

There are, of course, a variety of ways of defining social mobility. One may compare the social status of our respondents, as reflected in such indices as occupation and income, with that of their parents or of prior generations. This will give the long-run pattern as measured by external indices. Since the general hypothesis implies a connection with change in social status which is subjectively appraised as undesirable or threatening and which produces resentment that may be expressed politically, some measure must be given of this perception of status and status opportunities. It may be useful to compare with their expectations the aspirations for future careers which the respondents had at the time of joining the party. Here it would be of some importance to determine whether or not there were significant discrepancies between career hopes and expectations. It may also be useful to examine shorter-run career fluctuations, such as the impingements upon family life and career resulting from depression

[7] For example, Daniel Lerner, *et al.*, *The Nazi Elite* (Stanford, Calif.: Stanford University Press, 1951), pp. 3 ff.; Bruno Bettelheim and Morris Janowitz, *The Dynamics of Prejudice* (New York: Harper & Brothers, 1950), pp. 57 ff.

and unemployment, labor disorders, war, and enemy occupation.

If we compare the occupational status of the parents of our respondents with those which they themselves attained, the results are, if anything, negative for the general hypothesis which has been advanced. Taken as a group, these former party members did not have "lower" occupational statuses than their parents (see Table 10). Sixty-one per cent appear

TABLE 10

Comparison of Socio-economic Status at Time of Joining with That of Parents by Country
(in per cent)

	U.S.	England	France	Italy	All respondents
Improved	20	20	25	25	23
No change	65	58	64	57	61
Deteriorated	15	22	11	18	16
Total	100	100	100	100	100

to have been neither better off nor worse off than their parents. Substantially less than half manifested any change from the occupational status of their parents, and the larger proportion had improved themselves rather than declined in occupational status as compared with their parents. And this pattern seems to be more or less true for the respondents from each of the four countries. Indeed, a comparison of the occupational statuses of the contemporary members of the Central Committees of the Italian, French, and American parties with those of their parents suggests these same tendencies.[8] While the difference is not large, it does appear that more of the working-class respondents were on the downgrade as compared with their fathers than was the case for the middle-class respondents (see Table 11).

These data then indicate that we are not dealing with a social grouping which is declining in social status over the long run. However, this is by no means conclusive, since

[8] Holt, *op.cit.*, statistical appendix, Tables 1 and 3.

TABLE 11

Comparison of Socio-economic Status at Time of Joining with That of Parents by Class
(in per cent)

	Middle class	Working class	All respondents
Improved	33	13	23
No change	56	66	61
Deteriorated	11	21	16
Total	100	100	100

career satisfaction is rarely based on a simple comparison of one's own status with that of one's parents. Career satisfaction rests on the degree of correspondence between hopes and aspirations, on the one hand, and one's actual situation and expectations, on the other. The respondents were asked to describe their experience and career prior to joining the party, and to explain their motives for joining it. The great majority of respondents were employed (or students) at the time of joining. Furthermore, they were employed in occupations for which their training and education had prepared them, or were in process of being trained and educated. Only 29 per cent of the respondents were explicitly dissatisfied with their careers at the time of joining the party (see Table 12). Fifteen per cent were satisfied with their career prospects. And in 56 per cent of the cases, personal career factors were

TABLE 12

Discrepancy between Career Aspirations and Expectations by Country
(in per cent)

	U.S.	England	France	Italy	All respondents
Satisfied with career prospects	9	24	18	12	15
Dissatisfied with career prospects	40	26	29	22	29
Career prospects not relevant	51	50	53	66	56
Total	100	100	100	100	100

not referred to by the respondents or related in any explicit way to the act of joining.

The American respondents included the largest proportion of individuals who were explicitly dissatisfied with their career opportunities. This is probably due to the fact that more than half of the American respondents joined the party during the depression. For many of these "depression joiners," entering the party was in part a consequence of personal economic difficulties, or of the perception of a threat to their careers as a consequence of the depression. In contrast, dissatisfaction with career opportunities seems to have been least important among the Italian respondents, most of whom joined the party in connection with the general catastrophe of the collapse of Fascism and the German occupation of northern Italy in 1943.

Career prospects were least relevant among the middle-class former party members, and most relevant among the working-class respondents (see Table 13). Thus 40 per cent

TABLE 13

Discrepancy between Career Aspirations and Expectations by Class
(in per cent)

	Middle class	Working class	All respondents
Satisfied with career prospects	17	13	15
Dissatisfied with career prospects	19	40	29
Career prospects not relevant	64	47	56
Total	100	100	100

of the working-class group had been dissatisfied with their careers at the time they joined the party, as compared with 19 per cent of the middle-class respondents. This finding, combined with the one reported in Table 11, suggests that downward mobility and occupational dissatisfaction were factors which led many of the working-class respondents to join, but were of little significance in the affiliation of middle-class members. These findings may help to explain why work-ing-class party members have a better prognosis for long tenure and high party rank. In a great many cases, the party opened up career opportunities more satisfactory than those that were available outside. No significant differences in career prospects emerged from comparisons of earlier and later recruits and of the three party ranks.

Thus far, we have examined the long-run career trends of our respondents, and their evaluation of their career prospects as related to their decision to join the party. The factor of career, however, may enter into the decision to join the party in other ways. External events may result in short-run interruptions of career, or may cause damaging personal or primary group experiences which have career implications. Table 14 shows that a little more than half of the respondents had been negatively affected by political and economic events. Eleven per cent had suffered personally in the First or Sec-

TABLE 14

The Incidence of Social Damage prior to Joining by Country[*]
(in per cent)

	U.S.	England	France	Italy	All respondents
Damaged by social situation	48	48	57	57	52
Family or personal suffering in war	—	6	29	12	11
Affected by Fascism or enemy occupation	—	2	9	41	12
Affected by strike or labor disorder	16	10	18	2	12
Family or personal suffering in depression	34	28	2	2	17
Other	—	2	20	—	5
Not damaged by social situation	52	52	43	43	48
Total	100	100	100	100	100

* Multiple responses.

ond World Wars. This did not simply mean ordinary military service for the respondent or members of his family. Damage from war was defined as meaning some serious cost or sacrifice, such as the incurring of wounds or loss of life on the part of members of the family—in other words, war experiences which affected the structure and prosperity of the family and the respondent's mode of life. It was primarily the French and Italian respondents who reported such experiences and related them to the process of joining the party. Twelve per cent of the respondents were affected by Fascist suppression or Nazi occupation. Some of these cases involved imprisonment of the father, siblings, or of the respondent himself by the Fascist authorities. Others involved being called up for labor or military service by the Nazi occupation authorities. Forty-one per cent of the Italian respondents reported such experiences as being related to their decisions to join. Twelve per cent reported having been involved in labor disorders—strikes, factory occupations, etc.—prior to joining. And 17 per cent reported family or personal unemployment as a consequence of an economic depression as being related to their decision to join the party. This was especially frequent among the American and British respondents and hardly occurred at all among the French and Italian former party members.

The proportion of working-class respondents who had been personally damaged by military, political, and economic developments was higher than the proportion among the middle-class respondents (see Table 15). This finding, taken together with those on mobility and career expectations, suggests that for members of the working class joining the party is more frequently a response to personal damage and career frustration.

Similarly, those respondents who joined the party in the period prior to the Popular Front reported personal damage far more frequently than those who joined later (61 per cent for early recruits to 43 per cent for the later). This also confirms earlier findings as to the "deterioration" of Communist recruits in the post-1935 era. The later recruits tended to lack

TABLE 15

The Incidence of Social Damage prior to Joining by Class*
(in per cent)

	Middle class	Working class	All respondents
Damaged by social situation	42	61	52
Family or personal suffering in war	14	9	11
Affected by Fascism or enemy occupation	13	12	12
Affected by strike or labor disorder	8	16	12
Family or personal suffering in depression	14	21	17
Other	6	5	5
Not damaged by social situation	58	39	48
Total	100	100	100

* Multiple responses.

the motivational intensity resulting from personal damage attributable to the political, economic, and social order.

Most striking of all are the differences in experience of the three ranks in which the respondents were classified. It is quite clear that personal damage and suffering as a consequence of military, political, and social events prior to joining the party is related to later rank achieved in the party (see Table 16). Sixty-seven per cent of the high-echelon respondents had experienced such damage, as compared with 39 per cent for the rank and file. The low-echelon respondents were in between. This would seem to suggest that the suffering of personal damage inflicted by political or economic circumstances is related to later rank attained in the party. In other words, the act of joining in these cases is related to the impingement upon the individual of situations which are the classic themes of Communist doctrine—"capitalist crisis," "imperialist war," "the suppression of the proletariat by the bourgeoisie." To the extent that high-echelon Communists had personal experience of situations capable of being inter-

TABLE 16

The Incidence of Social Damage prior to Joining by Echelon*
(in per cent)

	Rank and file	Low echelon	High echelon	All respondents
Damaged by social situation	39	60	67	52
Family or personal suffering in war	11	8	16	11
Affected by Fascism or enemy occupation	8	25	2	12
Affected by strike or labor disorder	10	4	26	12
Family or personal suffering in depression	16	21	16	17
Other	1	7	12	5
Not damaged by social situation	61	40	33	48
Total	100	100	100	100

* Multiple responses.

preted in these terms, motivation for joining in these cases tended more often to have a political content.

Ethnic Characteristics

The stereotype of the Communist as a "foreigner" can be sustained only on the basis of the American data. Such data as are available show that the American party in its earlier years was predominantly a party of the foreign-born or of the first-generation native-born.[9] Even though the subsequent trend has been in the direction of recruitment of the older ethnic stocks, figures on the contemporary ethnic composition of the American party show that the party leadership and "cadres" are still substantially foreign-born or first-generation native-born.[10] The rank-and-file membership of the party,

[9] Francis X. Sutton, in *Ideology and Social Structure: A Study of Radical Marxism* (Ph.D. Thesis, Department of Social Relations, Harvard University, 1951, pp. 278 ff.), cites evidence showing that in the early 1920's more than 80 per cent of the party membership was organized in foreign language federations.

[10] See Testimony of Attorney General Clark in *Communist Activities Among Aliens and National Groups*, Hearings Before the Subcommittee

located as it is in a few large metropolitan centers, reflects the heavy concentration of newer immigrant stocks in those areas. That this foreign composition is a peculiarly American phenomenon is reflected in Table 17. Only 20 per cent of the American respondents were native-born of native parents. Thirty-six per cent were native-born of mixed parentage or of foreign parentage, and 27 per cent were foreign-born. In contrast, the English, French, and Italian respondents were

TABLE 17
Ethnic Origin by Country
(in per cent)

	U.S.	England	France	Italy	All respondents
Native-born of native parents	20	80	85	100	69
Native-born of mixed parentage	11	10	4	—	6
Native-born of foreign parentage	25	10	4	—	10
Foreign-born	27	—	7	—	10
Negro	11	—	—	—	3
Unknown	6	—	—	—	2
Total	100	100	100	100	100

on Immigration and Naturalization of the Committee on the Judiciary, United States Senate, Eighty-first Congress, on Senate Bill 1932, Part I, pp. 318 ff. In his testimony Clark reported the results of a study made by the Department of Justice in 1947 of the ethnic composition of the militant Communists in the American party. The Department files list some five thousand party members as militant (i.e., long-tenure members, "activists," and office-holders). Of these militant party members, 56.5 per cent were either born in Russia or countries adjacent thereto (Poland, Finland, Rumania, Lithuania, Turkey, Latvia, and Estonia), born of one or both parents from these areas, or married to a person of this Eastern European stock. Another 34.9 per cent were either of stock from other foreign countries or were married to stock from other foreign countries. In other words, 91.4 per cent of the American party militants were either foreign-born, first-generation native-born, or married to foreign stock. The percentages of these three categories are of interest. The American militants included 42 per cent foreign-born, 36 per cent native-born of foreign-born or mixed foreign and native-born parentage, and 13 per cent married to foreign-born or first-generation native-born stock. Only 9 per cent of the militants were native-born of native stock, and married to native stock.

almost entirely of native stocks..While these data cannot be taken as conclusive evidence of the ethnic composition of the American party, they suggest that recruitment to it may perhaps be understood in terms of the processes of acculturation.

From this point of view, it is essential to distinguish clearly between the foreign-born and the first-generation native-born. The foreign-born respondents among the American cases mostly came from Eastern Europe, and prior to their emigration to America had in many cases been exposed to or active in revolutionary movements. In the United States they tended to live in foreign neighborhoods. For many of them, joining the Communist Party simply represented a continuation of well-established political patterns, supported by the political atmosphere of their communities. Thus one respondent joined the movement in Greece while at school studying for the priesthood. On his arrival in America, he joined a Greek unit of the party and was assigned to work on a Greek Communist newspaper and to the Communist fraction of the food-workers' union. Another respondent who was Polish became involved with the socialist movement before the revolution of 1905, served as a party courier, and was twice imprisoned for political offenses. In his case also, joining the party in 1919 represented a simple conformity to his past. Another respondent said of his childhood in the Ukraine, "In those days revolution was in the air everywhere. I knew of the activities of the revolutionaries in the town. There were Cossack raids on the town. . . ." In many cases, the foreign-born respondents had been exposed to the socialist or Communist parties in their native countries. Perhaps the first assumptions made by such individuals were that the American setting was very much like that of the "old country," and that the same instruments for combating oppression were required. For such individuals, successful acculturation would involve learning that the American and old Tzarist social and political structure were different and that, as a consequence, different political methods were called for. No doubt, most of the foreign-born who joined the American party in the 1920's have since moved on, finding more suitable political instruments in the trade unions or in other more moderate political movements.

While a very substantial part of the leadership and membership of the American party is of foreign birth or parentage, the point ought to be made that the membership of the party at its peak never exceeded 100,000. Since that part of the American population which is of foreign birth or parentage is numbered in the tens of millions, the proportion of persons of foreign origin who joined the party was, at the very maximum, a minute fraction. In general, it would appear that some of those foreigners who did join the party had been exposed to the movement or its forerunners in their countries of origin, and many of the remainder were exposed to the party in the United States in foreign language associations led by persons who had had such revolutionary backgrounds in their countries of origin.

The acculturation problem of the first-generation native-born is far more complex.[11] Growing up in homes of foreign and often negatively esteemed cultural patterns, and exposed in the street and in schools to the dominant culture, they are almost inescapably involved in personal conflict to some degree. On the one hand, they tend to reject the values and behaviors of their parents and, on the other, they tend to feel rejected by the dominant American culture, which from its beginnings has been apt to rate the most recent waves of immigration as lowest on the scale of prestige. Among the

[11] On the psychological consequences of membership in minority groups, see, among others, Hoffer, *op.cit.*, pp. 49 ff.; Everett V. Stonequist, *The Marginal Man: A Study in Personality and Culture Conflict* (New York: Charles Scribner's Sons, 1937); Kurt Lewin, *Resolving Social Conflicts* (New York: Harper & Brothers, 1948), Parts I and III; Irvin L. Child, *Italian or American?* (New Haven: Yale University Press, 1943); Jurgen Ruesch, Annemarie Jacobsen, and Martin B. Loeb, *Acculturation and Illness*, Psychological Monographs, Vol. LXII, No. 5, 1949; David Rodnick, "Group Frustrations in Connecticut," *American Journal of Sociology*, Vol. XLVII (1941), pp. 157-166; W. L. Warner and Leo Srole, *The Social Systems of American Ethnic Groups* (New Haven: Yale University Press, 1945); particularly on the effect of ethnic marginality on political loyalty, see Jerome Bruner and Jeanette Sayre, "Shortwave Listening in an Italian Community," *Public Opinion Quarterly*, Vol. V, No. 4 (Winter 1941), pp. 640-656.

emotional problems induced by this difficult problem of adjustment and assimilation, a few may advantageously be commented on at this point. The first-generation native-born American may suffer from feelings of guilt because he is required to reject in some measure the authority of his parents in his efforts to assimilate to the dominant culture. He may suffer from a kind of confusion of identity and role because he is exposed to competing ideals, expectations, standards, and cues, and he cannot escape feelings of uncertainty, inadequacy, and ineptness. He may also suffer from feelings of isolation and estrangement, since he is literally between two worlds. To return to the world of his parents is to admit defeat; to be assimilated fully into the dominant world seems an impossibility. He may, therefore, despite his objective relationships, carry with him feelings of inescapable loneliness, of unbridgeable gaps between himself and others. If he is a member of an ethnic stock sharply distinct from the dominant ones and negatively evaluated by them, he may carry with him feelings of unworthiness, of being rejected. And, as often occurs, these feelings of being rejected may result in feelings of self-rejection, of being genuinely and integrally unworthy and undesirable. Finally, and perhaps most important, the situation confronting the first-generation native-born may, and usually does, induce feelings of hostility and resentment. The hostility may be directed primarily against his family and their culture, or it may be directed against the dominant culture, or it may pervade all of his relationships, including his attitude toward himself.

These feelings may be dealt with by the individual in various ways, depending upon their acuteness, the particular feelings which happen to be dominant, and the particular modes of expression to which the individual became accustomed during the course of his development. These problems will be discussed in greater detail below. Here it need only be said that for such individuals joining the party serves as a device for discharging and coping with some one or some combination of these feelings. It offers a strong and affirmative identity to those who are confused and reject themselves. It offers comradeship and community to those suffering from feelings of isolation. It provides a firm authority to which loyalty can be accorded, thereby reducing the feelings of guilt which arise from alienation from and rejection of parental authority. Finally, it provides an intellectual and moral structure for the expression and discharge of resentment.

This brief and rather extremely drawn description of the emotional problems of the first-generation native-born, and of the emotional uses of party membership in the light of these problems, has a primarily analytical purpose. It portrays the problem at the extreme or the margin for purposes of clarity. In actual fact, the degree of suffering and the kind of suffering varies within a wide range, depending on circumstances. It depends first on the differences between the foreign and the native culture. It is easier to learn new cues if they are not too different from the old ones. It depends also on the ranking given the particular ethnic stock by the dominant stocks. Certainly foreign-born Jews, Slavs, Italians, and Greeks have a lower prestige-rating than Northern and Western Europeans. Furthermore, much will depend on specific family circumstances, on the degree to which family cohesion has been undermined, on the extent to which the community setting minimizes or sharpens the problem of conflict or adjustment and, finally, on the intelligence, education, and personality of the individual. All that can be said is that this status is one in which such conflicts and problems are more likely to arise. This may in part explain the large proportion of first-generation native-born among the American Communist Party membership.

The significance of the ethnic factor in the American party brings into question the general applicability of one of the prevailing theories of susceptibility to Communism: the theory of social disintegration and alienation. Philip Selznick develops the thesis that the processes of industrialization, urbanization, and democratization have tended to corrode the ties and loyalties which relate individuals to the community and to create "an unstructured collectivity withdrawn from the normal, spontaneous commitments of social life . . . a glob of humanity, as against the intricately related, institutionally bound groupings that form a healthy social organism."[12] In addition to the long-run trends of industrialization, urbanization, and democratization as factors tending to produce "massness," Selznick cites prolonged unemployment, and other situations in which ". . . the culture is transmitted only weakly, as in the case of certain second-generation immigrant groups, and primitive peoples under the impact of white culture. . ."[13]

From the point of view of Selznick's hypothesis, the United States ought to be exceptionally vulnerable to subversion. Urbanization, industrialization, and democratization have certainly eroded older primary and community ties and loyalties on a scale without comparison. Yet the fact of the matter would seem to be that even during a period in which large-scale unemployment and a large, and only partially assimilated, foreign population accentuated these basic social trends, the Communist and other radical movements never gained a sólid foothold in the United States.

The Selznick hypothesis, while sound in the most general sense, is perhaps vulnerable in two respects. First, it tends to overlook the capacity of people to create new and comparatively satisfying primary and community ties to take the place of older ones which have been eroded by social mobility. In other words, the impairment of family, community, and religious relationships through social and political change does not necessarily produce "globs" of humanity. New forms of organization and social relatedness appear, as well as adaptations of old ones, and even though these new forms may be less aesthetically gratifying to an observer, and perhaps even less satisfying to the participants, they prevent the full development of the kind of "massness" and of alienation which Selznick describes.

Secondly, the Selznick hypothesis seems to rest upon a kind of sociological determinism. It tends to minimize the human capacity, not only for social creativeness, but for the

---

[12] Selznick, *op.cit.*, p. 284; see also Hoffer, *op.cit.*, p. 40.
[13] Selznick, *op.cit.*, p. 285.

rational employment of political instrumentalities as a means of improving conditions. These changes which Selznick stresses have not only weakened the hold of older leaderships; they have also created new leaderships. And the hold of the new leadership groups is not necessarily more "demagogic" than the hold of the older groups. To take only one illustration, industrialization laid the basis for the emergence of trade unions and the rise of a trade union elite with enormous political and social influence. The hold of the trade union leaders on their followings is hardly more demagogic than the hold of the old machine politician on the urban lower-class electorate. It would seem to be clear that urbanization, industrialization, and democratization do not necessarily produce the social disintegration and the susceptibility to activism and demagogy to which Selznick refers. They create problem situations which may or may not lead to new forms of relatedness and cohesion. In this respect, Rossi is quite right. The answer is in good part a political one.[14] For a variety of reasons, among which political patterns were of great importance, urbanization, industrialization, and democratization in England and the United States have not impaired the national consensus. The working class in both countries has maintained its basic loyalty to the national community. In France and Italy, on the other hand, the working classes have been historically alienated from their national communities and, consequently, as social groups have been susceptible to revolutionary movements. The French and Italian working classes were "alienated" and revolutionary long before the Communist Party arrived on the scene and took control of the working-class organizations. The difference between the continental European and the Anglo-American patterns are certainly not to be accounted for by the degree of, and the speed of, the processes of industrialization, urbanization, and democratization. The reasons for these differences have to be sought in the more complex patterns of political, religious, and social structure.

This digression is intended only to suggest that the con-

14 See Rossi, *op.cit.*, p. 230.

cepts of "alienation" and social disintegration, in the sense in which Selznick uses these terms, cannot by themselves adequately explain the success of Communist infiltration. Urbanization, industrialization, and democratization do not necessarily produce the kind and degree of disorganization and alienation which make a society vulnerable to Communist subversion. Societies may have within themselves the capacity to heal the wounds produced by economic and social dislocations. This is particularly true of the American case, where to stress merely the "alienative" and destructive side of the acculturative process would be to miss the essential point in American social development. In the course of the more than thirty years of its existence, perhaps several hundreds of thousands of people have passed through the American Communist Party. In all likelihood, a very large proportion of these have been foreign-born or first-generation native-born individuals for whom party membership constituted a learning experience in the long-run process of cultural assimilation. To be sure, they probably joined the party at a time when they felt themselves alienated from the cultural pattern of their parents and rejected by the dominant culture. But the great majority of those who joined the American party set it aside after trying it for a while, and turned to other methods of solving their problems. It is this, shall we say, constructive or learning aspect of party affiliation which is left out of the rather massive theory of vulnerability to Communism developed by Selznick. And if we fail to consider that the rate of turnover in the membership of the party has generally tended to be high, particularly in the West, this oversight may lead to a distortion of our conception of the Communist problem. Selznick's model of vulnerability is one in which a highly activistic movement is in a constant process of moving into psychological and social soft-spots. Actually, both individuals and groups have often used the party for their own purposes, and then set it aside when it no longer served these purposes. In other words, while the concept of alienation is useful in explaining susceptibility to Communism, the most important task of research and analysis in this connection is to discover the degrees and types of alienation which are related to different kinds and degrees of susceptibility.

Religious Characteristics

The religious denominations represented among the membership of the various Communist parties that are included in this study reflect, on the whole, the denominational composition of the urban industrial populations from which the party memberships of the various countries are primarily recruited. With regard to the character of the religious indoctrination received by our respondents, they appear to have come more often from pious or religiously observant families, rather than from atheistic or anticlerical ones (see Table 18). Twenty-three per cent of the respondents came

TABLE 18
Religious Attitude of Parents by Country
(in per cent)

	U.S.	England	France	Italy	All respondents
Pious	30	32	9	24	23
Observant	23	24	4	31	20
Indifferent	5	12	14	22	13
Antireligious	6	6	25	6	11
Other	2	—	—	—	1
Unknown*	34	26	48	17	32
Total	100	100	100	100	100

* The high percentages of "unknowns" are attributed to the fact that the question asked on religion was an "open-ended" one which could have been answered simply in terms of denomination.

from pious family backgrounds, and 20 per cent from families which observed religious tradition and ritual. Thirteen per cent came from religiously indifferent homes and 11 per cent from atheistic or anticlerical backgrounds. The French respondents included the largest proportion of persons coming either from religiously indifferent homes, or from aggressively antireligious backgrounds. However, almost half of the French respondents did not offer information on their religious background, so that these figures have to be taken with the greatest caution. The American, British, and Italian respondents came predominantly from homes in which religion was respected or positively cultivated. These findings may suggest that the popular stereotype to the effect that Communists are recruited from irreligious homes is on the whole incorrect. If these data reflect the general pattern, it would appear that more often than not Communists grew up in settings in which religious tradition was observed.

The most striking differences in religious background are related to rank in the party (see Table 19). The high-echelon

TABLE 19

Religious Attitude of Parents by Echelon
(in per cent)

	Rank and file	Low echelon	High echelon	All respondents
Pious	31	23	10	23
Observant	19	18	27	20
Indifferent	11	16	10	13
Antireligious	6	11	20	11
Other	2	—	—	1
Unknown	31	32	33	32
Total	100	100	100	100

respondents included the largest number of persons coming from antireligious homes, while the rank-and-file respondents included the largest number of persons who had been raised in an atmosphere of religious piety. The high-echelon respondents more often came to the party prepared to accept the antireligious features of Communist ideology. As we shall see below, there were other aspects of the ideological atmosphere of their early upbringing which had prepared proportionately more of the high-echelon respondents than of the other ranks to accept Marxist ideology with a minimum of conflict.

If we compare the religious backgrounds of our respondents with their religious attitudes at the time they joined the party, it is quite evident that many of them had rejected their religious training and upbringing in the course of adolescence or, at any rate, before joining the party (see Table 20). Thus,

TABLE 20

Comparison of Religious Attitudes of Parents with Religious Attitudes of All Respondents at Time of Joining
(in per cent)

	Religious attitudes of parents	Religious attitudes of respondents at time of joining
Pious	23	2
Observant	20	13
Indifferent	13	28
Antireligious	11	34
Other	1	—
Unknown	32	23
Total	100	100

while 43 per cent of the parents of these defectors had been pious or observant, only 15 per cent of the respondents were. In contrast, 62 per cent of the respondents were either indifferent or antireligious, as compared with 24 per cent for their parents. Generally speaking, there was a decline in church membership and religious feeling during the decades when our respondents were growing up. It is on the whole likely that the incidence of this decline was greater among those who joined the party than among those who did not. There is evidence to suggest that this was the case among persons susceptible to radicalism.[15] One can only say that a large number of our respondents had either withdrawn from religion or had rejected it before joining the party. In some cases, this was a consequence of a severe religious indoctrination in the home which antagonized the respondents, or simply one aspect of a general rejection of the family; in others, it was incidental to leaving the home or to attendance

[15] George Vetter, "Measurement of Social and Political Attitudes and the Related Personality Factors," *Journal of Abnormal and Social Psychology*, Vol. XLII, No. 1 (1947), p. 178; W. A. Kerr, "Correlates of Politico-Economic Liberalism-Conservatism," *Journal of Social Psychology*, Vol. XX (1944), pp. 61 ff.

at universities where a broadening of intellectual horizons impaired an earlier indoctrination. In many cases the shift was not a sharp one, but merely a matter of "drifting away." Although we would be in a better position to draw inferences if we had satisfactory data on trends in church membership and activity among the various social groupings in these countries, there can be little question that susceptibility to Communism is related in some way to the impairment of religious ties. But this study will hardly support extreme interpretations of Communism as the simple consequence of the decline of religious feeling and affiliation, just as at a later point it will fail to support the extreme view that persons leaving the party turn to religion as an alternative.

With the exception of the French respondents, the national groupings showed approximately the same distribution in religious attitudes. Just as the parents of the French respondents were more often antireligious, so were the respondents themselves, but again the high percentage of unknowns suggests caution in accepting these findings (see Table 21). The middle-class respondents included a sub-

TABLE 21

Religious Attitude at Time of Joining by Country
(in per cent)

	U.S.	England	France	Italy	All respondents
Pious	3	—	—	4	2
Observant	20	10	5	16	13
Indifferent	30	28	9	45	28
Antireligious	27	36	43	31	34
Unknown	20	26	43	4	23
Total	100	100	100	100	100

stantially larger proportion of persons who were anti-religious at the time of joining than did the working-class respondents. On the whole, this is consistent with both earlier and later findings which portray the middle-class respondents as having joined the party more frequently as a consequence of rebelliousness and emotional instability than was the case for the working-class respondents.

As might be anticipated, the high-echelon respondents included the largest proportion of persons who were antireligious at the time of joining the party (see Table 22). This is another datum supporting the picture of the high-echelon Communist, as compared with the other ranks, coming to the party with fewer values and loyalties which

TABLE 22

Religious Attitude at Time of Joining by Echelon
(in per cent)

	Rank and file	Low echelon	High echelon	All respondents
Pious	3	1	—	2
Observant	16	12	10	13
Indifferent	25	33	26	28
Antireligious	31	32	43	34
Unknown	25	22	21	23
Total	100	100	100	100

might stand in the way of a quick and complete assimilation.

On the whole, these data on the religious characteristics of our respondents supported the broad hypothesis suggested by Rossi, Selznick, Hoffer, and others as to the relationship between social disorganization and the impairment of "community" and susceptibility to Communism. What perhaps is lacking in these interpretations is an appreciation of the fact that this "social pathology" can take a "benignant" as well as a "malignant" form. Just as American immigrants or their children, unsure of themselves and unfamiliar with the possibilities of their environment, may join the party as a part of a general exploratory and learning process, so also young people whose religious beliefs have been weakened or destroyed for one reason or another may turn to Communism as a system of organizing beliefs, only to leave it when its requirements are found to conflict with other values and interests. Many of the respondents joined the party while in attendance at universities, during the heroic and simple days of the Spanish Civil War and the "struggle against Fascism," when joining the party sometimes meant very little more than a militant dedication to widely shared humanitarian values. It is certainly true that at the time of joining the party their condition might have been accurately described as "alienated." In many cases they were away from home for the first time, adapting to a new setting, exposed to confusing impressions, rejective and iconoclastic with regard to their pasts, and confronted with a political world in which militance might readily have appeared to be an appropriate attitude. The university students included in our group of respondents were not the types who were readily assimilated to the dominant university social groups such as fraternities or prestige clubs. Their class, ethnic, or regional origin and their personality characteristics made them unacceptable in these circles, or, when acceptable, their emotional needs and value orientations posed requirements which could not be realized within these groups. On most university campuses in Western Europe,[16] England, and the United States during the 1930's, the intellectually and aesthetically interested circles were generally linked with left-wing anti-Fascist interests. A young intellectually interested student, seeking a meaningful interpretation of the world and his mission in it, busily sloughing off the layers of parental or clerical admonition and rapidly absorbing magnificent and sweeping ideas, was readily attracted to the "Socialist Club" or the "Student Union," where he found spirits who shared his confusion and his interest in finding a gratifying intellectual and moral order. Most of these students who came into the party via anti-Fascist student societies of one kind or another left it when they left the university or soon thereafter, when the enchantments and transports of student life fell afoul of the requirements of career and family and of more mature views

[16] This was true even in the Italian universities during the 1930's and early 1940's. Magnani and Cucchi, for example, were first exposed to the Communist Party at the University of Rome, where they found themselves drawn to a group of intellectually interested fellow students which later took the form of an explicit anti-Fascist organization.

of what prospects the world held open. It is technically correct to describe these students as alienated from their families and their communities and unsure of their values, but it would be incorrect to view them as permanently alienated, as being capable only of "mass behavior." For, in actual fact, like the immigrants and children of immigrants who found in the party a momentary stopping place in the difficult and painful process of cultural adjustment, so also many of the university students who joined the party were engaged in a process of self-discovery and reality testing in which this experience was but an incident.

This should not be construed to mean that these individuals were innocent dupes of the party. On the contrary, in a great many cases, as we shall have the occasion to see in Chapters 9 and 10, they were persons with strong and compulsive needs to attack authority and the established order. The American and British respondents in particular included a large proportion of emotionally maladjusted individuals who were seeking to solve their emotional problems by attacking society, rather than face up to their personal inadequacies and conflicts. But, again, emotionally maladjusted people are also capable of learning, even though they seem to be predisposed to learning the hard way. As they matured, many of them became aware of the fact that their motives for joining the party were not political at all, and hence they moved on, seeking with more or less success other ways of solving their emotional problems.

CHAPTER 8

POLITICAL CHARACTERISTICS

THE COMMUNIST MOVEMENT requires an extreme degree of commitment from its members, strives to work a thorough-going transformation of their "mentality," and attempts to prepare them for any action against the prevailing social and political institutions. Like other totalitarian movements, the party has an especial interest in youth, since young people are relatively plastic and unstable in their commitments. With an older person, the party has to work against the grain. He tends to be occupationally or professionally committed. He has social roots in the form of family and social relationships. Furthermore, his values and general interests are more fully elaborated and supported by investments of one kind or another. We would therefore expect that Communist Party members would tend to be recruited at early ages.

Age at Time of First Radical Activity

In the absence of comparative data on other political parties, we can only describe the age pattern for our respondents as a group and for the various sub-groupings represented among them. And even here a problem arises, since many of our respondents are persons in their fifties and sixties who could not have joined the party in their youth. Since many of these individuals became members of radical organizations before the establishment of the Communist movement, we decided to record age at time of first radical activity for all our respondents, rather than age at time of affiliation with the party. This would appear to be justifiable, since in most cases the prior radical activity was either with an organization which moved in whole or substantial part into the Communist movement after its establishment, or with a front organization which led to affiliation with the party.

Twenty-one per cent of the respondents had engaged in radical activity before the age of sixteen; 49 per cent before they were eighteen; and only 25 per cent became involved after the age of twenty-three. A comparison of the working-class and middle-class respondents shows a larger percentage of the former who joined before the age of sixteen (see Table 1). However, taken as a whole, the age patterns of the middle-

TABLE I

Age at Time of First Radical Activity by Social Class
(in per cent)

	Middle class	Working class	All respondents
Before 16	15	26	21
16-18	30	28	29
19-22	25	23	24
23 and over	28	22	25
No information	2	1	1
Total	100	100	100

class and working-class respondents are similar. What is not brought out in this comparison is the fact that a substantial number of the middle-class respondents joined the party as university students and left the party when they left the university. In other words, their tenure in the party was short and related to the specific exposures of their university careers. This fact is brought out in an analysis of the relation between age at time of first radical activity and tenure in the party for the two groups of respondents (see Table 2). Thus,

TABLE 2

*Age at Time of First Radical Activity Related to Tenure
for Middle-class Respondents*
(in per cent)

	5 years or less	6-10 years	11 years or more	All respondents
Before 16	51	35	14	100
16-18	48	21	31	100
19-22	43	32	25	100
23 and over	55	26	19	100

among the middle-class respondents who engaged in radical activity prior to the age of sixteen, 51 per cent were in the party for five years or less, while only 14 per cent were in the party for eleven years or more. On the other hand, among the working-class respondents, 50 per cent of those engaging in radical activity before the age of sixteen remained in the party for eleven years or more (see Table 3).

TABLE 3

Age at Time of First Radical Activity Related to Tenure for Working-class Respondents
(in per cent)

	5 years or less	6-10 years	11 years or more	All respondents
Before 16	28	22	50	100
16-18	25	41	34	100
19-22	28	36	36	100
23 and over	75	21	4	100

Two points may be made with reference to Tables 2 and 3. For working-class respondents, early commitment to radical activity is clearly related to long tenure in the party. For both working-class and middle-class respondents, late involvement in radical activity (from age 23 and on) is clearly related to brief tenure in the party.

The pattern of engaging in radical activity at a very young age is most marked among those respondents who joined the party prior to the Popular Front period (see Table 4). Sixty

TABLE 4

Age at Time of First Radical Activity by Period of Joining
(in per cent)

	Early joiners	Late joiners	All respondents
Before 16	28	12	20
16-18	32	26	29
19-22	27	22	24
23 and over	10	40	25
No information	3	—	2
Total	100	100	100

per cent of those who joined before 1935 had become involved in radical activity before the age of eighteen, as compared with 38 per cent of those who joined the party after the Popular Front period. On the other hand, 40 per cent of the late joiners had not engaged in radical activity until the age of twenty-three or over. This confirms other findings as to the relative quality of the recruits in the pre-Popular Front and post-Popular Front periods of the party. The early recruits were younger, more assimilable, less committed to the "bourgeois" world, and better indoctrinated.

There would also appear to be a clear relationship between early involvement in radical activity and later achievement of high rank in the party (see Table 5). Thus 32 per cent

TABLE 5

Age at Time of First Radical Activity Related to Rank Held in the Party

(in per cent)

	Rank and file	Low echelon	High echelon	All respondents
Before 16	12	24	32	21
16-18	27	32	29	29
19-22	28	20	23	24
23 and over	33	20	16	25
No information	—	4	—	1
Total	100	100	100	100

of the high-echelon respondents had become involved in radical activity before the age of sixteen, as compared with only 12 per cent for the rank-and-file respondents. And 33 per cent of the rank and file had not engaged in radical activity until the age of twenty-three and over, as compared with 16 per cent for the high echelon. This relationship is also brought out in a comparison of our high-echelon respondents with the present members of the Central Committees of the French and Italian Communist parties (see Table 6). The patterns are strikingly similar. Thus it would appear to be a valid inference that persons who became involved in radical activity at an early age have a better prognosis for high rank in the party and, as we have seen at earlier points,

TABLE 6

Age at Time of First Radical Activity for Former High-echelon Communists and the Present French and Italian Central Committee Members
(in per cent)

	High-echelon former Communists	French and Italian Central Committee members
Before 16	32	32
16-18	29	19
19-22	23	21
23 and over	16	8
No information	—	20
Total	100	100

they are predisposed in other respects to assimilate successfully. Holt's study of Central Committee members shows that these individuals not only engage in radical activity at early ages, but also commit themselves fully and quickly to the party after joining. Thus 56 per cent of the present Central Committee members for whom these data were available became party functionaries within two years after joining the party.[1]

Political Background

The largest single group of respondents came from left-wing family backgrounds. Thirty-four per cent came from Communist, Socialist, Syndicalist, or Anarchist homes. Sixteen per cent came from "liberal" homes, i.e., pro-democratic and even moderately left. Sixteen per cent came from conservative families, and only 3 per cent came from monarchist or Fascist backgrounds. Fifteen per cent came from families which were indifferent or apathetic. On the whole, these data suggest that the membership of the party in the West consists to a considerable extent of persons whose backgrounds and upbringings would lead them to be receptive to Marxist and revolutionary ideology. For them, joining the party would be a matter of conforming to the past rather than deviating from it (see Table 7).

[1] Holt, *op.cit.*, p. 17.

TABLE 7

Political Attitude of Parents by Country
(in per cent)

	U.S.	England	France	Italy	All respondents
Communist	6	—	3	—	3
Other left	22	30	38	39	31
Liberal	11	28	10	17	16
Conservative	25	14	9	14	16
Aristocratic, authoritarian	—	—	3	2	1
Fascist	—	—	—	8	2
Indifferent	13	22	12	12	15
Unknown	23	6	25	8	16
Total	100	100	100	100	100

The pattern, however, differs from country to country. The French and Italian respondents included a somewhat larger proportion of persons who came from left-wing families than either the American or the British. That this difference is not greater may be due to the composition of the sample. In each country the sample included working-class and middle-class persons in approximately equal proportions. Such a selection is more representative of the composition of the British and American parties than it is of the French and Italian, the membership of which is largely recruited from the working class. Since, as we will see below, the working-class respondents come substantially more often from left-wing families, a representative sample of French and Italian party members would probably have shown a far larger proportion of persons coming from this type of political background. But even the present distribution suggests the hypothesis that the British and American parties are more deviant, i.e., a larger part of the membership has broken from family and community political patterns, while the membership of the French and Italian parties, on the other hand, consists in larger part of persons who are conforming to their ideological backgrounds. Table 7 shows that this is less true of the Italian respondents than of the French. But here the long Fascist interregnum and the sudden emergence of the Italian Communist Party as the leading movement of the resistance and one of the major parties of the postwar era accounts for the large proportion of respondents coming from liberal, right-wing, and Fascist backgrounds. It is likely that the present Italian party membership includes a far larger proportion of such persons than does the French.

It is also noteworthy that a substantial part of the American and British respondents also came from left-wing families (28 per cent of the American respondents, 30 per cent of the British), so that even in these countries joining the party often meant conforming rather than deviating from the politics of the family background. But the kind of conformity which was involved in the British and American cases was conformity within a group or community that was in itself deviant. In other words, the socialist and Marxist movements to which the parents of these American and British respondents belonged were confined to a few urban industrial areas, and in the American case primarily to foreign language groups. This supports the general characterization of the British and American parties as politically deviant movements, but the deviance is of two orders. They include a larger proportion of persons who have broken from their political backgrounds, and those who have not broken from their pasts come from deviant communities within the general society.

The middle-class respondents included a larger proportion of political deviants, i.e., persons coming from liberal, conservative, or extreme right-wing families, than the working-class group (47 per cent for the former, 23 per cent for the latter). This adds another detail to the general picture of the middle-class respondent as a social, psychological, and political deviant. Similarly, those who joined the party in the post-1935 period included a larger proportion of political deviants than did the early joiners.

Equally striking are the differences in political background related to later rank achieved in the party (see Table 8). The high-echelon respondents included the largest proportion of persons coming from left-wing backgrounds, and the rank

TABLE 8

Political Attitude of Parents by Echelon
(in per cent)

	Rank and file	Low echelon	High echelon	All respondents
Communist	4	1	2	3
Other left	19	38	43	31
Liberal	18	10	24	16
Conservative	18	21	6	16
Aristocratic, authoritarian	1	1	2	1
Fascist	2	3	—	2
Indifferent	16	15	10	15
Unknown	22	11	13	16
Total	100	100	100	100

and file the smallest. In other words, persons coming to the party from left-wing families move into it with a minimum of conflict, and with the strongest momentum, and hence are likely to gravitate to positions of leadership.

Situation at Time of Joining

The emphasis that has been placed on sociological factors thus far may tend to create a "deterministic" impression of the appeal of Communism. But all we have said so far is that certain kinds of social characteristics appear more often to be related to joining the party than others. Anyone who joins the party makes a decision, or a series of decisions, in a particular setting. This setting was typically defined by our respondents in terms of a specific exposure or sequence of exposures, and in terms of a general political situation. Choosing to join the party, then, involved a choice influenced on the one hand by a susceptibility, and on the other by a political exposure and situation.

More of the respondents joined the party via another organization such as a trade union, student organization, and the like than joined the party directly or via the Communist youth organization. Thus 54 per cent first joined a front organization, as compared with 35 per cent who joined the party directly and 11 per cent who first joined the Young

Communist League. For most of the respondents, therefore, joining the party cannot properly be described as a single act in time, but rather as a process involving a series of decisions stretching over a period of time. Even for those joining the party or the Young Communist League directly, the act of formal affiliation was infrequently accompanied by an awareness of the esoteric characteristics of the movement. Furthermore, these "front organizations," or the party units themselves with which our respondents affiliated themselves, were often locally influential groups. The student respondents, for example, were often confronted with influential "Socialist Societies" or "Student Unions." The working-class respondents were confronted with more or less powerful trade unions. Frenchmen and Italians during the German occupation of their countries were confronted with partisan movements, the heroism of which against the invader was widely supported among the general population. While it is true that when confronted by these political exposures some individuals were attracted and others were not, and some moved all the way into the party while others stopped with the front organization, the fact remains that the great majority of our respondents required a specific and influential exposure before they joined. This suggests that it would be a gross inaccuracy to conclude that only those persons join the party who have some special susceptibility related to social status or psychological characteristics. In a large number of cases, the political situation and immediate social pressure may be sufficient all by themselves to make persons join the party. The obvious illustration of this, of course, is seen in countries where the Communist parties are in power, and where career opportunities, prestige, and safety are primarily attained through joining the party. Similarly, during the war in France and Italy, individuals joined the resistance movements with the full support and even urging of peers, family, and community.

Finally, affiliation with the party has to be seen in terms of the general political situation obtaining at the time of joining. Practically all the respondents joined the party during periods of serious political threat, during general disasters, or in the aftermath of these disasters. Choosing to join typically involved immediate political pressure by trusted age-mates or occupational peers, in the light of an impending political threat or in the aftermath of a social or political catastrophe. Most of our respondents joined the party immediately after the First World War, during the depression of the 1930's, during the period of Fascist advance, or during enemy occupation of their home countries.

The content of susceptibility to Communism varies with the political situation. In the American and British settings, where the Communist movements are extremely small, and where other more effective opportunities for political action are available, susceptibility frequently involves some psychological and social deviance. In France and Italy, where Marxism and socialism have been deeply rooted, where the parties have been and are large and powerful, and where social evils are substantial and persistent, susceptibility often simply consists of a choice based upon reality calculations and confirmed by family and community pressures. The content of susceptibility varies not only with place but also with time. It was a quite different thing to have joined the party during the depression rather than during the late 1920's, or during the World War II alliance rather than during the post-Cominform period. Similarly, the content of susceptibility varies with the tactical orientation of the party. The Popular Front party and World War II alliance party appealed to different susceptibilities than did the party of the Nazi-Soviet Pact or the post-Cominform party. All of this suggests that the idea of a single pattern or kind of susceptibility is completely untenable.

An analysis of the periods during which our respondents joined the party may be of use in connection with some of the points made above. It may suggest how the political situation and the role of the party was perceived at the time of joining. Table 9 gives the periods of joining for our respondents as a group, as well as for the different ranks. Taking the group as a whole, there appear to have been three periods of heavy recruitment: (1) the years immediately after World War I and the formation of the Third International; (2) the period of the depression and the first years of the Popular Front; and (3) the World War II period

TABLE 9

Period of Joining by Rank
(in per cent)

	Rank and file	Low echelon	High echelon	All respondents
1922 and before	6	17	41	18
1923-25	4	4	20	8
1926-28	6	5	6	6
1929-31	4	10	6	6
1932-34	12	8	12	11
1935-37	15	17	9	14
1938-39	10	5	—	6
1940-41	9	3	—	5
1941-44	16	16	4	13
1945-47	16	15	2	12
1948 and later	2	—	—	1
Total	100	100	100	100

and the immediate postwar years prior to the establishment of the Cominform. This pattern is confirmed by other data on the fluctuations in the party vote in elections, as well as on fluctuations in party membership.[2]

The heaviest recruitment seems to have occurred in three kinds of situations. First, it has occurred at times when the party is protectively colored, as in the period of the Popular Front or the World War II coalition—periods when the party is identified with broad, moderate, and patriotic aims. Second, it has occurred at times of serious social breakdown, as in the depression, when the radicalism and militance of the party may be evaluated as an appropriate response. Finally, it has occurred in situations where the party appears

[2] See, for example, Sutton, *op.cit.*, pp. 313 ff., for a discussion of fluctuations in membership in the American Communist Party; and Domenach, *op.cit.*, pp. 112 ff., for the French figures. A paper specially prepared for the present study by Mark Abrams gives the British data on fluctuations in party membership.

to have good prospects for success, where it looks like the "wave of the future," as in the periods immediately after the First and Second World Wars. In short, it is in situations in which the party appears to be least deviant that it is most successful in recruiting new members.

Table 9 brings out a number of differences in the recruitment patterns of the various party ranks. The great majority of the high-echelon respondents came into the party in the years before 1925. More than 40 per cent came in before 1922. The periods of joining for the other ranks were more equally distributed among the very early years, the depression and Popular Front era, and the days of the World War II coalition. The recruitment pattern manifested among the high-echelon former party members is very similar to that of the present Central Committee members of the French, Italian, and American parties (see Table 10). Both groups

TABLE 10

Comparison of Period of Joining for High-echelon Former Party Members and Present Central Committee Members
(in per cent)

	High-echelon former Communists	Present Central Committee members
1922 and before	41	37
1923-25	20	15
1926-28	6	8
1929-31	6	6
1932-34	12	6
1935-37	9	6
1938-39	—	3
1940-41	—	1
1941-44	4	3
1945-47	2	1
1948 and later	—	—
Unknown	—	14
Total	100	100

show an extraordinarily large concentration of persons who joined the party in the aftermath of World War I and during the period when the *mystique* of the Bolshevik Revolution exercised its greatest attraction. While this reflects the effects of seniority, and a policy of recruiting top leadership from within the party organization, it is of interest in another connection. The period after World War I differed from all subsequent periods in the sense that there was the least ambiguity in the position of the Communist movement, and the party seemed to have immediate prospects for success. These early recruits affiliated themselves with the party at a time when the mission of the party was "pure," and when it appeared to have the future on its side. It is, of course, necessary to point out that many of those who came into the party during this period, and reached the higher echelons, either left it or were expelled in the great factional struggles of the 1920's and later decades. But for those who picked the Stalinist side and who now are masters of the party apparatuses, this memory of the time of their original affiliation, during the heroic era of revolutionary innocence and success, may serve as a means of renewing their faith and carrying them through days of difficult choices and depressing prospects. This is not at all to argue that the memory of the original "purity" of their commitment is the most important factor accounting for their loyalty to the party. It is quite clear that other factors—such as the unavailability of alternative careers and positions of political influence, and the material advantages of party office—play important roles. One can only say about the memories of these high-echelon Communists, in contrast to those of the lower ranks, that they more frequently contain this layer of "revolutionary purity," and that it may be possible for them to continue to believe, despite all the contaminations to which they have been exposed, that the feelings and aspirations of this period constitute the essential truth of the movement. That this may be the case is reflected in the fact that our high-echelon respondents when leaving joined or formed dissident Communist movements more often than did the lower ranks. These dissident movements lay claim to the pure, original doctrine and reject the impurities and deviations of the Communist movement. But this is a theme which will be developed in the later discussion of the process of defection.

CHAPTER 9

SUSCEPTIBILITY TO COMMUNISM

So MANY VARIETIES of human experience are encompassed in susceptibility to Communism, so many different kinds of needs, interests, and values enter into decisions to join the party, that it may be useful at the outset to provide a system of classification, a kind of card index, of levels, types, and patterns of susceptibility. By *level* of susceptibility we mean the degree to which an individual is aware of and positively chooses to join the party in terms of its inner characteristics and requirements. By *type* of susceptibility we mean the particular need or set of needs and interests which the individual seeks to satisfy by joining the party. By *pattern* of susceptibility we mean the particular combination of level and type characteristic of specific individuals, or occurring with significant frequency among the various strata and groupings within the party.

Levels of Susceptibility

Certain distinctions between levels of susceptibility have already been suggested at earlier points in this study. In our analysis of how the party is perceived we found that certain individuals—particularly those who later moved into the higher echelons of the party—had been exposed to the party doctrine before joining. These recruits were relatively aware of the esoteric properties of the party. On the other hand, there were many respondents who were unaware of the esoteric character of the movement, who were attracted to the agitational or tactical representations of the party. Those who joined in the Italian and French resistance movements are good examples of the latter type, as are some of the British and American trade unionists who saw in the party little more than a militant trade unionism.

Again, in the analysis of the social origins and political background of our former party members, it was clear that some, particularly those who later became party leaders, came from families and community settings in which anticlerical-ism, Marxism, Leninism, and even Stalinism were already deeply rooted and taken for granted. Some of these persons were exposed to the esoteric party at the breasts of their mothers, so to speak. On the other hand, there were many respondents who came to the party with attitudes and expec-tations in full conflict with esoteric party ideology and prac-tice, and who consequently could only have been susceptible to the exoteric representations of the party. The latter group may be referred to as "dupes" of the party, persons caught up in the party's agitational net, material unsuitable for the party cadres and constituting a considerable part of the rank and file of the Communist movement. The adherence of this group to the party may be based upon an acceptance of some part of the party's demonology and of some one or combina-tion of the exoteric goals to which the party lays claim.

We may for purposes of brevity refer to the two levels described above as esoteric and exoteric susceptibility. They are the extremes in the ideological continuum. Actually, most persons joining the party fall somewhere in between these two extremes; they are in the middle range of ideological susceptibility. That is to say, they are not aware—in the sense of being experienced and "steeled"—of the esoteric require-ments of the party. At best, their awareness of the esoteric party is an intellectual one, consisting of knowledge of a few slogans, or of hasty exposure to some of the classic Com-munist writings. At the same time, it would be incorrect to view this group as innocent dupes of the party. This middle range of ideological susceptibility consists of persons who are not explicitly aware of the esoteric requirements of the party, but who register the fact that they are affiliating themselves with something that is esoteric, outlawed, iconoclastic, pitted against society. This was the significance of the earlier finding that more than half of the respondents saw the party at the time of joining as a means of solving some of their own non-political problems. In many cases, these non-political prob-lems involved impulses to deviate, to reject parental and religious patterns, to do something exciting, romantic, bohemian, antagonistic. This was especially frequent among the middle-class recruits in England and the United States, most of whom knew little of the party doctrine and operating code when they joined and were hardly aware of the implications of their decision. For them, there was an awareness of an esoteric and deviant discipline in the movement they were joining, but not an awareness of the specific properties and demands of this discipline.

This distinction between levels of susceptibility is useful for purposes of prognosis. Individuals who come to the party aware of its esoteric requirements and discipline have a better prognosis for long tenure and high rank, while those who have been exposed only to the exoteric images of the party will require substantial "remodeling" before they can enter the inner party. It is also useful as a rather simplified description of the ideological stratification of the Communist movement, and hence suggestive of the problems of cohesion and coordination which confront the party leadership. Since the rank and file of the Communist movement, and even many of the low-echelon officials and some of the higher echelon, are not fully adapted to the inner discipline of the party, they limit and confine the freedom of maneuver of the party, unless the leadership decides, as it sometimes does, that a particular action is necessary despite the losses in party membership that may result. This existence of a large bulk of unassimilated party members and "untested" party leaders accounts for the extraordinary emphasis placed upon the training of the cadres which one finds in all the elite periodicals of the movement. In a sense, the party is a prisoner of its own tactics; persons who have been attracted to the party because of its tactical espousal of trade union objectives, for example, or of patriotic interests are possible defectors when the party acts in conflict with these interests. Admission into the cadres, on the other hand, signifies a degree of submission and loyalty to the party which involves the suppression of these earlier exoteric "illusions" and "self-deceptions."

The ideological stratification of the Communist movement is of course affected by the tactical orientation of the party.

In left revolutionary periods, the esoteric discipline of the party becomes more obvious, the concealment of the party's inner code becomes more transparent. Thus it was in these left periods, such as the years immediately after World War I and the early years of the depression before the Popular Front, that the party tended to recruit persons who were aware of its esoteric discipline and who were therefore more likely to move quickly into the cadres and the upper leadership of the party. In Popular Front periods, on the other hand, the party draws in a more mixed collection of recruits, most of whom are unsuitable as leadership material.

Another factor which will affect the ideological stratification of the movement is the general political and social situation. In periods of catastrophe such as wars and their aftermaths, or in serious depressions, the militance and power emphasis of the inner party will tend to "make more sense," and, at least as long as the crisis obtains, the ideological differences between the inner and outer party are of less importance. Once the crisis is over, however, the party will return to its more typical pattern of an inner core integrally committed to the complete destruction of the established society, and an outer party consisting of individuals and groups whose attachment to the party is based upon an acceptance of its exoteric claims and at best only a partial awareness of the requirements of the inner discipline.

As a consequence of experience, the effectiveness of these recruitment tactics among certain groups has declined through time. This is particularly the case with Western intellectuals; more exposed to communication and more trained to draw inferences from knowledge, they learn more rapidly and more effectively than workers or peasants. Western intellectuals came into the party in significant numbers in the years of the revolutionary *mystique* after World War I, in the years of the depression and the Popular Front, and in the period of the Russian-Western Alliance during and immediately after World War II. However, the duplicity and concealment of the party and its integral power orientation have become more obvious to intellectuals with each of the great changes in line, and particularly with the Nazi-Soviet Pact in 1939 and the establishment of the Cominform in 1947. Thus Communism has very little attraction today for intellectuals in England and the United States, since few of them can be taken in by the exoteric picture of the party as the "savior of the peace" and as the embodiment of "true democracy."

At the same time, the party has tended to hold its ground among the dissatisfied working classes of France and Italy, since there the agitational tactics of the party appeal to immediate and pragmatic interests and needs, and the exposure of the working classes to communication and their capacity for drawing inferences from knowledge is more limited. Indeed, the party has gained substantial ground in recent years among the French and Italian peasantry simply on the basis of its advocacy of their immediate interests, and with little prospect of recruiting peasants into the cadres and inner core of the party.

Thus the party continues to have its inner and outer ideological layers, but the tactic of concealment tends to lose its effectiveness as it becomes obvious. It becomes obvious for some sooner than for others, depending upon their learning capacity and their exposure to communication. The point ought also to be made that persons may learn and still not act on the basis of this learning, since the alternatives confronting them may be unsatisfactory. French intellectuals certainly share a capacity for learning with their British and American colleagues, but the orientation of the French intellectuals to Communism differs radically from that of the Anglo-American intellectuals.

The continued attraction of Communism for intellectuals in countries such as France and Italy may be attributed to the deep and apparently chronic social crisis characteristic of those countries, which confronts the intellectuals with problems of decision which are more complex and exacting than those which confront their colleagues in England and the United States. In England and the United States, a political tradition of compromise has made it possible to bring the working classes into the family of political power and has won their loyalty by granting them a share in the available values and opportunities. In France and Italy, the working classes have tended to be alienated from the political community and revolutionary in their orientation. Many French and Italian intellectuals who are confronted with this deep social and political division reject the middle class and identify themselves with the working class. They find in the working class a hope for morality and progress which they can find in no other sector of the society. This attitude toward workers as holding the hopes for a future of morality and dignity was a common pattern among all intellectuals in the 1930's, when middle-class society in general appeared to be shaken to its foundations and unable to find a moral purpose or the energy and conviction necessary to achieve one. The reforms in British and American society have renewed the faith of the intellectuals of those countries, but such reforms have not been achieved in France and Italy. Thus, in these countries, a permanent social crisis and the weakness and ineffectiveness of political alternatives to Communism confront intellectuals with a difficult problem which many of them have solved by adherence to the party, by fellow-traveling, or by "neutralism."

Types of Susceptibility

By type of susceptibility we mean the various kinds of individual needs and interests which may enter into decisions to join the party. For the purposes of the present study, these needs have been classified into four major groupings: (1) neurotic needs, (2) self-related interests, (3) group-related interests, and (4) ideological interests. Neurotic susceptibility to Communism will be discussed in detail in the chapter which follows. However, some explanation of the "emotional" factor is necessary if the classification employed in this study is to be understood.

It is obvious that all action involves feeling and emotion. In the case of persons joining the party outside the Communist orbit itself, alienative feelings are typically involved— that is, feelings of rejection and resentment, impulses to attack and withdraw, or some combination of these. Such negative impulses may be partly unconscious, chronic, a consequence of the maladjustive way in which the individual seeks to relate himself to others, or they may be the result of some situational impairment or damage—the consequence, in other words, of some event or development which is initiated outside the individual. Thus unconscious hostility in the neurotic might influence the decision to join the party. In a normal person, resentment of a situation in which he was unemployed through no fault of his own might also lead to joining the party. In a neurotic person, withdrawal from interpersonal relationships and feelings of isolation and loneliness resulting from this tendency may contribute to susceptibility. In a normal individual, the loneliness and isolation which result from moving into a new social setting may have the same effect. In a neurotic individual, deeply rooted feelings of unworthiness and inadequacy may lead to joining the party. In a normal individual, experiencing a society or social situation which rejects him, which disqualifies him from certain kinds of roles and participations, may create a readiness to join the party. In a neurotic person, feelings of confusion, of conflict, and of uncertainty may contribute to the attraction of the party; and confusions and uncertainties which are the consequence of the objective situation in which a normal person finds himself may have the same effect. However, the neurotic person will join the party in response to the pressure of internal needs, and often in defiance of the modal patterns of his social grouping. The normal person who has suffered some situational damage will join the party in response to the situation, and often (but by no means always) in conformity with patterns prevailing in his social grouping.

Where the feelings reported in or inferred from the interview material appeared on careful appraisal to have been chronic, unconscious, and maladjustive, they were classified under the heading of neurotic needs. Where the feelings appeared to be situationally induced, they were classified according to the objects and interests with which they were associated.

Self-oriented Interests. Three main types of self-oriented interests were reported by the respondents: (1) career, (2) social relatedness, and (3) intellectual clarity. Some 19 per cent of all the respondents reported career interests as related to joining the party. It was the rare case, however, in which career interests all by themselves accounted for the act of joining. Career factors can enter into the decision to join the party in a variety of ways. They may, for example, be the crucial interest which results in affiliation. One American respondent said, "I read the Manifesto and thought it was wonderful, but didn't do anything about it, but when the X group began to publish my poetry and told me I had great talent, I joined. I had the predisposition, but I needed a bridge." Quite a few of the Italians who joined in 1945 or later spoke frankly of the job opportunities offered them by the party. In the words of one of them, "I was listened to, well treated by the comrades and especially by my superiors, who held out inducements that with my temperament and my abilities I might one day become an important man in the party." Other Italian respondents referred to the practice of the Italian Communist Party of paying the tuition and expenses of the more active Communist university students. In some cases, trade union functionaries were told that they would have to join the party if they wished to keep their jobs. For some artists and intellectuals, career interests entered into the decision to join the party through a desire to be associated with Communist *avant-garde* writers and painters. This was particularly true of the 1920's, when there was an artistic ferment in the Soviet Union. A Frenchman commented, "One important thing for intellectuals in moving to the party was the revelation of the first Soviet films. We had the feeling of an aesthetic revolution. It was a rich period from the intellectual point of view." An American writer reported, "When I came back to New York in 1935, I found that many of my friends were deep in the Communist movement. One in particular had become a CP member and had written a proletarian novel which was hailed as the thing. I felt utterly empty. These people had something which filled them with importance."

The cases recorded here under "social relatedness" were persons who were "situationally lonesome." That is, they were not chronic isolates or "withdrawn" people, but were in situations where their ethnic or social characteristics made it difficult for them to affiliate themselves with the dominant groupings. Some 20 per cent of the respondents reported needs for group relationships as contributing to their decisions to join the party. An American woman Communist spoke of her college experience in these terms, "My social life was very unstable and the Communist Party provided group relationships around ethical themes. I had a need for a place to belong to—some organization with a moral goal. Working as I did with intellectuals, it was the most satisfying experience." An English respondent, away from home for the first time, made his first friendships with a small group of Communists. "I wasn't particularly interested in politics, but I went along with them, mainly because they were nice people and I wanted to retain their friendship."

Finally, there were some 12 per cent who were attracted to the movement because of an interest in its intellectual aspects. At one extreme in this dimension were those who were seeking a complete intellectual pattern. In the words of an American artist, "I wasn't interested in Marxian economics. The appeal was primarily artistic. It was a pattern. It was a neat sequence of inevitability—like the resolution of a problem in painting. . . . This appeal was greater than compensation, sour grapes, hatred, and the like. I had none of these latter reactions. I liked my society and life. By nature I was an optimist." At the other extreme was the more simple interest in being an informed person, having a position on social and political questions. This kind of interest was characteristic of some young university students who were attracted to the party for short periods since it gave them a kind of claim on "knowing the answers."

Group-related Interests. Thirty-nine per cent of the respondents reported that they joined the party because it was a more effective way of realizing the objectives of groups with which they were already identified. Here the most common type (30 per cent of all respondents) was the trade unionist impressed by the militance and efficiency of the Communist trade union leaders. As one American respondent put it, "We needed an organization, but didn't know what to do or how. The CP had the superiority of organizational knowledge and political understanding. . . . The CP did more than talk. They always reported some kind of concrete progress at each meeting." Another American trade unionist remarked, "If there was one Commie in the shop, the boss would be scared to death and would listen to reason. The Commies wouldn't let him take advantage of anyone." While in the United States the Communist approach to trade unionists emphasized how useful Communists could be in realizing trade union objectives, on the European continent there was a tendency to stress the identity of interests of union and party. A Frenchman reported, "I was the secretary of the federation, but all the rest of the administrative committee were Communists. . . . My colleagues were amazed that I could find any difference of interests between party and union. They said, 'Come and join us, there's no conflict between political action and union action.' "

Only the American cases reported joining the party in order to facilitate the work of minority group organizations with which they were already identified.[1] A Negro woman teacher who was active in a well-known Negro organization was approached by Communists and appealed to completely on the basis of anti-prejudice. "Two or three sort of picked me out to discuss things more political," she said. "There was always an insidious attempt to appeal on the basis of the Negro problem. Finally, one particular fellow got around to really discussing the Negro question. I had long arguments with him. He gave me several things to read. Something was going on at the time—not the Scottsboro case, but something very revolting in the South. Then it was shown to me that

[1] Three per cent of all respondents reported minority group interests.

the CP was the only group truly interested in democracy for the Negroes. I got all the clichés, for which I fell, and joined. . . ."

Only the French and Italian respondents reported patriotic interests as related to their decisions to join the party.[2] During the German occupation of France and northern Italy, many Frenchmen and Italians were attracted to the movement because it was a militant force fighting for French and Italian freedom and against the invader. Thus a Frenchman commented, "They [the Communists] were the only ones to take a stand in the difficult days before 1944. After that there was a rush of new members. . . . At the liberation the CP seemed more French than the other parties. It was the French aspect, the national front aspect, of the party which attracted me. The Nazi-Soviet Pact had become a nebulous thing." An Italian who had joined during the liberation commented, "My position was that of a lively sympathy for the Italian Communists, because they were Italians, anti-Fascists in the true sense of the word and, therefore, to my way of thinking, defenders of our national interests."

Ideological Interests. Practically all of the respondents (91 per cent) reported some political or ideological interest as related to joining the party. The party was identified as being opposed to certain political and social evils, and as a means to certain desired political goals. In the analysis of perceptions of the movement we have already seen that only a minority of the respondents had been exposed to the esoteric party doctrine and were ideologically involved, in this sense of the term. The exoteric goals cited by the respondents as influencing their decisions to join the party fell into four main sub-categories. These were (1) racial and ethnic equality, (2) economic and social equality, (3) freedom from oppression, and (4) pacifism and internationalism.

It would be a great mistake to view these ideological attractions of Communism as simple "rationalizations" of other types of needs, such as those resulting from emotional

---

[2] Eight per cent of all respondents reported patriotic motives in joining the party.

problems and personal interests. There were indeed many instances in which ideological interests were transparent cloaks for personal motives of one kind or another, but there were also many cases where there could be little question of the genuineness of the ideological interest. A few comments may make this clear. An Italian woman whose father had been beaten to death by Fascist "Squadristi" in the 1920's commented, "My father's death was at the door of Fascism and I carried in my flesh and in my heart all the sufferings and the misfortunes which this regime had caused in the world." Some of the Italian intellectuals who joined the party in the 1930's as university students spoke of the impact of the Abyssinian War, of the Spanish Civil War, and of the appeasement policy of the democracies. The oppression of Fascism was an intimate experience for them. On the one hand, there was the Fascist tyranny which intervened directly in their lives in the university, and on the other the "decadent democracies" which did nothing against these evils. Their ideological interests were hardly "projective" in the psychological sense. They were based on personal impingements and expectations. One of these Italian intellectual anti-Fascists remarked, "In my opinion it was logical that human beings, young and not yet overtaken by the disease of ambition spreading under the dictatorship, should be attracted to Communism. . . . We studied [Marxism] as famished people eat when they suddenly come upon a table set forth with food."

Among those joining in the early 1920's were many who had lost members of their families in the First World War. Some of them expressed feelings similar to that of the British respondent who commented, "One of my earliest memories is of my father returning from the hospital in 1919. He was a big strapping fellow and he came back on crutches with a flapping leg. It burned a picture in my mind that I've never forgotten. Ever since I've had a deep hatred for war, though I'm not a pacifist." There were other kinds of direct exposures to disturbing impressions and experiences which led to susceptibility to Communism on this simple ideological level. Seeing the consequences of depression and unemployment or witnessing police action against strikers and demonstrators were reported with some frequency as influencing choices to join the party. In other words, there were many cases in which the ideological interest seemed clearly to be a response to experience and knowledge. Since in these cases the party was perceived not as a power-oriented conspiracy, but as an advocate of specific aggrieved groups and as a militant opponent of immediate evils, the response appeared to be appropriate.

These findings as to the kinds of ideological interests involved in joining the party point again to the fundamental problem of assimilation into the Communist movement. It appeared that most people come into the party not only with alienative feelings but with positive and constructive expectations as well. These positive and constructive expectations are a part of the susceptibility to the exoteric appeals of the party. As individuals come closer to the esoteric party and begin to appreciate the essentially tactical character of these exoteric appeals, conflicts arise and defection often results.

Patterns of Susceptibility

National Differences. Certain differences in level of susceptibility among the national groups of respondents have already been brought out in the analysis of the ways in which the Communist Party is perceived. Thus the French respondents were exposed to the esoteric doctrine more frequently than the other national groupings. It might be said by way of hypothesis that the French party conforms more to the esoteric Communist model. The Italian group included the smallest proportion of persons who had been exposed to the esoteric doctrine at the time of joining, and hence may be viewed hypothetically as conforming to the exoteric model of the party. The American and British respondents, and particularly the American, included the largest proportion of persons who, while not perceiving the specific properties of the esoteric model of the party, registered its deviant character. Thus the American and British parties may hypothetically be described as falling in the middle range of susceptibility, i.e., the level at which the esoteric model is not specifically perceived, but at which its generally antagonistic and deviant properties are registered.

The need patterns manifested by the different national groupings are consistent with these findings as to level of susceptibility (see Table 1). Thus the incidence of neurotic

TABLE I

Types of Needs and Interests Related to Joining the Party by Country*
(in per cent)

	U.S.	England	France	Italy	All respondents
Neurotic needs	58	48	25	31	41
Self-oriented interests	70	34	39	35	47
Group-related interests	42	26	54	25	39
Ideological interests	88	94	86	94	91

* Multiple responses.

needs was highest among the American respondents, next highest among the British, and lowest among the French. In other words, about half of the American and British respondents sought to realize some unconscious, maladjustive emotional need in joining the party, in contrast to the French and Italian respondents, for whom the proportion was substantially lower.

Similarly, with regard to self-oriented interests the American respondents stand out among the national groupings. The interest most frequently involved here was that of social relatedness, which reflects again the ethnic character of the American party. Since so many of the American respondents were foreign-born or first-generation native-born and living in situations in which they did not have satisfactory access to social relationships, they often sought to solve problems of loneliness and isolation by affiliating with the party.

With regard to group-related needs, efforts to realize minority group interests were unique to the American party, while efforts to realize patriotic interests occurred only among the French and Italian respondents who joined during the anti-Nazi and anti-Fascist resistance periods.

The distribution of exoteric ideological interests among the national groupings is of considerable interest, since it suggests a number of special attributes of the various national parties. Thus only the American respondents sought to realize social or ethnic equality by joining the party. Political freedom and anti-Fascism occurred with exceptional frequency among the Italian respondents. This suggests that both nationalism and libertarianism may be significant factors in limiting the freedom of maneuver of the Italian party leadership. On the other hand, anti-militarism and pacifism were reported most frequently by the French respondents, many of whom had joined the party in the wave of pacifism which swept France in the years after World War I.

It is quite clear that at the exoteric level the various national Communist movements differ significantly from one another. At this level they are saturated, so to speak, with the local color, the special attitudes resulting from national historical experience, and with the special problems and orientations current among particular groupings of the population. A certain homogeneity is maintained at the esoteric level of the various parties, but even here it more than occasionally becomes clear that this esoteric indoctrination is only skin-deep and is cast off at the first difficult test, at the first real impingement of esoteric requirements on outside interests and commitments.

Class Differences. We have already seen in the analysis of how the party is perceived that relatively few working-class respondents had been exposed to the esoteric doctrine of the party before joining, and that they tended to remain unindoctrinated while in the party. In contrast, the middle-class respondents were more often exposed to the esoteric doctrine before joining, and more often experienced formal indoctrination while in the party. At the same time, far more of the middle-class respondents perceived and were positively attracted to the deviant and iconoclastic characteristics of the esoteric party. Thus the working-class Communists appear to cluster at the exoteric level of susceptibility, while the middle-class Communists appear to cluster at the esoteric level or at the middle range, at which the deviant character of the esoteric party is emotionally registered, though not explicitly perceived. In an analysis of the social characteristics of the respondents, we also found that the middle-class respondents were deviating far more frequently from their social, political, and religious backgrounds in joining the party. This suggested the hypothesis that the middle-class respondents would include a larger proportion of persons with psychological problems and difficulties which they sought to solve by joining the party.

This hypothesis is confirmed in Table 2, in which it is shown that more than twice as many of the middle-class respondents as of the working-class group manifested neurotic problems.[3] Since joining the party in countries such as Eng-

TABLE 2

Types of Needs and Interests Related to Joining the Party by Social Class*
(in per cent)

	Middle class	Working class	All respondents
Neurotic needs	56	26	41
Self-oriented interests	51	43	47
Group-related interests	24	53	39
Ideological interests	92	89	91

* Multiple responses.

land and the United States constitutes far more of an act of deviation than is the case in France and Italy, it was also expected that the American and British respondents—both middle- and working-class—would manifest neurotic difficulties more frequently than their French and Italian colleagues. This hypothesis is confirmed in Table 3, which shows that neurotic deviance is practically the rule (75 per cent) for American

[3] For a preliminary comparison of working-class and middle-class needs and interests based on our American cases, see Herbert Krugman, "The Appeal of Communism to American Middle Class Intellectuals and Trade Unionists," *Public Opinion Quarterly*, Vol. xvi (Fall 1952), pp. 331 ff.

and British middle-class respondents, and while far less frequent for the French and Italian, still is fairly common. On the other hand, the incidence among the working-class respondents of both regions is low, but higher among the British and American respondents than among the French

TABLE 3

Comparison of Incidence of Neurotic Needs among American-British and French-Italian Respondents by Social Class
(in per cent)

	Middle class	*Working class*
French and Italian	35	21
American and British	75	32

and Italian. That so few of the American and British working-class respondents were deviants in the psychological sense may be attributable to the way in which the party is represented and perceived among the working class. In England and the United States in particular, the party is represented and perceived as instrumental to trade union goals and objectives, as oriented toward the immediate needs and grievances of the working classes. Hence the act of joining may appear to be a response appropriate to the situation and to the goals prevailing among working people.

This strikingly high incidence of neurotic needs among American and British former party members should not lead one to the conclusion that all middle-class neurotics are susceptible to Communism. It does appear that middle-class persons with emotional problems who have become accustomed to dealing with problems, conflicts, and emotional difficulties by means of a more or less complex pattern of intellectual rationalization, and who are under pressure to justify the expression of resentment in moral terms, are more likely to be susceptible than those who cope with these problems through simpler forms of action such as the direct expression of resentment, or through physiological narcoses such as alcoholism and sexual promiscuity. Again and again, our American and British middle-class case material reveals this

pattern of intellectualization as a means of coping with alienative and maladjustive feelings and impulses.

The results of social psychological studies on the relationship between emotional factors and radical political attitudes
on the whole give some support to this characterization of
the middle-class Communist. These attitude studies, which
were conducted primarily during the 1930's (at which time
most of our American middle-class respondents were joining
the party) and among American college student populations,
tended to describe the liberal-radical college student as better
informed and more bookish than his conservative peers, more
inclined to introversion, and more often marked by feelings
of inferiority, hostility, and isolation. These correlations were
in every survey small and inconclusive. But if such tendencies
were manifested somewhat more frequently among persons
holding liberal and radical views, it may be a sound hypothesis that persons who joined the party in these same milieux
possessed these characteristics more frequently and to a more
pronounced degree. At any rate, this is strongly suggested by
our data on the American and British middle-class former
party members included in our sample.[4]

An illustration or two may be of value at this point.

Thomas grew up in an English port city, the son of a dock
pilot who earned good wages but drank heavily, so that the
family was usually badly off. His parents were unhappy together and fought over the father's drinking and general unreliability. They separated when Thomas was seventeen. He
left school when he was fourteen and went to sea at sixteen.
He worked on liners for a while and felt a terrific resentment
at all forms of snobbery. He could not give any examples
of rudeness on the part of the passengers, but said he felt

---

[4] See, among others, Kerr, *op.cit.*, p. 65; G. Murphy, L. B. Murphy, and
T. M. Newcomb, *Experimental Social Psychology* (New York: Harper
& Brothers, 1937), p. 944; Emily Dexter, "Personality Traits Related to
Conservatism and Radicalism," *Character and Personality*, Vol. VII
(1938), pp. 230 ff.; M. H. Krout and R. Stagner, "Personality Development in Radicals: A Comparative Study," *Sociometry*, Vol. II (1939),
pp. 31 ff.; Ralph H. Gundlach, "Emotional Stability and Political Opinions
as Related to Age and Income," *Journal of Social Psychology*, Vol. X
(1939), p. 577.

all the while ". . . that people knew he had no education from the way he spoke." After four years at sea, he went to a seaman's school and passed his officer's examination. And while on shore he began to read. He said, "I enjoyed wallowing in abstruse mental gymnastics." He read, among other writers, Kant, Schopenhauer, Hegel, and Nietzsche. From philosophy he developed an interest in religion and atheism, and then began to read Marx and Engels. He came across Marxist writing himself. He used to buy books in Charing Cross when ashore and read them aboard ship.

He was quite successful as a ship's officer and rose to second in command by the time he was twenty-eight. At the same time, he was a withdrawn and taciturn man who stood out among his associates because of his intellectual and political interests. He was attracted to Communism because it had an intellectual aspect, as well as one of militance and dedication. He had been much influenced, when his reading had taken a political turn, by meeting two Communist sailors on a ship lying in port alongside his own. They were particularly intelligent and high-minded, good sailors and admirable men. "I asked them questions and talked over the question of the Communist Party with them. They told me that to be a real Communist, one had to inspire others by force of example. One had to be a good sailor and do the dangerous jobs, use the capitalist system as training to become a leader in the best sense of the word. When other sailors went ashore, these two would stay behind and scrub out the forecastle." Their character and attitude of dedicating themselves appealed to Thomas. This helped to give him the feeling he ought to take a chance. The party was the first organization he had ever joined.

In Thomas' case it is quite clear that the prior development of a pattern of intellectual interest and activity, stimulated in part by feelings of inferiority and isolation, had led to susceptibility. In his situation the simple presence of alienative feelings would hardly have resulted in contact with or interest in the Communist movement.

This adaptive pattern is even more clearly manifested in

the development of Jerome, the son of a Middle Western American musician. His father was a hard man who forbade him to play with other children, and made him study music instead. His mother died when he was a child. "I had a great emotional problem as a child. For the most part I was rejected by other children in the neighborhood. My father didn't permit me to play games, sports, and the like. Father was regarded as a queer person in the neighborhood. I played the piano, and couldn't play games, so I was quite an oddity among the other children and very miserable and unhappy, yet feeling superior because I could play Mozart or read poetry. When the sex years came on I wasn't invited to parties. This disturbed me very much. By conceiving of myself as an intellectual, however, I got a great deal of gratification. I took on all the affectations, read obscure poets and philosophers, and got very involved."

Jerome was "developed" by his only friend, an older person who was ". . . emotionally maladjusted . . . lonely and unattractive." His friend was a member of the Young Communist League. Jerome joined the YCL when he was thirteen, despite his father's opposition. His father refused to give him food, and on several occasions threw him out of the house. After being in the party for a year, he left home entirely and lived on handouts from the party. He took great pleasure from the fact that while other boys were in high school and under the thumbs of their parents, he was a free person, performing an adult role. While in the party, Jerome considered himself to be a great theoretician, "devoted to the movement and willing to sacrifice his life to it."

In the two cases cited and in many others it is quite clear that the intellectuality involved was hardly a disciplined activity. It involved "swallowing books whole," reading difficult philosophical works without prior training, or it was essentially an aesthetic kind of intellectuality. In other cases, it was clear that when serious and disciplined intellectual activity began, particularly in the social sciences, faith in the movement often was shaken, and the process of defection set in motion. Thus a British student who had joined the party

at the beginning of his university career found his faith
weakening when he began to study economics seriously. "I
found it hard to reconcile the course I was studying with the
party's economics. Marx's labor theory of value didn't seem
very useful and the party criticism of Keynes wasn't satisfactory. . . . Then I came to look on dialectical materialism
as rather queer. The Marxist doctrine of the state seemed
purely a quibble." Another British respondent began to lose
faith in the party when he left the university and undertook
a research job. "I suddenly found that I was interested in
questions of social history, which was my research topic, for
its own sake. Probably this is what started the rot. . . . The
majority of people who kept up their party membership indefinitely are those who have not been subjected to any kind
of intellectual discipline."

While the incidence of psychological deviation was relatively high among the middle-class intellectual respondents,
it goes without saying that there are conditions and circumstances in which quite "normal" intellectuals may decide to
join the party. In the satellite countries, where intellectual
careers and personal safety are conditioned upon political
factors, the soundest of intellectuals may succumb for understandable reasons. Indeed, under these circumstances, where
the opportunities for study are so closely supervised and the
Communist perception of the world is inculcated from earliest
childhood, the motive may not be careerist at all, or only
partly so. The individual may believe in the picture of the
world to which he is exposed simply because he has not been
confronted with alternative interpretations.

Outside the Soviet orbit, in a country such as Italy during
the years of Fascism, an emotionally healthy and courageous
intellectual might join the party simply because he has perceived and experienced the evils of Fascism but has not perceived and experienced those of Communism, or, on balance,
prefers the risks and evils of Communism to those of Fascism.
Or, in the contemporary French and Italian political situations, as we have already suggested, where the Communist
parties control the trade unions and are the largest move-

ments among the working classes, and where Marxist ideology has had a great influence for many decades, joining the party or sympathy for it may be based on a "plausible" kind of intellectual and moral analysis which does not imply an unequivocal commitment to the party. Such, for example, is the position of some intellectuals in the French Communist Party, who justify their adherence to, or sympathy for, the party in the following terms: The intellectual must have a moral goal if his work is to be meaningful. The bourgeoisie is self-centered and corrupt; all idealism has left it; it cannot lead the way to justice and progress. Only the working class has an ethical impulse and promise for the future. Since the working class follows the Communists, the intellectual may not oppose the Communist Party without violating his obligation, his "engagement," to the working class. In intellectual circles in France such a position as this is hardly viewed as the reasoning of a crank. It is a plausible point of view which is entertained among certain party intellectuals, sympathizers, and "neutralists."

On the other hand, in the United States and England, where the party has never taken deep root, where the trade unions are non-political or allied with the moderate left, affiliation with the Communist movement has generally been viewed as "deviational" and extremist. The only exceptions have been among certain social groupings, and in certain periods such as the early years of the depression when capitalism appeared to be "doomed," and when there was a widespread collapse of confidence in the future. In this atmosphere of crisis and the general collapse of expectations, joining the party at certain universities and among certain professions— particularly among social workers dealing with the unemployed—had a kind of plausibility. But even among these groupings and during this period, only a minute proportion of the people exposed to the party or its front organizations actually joined.

It would appear, on the basis of our interviews with British and American professional and middle-class respondents, that the kind of intellectualization which seemed to enhance susceptibility to Communism in these countries was one of two types. It was the intellectual self-intoxication, for example, of the young college student, or self-taught person, whose mind was filled with an excited confusion and who saw in the party and its doctrine a system which provided answers. Or it was a kind of cognitive and evaluative distortion which served to rationalize powerful needs for the expression of resentment, needs for relatedness and acceptance, or needs to overcome feelings of weakness and inadequacy. In the first case, joining might be described as the consequence of error; in the second, the most powerful pressures for joining were compulsive and in large part below the level of the individual's awareness.

A number of other points of contrast emerge from a comparison of the need and interest patterns of the middle- and working-class respondents. To refer back to Table 2, "self-oriented interests" occurred with approximately equal frequency among both groups, but the need for intellectual clarity was, as might be expected, especially common among the middle-class respondents and rare among the working class. Group-related interests were especially frequent among the working-class respondents. Forty-six per cent of these respondents were members of trade unions when they joined and viewed the party as a means of realizing trade union goals. Finally, even though the overwhelming majority of both groups reported ideological interests, the middle-class respondents reported more ideological interests on the average than the working class. Typical intellectual respondents listed several ideological interests such as opposition to discrimination, belief in peace and internationalism, anti-Fascism, and the like, while the typical working-class respondent was more likely to report a single and more locally oriented interest such as "improving conditions of work in the mining areas."

In summary, the need and interest pattern of the working-class respondents was more in response to situational problems, more pragmatic and immediate in content, while that of the middle-class respondents was more likely to be projective, generalized, and "cosmopolitan." This confirms evidence brought out in the preceding chapter, which portrayed the working-class respondents as having more objective grievances, as having suffered personal damage through social and economic causes more frequently than the middle-class group, and as having perceived the party in a local context.

Differences Based on Time of Joining

We have already seen that those respondents who joined the party in the period before 1935 had more often been exposed to the party doctrine before joining. These early recruits also were less frequently drawn from middle-class backgrounds and from religious and conservative political homes. In general, they appeared more often to be conforming rather than rebelling in joining the party. The types of needs and interests manifested by the two party generations appear to be consistent with their ideological and socio-political characteristics (see Table 4).

TABLE 4
Types of Needs and Interests Related to Joining the Party by Period of Joining*
(in per cent)

	Early joiners	Late joiners	All respondents
Neurotic needs	38	44	41
Self-oriented interests	42	51	47
Group-related interests	44	33	39
Ideological interests	94	87	91

* Multiple responses.

Thus a somewhat larger proportion of the later recruits manifested neurotic problems. More of the late recruits were attracted by self-oriented interests, while the early recruits were more frequently attracted by group-related interests. In particular, more of the late joiners were recruited because of career interests, a finding which would seem to reflect the fact that the parties had more patronage and other career opportunities to offer in the period after the Popular Front. The early recruits in a large number of cases were attracted on the basis of trade union interests, which reflects the higher proportion of working-class respondents in the early group.

The ideological interests of the two groups reflected differences in time and political situation. Pacifism and internationalism were more characteristic of the joiners of the 1920's, while anti-Fascism was almost entirely restricted to the post-1935 group.

Differences Based on Rank

The differences based on rank were more striking. We have already seen that a substantially higher proportion of the high-echelon respondents had come from Marxist or left-wing backgrounds and that they were more frequently exposed to the esoteric doctrine before joining. Thus the high-echelon respondents clustered at the esoteric level of susceptibility and, more frequently than the other ranks, were conforming to their backgrounds and communities rather than deviating. Consistent with these social and ideological patterns is the finding that the high-echelon respondents manifested neurotic needs far less frequently than the other ranks (see Table 5). Only 22 per cent of the high-echelon

TABLE 5

Types of Needs and Interests Related to Joining the Party by Echelon*
(in per cent)

	Rank and file	Low echelon	High echelon	All respondents
Neurotic needs	46	48	22	41
Self-oriented interests	55	41	37	47
Group-related interests	40	32	45	39
Ideological interests	87	93	94	91

  * Multiple responses.

respondents manifested neurotic problems, as compared with 48 per cent for the low echelon and 46 per cent for the rank and file.

The only emotional problem which occurred with any great frequency among the high-echelon respondents was neurotic hostility—that is, chronic antagonism and need for dominance in personal relations—while the low-echelon and rank-and-file respondents manifested a greater variety of types of emotional maladjustment. (This will be brought out in greater detail in the following chapter.) That the low-echelon respondents should manifest neurotic problems as frequently as the rank and file is not surprising. Movement into the position of cell secretary, or even "branch" office, does not ordinarily call for strong commitment and sustained motivation. This kind of office can be attained without much difficulty and held for fairly long periods of time by persons who have serious conflicts in motivation. On the other hand, high party office involves capacities for stability and sustained productivity which persons suffering from emotional problems and conflicts are unlikely to possess. The only type of neurotic problem which appears to be consistent with high party office is hostility, particularly where the individual does not have conflicts about its expression. This is because high party office offers frequent opportunities for aggressive actions and for the dominance of others, and hence is congenial to certain forms of disciplined hostility. Extreme hostility and conflict and guilt over its expression are likely to produce instability and unreliability under pressure, behavior patterns which the party is likely to test out before promotion to "responsible" tasks.

If we separate the respondents into American-British and French-Italian, we find that the incidence of neurotic needs is uniformly higher for all the ranks of the American and British respondents, but that the distribution among the ranks is the same for both regions (see Table 6). Generally speaking, the American and British rate is double that of the French-Italian. And for both regions the incidence among the high echelon is approximately half that of the lower ranks. It is of particular interest that the high-echelon respondents in the United States and England showed such a comparatively low incidence of psychological deviance. This may in part be attributable to the fact that a substantial proportion of the high-echelon respondents in the Anglo-American region came from communities and families in which Marxism or extreme left labor tendencies were quite common—in

TABLE 6

Comparison of Incidence of Neurotic Needs among American-British and French-Italian Respondents by Echelon
(in per cent)

	Rank and file	Low echelon	High echelon
French-Italian	30	37	16
American-British	57	60	32

other words, from politically deviant communities. The act of joining in these cases, while deviational when viewed from the point of view of the nation as a whole, was not deviational from the point of view of the specific setting in which the decision was made.

The only other significant differences in the need pattern of the various ranks were ideological in character. Since the high-echelon respondents were almost entirely recruited in the early years of the movement after World War I, they were attracted by the exoteric appeals of the party which were current during these years. Their original adherence to the party was in part based on the conviction that it would eliminate war and what they understood to be the causes of war—capitalism, nationalism, and imperialism.

Our findings thus far have demonstrated with cumulative impact that emotional maladjustment[5] as a factor influencing adherence to the Communist movement seems to be especially characteristic of the American and British middle-class intellectuals. In addition, the Communist movements in England and the United States[6] have a much larger proportion of middle-class intellectuals in their memberships than the

[5] Cf. Ernst and Loth, *op.cit.*, pp. 127 ff.
[6] *Ibid.*, p. 3; Sutton, *op.cit.*, pp. 277 ff.

parties in other countries. Hence, if we are to understand the type of Communist movement which is "closest to home," we shall have to examine in greater detail the ways in which different kinds of emotional problems and maladjustments can lead to joining the party. This is the theme of the chapter which follows.

CHAPTER 10

TYPES OF NEUROTIC SUSCEPTIBILITY

IT WOULD BE TEMPTING to suggest that some particular type of emotional maladjustment or some unique pattern of psychological development lies at the basis of neurotic susceptibility to Communism. What actually appears to be involved in this type of susceptibility is the presence of any one or any combination of the common types of disturbances of personal relationships, occurring in conjunction with certain intellectual and moral patterns, and occurring in a setting in which there is an exposure to the party. Thus two college students may be affected by economic circumstances in the same way, and both may perceive politics in the same terms. They may both be confronted by the same student organizations, and both approached by party representatives and asked to join. If one of these students is unconsciously hostile and destructive, there is a higher probability that he will join the party than that his more "normal" friend will do so, since the party appeals not only to his conscious, rational, political interests, but to his unconscious feelings as well. Similarly, during a party crisis resulting from a change in line, as between two party members, one neurotic and one normal, the "normal" one will feel freer to withdraw from the party if it no longer adheres to the position it held at the time of joining, while the neurotic one will tend to be held to the party by his underlying destructive feelings.

The problems of interpersonal relationships most commonly manifested among the former Communist respondents were hostility and withdrawal; in other words, there was a relatively high incidence of persons who were chronically rebellious and antagonistic, and of persons who were poorly related to others and to their surroundings. The case material submitted by the psychoanalysts who cooperated with the study brought to light other patterns, such as excessive submissiveness and dependence in personal relations, and feelings of self-rejection of one kind or another (e.g., guilt feelings, inferiority feelings, etc.).

If we take both our interviewing material and our psychoanalytic case histories, it is evident that any of the common patterns and problems of personal maladjustment can contribute to joining the party. The interviews with former party members, since they represented self-portraits and appraisals, tended to reveal only the grosser forms of behavioral maladjustment—a record, for example, of constant rebelliousness or of constant withdrawal from personal relationships. The psychoanalytic cases, on the other hand, consisted of clinical appraisals, and hence tended to bring to light types of feelings and attitudes which would be held in repression or suppression. Thus the two types of data are complementary and suggest the range of different kinds of emotional problems which can be "solved" by joining the party.

A further point as to the uses of the two types of data may be made. The interviews with former party members suggest hypotheses as to the distribution of different types of emotional problems among different types of party members. The psychoanalytic cases cannot be used for purposes of estimating distributions since they are such an unusual group of Communists. However, they are of great value for illustrative purposes, as studies in depth of the ways in which neurotic difficulties contribute to joining the party. In general, the percentage figures cited in the material which follows should be taken with considerable caution. While the coding was conservative, a depth interview is hardly a satisfactory basis for making clinical appraisals.[1]

[1] The psychoanalytic material consisted of 35 cases contributed by 22 analysts in New York, Los Angeles, Washington, D.C., and New Haven during the period of October 1950 to June 1951. The analysts were mainly orthodox Freudian in their approach, although several from the Washington School were included. Typically, the presentation of a case involved a two-hour session with the analyst, with an open-ended interviewing guide which covered the patient's life history and personality problems, the political history of the patient, and appraisals by the analyst of the functions of Communist affiliation in the personality system of the patient. The 35 cases included 20 men and 15 women. Eight were from the medical profession, 6 were social workers, 6 were in the theatrical

Hostility

In the areas outside the Communist orbit, the most common, if not universal, feeling related to joining the party is that of resentment. In the discussion of the ways in which the party is perceived, it has already been pointed out that the great majority of our respondents account for their decision to join by referring to some aspect of the party's militance, its trade union militance, its militance in the interest of minority groups, its militance in striving for a variety of different kinds of political and ideological objectives. Affiliation with a "militant" political movement almost by definition implies conditions, situations, or groups which are negatively appraised or "resented." We have also seen that militance is the attribute of the party which is most frequently stressed in the party classics and other media of communication. In particular, the analysis of the American *Daily Worker* showed the enormous emphasis which the party places on the evils of society, and the relatively slight emphasis given to constructive themes. It was there suggested that the first stage in assimilation to the party, if one were to accept the party's own picture of itself, involved the adoption of the Communist exoteric demonology in whole or in part, far more than the acceptance of positive and explicit goals. In other words, the party on the mass level appeals almost entirely to resentments, or tries to create them where they do not already exist, and in either case tries to focus these resentments on particular objects.

Given this enormous emphasis on rejection, resentment, and militant combat against evil antagonists, it should hardly

---

professions and the fine arts, 5 were academic people, 5 in the applied sciences (mainly engineers), and 5 miscellaneous. Twenty-nine of the 35 were of foreign-born parents. In almost all cases, the analyses took place after the end of World War II. Twenty-six were party members at the time of their analyses, and 9 were ex-members. Of the 26 who were in the party at the time of their psychoanalytic treatment, 15 withdrew from the party during their analysis, and 11 remained. For a more detailed description of this selection of case histories and for a more detailed analysis of the role of hostility, see Herbert E. Krugman, "The Role of Hostility in the Appeal of Communism in the United States," *Psychiatry*, August 1953, pp. 253 ff.

occasion surprise that the feeling most commonly manifested among respondents was resentment, antagonism, rebelliousness, and hatred. In the majority of cases the resentment appeared to be situationally induced and in conformity with community patterns. But in a substantial number of cases it appeared to be a pattern of chronic and unconscious hostility resulting from family and childhood experiences. While the incidence of neurotic hostility was relatively higher among the British and American cases, the middle-class respondents, and in the lower echelons, it also occurred with some frequency among the French and Italian respondents, the working-class respondents, and in the higher echelons (see Table 1).

TABLE I

*The Incidence of Neurotic Hostility among
Different Party Groupings*
(in per cent)

Country

United States	33
England	34
France	20
Italy	24

Social Class

Middle class	41
Working class	16

Echelon

Rank and file	33
Low echelon	34
High echelon	13

It is also of interest that in 20 out of the 35 psychoanalytic cases, the psychoanalysts explicitly related unconscious hostility in their patients to the attraction of the Communist Party. A number of illustrative cases taken from the interviews and the psychoanalytic material will show how neurotic hostility may contribute to susceptibility to Communism.[2]

[2] In order to protect the anonymity of the respondents, certain of the facts pertaining to place and similar points of information have been scrambled.

The Case of Luigi. A case of rebellion against the family almost classic in its simplicity and grand opera in its denouement is that of Luigi. He was born in Naples in an upper-middle class family. His father was a professional man, and his mother a leader in Neapolitan society. He was obviously neglected by both of his parents, who were primarily concerned with their social life. From childhood he detested their entire way of living. His father was a fervent Fascist and had taken part in the march on Rome. His home was always full of guests, the best people of Fascist society.

Luigi remembers that when he was five years of age, his mother took him to see a parade of "Black Shirts." Among the first in the parade was his father, dressed in a "resplendent uniform," and occupying a post of honor. One of the workmen watching the parade turned his back on the great procession and spat on the pavement. He was immediately attacked by Black Shirts, who beat him up and then took him to prison.

Luigi's father did not join the armed forces during the Abyssinian War, nor did he go to Spain. Luigi became convinced that his father was not only detestable, but also a coward. When the Second World War broke out, his father urged him to volunteer for the Tenth Division, the elite outfit of the Fascist army. Luigi refused. He told his father he would do his duty as an Italian soldier when called up, but that no one could force him to enroll with the "assassins of the Italians."

His father threw him out of the house, disowned him. His mother stood by in tears while Luigi reproached her for never having taken care of him. He went to live with a school friend whose father was a skilled workman. Here he found friendship and an opportunity to work as an apprentice mechanic. In these surroundings he became aware of underground anti-Fascist activity, and was an enthusiastic convert. A Communist workman in his shop showed a liking for him and invited him to an underground cell meeting. The thought of taking arms against Fascism filled him with enthusiasm and excitement. He studied hard and tried to rout out of his mind ". . . every memory and trace of his bourgeois origins." He experienced profound joy when he learned that the enemies of Fascism were on the move, and that the Fascist suppression which his father approved had not been effective.

After a period during which Luigi had to prove his loyalty, he was given an espionage job because of his knowledge of the Fascist leaders and organization in the Neapolitan region. His function was to pick up information on troops and munitions movements. He was caught with false papers in a police round-up and tried for high treason. His father was present at the trial and stated that he had disowned Luigi. His mother cried and told him that she regretted having abandoned him. He was convicted and sentenced to fifteen years in prison, five of which were to be in solitary confinement.

With the liberation of southern Italy he was freed. "I was happy but felt a terrible need for revenge." He heard that his father had escaped and joined the Fascist Republic in northern Italy. He was assigned by the party to act as a courier and liaison man for a group of partisan formations. He was caught with a group of partisan units by German forces and taken prisoner in 1944. The Germans turned him over to the Italians and he was beaten by his guards until the blood ran, and then placed in a prison. His father paid him a surprise visit in the prison, insulted him, called him a traitor and a coward, and told him that he would be tortured if he did not reveal the location of the partisan units.

Luigi pretended to make peace with his father, and offered to act as a spy on his own partisans. He asked his father where his unit was located, so that he might get the intelligence to him. His father gave him this information. Luigi sent a message to a squad of partisans through a contact in the prison, informing his men of the location of his father's unit. They carried out a surprise attack, and killed his father.

The Case of Maureen. Although lacking in the Latin overtones, the atmosphere of violence, and the neat dove-tailing of the plot, the case of Maureen also was one of extreme rebellion against the family. Maureen was born in a medium-sized New England town in 1910. Her mother and father were badly matched; they quarreled and were quite unhappy together. Maureen was exposed to several different kinds of conflict in her childhood. There was especially intense hostility and misunderstanding in her relationship with her father. Her own parents were aggressively atheistic, while other members of her family with whom she lived after the death of her mother were pious Catholics.

When Maureen was eight, her mother died and she went to live with relatives. Her memories of her childhood were acutely unhappy. Confronted by the strong and clashing personalities of her mother, father, and other members of her family, she took refuge in aesthetic interests. She began reading at four years of age and wrote her "first novel" at nine. When she was fourteen she ran away from home and never returned to her family. "Father's policy was that if I came home he'd support me, but not before. We get along fine now, though when I was young I used to go without food at times."

She worked her way through high school and college, and from her own account was rather difficult to handle. "I never paid much attention to rules. I was the terror of the university." After leaving college she went to Chicago, where she got a job as a reporter. It was while working as a reporter (and a very successful one) during the first years of the depression that she became interested in politics. She attributes her conversion to Communism to her experiences with suffering and chaos in the Chicago of the depression. Having made up her mind to act, she sought out the party. She was in favor of doing something violent about the depression and thought the party would offer such an opportunity. When she finally made contact with the party, she asked that she immediately be assigned to underground and dangerous tasks. The party had other plans for her. It wanted to use her as an underground member in a front organization. She fought bitterly with the party officials, begged to be permitted to leave her journalistic work and be given some active and tough assignment, but she was prevailed upon to use her talents in her own field.

Though Maureen's tenure in the party was long, she was

constantly resigning or threatening to resign, and then going back since she had committed herself so deeply and had acquired a husband who was a party functionary. She said about her antagonist in one party quarrel: "I would have shot him if I had had a gun at the time." At the same time, she got a great sense of security out of being in the party. "I never had a real family and, though you didn't have to like the CP family, at least you were all together against the world. Persecution won't drive them away from the party; it only makes them closer."

The Case of Max. Max was born in 1895, the child of poor French peasants. His parents abandoned him when he was four years old and he was brought up by a neighbor. He had only three years of schooling and then was put to work by other farmers. His childhood was hard and barren of affection. He found work in a factory after the end of World War I. He had moved to a part of France which was traditionally left and in which the newly formed Communist Party was successful in recruiting. In explaining his decision to join, he said that his ". . . unhappy childhood had produced in me an implacable hate for all those who from their childhood had enjoyed all the good things of life and who never experienced what hunger, cold, and poverty meant. I never tried to think why I hated them so much. I gave myself up to these feelings without reasoning, and instead put all my cunning and the shrewdness of a wild animal at the service of an idea that promised me vengeance." His reputation for violence is reflected in the fact that his party nickname was "The Fist." He served a prison sentence between 1930 and 1939 for violence done to a member of the *Croix de Feu*.

In 1942 Max joined the *Maquis* and had the command of a small group of partisans. His unit was known for its cold-bloodedness. Max himself was assigned to punitive action against the collaborationists. He carried out a number of night raids. "Several times I was forced to kill these individuals when they offered resistance or when they called me a thief and assassin. I always had a sense of satisfaction in killing the rich, the Fascists."

Apparently Max was not too careful in his selection of victims. After the war, the mother of one of the men whom he had killed accused him of the murder. The party provided him with legal defense, and got him off with a one-year sentence. At the end of his prison term, he was called to the federation headquarters of the party and told that the party would have to expel him because of his criminal record. He was expelled with the understanding that the party would call on him whenever they needed his special talents. He considers himself a loyal Communist and holds himself in readiness for "violent days."

It is evident that in both the case of Maureen and that of Max, feelings of hostility were of an extraordinary intensity. Maureen was barely capable of controlling her rage reactions and had as unstable a career in the party as out of it. Max's indoctrination appeared to be the simplest veneer over violence and other forms of criminality. Despite the militance of the Communist movement, extreme hostility in a member would appear to come into conflict with the need for a stable, controllable organization and a disciplined policy. As long as the party needed a desperate and courageous executioner, Max had a place in it. But in the more subtle and law-abiding days of peace he was a dangerous man to have on the party rolls. Maureen could remain in the party for a very long time, since she was able to control her resentment and found it possible to discharge some of her hostile feelings in the writing of articles for the Communist press and in the training schools of the party. Often the party is the factor which makes it possible for individuals to control their hostility, by offering opportunities to express it under "socially acceptable" terms, by permitting hatred to be discharged in speech and in writing, and providing occasions for incurring danger, such as passing out leaflets at points where violence might occur, haranguing workers outside plants, and the like. Sometimes the party is the factor which keeps people from flying apart because of the intensity of the hatred pressing for discharge.

The Case of Jack. Such a case was Jack, of whom his

psychoanalyst said, "He was defending himself against violent impulses—all his gentleness is a struggle against hostility. . . . He had no inner authority over himself. The party gave him something he never had—consistent authority. It gave him a way of looking on the world as an orderly place. Otherwise, he would regard it as chaotic and violent." His analyst hazarded the guess that if it were not for the party he might have been ". . . a criminal, a ruthless big-time swindler, or something of the sort." Jack came to his psychoanalyst suffering from great anxiety, spells of unjustified rage, and inability to sleep or work. The analyst described him as "a very disturbed person—at times on the verge of psychosis and at times on the verge of violence."

The analysis brought out the following picture. Jack was first-generation native-born of Eastern European Jewish parents. His father was pathetically ineffective as a wage earner and as a family authority. He had two brothers, one older and one younger, toward whom he felt extremely rivalrous and hostile in childhood, and whom he still holds in complete contempt. He grew up in a poor, foreign section of a large city. There was always the danger of attack from other non-Jewish groups of boys who lived in nearby neighborhoods. He was always afraid until he learned to fight well. He failed to finish high school because he wanted to be independent and make money.

At around this time he decided to become a playwright, and moved to New York. He refused to take help from his family and spent several hard years breaking into the theater. He married a woman with independent means. Much of the time in the analysis was taken up with therapeutic work on his rages, which were directed against his wife, superiors, and literary agents. If he did not think he was being treated fairly, he had to hold himself in to keep from attacking the man in authority. Most of the time, on the surface, he was mild, quiet, gentle. His rage would break out suddenly after an accumulation of irritations. For example, his wife was a poor housekeeper. After a period of household neglect, Jack would suddenly become violently angry. "He was always under tension, always on the point of rage, and a little detail might set it off."

In the party Jack thought of himself as a master of the ideology, ". . . arrogant and aggressive about correcting others for ideological slips." His fantasies about his political role were completely ruthless. His analyst pointed out that the party made it possible for him to impersonalize his hatred. "His need for the party is very great. He has no faith in anything else, no other community ties. He doesn't fit into society in any way except through the party, and through its ideology."

A number of points may be made as to the ways in which the party meets the needs of neurotically hostile people. In the first place, the party is a hostile organization; it is an "outlaw," an organization which fights established authority. The mere act of affiliating with it may be an act of defiance, and hence satisfying to persons who have these needs. Within the party there are many opportunities to express hatred, to discharge the tensions resulting from pent-up hostility. The tone of the party press, the atmosphere of party discussions and mass demonstrations, serve to drain off and discharge this hostility. Furthermore, the party makes it possible to dignify and ennoble these hostile impulses and hence make them "fit" for expression. Since the feelings are often extremely powerful and directed originally at quite inappropriate objects, such as mothers, fathers, and siblings, most individuals feel the need to displace these feelings, to direct them upon other and safer targets, to rationalize them in political, intellectual, and moral terms, to project the hatred upon other objects, which thus makes one's own hatred permissible. The party offers a hostile person an attractive self-image of one who understands the cause of evils and the effective ways of combating them. Thus it permits a man to transform himself from a hating and hence hateful individual into a person whose hatred is based upon and supported by knowledge. It also tends to allay the guilt feelings that are usually associated with hostility: one can not only hate with "reason" but for morally good reasons. The psychoanalytic data were especially revealing on this point. In many cases the analysts referred to the ways in which party membership took care of these guilt feelings. A few quotations may serve to make the point. The party supplied one person with "the opportunity to be ruthless without guilt"; it gave another "his one and only outlet for aggression without guilt"; it provided a third with "the right to hate without guilt"; a fourth was permitted "to destroy without guilt, to commit aggression without responsibility." Such comments occurred with great frequency in the psychoanalytic cases and in many of the interviews with party members.

The party is also of use in allaying the anxiety that is usually associated with neurotic hostility. Persons who are constantly under the pressure of hostile feelings ordinarily suffer from anxiety over the destructiveness of their feelings and the dangers of retaliation. It is dangerous to them to have such feelings. The party provides group support, and hence a certain safety.

Thus the party is hospitable to neurotic hostility and to the feelings and emotional needs which are often associated with it. It satisfies the need to express hostility even when the hostility is unconscious, and when the general pattern of the individual's overt behavior is genial, compliant, dependent, and passive.

In his analysis of the place of hostility in the appeal of Communism which is based upon our psychoanalytic interviews, Krugman points out that in a number of these cases, hostility was a latent rather than a manifest pattern.[3] These particular individuals had found it impossible in their childhood to carry off revolt successfully. The patterns of family life to which they had been exposed had made it necessary for them to repress their hostility and to adopt conciliatory approaches in their relations with parents and other persons. They had resolved the problem of how to respond to cruel, exploitative, or unloving parents not by attacking, defying, or breaking away, but by repressing these dangerous impulses and by developing a yielding or detached overt behavior pattern.

[3] Krugman, *op.cit.*, pp. 259 ff.

But the hostility continued to influence behavior in subtle ways—through not giving one's self in personal relations, through lying and cheating, evading and thwarting, rather than attacking and rebelling. After joining the party, these individuals remain passive. In fact, the authoritarian pattern of the party permits them to be passive at the same time that it satisfies their unconscious needs for rebellion and defiance.

The Case of Ralph. Ralph was that kind of Communist. His analyst described him as a basically passive, feminine individual. For him, the party ". . . was a rebellious group in which he could play a passive part." Ralph was the oldest of three children. The father was a weak and passive person, the mother dominant, nagging, always critical of the father's ineffectiveness. In this unstable and threatening family atmosphere, Ralph developed the pattern of being the "good boy," running errands, working part-time to add to the family income. He could not identify with his weak and ineffective father, and was outwardly passive but inwardly resentful toward his mother. In general, Ralph had few friends. Those whom he had were generally selected because they were more dominant than he, and were likely to impose on him.

In later life he married a woman older than himself, apparently in the hope that he would find a good mother. Since he could not meet his wife's expectations of effectiveness and masculinity, and she could not provide him with everything he had missed in his childhood, the marriage deteriorated rapidly. Ralph crawled into his shell and made no demands. He lived in the same house with his wife, but otherwise withdrew. After a time he left his wife for a more motherly girl friend, but this relationship also was of short duration. He followed the same pattern with friends: "He was hoping for love but had an underlying hostility."

In the party he was similarly passive and ineffective. He found it hard to approach people in fund-raising. He put his own money in instead. Being in the party made it possible for him to maintain his passive adjustment, while at the same time satisfying his underlying and devastating hostility to his environment.

The theme of hostility is so pervasive in all this material that its crucial role in neurotic susceptibility to Communism is inescapable. It is also true that hostility is a central factor in all neurosis, even when the overt behavior manifestations do not appear to be hostile at all. This would seem to suggest that any neurotically hostile person is susceptible to Communism. But this would be as incorrect as saying that any person resentful because of some damage to his position and status is susceptible. In the case of the situationally resentful person, as well as in that of the neurotically hostile one, the mediating factors which make for susceptibility are the adaptive patterns which require an intellectually and morally satisfying solution, and a perception and exposure to the party which is congruent with these feelings and patterns. In the case of the neurotically hostile person, the mechanisms of defense are of special importance, since the individual is responding not so much to problems outside of himself but to needs which are within and which press him antagonistically against his environment. The man who joins the party because he is unemployed or employed at an inadequate wage, or because his father has been killed in a war, may try to adjust himself to his external situation by joining the party. The mechanisms of learning and reality-testing are central in this adjustment. If the party fails to deal with the external situation in accordance with his expectations, then he may leave it and seek adjustment by other means. The party appears to be a way of getting employment or eliminating war by social and political reforms of one kind or another. The man who joins the party because of neurotic hostility or other neurotic needs is dealing with a threat which is inside himself, as well as with threats and problems which are external. Hence his political orientation represents a jerry-built structure of adjustive and defensive measures. The apparent threat may be a depression, a war, or social and religious discrimination, but there may be available in the situation a variety of devices and instrumentalities to deal with these problems. If a man is neurotically hostile, he may select the Communist Party because it satisfies his unconscious need to express extreme and integral hatred. This will involve displacing his hatred from such objects as parents, siblings, spouse, or individual authorities, impersonalizing it and focusing it on capitalism, the ruling class, and the like. It may also involve projecting onto the political arena his unconscious conception of personal relations as being unamenable to mutuality and compatibility, as involving integral incompatibility, the destruction or absorption of one antagonist by the other. It will also involve rationalization. Thus, instead of recognizing hostile and destructive feelings in himself, he may create an image of an alert and militant leader chastising evil and rewarding virtue.

Isolation

While hostility and resentment appear to be all-pervasive themes in the appeal of Communism, the attractions of the party typically involve other emotional problems and needs. Rossi makes much of the community aspect of the Communist movement.[4] In the classics and in the Communist media of communication there is constant emphasis on organization, community, relatedness. The ideal image of the Communist conveys the impression of a man who has his place in the meaningful progression of time, and who is surrounded by steadfast and loyal comrades. The Communist militant is not only related to a group; he also shares in a kind of mystical body, he merges himself in the *corpus mysticum* of the party, acquires a larger identity from it and even a sense of immortality. This stress upon union and unity, sharing in communion and community, has an especial impact upon those who are unrelated or inadequately related to their fellowmen, upon the lonely and the isolated. It can appeal to the one whose loneliness is situational—for example, to the college freshman away from home for the first time, who may lack the necessary introductions and contacts—as well as to the one whose loneliness is self-imposed, who rejects and withdraws from others because of some deep distrust of men, some fear of being improperly used and hurt.

[4] Rossi, *op.cit.*, pp. 230 ff.

That the party appeals to such withdrawn people is reflected in Table 2, which reports the incidence of neurotic isolation among the various groupings in the party. As might be anticipated, the incidence of neurotic isolation was higher among the American and British respondents, among the middle-class and intellectual respondents, and among the rank and file and the low echelon. If there is a kind of detachment in the role of the intellectual, it might be expected that persons who already have these withdrawn and alienative tendencies would be more likely to opt for intellectual professions. Persons whose relationships are more or less impaired may find science, philosophy, and the arts a possible way of relating themselves to life and purpose.

In contrast with neurotic hostility, which had some incidence among the high-echelon respondents, isolation seems

TABLE 2

The Incidence of Neurotic Isolation among Different Party Groupings
(in per cent)

Country	
United States	27
England	26
France	18
Italy	8
Social Class	
Middle class	32
Working class	5
Echelon	
Rank and file	25
Low echelon	29
High echelon	2

to be almost non-existent at this level. This may be due to the fact that the high-echelon Communist is under pressure to produce a high output of energy; he has constantly to deal with people, manipulate them, give them orders, inspire them, and the like. He can be antagonistic, autocratic, sadistic, but he cannot be shy, withdrawn, fearful. The neurotic isolate is more likely to be in the rank and file, or to occupy some low-echelon position involving routine actions.

How withdrawal may enter into the appeal of Communism is the theme of a number of illustrative case histories.

The Case of Julia. Julia grew up in a small Ohio town, the daughter of two professional musicians who were quite temperamental and unstable. "My parents have been warring for forty years. From the early days, my sister and I were both very maladjusted, especially me. I never went out with anyone at school, but rushed home to play the piano. . . . Our parents' rivalry almost wrecked us. It's a wonder we didn't have nervous breakdowns. . . . I took my father's side and sister took my mother's. However, father pushed me away because I was a girl, and mother pushed me away for siding with him."

After leaving school, Julia came to New York, where she got a job playing in a small hotel orchestra. Some of her fellow musicians were party members and sympathizers. She was asked to help in a strike which was then going on, and got great satisfaction out of working in the soup kitchens or helping the men in other ways. After this experience she joined the party. She said, "The attraction was heavily emotional. A group of friends attracted me—a need to belong— a feeling that perhaps I would do something to improve conditions, to be a hero of some kind. . . ."

She was always attracted to simple people, ". . . seamen, garage mechanics. . . . Maybe it's due to some inferiority of my own—probably so." These were the only types to whom she could relate herself. For a short while she was in a party cell with intellectuals. "We were mighty glad to get rid of each other. They were mighty stuffy." She was too shy to do recruiting or sell the *Daily Worker*. "My usual reaction was to give my own money, and give the newspapers away. I couldn't go out like the others and make speeches while selling the *Daily Worker*."

Julia's way of dealing with difficult situations was to run away. She wanted to divorce her first husband, but was afraid to face him and ran away to Chicago where she became a waitress. She returned to New York several years later and went back into the party. Throughout her interview she emphasized her loneliness. She had had no friends before joining the party, and apparently did not acquire any real friends after joining. Although she joined because of loneliness along with many others who joined for the same reason, she claimed ". . . it doesn't solve loneliness problems at all."

The Case of Matthew. Matthew was both withdrawn and hostile, but in accounting for his joining the party he especially emphasized the group attraction. He was born in a Glasgow slum, the son of a small merchant. His father died when he was three and his mother when he was seven. He was placed in a Poor Law institution for children where he remained until he was fourteen. He claims to have been badly treated in the home, "knocked about quite a lot," and the food was very bad. His first job was as a house and garden boy for a stockbroker who was having a bad time in the 1921 crisis and wanted cheap labor. He got up at six o'clock in the morning and did a housemaid's job in the morning, doing the rooms, preparing and waiting at lunch, and working in the garden in the afternoon. He finished at ten p.m., and worked seven days a week. When he asked for time off, he was given permission to go to church on Sundays. He was paid seven shillings and sixpence a week.

He remained at this job for a year, until he could not take it any longer, and then did farm work and odd jobs. When work gave out, he applied for relief and was told that he would have to go to the workhouse. He refused this and for a period simply slept in the open and nearly starved. He finally went to the workhouse, where he remained for nine months. While in the workhouse he met a vagabond writer who was a member of the ILP. His friend tried to proselytize him, but without success.

Matthew then got a job in the building trades and gradually became interested in the Labor Party. He came into contact with some YCL members and was attracted to them because of their informality and carefree dress. He felt more at ease with them because he himself could not afford to wear anything better than slacks and an old coat. He commented several times in the interviews that he was very shy and ill at ease with other people. When he lost his first building job he was out of work for almost a year. He spent most of his time in libraries and parks reading. He read almost a book a day, mainly novels. His favorite author was Jack London.

It was during this period of unemployment and reading that Matthew decided to join the party. He said that in making the decision he was especially moved by remembering his early life and being convinced that that sort of thing could not happen in a Communist state. His mother had died of tuberculosis after a life spent mostly in public houses. He was convinced by his Communist friends that capitalism was the cause of poverty and disease. What especially attracted him about the Communist group was their liking for singing. The party members made unending efforts to talk him into joining but for a time were quite unsuccessful. Several attractive girls joined in this effort, and what impressed him about them was their sincere earnestness as well as their attractiveness.

The Case of Alvin. Alvin came to his analyst complaining of great insecurity in his relations with people, a problem which he had had from childhood on. He was the second of three boys, the son of a foreign-born Jewish painter and decorator. The family lived on the "West side" of Chicago in a "tough" neighborhood. He avoided getting into fights by running away; he was very nimble and fast. His parents quarreled constantly. The father was worried about business, and the mother was bitter toward those in the block who had more than they had. There was no tenderness between the parents; after the birth of the children they no longer slept together. The mother gave Alvin no tenderness at all, no care, not even when he was sick. She would not let him play with other children or visit their homes. Alvin viewed his father as a failure, a flop. His older brother had rebelled a little and gotten hit for it. Alvin learned to get along by being compliant, by keeping his mouth shut.

Alvin was good in school, but recalls that he used to lie

about his grades (said he got "B's" or "C's" instead of "A's") in order to deprive his mother of satisfaction. Until he became involved in the Communist movement, Alvin never joined anything. It was out of loneliness that he became a member of the Communist Party. He felt no resentment against society or his family. The hostility was deep underneath, but he protected himself from it and from outside hurts by the techniques of withdrawal. The few friends he had were either persons who went out of their way to be friendly toward him, or persons who were unhappier than he. One of these friendships was with a Communist who was very bitter and very aggressive. Alvin got a vicarious kick out of his friend's aggressiveness, but would not dream of behaving that way himself. He was quiet and often rude, but never antagonistic. If he could not think of a direct answer to a question he would say nothing. He had no life goals, no desire to get ahead. His hostility was held in repression, and affected his behavior mainly through withdrawal and "negativism," i.e., hurting himself and depriving others of himself rather than attacking others. His analyst summarized his case history as "simple schizophrenia—just a lonely, isolated, bitter, self-defeating person."

The Case of Frank. Frank also reported a background of constant quarreling between his parents, although there were affectionate relations between them. The mother tended to dominate, but the father had fits of temper. The mother had the reputation of being a noble and self-sacrificing person, but was capable of doing dreadful things to her children. When Frank was four years old his mother "forgot" him and left him asleep on a beach after a picnic. She would frequently tease him, telling him that he was not really her child. He apparently lived constantly in fear of abandonment. Throughout his life he feared and obeyed her, and at the same time tried to avoid her.

In his overt behavior Frank was a "good boy," but he developed techniques of evasion and thwarting which entered into his adult life. He got away with lies and was detached in almost any kind of situation. He had girl friends, but broke off these relationships when they got too close. He had a series of three wives, but was happy with none of them. He was ashamed of showing his feelings, partly because he was not aware of what they were and feared to let them come to the surface. He was aware of the fact that he was not a good or "giving" person, but at the same time wanted to be good. He could help people who were really in trouble, but not himself or other people who were strong and healthy. Frank's analyst concluded his appraisal by saying, "His main drive was utter withdrawal, accompanied by a lending of his shell to people to do with as they pleased. His political activity was built around the ideal of making a world where people could have fun and have what they wanted and needed. But this did not apply to him, the fulfillment was for others. . . . His chief defenses are withdrawal, detachment, aloofness from others and from his own feelings and activities."

The chief defense mechanism involved in withdrawal is repression. The neurotically aggressive person strikes back, attacks, not only when he is situationally threatened but in most relationships. The withdrawn person represses his hostility and in a sense anesthetizes himself and defends himself against his feelings. Hostility was often reported in our withdrawn cases, but the withdrawn person may have been confronted with a family situation in which attack and retaliation were simply impossible. Hence the only possible way of dealing with his rages and hostilities was to drive them below the level of consciousness. His hostility, instead of pressing against others, presses in a subterranean way against himself, pulls him out of contact with people, and to a considerable extent out of contact with his own feelings. The withdrawn person is a "shell," lacking in spontaneity and direction. In the ultimate catatonic state of schizophrenia, the withdrawn person comes close to being emotionally dead.

But, short of these extreme states, the neurotic isolate feels some need to relate himself to people and to events. He knows he is alone and lonely, and tries to overcome this situation. But as long as his feelings are repressed, his efforts to relate himself are futile. He goes through the motions, but he just is not there. He may be led to the choice of Communism through his unconscious feelings of hostility and self-rejection, and through his external adjustive problem. The party is not only a community; it is a hostile community, and it is a community for outcasts. In most of the cases of neurotic withdrawal, the party was the first real group which was joined. The party can offer such an individual the illusion of being related. It prescribes tasks for him, gives him a role, gives him comrades, prescribes the mode of his relationships to the outside world as a whole. It helps him keep his hostile feelings in repression, by being hostile for him. This may involve the mechanisms of displacement and projection. It helps him evade his own anesthesia by giving him goals and the illusion of purposeful action. And this may involve the mechanisms of reaction formation, and of rationalization. The stronger the need to withdraw, and the greater the impairment of the capacity to feel, the more likely is such a person to be a passive rank and filer in the party. At best, such persons tend to hold low-ranking offices or perform functions which require little initiative.

Self-rejection

Thus we have seen that Communism may appeal to persons who are overtly hostile toward or resentful of their environments, to persons who are neurotically passive and dependent, and to persons who are withdrawn from or isolated in their environments. It would also appear that Communism may appeal to persons who feel rejected or are rejected by their environments. The image of the Communist militant is of a dignified, special person, dedicated, strong, confident of the future, a man who knows his objectives, does his duty without hesitation. These aspects of Communism have an obvious attraction for persons who carry within themselves feelings of being weak and unworthy as a consequence of early childhood experiences, as well as for persons who have been objectively rejected by their environments. The Negro, the Jew, the foreign-born, and the first-generation native-born, the unemployed, the native intellectual in a colonial country, may respond to their social situation by feeling rejected, unworthy, lacking in dignity and esteem. In this sense, any negatively discriminated status may contribute to susceptibility. Throughout the interviews, even when neurotic problems were not indicated, this theme of rejection occurred with some frequency. In some cases, the emphasis was on weakness and inadequacy; in others, on ugliness, unworthiness, unassimilability. In either case, the basic provocation was rejection, either rejection in the situation, such as the Negro who is deeply hurt by an experience in school or college, or rejection in early childhood which has left inner and chronic doubts of one's strength and worth. The healthy child or adult who experiences some rejection at the hands of the environment may respond to such provocations by adjustive behavior. The neurotic adult whose damaging experiences occurred in early childhood may carry with him permanently the consequences of such mistreatment in the form of feelings of inadequacy and inferiority, confusions of identity and of role, feelings of worthlessness and of sinfulness. Regardless of his objective situation, he is constantly under pressure to defend himself against the defects which he feels inside himself.

As has already been pointed out, these self-rejective feelings were manifested with far greater frequency in the psychoanalytic case histories than in the interviews with former party members. Twenty-one of the 35 psychoanalytic case histories (or 60 per cent) indicated the importance of feelings of weakness in the attraction of Communism, and 16 (or 46 per cent) stressed unworthiness. On the other hand, Table 3 shows that only 11 per cent of the former Communist respondents manifested feelings of weakness and inadequacy, and 10 per cent feelings of unworthiness.

The incidence of these feelings follows roughly the same pattern as was the case for feelings of hostility and isolation —relatively high among the American and British, the middle class, and the lower echelons, and relatively low among the French and Italian, the working class, and the high echelon.

The reason for the relative infrequency of reference to

these feelings of self-rejection in the self-appraisals of former Communists would appear to be clear. These are the very feelings which many of them are fighting against, which they are unwilling to admit, and which they hold in repression. In many of the rebellious cases, it was quite evident that the hostility represented a kind of compensation for and defense against inner feelings of weakness and dependence. And in many of the "withdrawn" cases, it was evident that the with-

TABLE 3

The Incidence of Neurotic Feelings of Weakness and Unworthiness among Different Party Groupings
(in per cent)

	Weakness	Unworthiness
Country		
United States	19	14
England	18	8
France	5	7
Italy	2	8
Social class		
Middle class	14	14
Working class	8	5
Echelon		
Rank and file	14	9
Low echelon	11	12
High echelon	6	6
Total for all interviews	11	10

drawal represented a defense against feelings of hostility, inadequacy, and unworthiness. Thus one would expect that clinical but not self-appraisal would bring to the surface the "weakness and vulnerability" aspect of hostility, and the hostile and self-rejective aspect of withdrawal. Then again, hostility and withdrawal are overt behavior manifestations. In describing one's career and social relations it is hard to conceal a chronic pattern of antagonism or withdrawal. And, in addition, these qualities are not necessarily negative ones. One can speak of being "shy," "proud," a "lone wolf," or "tough" and "hard-boiled," without creating the impression of being "queer." On the other hand, for men to speak of feeling passive, weak, or feminine, of feeling morally worthless or perverse, does involve an admission of being queer. Hence, it may be a safe inference that the incidence of these feelings of weakness and unworthiness was higher among the respondents than was manifested in their interviews, but that they were in some measure unconscious feelings, or the respondent was unwilling to speak of them.

The Case of Alice. Alice was the child of foreign-born Jewish parents who grew up in an anti-Semitic community. In her childhood she "wanted to be accepted by all," and went to great lengths to deny her Jewishness and foreignness by taking on the interests and mannerisms of the Gentile children. She was mainly interested in sports and was a cheerleader. But she apparently always suffered from a lingering feeling that there was some fraudulence in her credentials. In addition to feeling "out" because of Jewishness, the family went through economic "ups and downs," sometimes well-off, and sometimes at the point of dispossession. There was much conflict in the home. The need for acceptance and recognition appeared to be dominating themes in her efforts at adjustment.

In college she went through the typical process of being "developed." She found the Communist boys had a sense of direction. They brought her problems down to size. She was able to solve her problem of Jewishness by denying its importance, by assimilating the problem itself into much larger, "truer" problems. To still the feeling of being without roots, she developed a sense of having roots in something that was world-wide, meaningful, and powerful. "I had been running away from my Jewishness before college. . . . There was the pain of being Jewish and the hurts suffered at home. . . ." She described her mechanism of escape from the Jewish problem in the following terms: "If you can't belong to any country, then belong to no country, and then nobody should belong to a country. . . . If you are not accepted by Gentiles, why not join the most different group, give it some meaning . . . revel in your isolation?"

The Case of Emile. This theme of deliverance and redemption from an unbearable state by merging one's self in the party and the working class comes out with even greater clarity in the case of Emile, a French Communist. He was the son of a watchmaker, a *petit-bourgeois* and narrow-minded man. "I remember his little shop, the strange smell, the overpowering sense of being fated to go on with such a life. I felt miserable in this atmosphere. . . . I was unhappy in my family. I felt the need to create, to do something. My parents wanted me to go into business. I did not do well in school. I left school at fourteen and got a job in a store, selling silk goods. I remember how I hated my boss. He would change his suit every day and he smelled good. I suppose he put perfume on. . . .

"My first revolt was when I went to the *Café Rotonde* when I was fifteen or so. There I would drink *café crème* and read the literary papers. This was my first break on the aesthetic plane. There were cubist and surrealist pictures on the wall. My aesthetic sensibility was already highly developed."

His family expelled him from home when he began going left, and he was taken into the home of a workman. "There I found the people, love for man. It was admirable to work with simple people. What beauty there was in them! I lived with very little money. We would meet in little cafés. There I fulfilled my need for communion with people."

When he joined the party he bought a workman's cap. "I rediscovered the nobility and dignity of the proletariat in workers' restaurants. It was a very rich life. I ate with the unemployed. They would speak to me as a comrade. I knew the sense of fraternity between men." One day while selling Communist literature he met a rich cousin. She said, "Aren't you ashamed?" He felt very proud. He was humiliating his class.

Emile's motivation was very much like that of a young Jewish boy whose parents were prominent in the religious community of his home town. Before joining the party, he wrote an autobiography in which he bitterly attacked the Jewish community. He made no effort to disguise characters or occurrences. It caused dreadful suffering to his parents. The rabbi officially read him out of the congregation.

The Case of Neil. In some cases, feelings of worthlessness and vulnerability may be so strong as to lead to suicidal impulses. When Neil was seventeen he volunteered for the RAF as a rear air-gunner with the conscious intention of getting himself killed. Neil was the youngest of three children, the some of a well-to-do Manchester physician. From early childhood he disliked his father. He was terribly afraid of him and his rebellion took the form of sulking, which apparently only increased his father's contempt for him. He still dislikes his father intensely. He describes him as an autocrat, a little ridiculous, and forever talking about his own achievements. Neil was educated at a public school, ". . . one of those which just manage to scrape by as a public school, and in consequence are especially snobbish and authoritarian." Neil "loathed" it.

It was after failing in his first effort at matriculation that he decided to join the RAF in the hope of being killed. After demobilization he went to a university with the intention of going into journalism. It was during a difficult relationship with a girl that he decided to join the party, to make a break from his family and the past. The girl was a refugee. Apparently all of his girl friends had been persecuted European refugees. And he seemed to have a preference for older women who would take the initiative and look after him. His parents reacted to his decision to join the party with impotent horror, and he left home to live on his own. Joining the party gave some value to his life. "Being in the party was the first social thing I had done since demobilization. It raised my self-confidence, which had sunk to a low ebb before the dreary view of being a student with very little money and damn-all prospects at the end. At least I could be a good party member. All my life I have been attaching myself to people or institutions to improve my prestige. Then I jettison them when they have served their purpose, and look for something better."

The effort among middle-class intellectuals and artists to

erase their own identity and find a new and "instinctively sound" identity in the working class is frequently seen and it is not without its comical aspects. Emile bought a working-man's hat. A San Francisco girl who did early morning recruiting on the waterfront used to take along a little bag with stylish clothing in it, for a quick change from her blue jeans. She worked for a fashion designer. The British apparently handle this problem with a sense of proportion. A British girl Communist asked leave from her colleague on a picket line because she had to dress for a reception at Court. Another British respondent referred to a fellow Communist as ". . . a chap from a wealthy home who had broken with his family, and 'gone native,' living in a filthy garret and dressing as a workman. I discovered later that he lived a double life. Every once in a while, his expensive tastes would get the better of him and he would have a night out in the West End. I bumped into him once in Paris, coming out of one of the most luxurious restaurants, exquisitely dressed. He was most embarrassed."

The role of feelings of inferiority and unworthiness, as well as the developmental patterns and emotional problems which give rise to them, are brought out with greater sharpness in the psychoanalytic cases. To be sure, this material stresses the importance of sex-role conflict. And it is important to point out that feelings of inferiority and of unworthiness may arise out of situations of social discrimination and rejection, particularly if these problems impinge on a person in early childhood, and in situations where the family is particularly vulnerable—in the case, for example, of Jews who live in unfriendly Gentile neighborhoods, or of children who grow up in families which deviate from the neighborhood patterns. The problem in these cases may not be a family one. The relations within the family may be comparatively sound. Similarly, organic defects such as lameness, blindness, ugliness, exceptional clumsiness, may result in feelings of inadequacy and unworthiness which lead to a potential susceptibility. In other words, the inferiority may be objective, the consequence of social ratings or of organic shortcomings, or it may be the consequence of an inner conviction of inferiority owing to some early laming experiences.

The Case of Walter. Walter came for treatment because of a general dissatisfaction with his personal relations. He felt that he got along with people by being a phony, that nobody really liked him, and that he didn't really like anyone either. His father was a successful businessman, emotionally dependent on his wife, who ruled him through martyrdom and tears. The father was greatly concerned with what people thought of him, constantly tried to maintain appearances. There was no real warmth in the family, no strength or stability. He had no admirable father to identify with, and his mother's hysteria made him distrustful of women, a pattern which led to difficulties in marriage and to promiscuity.

He had many friends, but his relationships with them were overanxious. He was constantly worried about whether he was good enough for them. "He is always acting as though trying to prevent them from finding out how unworthy he is. They visit him, he thinks, because they can't think of any excuse to get out of it." In depressed moments, he thought of himself as a dirty, loathsome, and unpleasant person, essentially unlovable. At other times, he conceived of himself as very powerful, capable of taking any blow, capable of manipulating any situation. He had a dreadful need of being loved and approved by people, but at the same time felt that he could obtain their approval only by fooling or tricking them into it. He did not feel he could be liked spontaneously and for his own sake.

In college Walter was identified with all the extremist groups—the gamblers, the bohemians, and the Communists. His affiliation with the party was based upon a belief in the fundamental evil of the present "system" and of himself. He had few thoughts about the future of Communism. He mainly saw it as a powerful and cunning force with which to fight the evil of the world.

The Case of Joan. In some Communists, this feeling of the evil and depravity of the self and of the world which made it so, leads to an almost Gothic posture of prayer for forgiveness and redemption. Joan came from a poor foreign family. The father was a shoemaker. They lived behind the shop. The mother became an invalid when Joan was twelve, and died after a year of painful illness. Her father died when she was sixteen. In school Joan was bright, but had no friends. She was unpopular with her age mates, who teased her and made fun of her foreign background.

After the death of her parents she and her sister went to live with a well-to-do aunt. Joan did not get along well with her aunt. She felt that her sister was given better treatment than she. She left her aunt when she was seventeen and went to work. She became involved very quickly with an arty and bohemian group, the first group which gave her a feeling of being wanted. She had a series of love affairs, none of which lasted or gave her any satisfaction. Her last affair was with a deeply disturbed man who was cruel to her. After this experience, she went to live with an older woman who was a homosexual. She was not satisfactorily involved in any of these relationships, since she was frigid and incapable of give-and-take.

One summer she attended a Communist labor school during her vacation. The impression on her was enormous. Here were robust, healthy, purposeful, and friendly people. The party appeared to her as a kind of sanatorium, a way out of bohemian perversion. She was aware that she was emotionally ill, and developed the belief that there were no neurotics in Russia.

Joining the party had a number of meanings for her. Perhaps the most important was her belief that it was a way out of illness and moral corruption. It was a way of attaining respectability through being identified with morally justifiable causes. It was also a way of breaking out of her emotional anesthesia into a world of positive feeling and spontaneity.

These feelings of self-rejection, of inadequacy, of moral depravity, are often, but by no means always, associated with conflict and confusion in sex roles. The developmental pattern which seems to be involved in these cases is that of a family situation in which the child's efforts to use his parents as images after which to model himself are thwarted. Thus, in the American culture, which stresses success and conformity in the outside world as the proper male role, many of the families described involved weak fathers and dominating mothers. Neither fathers nor mothers had the capacity to develop in their sons any confidence in their ability to fulfill male roles in relation to other males, or in relation to women. The individual's capacity to develop and sustain in later life warm and responsive relationships with persons of the same sex, or of the opposite sex, are crucially influenced by the "rehearsals," so to speak, of childhood relationships in the family. A strong and stable father may provide a son with a bridge to later relationships with authority and with other males. A warm and stably loving mother may give him confidence in women, and lay the basis of good relationships with women and a sound marriage.

A common pattern among the psychoanalytic cases and American respondents was the impairment of family relationships as a consequence of culture conflict.[5] Thus a large proportion of both groups were children of foreign-born parents. In these families, it often happened that the foreign-born fathers failed or did poorly in business and were inadequate in other respects. They spoke with foreign accents; they were extremely insecure in their social positions; they tried to prevent their sons from conforming or adjusting to the outside culture patterns, or made fools of themselves in trying to conform to these patterns themselves. Often the mother led in deprecating the father, urging her sons on to achieve what the father obviously could not attain. In other words, the mothers minimized the fathers and exploited the sons, pushing them beyond their capacities, using them, rather than permitting them to find their own levels. Thus a quite common pattern in our case material was the boy who had contempt for his father, and who distrusted his mother, who

[5] See the discussion of the ethnic factor in the American party in Chapter 7, and the analysis of family structure and role conflict in Krugman, *op.cit.*, pp. 255 ff.

felt cheated by his family, and cheated by his society because of his foreign origin.

For such individuals as these, joining the party may represent an escape from an inner role confusion into something that is strong, integrated, dignified, and confident. If there is real internal doubt of one's capacity to behave as a male, joining the party may on the one hand serve as an act of defiance against a world which has denied him a secure sense of his role, and on the other hand provide a spurious sense of strength and maleness. The party and its authorities, such as Lenin, Stalin, or the national party leaders, or the individual Communists who recruited these people, often appeal to them as substitutes for the good, strong fathers whom they never had. And by giving their loyalty to these new fathers they allay the grief and guilt which those who reject their fathers cannot escape.

The Case of Arthur. Arthur's father was born in Europe and never really learned to speak English. He was a meek man who always looked as though he were about to cry. Arthur hated his father for his weakness, and refused to take presents from him. The mother always won arguments in the family. She spoke English and was intelligent. She was hard on Arthur, refused to give him sympathy when he got involved in fights, told him to fight his own battles. In his adolescence Arthur began to avoid his mother. He became furious when she cooked his favorite dishes. He was afraid she wanted to dominate him, and he refused to give an inch.

He never developed any lasting friendships, but he was always a good boy and did what he was supposed to do in school. He had no confidence in his ability to be adequate with women, and was unmarried at the time of his analysis. He was afraid of women, feared they would dominate and destroy him, just as his father was destroyed by his mother.

His analyst commented about the meaning of the party to Arthur in these terms: "His personality is dominated by confusion. For example, he thinks he wants to get married, but when you get closer you find that he can't imagine what it's like to be a father or a husband. The party is the group that knows what's right and what's wrong. He became a Communist because men were humiliated and dominated by women. He hated his mother for her domination and his father for permitting it. He felt helpless." He defended himself against feelings of inadequacy and impotence by intellectual snobbery which had no real basis in fact. He really was not interested in intellectual problems. In college the sophisticated people were Communists. They made an "equal" out of him.

Arthur was typical of many of the male psychoanalytic cases for whom joining the party represented an effort to remedy defects in themselves, such as an incapacity to assert themselves professionally or to obtain satisfactory love and friendship relations. The basic problem appeared to arise out of role conflict and confusion, which in turn was attributable to a family situation in which neither parent played his nor her proper role as parents or as husband and wife, and in which the child was unable to develop a stable and secure sense of identity.

The Case of Frances. The family pattern among some of the female psychoanalytic cases was similar. Frances came to analysis in a state of acute anxiety. She said that she disliked her parents intensely, and wanted to leave home but was terrified of doing so. She was afraid at night, terrified of being alone, had feelings of unreality and moments in which she could not remember who she was.

Her father was a successful businessman who was very dependent on his wife. The strong partner was the mother, who viewed Frances as a competitor for her husband's affection. She was envious and vain, and in a subtle way a complete tyrant. Frances both feared and hated her mother, and viewed her father as a poor weak man in the control of her mother. By the time Frances was seven, her parents considered her a problem child. She was deviant and rebellious. In school she associated only with the lonely and queer children.

After puberty she began to develop a hatred and contempt for women and for being a woman herself. She loathed and feared her own body. In her fantasies she thought of herself as being without a body. She fought her own sexual feelings since they always reminded her that she was a woman. She had no confidence that men could love her, since she felt that she was a disgusting object.

Joining the party made it possible for Frances to have sex relations, not because they gave her satisfaction, but because she could show contempt for the ordinary laws of society. The Communist doctrine of sex equality helped her reject her femininity. Being a party member also meant that she could wear blue jeans, do common labor, in fact, do everything that was prohibited to middle-class girls. After she left school she went to work in a factory.

She liked art, music, bohemia, and periodically had intense attachments to one or two neurotic girl friends, bound to them by a common hatred. The party provided her with a supporting structure for her self-rejection and hatred. Though on the surface she was defiant and assertive of her views, underneath she was tormented by doubts about everything. The party gave her absolute answers to everything. There was no need for decisions, for doubt; it gave her real relief.

Being in the party supported Frances' effort to deny that women are different from men, and in particular it made it possible for her to think of herself as a strong male. The party enabled her to project her distrusts and hatreds into politics. She could interpret the world in terms of dog-eat-dog, struggle, and violence, without feeling irrational. The party in a sense confirmed and elaborated and justified her private paranoid ideas. In the words of her analyst, "There is violence and hatred everywhere and every act, no matter how small, can be interpreted in terms of the struggle. Her affiliation provided a chance to deny personal failure and make it world failure. She could identify herself with a group of underdogs —the mistreated ones . . . who have the right to counterattack. It took care of her conscience. . . . You don't have to consult your conscience, but only your memory for slogans and manifestoes." Frances' way of dealing with her hatreds and confusions was defiant and rebellious. She sought to destroy herself—her social class and her sex—and bring the whole world down in the process.

The pattern manifested in Frances' case represents in extreme form the impulses which lead individuals to go bohemian. Promiscuity and iconoclasm are means of defying rigid and rejective parents and of overcoming inner feelings of inadequacy and shame. As in the cases of Emile, Frances, and a number of others, an important aspect of this bohemianism is to be understood as an effort to humiliate one's parents by rejecting their class, their manners, their entire code. But it is also to be understood as an effort to find and establish an identity. And since one's internal appraisal of the self is low, it is possible to attain identity and relatedness only among similarly fallen persons. Bohemia is a kind of society of rejects and outcasts seeking for standards and ideals which will resolve and satisfy impulses which are in full conflict with one another—impulses to conform and be related, impulses to reject and withdraw, impulses for health and integrity, impulses to demean and debase the self. Often the party can serve as a kind of resolution of these conflicting impulses by appearing to satisfy the destructive and constructive impulses at the same time. For individuals unable to escape from these cruel dilemmas and confusions, the party makes possible a positive and constructive image of the self: for the wounded and aggrieved, a day of reckoning; for the lonely, community; for the weak, strength; for the humiliated, dignity; for those who have lost their way, certainty and clarity; for those burdened down with guilt, safety and redemption.

Conclusions

Thus the presence of alienative feelings which have resulted from serious deprivations and thwarting of expectations in early life may contribute to susceptibility to Communism. These feelings may be "engaged" and to some extent satisfied by joining the party and participating in its activities. At the same time, it would be a great mistake to believe that the mere presence of such alienative feelings creates susceptibility. Other aspects of the individual's orientation, such as his information and knowledge and his values, as well as the particular manifestation of the party to which he is exposed, may enhance or reduce the probability of his joining.

If it is incorrect to argue that all emotionally maladjusted persons are susceptible to Communism, it would be equally inaccurate to say that a particular type of maladjustment or developmental pattern is congruent with the appeal of Communism. If anything can be said along this line, it would be that among the various patterns hostility, if amenable to discipline, may contribute to the kind of motivation which leads to rapid and successful assimilation in the party. In other words, if the individual is overtly aggressive but not to the point of being incapable of a stable interpersonal role, he would appear, on the basis of our data, to have possibilities for party leadership. The same cannot be said for persons who are primarily withdrawn or self-rejective and whose hostility rarely, if ever, comes to the surface or, when it comes to the surface, takes on explosive proportions.

It did not appear from these data that any particular "oedipal" pattern contributed to susceptible personality tendencies. There were family situations in which the father was authoritarian and the mother weak, where it appeared that the party symbolized a revolt from the father. Among the American first-generation native-born of foreign-born parents a quite frequent constellation was one in which the father was weak and the mother dominant, and in which joining the party appeared to symbolize a revolt from the mother and a search for a strong father. And there were cases in which intense sibling rivalry appeared to be the main focus of family conflict.

A number of aspects of the developmental pattern appeared to be significant. One of these was whether or not the individual was able to mobilize and express his hostility. This would in part be determined by temperamental and constitutional factors, and in part by the possibilities within the family and other primary institutions of expressing this hostility. If the childhood pattern was such that the major direction which the maladjustment took was rebelliousness and antagonism, such an individual might find the party congenial to his emotional needs and gravitate to a responsible post. Other feeling patterns might lead to joining the party, but rarely to high-echelon status. In addition, the cognitive and value patterns of the family, the community setting, and the individual's own orientation are crucial to the whole problem of susceptibility. If the family cognitive pattern placed a premium on intellectuality—that is, knowledge and the capacity to generalize—or if the individual himself developed this mode of relating himself to the world in the absence of such a family pattern, and if the family moral pattern set obstacles to the more direct and simpler methods of expressing hostility, then such an individual might find the "moral militance" and the "theoretical" properties of the party congruent with his needs. The party supplies the supporting intellectual structure which for neurotics can transform hostility and antagonism into "fighting intelligently and with knowledge for good goals."

This factor of emotional maladjustment affects not only susceptibility to Communism, but also the process of adjusting to the party and the process of defection from it. Thus persons who find affiliation a means of coping with emotional difficulties may cling to the party long after it conflicts with their ideals, their career, and other personal interests, or when leaving the party may experience the most extreme suffering and disorientation. How the factor of neurotic needs affects the processes of assimilation and defection will be treated in Chapters 11 and 12.

CHAPTER 11

TYPES AND PATTERNS OF DISSATISFACTION

ONE of our more perceptive respondents, commenting on the process of assimilation into the Communist movement, referred to three stages which he held to be typical of the great mass of party members who never get beyond rank-and-file or low-echelon status. The first of these is the act of commitment or joining, which, as we have already seen, only rarely involves a clear perception of the significance of the esoteric party. "Typically, a person comes into the party before becoming a Communist—makes a commitment before realizing the basis for it—becomes something, and then goes about learning what it is that he is supposed to have become. . . . The party is set up for such people; it does not expect to receive Marxists. It accepts non-Communists and gives them the title in order to make them what the title implies. . . . The party is broader than the church in its willingness to accept 'anybody.' "

But while the new recruit is not a Communist, there is one thing he can do immediately: become involved in "activities." And so the second stage of assimilation into the party is the stage of being "activated." The recruit is given tasks. Indeed, the pressure on him to undertake tasks is ordinarily so great that he is left with little leisure to appraise his new experiences. In the words of our informant, "He can take part in almost any activity and he is in motion on a suitable level— everyone is capable of meeting the demands of the CP in action, if not in thought. He gets a feeling of participation and identification through the acceptance of responsibilities. He gets a feeling of contributing to the movement. This is commitment without indoctrination, and only the individual intellect will determine how far he can go on this basis. The devoted party member may be extremely naive politically. That is why he is so humble at meetings. His mood is one of acceptance of the answers his questions get. His sense of identification is very strong, and he has been reached through activity, not thought."

The third stage, according to our informant, involves "sloganization." "The CP is ready for our man with slogans. It reduces a policy to manageable proportions for him. All it requires is memory of one or two words, hammered away and repeated endlessly. If you use the right slogan, you're on the line; and if you use the wrong one, you're off. . . . The typical stage of indoctrination is the slogan stage. Most party members don't get any further than this. . . . This explains in large part the ritualistic atmosphere of the party. That is, you say the right things in the right way and you get along. Hence many people become very good Communists without ever having a serious political thought."

Thus most party members live in a world of "activities" and "slogans." They lack the time, energy, skill, and courage to break through this powerful organizational pressure which devours their time and provides them with a rigid and simple intellectual structure. To make progress beyond this point is to "break through" or "break away." To "break through" means to become privy to the esoteric party and to accept its integral reduction of all goals and values to the power of the party. To "break away" means that the dawning realization of the character of the esoteric party produces repulsions which ultimately lead to defection.

But dissatisfaction with and defection from the party may occur at any point in the process of assimilation. In some of our cases, dissatisfaction began at the point of affiliation, even before any involvement in activities. This, for example, was the case with a young college student who joined a group of fellow students in picketing at a neighboring plant. At the picnic which followed, and after having consumed his tenth bottle of beer, he accepted a party card. In the mood of the morning after, he regretted his decision, and never attended party meetings or renewed his membership. Similarly, there were those who defected in the "activation" phase, mainly because party activities took too much time, or took them away from other pursuits. Most of the cases, however, went through all three stages and defected at the point at which the party directly impinged on some one or some combination of their interests and values.

For most of our defectors, multiple dissatisfactions were involved. Similarly, for most of them, becoming dissatisfied with the party was cumulative. Thus an individual may join the party in some doubt as to the wisdom of his decision. He may resent the impact of party activities on his non-party interests and relationships. He may be offended by the process of indoctrination by slogans. But even though dissatisfactions may accumulate at each one of these stages, his original momentum and party pressure keeps him in line until some sharp impingement on his interests, feelings, or values takes place. Even at this point inertia may keep him in the party, even though he has already defected in spirit. He may wait until a general party crisis makes it possible for him to withdraw with a minimum of conflict and publicity.

What is interesting in our findings as to these processes of assimilation into and defection from the Communist movement is that so few of the respondents fully perceived the esoteric party at the point of defection or in their subsequent thinking about their experience. In other words, most of them did not perceive the esoteric party when they joined and were not fully aware of it when they left. To the extent that perception of, and repulsion from, the esoteric party was involved in defection, it typically took the form of a realization that the "real" party to which they had finally become exposed was different from what it had been represented as being, and that this "real" party either involved risks and costs which the respondents were unwilling to incur, or was felt to be intrinsically evil in some general way. But it was the rare case who could generalize about the party or explicate this feeling beyond offering such vague characterizations as "The leaders are all corrupt"; "They're out to line their pockets"; "What these boys want is power"; "They're just Russian puppets"; and the like.

This finding should not occasion surprise, since clarity in the perception of one's political associations and affiliations is generally rare. What is of importance in this connection is that this is probably as true of most Communists as it is of other groups. This may suggest that the widespread view that all party members are, or that all former party members were, in the same sense participants in the "conspiracy" is quite inaccurate.

The variety of meanings which Communist affiliation may have has already been discussed. Our problem now is to describe the varieties of needs, interests, and values which may come into conflict with assimilation into the party, and contribute to defection. We have classified dissatisfactions with the party into five categories: (1) career-related dissatisfactions; (2) pressures on personality and personal relations; (3) pressures on other group loyalties; (4) pressures on values; and (5) pressures on moral standards. The task of the present chapter is to describe and illustrate these types of dissatisfaction, and then to indicate how they are distributed among the various party groupings.

Career-related Dissatisfactions

Considerably more than half of our respondents had made their careers as party functionaries or as paid officials of party-controlled organizations such as trade unions. A good many others held low-ranking unpaid positions in the party apparatus. A common cause of defection among these functionaries and unpaid officeholders was some interruption or disturbance of their party careers. Twenty-two per cent of the respondents attributed their defection in whole or in part to career reasons. Sometimes these career-related dissatisfactions simply involved a party decision to replace a man in his post. Thus an English respondent reported that after his war service, ". . . I returned to the Midlands and found that new people had taken over control of the party there. I naturally resented that these people had usurped my place and I was now only part of the machine." An American trade unionist remarked, "In the shop unit I was frequently asked to step aside when due to become a full-time paid union organizer in favor of someone brought in from the outside. They asked me as a 'true member of the proletariat' to step aside, and told me that I was best in the rank and file. I swallowed this to the very end." A similar situation arose with a British trade unionist, but the conflict had a different outcome: "I was informed by a party member just before the annual union election that they had decided to put up another nominee as union delegate. I told them I would go forward and stand or fall by the judgment of the men. At the time of the nomination meeting I was away convalescing after illness and the party tried to have me ruled ineligible. But the meeting went against the opinion of the Communist chairman, and at the pit-head ballot I was re-elected by a substantial majority. I left the CP and applied to join the Labor Party. I was accepted with cheers." There were several cases involving intra-party struggles for power, as in the instance of the British high party official who was accused by a colleague of having misappropriated party funds. ". . . I tore into him and knocked him unconscious. After that, the party decided I was run down and needed a long rest."

In Italy the high rate of defection from the party for career reasons was due to the fact that the party bureaucracy was hastily recruited after 1943 and had not been fully trained and indoctrinated. Thus many officials withdrew when party discipline began to be imposed. Such was the case of the Italian woman who was assigned the job of organizing a unit of the Communist-controlled Union of Italian Women. She was quite successful and recruited women of all political persuasions, and instituted an effective and popular educational program. After getting the unit under way, she was ordered to turn over the job to a woman who had just completed a course at the party training school in Bologna. She herself was sent on to another village to organize a new unit. She soon learned that the work she had undertaken in the first village was being undone by the new party leader, who followed a policy of declaring war on all the non-Communists in the village—the priest, the mayor, the doctor, and the pharmacist. All of the Catholic women were ordered to withdraw from the organization by the priest. She went to the federation headquarters to protest, and explained that all her work had been undone and that the party had lost an excellent opportunity to carry its propaganda among all classes in the village. She was bitterly critical of the party training school, stating, "If in the party schools they implant confusion in the minds of the comrades, I am proud of never having gone there." She was interrupted by the federation secretary, who asked her, "What use are the non-Communists? You come from a family of property owners and of exploiters of the poor and can never be a real Communist; that is the reason you kept reactionary elements in our ranks." The following day her expulsion was announced in *L'Unita* and party members were instructed to avoid her because of her reactionary affiliations.

An Italian party intellectual who was used in propaganda work was summoned to cell headquarters, where he was told that he deviated from the directives in his speeches. "From that day," he said, "I was conscious that there was an extra listener to my speeches who would report any deviation." He refused to mend his ways and was suspended from his duties for fifteen days. He thereupon resigned.

Activity in the party often conflicts with one's career outside the party. Some 13 per cent of the respondents reported that their defection was influenced by conflicts between party activities and career interests. This is particularly the case with individuals who are moving ahead in their work and find the party a handicap. One British party intellectual got a university post and ". . . didn't like pushing rather crumby pamphlets around the senior common room." Another Britisher who had a bright future as a member of a local council reported, "I felt I could be of more use if I were free of ties with the CP. I realized I ran the risk of being accused of being a Communist and getting kicked out." There was a French Communist who was given a government post because of his outstanding services in the resistance movement. While doing this work, he was summoned to Paris by the party to take part in the formation of the French Communist youth organization. He replied that since he had been sent by the government he could not return until his mission was completed. When he finally did come back, the party broke him to the ranks for punishment. He gave up all party activity and at length resigned.

Sometimes this disruption of careers by the party involved efforts to force individuals to engage in work which conflicted with their professional interests and values. There were many cases of writers who felt that party activities were destroying their talents. Thus, an American writer remarked, "In the movement you always ran across the 'leather jacket' party people who looked with scorn on the writer and admired the proletariat. I felt that I was doing something good, ethical, but the price I was paying was the abortion of my talent. I had no time to write, to brood, etc. As time went on, I began to ask for leaves of absence to do writing. To get these leaves I had to get into more and more arguments. Finally, the thing that made me break was the realization that I would kill something very precious in me if I stayed in the party."

A British writer who had the same problem said, ". . . my writing seemed to be getting worse. There were two things conflicting for my energy. I only spent a quarter of my time on party work, but the effect was bad. I had to choose between being a writer and a politician. I just went to live in the country, very largely to break contact with the party. They never bothered to keep track of me."

A young French historian was forced to make a choice between the study of history and the party. "The party asked me to show them the first draft of my thesis. I was summoned to party headquarters and told that I had to choose between going on with my thesis and remaining a Communist."

Party Demands and Personality

The party often makes demands on people which force them to act out of character, to violate personal standards of conduct. It may require that they act without mercy, that they manipulate other people, tell them one thing while meaning another. It also may require that they sacrifice their own individuality, give themselves up fully to the party's purposes. Nine per cent of the respondents reported that their defection was influenced by being required to do "cruel" things, or by witnessing them; 17 per cent were revolted by being compelled to manipulate other human beings or by observing the manipulative patterns in the party; and 24 per cent were repelled by the destruction of individuality in the party, the depersonalization which they were forced to undergo or which they observed taking place about them.

Some of the French and Italian Communists were revolted by acts of cruelty during the liberation purges, and carried these memories on their consciences. An Italian partisan had been set to guard a Fascist prisoner whose face had been beaten to a bloody pulp. Two of his comrades asked to be permitted to finish the prisoner off. He refused to permit this. ". . . they returned with a political commissar, who commanded me to let them pass. When I opposed this, they called me a reactionary and I was obliged to threaten to open fire to force them to leave. . . . Another time I assisted at the destruction of all the furnishings, goods, and chattels in a house owned by a Fascist. The Fascist had escaped, but his wife and little girl were there and were insulted and maltreated." He commented that the cruelest among the liberators were those who had suffered least. Those who had returned from the concentration camps had really suffered and were more inclined to understand and forgive.

Some of the respondents reported incidents from the Spanish Civil War which had horrified them. A French party leader visited the French battalion of the International Brigade and made a speech. "After the speech some men came to see me and gave me letters for their relatives in Paris. Later on I had dinner with André Marty in his sumptuous villa, where he was guarded very heavily (he was always afraid). He told me, 'Give me those letters! I know that you have several, and they must be censored.' I refused. He said, 'This is an order. It is necessary for security reasons.' I gave him the letters and later learned that one of the men had been shot."

One of the British International Brigade leaders had a subordinate who was having difficulties with the party leadership. He instructed his subordinate not to expose himself in action. "A little later I heard that G. had been killed in a Fascist ambush. There were conflicting stories about his death. One of the American Communist leaders who had been wounded in the same action told me that G. had been shot in the back. I sent my men to find G.'s body. After some trouble they located it and found it had a small hole in the back of the head and a large one in the forehead. He had been shot in the back of the head at close quarters."

The cruelties involved were not always acts of physical violence. These were, on the whole, rare events and usually occurred in war situations. More frequent were comments about the humiliations imposed on party members for minor acts of deviation and disobedience. Individuals committing such offenses were often required to confess their errors publicly. Some of the British respondents first began to doubt the party when British soldiers and officers who had been stationed in Russia during the war and had married Russian girls were refused permission by the Soviet Union to take their Russian brides home with them.

The problem which troubled the consciences of quite a few of our respondents was the party's practice of using people, manipulating them, misrepresenting the party's purposes. Seventeen per cent of the respondents referred to these manipulative practices as factors contributing to their defection. A British trade unionist remarked, "Before I joined the CP, I could go to a meeting, sum up what was being said, and make up my own mind. But when I joined the party I found it was all worked out beforehand, who was to say what, who was to get up and second. . . . They tried to work up the feeling that anyone who disagreed was disloyal to the rest of the men. Then the vote would be taken by a show of hands. The last thing they wanted was a ballot. So about half a dozen could carry a meeting of two thousand."

An Italian intellectual developed this theme of manipulativeness more explicitly: "I sincerely loved the masses whom

I addressed, but little by little I became aware that the party machine—that is, the whole hierarchy—did not love them at all, but was merely maneuvering them as a shapeless mass, absolutely lacking personal or, rather, individual intelligence. In fact, the party needed only a collective brain, and wanted of me, as an intellectual, aid in this depersonalization."

More common among the respondents were reactions against threats to their own individuality. A simple Italian fireman, who had joined the party during partisan days, remarked after serving for a few years in the party, "I felt that my personal character was becoming, day by day, more styled and repressed. . . ." Another Italian said, ". . . to express my own personality had become almost a physical necessity. And it was my personality which was opposing this absorption of personality which the Communist Party was trying to obtain from the masses." An Italian intellectual spoke of the party as tending to "crystallize my brains." Still another remarked, "Leaving the party gave me the feeling of having reacquired the right to my own personality." A French intellectual who had served eighteen years in the party talked about the changes he observed among his intellectual comrades. "They spoke like characters out of Kafka; they were dried up; they read only *L'Humanité*. I felt hideously alone among these French comrades, and I could not stay with them. For them, if you have a single doubt you ought to be killed. Their humanity is deformed, atomized, disintegrated. They are monstrous people. They have lost their souls." An American commented in similar terms: "These people interfered most viciously in my personal life. They were the ones who destroyed my spontaneity, who made me express myself in the most stereotyped forms."

The most common class of dissatisfactions with the party were simple repulsions from the atmosphere of the party and from party associates. Almost half of the respondents described their problems of adjustment in the party in these terms. Middle-class party members often felt uncomfortable while working in the same cells with unemployed or foreign workmen. Working-class party members were repelled by the pedantry and intellectual gymnastics of the intellectuals, or the bohemianism of some of the middle-class members ". . . who found it exotic to be Communist." Some of the British and American respondents were offended by the bohemianism and sexual immorality of groups with whom they came in contact. Others felt that many of the party members were "queers," neurotics, misfits. Still others were repelled and frightened by the dogmatism and fanaticism of the party militants. A young Negro remarked, "The regular party people were so intense, like maniacs, they scared young people." A Britisher was offended by the dogmatism and humorlessness of the party atmosphere: "I found the word 'comrade' repellent, with its heaviness and artificiality. The first time someone said, 'Comrades, we are in a revolutionary situation,' I expected something to happen. But not the tenth time. . . . I was prepared to work quite hard for the party, but found it quite a strain that no one could ever think the CP funny."

There were those who were troubled by the conspiratorial atmosphere. An American remarked, "They said Communism was twentieth-century Americanism, but couldn't make a phone call without making it sound conspiratorial." Others referred to the scruffiness and dirtiness of the comrades. Still others were appalled by the inefficiency of the party. This was particularly true of the British and American respondents who came into contact with the upper echelons. An American who worked for a while in the party headquarters in New York reported, "I was almost immediately appalled by the bureaucracy. The party functionaries were wasteful, inefficient, slovenly. They had no files, did no research. The top men came in at 11 a.m. and went out for two-hour lunches. They didn't look like professional revolutionaries to me."

Pressure on Personal Relationships

If the ideal of the party is to have the individual give up his personal moral standards and individuality, it also tears at his personal relationships—with parents, siblings, spouse, and friends. Twenty-nine per cent of the respondents cited pressure on personal relationships as factors leading to defection. There was an Italian engineer whose father was the manager of a plant, apparently a man of simple dignity who had not opposed his son's decision when he joined the party. When the Cominform was established, the plant was struck and the son took his turn on the picket line. When his father came out for lunch at noon, forty Communist pickets sent from a neighboring town surrounded him and his car. "My father leaned out of the car window, asking what they wanted of him. No one spoke, but as he got out of the car one of the pickets spat in his face. Offended and furious, careless of the fact that he was one against forty, he invited the coward who had spat to come forward and settle it man to man, saying that he was talking not as the factory manager but as a man offended in his personal dignity." The pickets withdrew. After this incident, the son found his membership in the party intolerable and resigned.

Many of those who defied their parents when they joined the party had uneasy consciences which troubled them until they finally left the party and rejoined their families. Certainly, many of the children of Catholic families in France and Italy must have experienced tragic scenes similar to that described by an Italian respondent: "My mother appealed to my Catholic sentiments, asking me how I could deny the religious principles in which I had been raised. She saw in the party a movement which would destroy the family and society, and was heartbroken when my young brother followed my example and joined the party." A number of the respondents reported as causes of defection actions taken by the party against wives or husbands or friends.

Conflicts of Group Loyalties

Most individuals when joining the party are not fully aware of the integral loyalty demanded by the movement. They consider that there is an identity of national or trade union interests with that of the party, or at least that the two interests do not conflict. It is quite evident that this exclusive claim upon loyalty is not fully perceived by a large proportion of party members at the time of joining, since so many defections occur at the point at which the party insists that national loyalty, trade union loyalty, or minority group loyalty be subordinated to party loyalty. Thus the Nazi-Soviet Pact reduced the parties in the West to mere fragments of themselves, since the subordination of the various national movements to Russian policy was made so dramatically clear. One French respondent who was a top party leader in the 1930's reports that even Maurice Thorez was sympathetic to the idea of a party independent of Moscow after the announcement of the pact. He went to see Thorez, who was then in the army serving as chauffeur to an officer. They had a long talk about their common ideas and Thorez seemed to agree with the proposal that the French party ought to become autonomous and support France in its war against Hitler. Party loyalty won out in Thorez' case. Shortly after this meeting, he deserted from the French army and went underground.

Since the end of World War II the establishment of the Cominform has posed a similar problem for party leaders and members. Both Thorez and Togliatti were required by the Cominform to make public statements that in the event of a war with the Soviet Union, Communists would not fight against Russia. This policy had an especial impact in Italy, where a number of provincial party leaders, led by Magnani and Cucchi, resigned and formed a rival "national Communist" organization. Magnani had previously presented a resolution at a provincial congress of the party in Reggio Emilia in 1951. The resolution supported the opposition of the party to the Atlantic Pact, but also declared that Communists would defend their national territory from aggression from any quarter.

The subordination of trade union interests to the interests of the party also is a common cause of defection. In recent years, the political strikes in France and Italy that were called to protest the participation of these countries in the Marshall Plan resulted in the defection of large numbers of party members and a general loss of membership in the Communist-controlled trade unions. An Italian trade union leader commented, ". . . the moment always comes in which one recognizes that the Communist Party is not trying to help the masses to better their condition, but to endure in their present poverty. . . . As a union official, there came a point at which I felt shame at the use of such weapons as 'chain strikes,' 'quickie strikes,' and the like." He felt that the entire purpose of the unions was being subverted, that the discipline essential to production was being destroyed without any material advantage to the working class.

Similar efforts to use the unions for political purposes provoked crises in the British and American trade unions. A Scottish trade union leader reported that in the postwar period the Scottish Communists had captured the Glasgow Trades Council. "Having gained control, they recklessly steam-rollered resolutions that had nothing to do with trade union work, for instance, about peace and the Americans' handling of Scottish students going through Austria to the Berlin Congress. This was going against the declared policy of the Scottish Trades Union Congress and they must have known they were risking a head-on collision. Now the Scottish T.U.C. has withdrawn its support from them and is forming a new Trades Council." Similarly, the efforts of the American party to use the Communist-dominated trade unions in the Wallace campaign precipitated a crisis. One union leader recalled, ". . . a few of us decided that the third-party idea was bad and that the gains under FDR would be lost. We wanted the union not to take a stand but the leaders jumped on us to plug for Wallace regardless of how the union felt. About half a dozen of us dropped out all at once, and they went after us hammer and tongs. It really busted the union up."

Another American trade union leader said, ". . . the CP got the union to take many rash steps after Korea. . . . I got disgusted, went out for a double rye, and decided that I wanted nothing more to do with the CP. I went on working as a business agent."

Similar resistances are created when the party subordinates group interests to its purposes. Some of the Negro and Jewish respondents reported that they left the party when it became clear to them that the party had no real interest in Negro or Jewish problems as such, but was simply using them as a basis for propaganda and recruitment. One young Negro was sent to Moscow to participate in the making of a film on the Negro problem. For some reason, the Russians changed their minds about producing the film. He protested the decision and was invited to spend a weekend with a top Russian party leader. In the course of a long discussion, the Russian asked him, "Are you a Communist or a Negro?" He told the Negro he had to forget his birthright, that the problem is the same for black or white, Christian or Jew. "That was too much. I couldn't agree and said so." Other Negroes working with non-Communist Negro organizations complained that the party could never be relied on. Sometimes it took a stand on race questions and sometimes it didn't. Gradually they became aware of the fact that the party used the Negro problem when it suited the party's purposes, and not when it suited the needs of Negroes.

In a country such as Italy many party members are believing Catholics. In the years after the liberation of Italy neither church nor party forced the issue. The party statutes did not require that a member leave the church, and the church did not formally prohibit party membership. Since 1947, the pressure of the church has increased, and threats of excommunication have been directed at Catholics voting the Communist and Left Socialist tickets. This threat, however, has not been effectively enforced and there continue to be many Italian party members who are believers, churchgoers, and even continue to receive the sacraments. Sometimes this conflict between religious faith and Communist faith becomes clear only *in extremis,* as was the case of an Italian who fell ill: "I grew worse and was at the point of death, and then my old religious faith, the constant support of my family, came back stronger than ever. . . . I commended my soul to God . . . and took a vow to quit Communism if my life would be spared. . . . God granted me my life. I had been a long time in the hospital, which gave me the opportunity to think over my purposes much more clearly than I had thought at the time of my joining the CP."

That religious feelings of many party members in Italy are still alive is reflected in the reported successes of a Catholic lay organization specifically active among Communist workers and peasants. The organization was founded by former Communist Party members who had left the party for the church. Members of the organization are on a constant lookout for Communists who still show signs of the persistence of their religious faith. Such individuals are approached on admittedly false pretenses. They are invited to spend three or four days on a free vacation where they can play cards, bowl, listen to accordion concerts, and the like. An Italian whose defection was precipitated by such a "vacation" described his experience as follows: "The house was large and very beautiful, profoundly silent, and surrounded by a garden with tall pine trees. We entered a long corridor and each one of us was assigned a small bedroom with a window opening on the garden. The exercises lasted three days. A Jesuit gave about four lectures daily in a chapel, sermons in which from time to time he touched on all those subjects which were most stinging to us who had denied the faith. . . . The rest of the time was spent in our rooms in meditation, alone and in absolute silence.

"In this complete solitude, the priest's words kept running in my brain and repeating themselves, until all resolved themselves into one phrase: I had denied God, that same God who had sustained me in the most unhappy of my days of imprisonment, and in whose name my mother reproached me for my friendship and work with Communists. Nevertheless, something in me resisted that constant call to redemption, something which was probably due to the unfeeling iron discipline to which I had been subjected in the past years; so that while almost all who had taken part with me in the spiritual exercises ended by confessing and taking Holy Communion on the second day, I resisted in a state of anguish until the third day: only then was I able to break down all reserve and void my soul of all that had weighed it down. Not one of those who were with me refused or abandoned the 'Villa del Sacro Cuore' before the termination of the three days and all of us left restored, after having undergone the same process of conversion. Up to three days before, if we wanted to insult someone, we called them 'priest.' Today we saw in the priest the benefactor, the liberator."

Value Conflicts

Loyalty to the party and its decisions often puts pressure on ideals and principles other than those already implied in the material discussed above. The value conflicts reported by the respondents could be classified under the headings of intellectual, aesthetic, political, and economic. Intellectual and aesthetic conflicts were primarily reported by party journalists, scientists, and artists. Conflicts over economic values were mainly reported by trade unionists, factory officials, or administrators of such party enterprises as cooperatives. Political value conflicts were generally reported among all groups of party members.

The Nazi-Soviet Pact created a crisis of conscience among many party journalists. In their capacity as journalists, they had to elaborate and defend a policy which flew in the face of everything the party had stood for in the period of the Popular Front and "collective security." Even party journalists who had the reputation of being "tough Bolsheviks" found it difficult to stomach this role. Thus one of them remarked that when he first heard of it, he viewed it as "hard-boiled realpolitik." ". . . the Western powers deserved what they got. They would have turned the Germans on the Russians if it had been possible, but the Russians turned the tables." But, as time went on, his troubles began. While he could accept the pact as tough politics, he could not go so far as to view the Western powers as responsible for the war. He was too much of a journalist. "I couldn't take this intellectually." He protested among his colleagues and was told to "trust Stalin," take matters on faith. This he could not do, and when the fall of France showed him dramatically what the consequences of the pact had been, he resigned from the party.

In the post-World War II period the cultural purges, the attacks on "cosmopolitanism," also had a disquieting effect upon party intellectuals. A British scholar felt that the attack on cosmopolitanism was directly contrary to the international traditions of learning. As a scholar he felt threatened in his vocational interests and values.

The Lysenko controversy in the Soviet Union provoked a crisis among the British geneticists who had been party members or sympathizers. What is so striking about this incident is the fact that the defection of the British geneticists did not occur in connection with the general cultural purge in the Soviet Union, or even when the official Soviet position attacking orthodox genetics was first announced. It was not until the British party, backed up by the Soviet Union, attempted to compel acceptance of Lysenkoism by the British geneticists that defection occurred. A report by one of the participants in this controversy is instructive.

The first reports received by the British geneticists of the decisions of the Soviet Academy of Agricultural Scientists were garbled. "The British party published a speech by Lysenko. I read it and found it completely unintelligible. There was a lot of discussion among geneticists at this time. The B.B.C. organized a symposium between four speakers, including Haldane. Haldane was very cagey and refused to take sides, though he tried to defend the Soviet Union against attacks made without knowledge of the evidence. The first thing that infuriated me was an article in the *Daily Worker* by Clemence Dutt, reviewing a book by Lysenko and attacking the orthodox geneticists. This at a time when Haldane, the leading party scientist and geneticist, was refusing to commit himself. The *Daily Worker* also published a false account of the B.B.C. symposium, implying that Haldane had given complete support to Lysenko.

"Meanwhile, I had had one or two discussions with party zoologists, who were not geneticists, but had jumped on the Lysenko bandwagon. I was never more surprised in my life than when one of them told me that Lysenko's book was one of the most remarkable he had ever read, while I, a geneticist, could not understand a word of it.

"Then the party called a meeting of its geneticists. There were about twelve or thirteen of them. The only other people who attended were Maurice Cornforth and another party leader whose name escapes me. Much to Cornforth's disgust, the party geneticists were up in arms and in particular attacked the *Daily Worker* for falsifying its account of the broadcast symposium. Cornforth said there had been a typographical error, or something like that. Haldane's particular line and the line the group supported was that here was a great opportunity for the British party to take an independent and critical, but sympathetic, attitude, and so make it clear that we did not follow Moscow slavishly. Cornforth didn't say very much, but he implied that all this was going to be steam-rollered. I think the party had hoped the geneticists would pass a resolution approving Lysenko's position, but since this didn't happen no resolution was taken at the end of the meeting.

"Then the *Daily Worker* put out an 'educational supplement' about Lysenko, attacking orthodox genetics. Haldane, at the time still chairman of the *Daily Worker* board, wrote a reply, attacking the supplement point by point. He had this reply cyclostyled and circulated. Previously there had come into existence as part of Marx House three organizations which were intended as platforms for theoretical discussion. These were the Engels Society (scientific), the Sigerist Society (medical), and a legal society. I think these were all postwar foundations.

"After the appearance of the 'educational supplement' and Haldane's reply, the Engels Society called a small meeting of the Society. About thirty to forty scientists from various fields were present, including Bernal and Haldane. By this time the line-up was beginning to be clear. The geneticists were all hostile to the party line. Most of the other scientists were confused, though one or two had climbed on the bandwagon, including Bernal and some biologists. All the geneticists and biologists at the meeting, apart from Haldane, were comparatively junior people. The meeting was opened by a biologist who read a prepared statement in favor of the Lysenko position. It was agreed that Haldane would reply. Then an extraordinary thing happened. Before the old man could rise to his feet, someone whom none of us had ever seen before got up and began to explain elementary genetics to the boys. He appeared to be under a complete misapprehension as to the nature of the meeting and obviously thought we were all convinced Michurinists in support of the party line, which he believed to be wrong. We were all waiting to hear Haldane and tried to shout him down. Eventually he sat down, protesting that he would take the matter up with higher quarters. Then Haldane got up and attacked the first speaker. Other people spoke and tempers ran quite high, but the position wasn't yet formalized. At the end of the meeting, Bernal made a soothing statement and intimated there would be further discussion. Again no resolution was taken.

"What I couldn't stomach about the Lysenko theory was the lack of coherence in its presentation. There are a lot of quite reasonable criticisms that could be made against orthodox genetics. It is a young science, still passing through a period of violent controversy. But this wholesale abuse disgusted me. The next thing was that in February 1949, the Engels Society called a two-day 'school' on the genetics controversy. This was held at the Society for Cultural Relations with the U.S.S.R. and was a full-dress affair. Emile Burns was in the chair, with Bernal sitting beside him. There were from seventy to eighty scientists present. The meeting was opened by two statements, one by an orthodox geneticist, the other by a Lysenkoist called Morton, a botanist who appeared out of nowhere, but has since become the party's great expert on Michurinism. Again the meeting was too divided for a resolution to be taken.

"Subsequently there was a series of meetings. I didn't go to all of them because I was beginning to be sick of the whole affair, but I did go to a meeting of the Engels Society at Marx House. By now, Maurice Cornforth had collected a dossier on Haldane, who was not at the meeting. He put across the extraordinary line that Mendelism and Nazi race theory had the same origin, and that was why Haldane and the other party geneticists had failed adequately to attack Nazi theories. This was a complete distortion of history. Some of the most crushing prewar indictments had come from Haldane, e.g., in *Heredity and Politics* and constant writing in the *Daily Worker*. I got up and had a row with Cornforth, accusing him of being a bloody liar. So far as I know, only one geneticist supported the party in this controversy and he was a plant geneticist. I suspect that all the rest must have drifted out of the party.

"Then a delegation came over from the Soviet Union, including Gluschenko, Lysenko's right-hand man. I went to one or two meetings where he spoke and also talked to him. He gave a curiously unsatisfactory impression. He didn't have much to say, but yet he seemed to know what the game was all about. Talking to him privately, we asked whether there was any research in human genetics taking place in the Soviet Union, as there had been a flourishing school there in 1935-1936. He said he knew of no research in human genetics at the present time. Then we asked him if he knew anything about the recent work on blood groups. He said no, he was a plant geneticist. But next night at a public meeting he gave a great diatribe against orthodox human genetics. It is illustrative of the curious level at which crosstalk went on during Gluschenko's visit that in spite of the emphasis on the practical results of Lysenkoism, the main example given was that they had somehow found a method of producing apples that looked like pears. The incredible thing was the intangible nature of the whole controversy. In arguments put forward by the Lysenkoists any particular sentence makes sense, though there are some bizarre statements, but in the end you don't know what it's all about. It's certainly not the cold reasoning of classical Marxism, but a kind of mysticism.

"In the summer of 1949 Haldane publicly stated his position in the *Modern Quarterly*, in an article defending orthodox genetics. This was followed by a much longer article by Bernal which I couldn't understand, except that it made the issue one of confidence in the Soviet Union."

There were a number of cases in which party journalists and scholars were repelled by the shoddiness or the simple immorality of Communist journalistic practice. One British party member who was a specialist on East Africa was horrified at an article written by a party official on East Africa: "I was angered at the presumption of people who had never been to East Africa pretending to have firsthand knowledge of conditions there. The most disturbing thing was that here, in the leading Marxist intellectual journal, in place of evidence they were simply lifting ideas out of Lenin's *Imperialism*. I wrote a counterattack . . . disputing some of their facts. My article was published, but no reply was forthcoming. As a result of writing this article, I felt for the first time that it was stupid to pay any attention to party theoreticians such as Palme Dutt, if they made up their stories this way."

Although the party tends to distrust intellectuals, viewing them as unstable and unreliable, it generally holds them on a loose leash, since they are of value, particularly if they have big reputations. An Italian artist of considerable fame who was employed as an art critic on *L'Unita* began to get restive after the establishment of the Cominform. He expressed his views to the editor, arguing that art and politics were incompatible and that he could not sacrifice his personal views. When the editor failed to convince the art critic that he ought to remain, the top party leader Pajetta was called in to try his capacity for persuasion. "Pajetta said that I might persist in my views regarding culture, art, and all the manifestations of the spirit. I could also defend the Western tradition as against the Oriental, he indicated, and concluded by saying that it would not matter so long as I maintained in my articles the greatest prudence possible, leaving my criticism to oral discussion."

A number of poets, musicians, and painters reported party decisions and attitudes on aesthetics which conflicted with their own aesthetic conceptions. An Italian composer and conductor, a prize possession of the Italian Communist Party, complained about interference in his work: "Just to give one example, when I was commissioned to compile the programs for the opera season . . . they tried to make me exclude the Wagner operas from the program because Wagner's music is contrary to the Communist conception." He refused to accept these interferences and ultimately found it impossible to remain in the party.

A British poet came up against a similar problem, but party discipline was applied against him with greater force: "I had written some poetry which a number of party members happened to see and realized was introspective and defeatist. They suggested I tear it up, but I refused. Following this, I had a great argument with the cell secretary about poetry and later was informed there would be a special lecture by L. on Marxism and art. It was announced in the ordinary way, not put as anything personal, but I was asked to attend. I arrived rather early for the lecture and found the room laid out in an unusual way. In front of the lecture-table and between it and the rows of chairs, there was an armchair out all on its own. I sat down at the back of the room. When the comrades arrived, they told me the armchair was for me. I went and sat down in it, rather amused. I could see what was coming. When L. arrived and began to speak, it was to me that he addressed himself, as though there were no one else there. He had been briefed and so had the group. They all sat looking at me very grimly.

"When L. had finished speaking, the chairman asked if there were any questions. Everyone sat silently, waiting for me to speak. They all had their eyes fixed on me. I got up and began to argue with L. I was thoroughly worked up by now and didn't give a damn. I brought in all the reactionaries, including Eliot and *Horizon*. L. pretended never to have heard of *Horizon*, and asked who edited it. When I said Cyril Connolly, he looked at me pityingly. We finished by shouting at each other. An Indian girl, of whom I had asked a question about Hindu philosophy a couple of weeks before, got up and said I was obviously a bad lot, interested in decadent philosophies. None of the others took part in the argument, though from time to time they murmured their disapproval. At the end the chairman wound up. He said it had been a most regrettable discussion and told the comrades to take a warning from the way I was going down the drain. They all walked out without speaking to me."

The most common type of value conflict among the respondents resulted from experiencing or observing the authoritarian and manipulative political practices of the party. Some respondents were troubled at the ways in which a small party caucus could dominate a trade union or other organization. Others had difficulty accepting the internal electoral procedures of the party in which the upper echelons determined elections at the lower levels. A British respondent states that in all of his twenty years as a party member he had never observed an open and free election for any committee or council. "It sometimes appeared free, but the leaders would submit a panel of names which everyone voted for. There would be a list of fifty nominations sent to the panels commission, but twenty of these would be recommended by the panel, and everyone voted for the twenty." Others were troubled over the ways in which party discussions were rigged. An American trade union leader participated in a discussion between two unions—both Communist-dominated —about the amalgamation of the two unions. "I got up to say something but was told to sit down. They had already picked out all the speeches."

A less common basis of dissatisfaction with the party arose from situations in which party decisions resulted in losses in economic efficiency and productivity. This kind of criticism was made by trade union leaders forced to call political strikes, or by Communist managers of business enterprises. An Italian respondent who had been placed in charge of a system of party-owned cooperatives often had to hire incompetent workers sent from party headquarters. At the same time, he was expected to do an efficient job and contribute to the party's income. Persons who held managerial posts in private industry were also often caught in the cross-current of party decisions and their effects on productivity and efficiency. Thus a Frenchman who was the director of personnel in a factory dismissed an inefficient workman who was also a party member. The Communist factory organization ordered him to reinstate the man and called a strike against him. The personnel director held his ground, and although he was ultimately upheld by the Central Committee of the party, he had already become completely disillusioned.

It is an interesting lead to possible bases of dissatisfaction inside the Communist orbit that in the cases of those respondents who were in managerial posts in party or private business enterprises in France and Italy, tension almost always occurred between the managerial interest in productivity and party attitudes affecting personnel and labor policy. In some instances, trade union leaders had the same reactions, turning away not only from the party, but from the continental European tradition of political unionism. A former top Communist trade union executive in France commented, "We must fight the battle for productivity on two fronts, against the C.G.T. and against the reactionary bosses. It will not be easy, but it is necessary. There are enormous possibilities. In 1927 France had 1,200,000 textile workers; today there are only 638,000, yet production is 30 per cent above that of 1927. One worker can take care of thirty looms, as against eight, fifteen years ago. Wages ought to go up as productivity goes up. . . . It is a question of educating the workers, of making a reality of the factory committees, and of getting the support of the more enlightened employers . . . a question of forming leaders at the level of the plant, real militants in the tradition of the trade union movement."

General Appraisals of the Party

The preceding types of dissatisfactions with the party all represented negative reactions to specific experiences with the party. They did not involve explicit general appraisals of the party. This in itself is a significant finding, for it would appear from the preceding material that disaffection typically tends to result from direct impingements of party policies and party decisions on the interests and relationships of the individual, rather than from general rejections of party theory and policy. In fact, this latter type of disaffection, when it occurred at all, seemed to follow after experience of more specific party actions. For example, an individual's first dissatisfactions might have resulted from seeing some corrupt or dishonest action in a trade union. From this he would conclude that the party as a whole was a corrupt organization.

Leaving the party thus seems typically to involve not a general appreciation of the character of the party, but a response to specific experiences with certain aspects of it. Often the disillusionment with the party had the same basis as the original "illusion." Thus many trade unionists joined the party because they felt there was a coincidence in goals between the party and the union movement, and left the party when they found that it was subordinating the union or unions to its own purposes. Often intellectuals who were attracted to the party because they were impressed with its theoretical and intellectual aspects left the party when they found that it violated and destroyed intellectual values.

Generalizations about the party usually appeared to be *post hoc* efforts at providing an intellectual and moral structure for a decision which was typically based upon a series of conflicts and dissatisfactions. Most of the generalizations offered by the respondents were of a simple order. Thus the party was described as being essentially concerned with power rather than with moral and humanitarian goals. Twenty per cent of the respondents described it in these terms. Seventeen per cent felt that the party was corrupt, that the leaders were in it for their own gain. Thirty per cent felt that the sacrifices demanded by the party were too great, that the means were too costly, or that the means used by the party destroyed the possibility of achieving its goals. Only a small number (12 per cent) of the respondents, and these were mainly among the early defectors, attacked the party as deviating from Marxist-Leninist doctrine.

An Italian trade union leader described the way in which he came to the conclusion that the party was simply power-oriented in the following terms: "During my experience as a trade unionist I had seen that the central point of Communist policy was agitation for the sake of agitation, that is, to bring up problems constantly in order to arouse more discontent, without really offering any solution to the problems—the real purpose being to gain power by means of this agitation." Another Italian came to the conclusion that "The Communism of today is nothing more than a process of mobilizing the social order under the elite of a new type—in other words, a simple power dictatorship." After a year in Moscow, an American Negro said, "I decided there was such a thing as a Russian Tammany Hall."

The theme of the corruption of the party was developed in a variety of ways. A French intellectual discussed the motives underlying the continued loyalty of some of the party intellectuals: "For instance, Victor Marguerite was obtained through royalties. Vanity plays a greater role than money— a terrific appetite to climb the ladder. There are some intellectuals who join without having anything to gain from the party. Others make a career in the party—for instance, Aragon, who is not a Communist at all."

An American trade union functionary commented, "I guess you have to be on the other side of the fence before you realize how rotten they are. They used every trick in the book to get me to change my mind, everything from an offer of a three-week paid vacation to an offer of the most attractive girl in the union." Other party members were revolted by corrupt practices such as stuffing ballot boxes, taking names from the telephone book to forge on petitions, and the like.

Some of the British respondents were disillusioned by what they viewed as the cowardice of the party leaders. One remarked, ". . . during the war most of the leadership had 'disabilities.' There used to be a crack, 'Comrades, you have nothing to lose but your ulcers.'" Similarly, during the Spanish Civil War many party members were repelled by the way in which the leaders retained safe berths at home while sending humble militants to the battlefields. A Scottish woman member once asked a party leader, "Tell me, are the Moors here in Glasgow? I see all the party leaders here."

The closest some of the respondents came to considered moral judgments of the party involved the problem of means and ends. An Italian admitted that all progress called for costs and sacrifices. Revolution could not be had free of charge. However, as time went on, he began to distinguish between what he called necessary and unnecessary costs. "I have well-founded doubts, when Russia uses a million workers in forced labor to build a dam in six months, that these are necessary sacrifices. Doesn't the doubt arise that the 'harm' done to others is at least disproportionate to the 'good' which the party may derive?" A Frenchman said that he ". . . realized as early as 1946 that the party dismissed some essential and painfully acquired things, such as friendship, love, knowledge, that it showed an astonishing fear of science. . . . At the beginning I was convinced that through Communism new norms of freedom would be created, but soon I realized that it was a hopeless situation."

Often the cost in means was seen in immediate and personal terms, as in the case of the American trade unionist who said, "Many people break from the party because they are given tasks which are either impossible to carry out or are obviously impossible morally, such as wrecking a union you had spent ten years building up." A British intellectual put his problem in terms of growing up and realizing the human aspect of the problem: "I felt that it demanded too much human sacrifice to achieve its ends, and that it was no longer possible to argue that the ends justified the means. . . . Perhaps also I became more interested in people and less in abstractions—maybe the same reasons why at that time I changed over from science to psychology."

Patterns of Dissatisfaction

Thus we have seen that defection may be influenced by the pressure of the party on any one or a combination of the interests, values, and relationships which the individual brings with him into the party. But these types of dissatisfaction are not distributed in a random manner among the various types of party members. It was of interest that the Italian respondents complained with particular frequency of threats to their individuality. Forty-five per cent of the Italian respondents were repelled by this aspect of their experience. This especially high proportion may be due to the fact that the Italian respondents came into the party in 1943 largely as a reaction against Fascist suppression. To them the party meant liberation. The impact of party discipline would be felt with especial poignancy by persons coming to the party with these libertarian expectations.

The American and British respondents were repelled far more frequently by the atmosphere and associations of party life than the French and Italians. This may be accounted for by the fact that the conspiratorial, dogmatic, and authoritarian pattern of the party clashes most sharply with the political and associational patterns of British and American society. The especially high proportion of American respondents who were repelled by the associations and atmosphere of the party may be attributed to the ethnic and social heterogeneity of the American movement. The French, Italian, and British respondents were largely of native stock and of the dominant religions. The Americans, on the other hand, were very frequently foreign-born or first-generation native-born (and of many different national origins), the religious mixture was not like that of the society at large, and the proportion of bohemian intellectuals was substantial. Hence almost every group found something in the party which was repelling. Those from the older ethnic stocks were sometimes repelled by the foreign aspect of the party. Working-class members were repelled by the bohemian intellectuals and artists. Some of the whites were uncomfortable among the Negroes and the Negroes were ill at ease among the whites.

Social Class and Patterns of Dissatisfaction

A number of interesting differences emerged from a comparison of the dissatisfactions of the middle-class and working-class respondents. Table 1 groups together the types of dissatisfaction most characteristic of these two groups. More of the working-class respondents complained about conflicts in connection with their party careers. This probably results from the fact that a greater proportion of the working-class respondents were employed by the party or by party-controlled trade unions. Complaints about pressure on individuality occurred twice as often among the middle-class respondents. This is not a difficult finding to interpret, since middle-class people tend generally to be more individuated, to have more elaborate interests than working-class people.[1]

TABLE I

*Types of Dissatisfaction with Party by Social Class**
(in per cent)

	Working class	Middle class	All respondents
Disruption of party careers	27	17	22
Loss of individuality	16	32	24
Party associates and atmosphere	40	53	47
Trade union—party conflict	46	14	29
Russian domination of party	19	28	24
Party vs. intellectual values	11	47	29
Party vs. aesthetic values	1	12	6
Party vs. political values	25	34	29
Party vs. economic values	10	7	9

* Multiple responses.

Hence they are more likely to feel the threat to their individuality resulting from party discipline and to resent the pressures for conformity.

As might be expected, the working-class respondents were caught in trade union—party conflict far more frequently than the middle-class respondents. On the other hand, the middle-class respondents were more troubled by the Russian domination of the party. This may be due to the fact that the middle-class party member tends to see the party in its general and international manifestations, while the working-class party

[1] See Richard Centers, *The Psychology of Social Classes* (Princeton: Princeton University Press, 1949), pp. 141 ff.

member tends to be more locally oriented. Conflicts with intellectual and aesthetic values were more characteristic of the middle-class members, while the working-class members complained somewhat more frequently of the effects of party policies on the efficiency and productivity of enterprises with which they were identified. In general, the repulsions from the party of these two groups resulted from the party's impingement on their vocational interests. In the case of the middle-class respondents, many of whom were intellectuals, the impingement was on such values as honest reporting and interpretation of news for journalists, or aesthetic freedom for artists. In the case of the working-class members, the impingement was on career interests (as trade union functionaries, in most cases), or on trade union interests in general.

Echelon and Patterns of Dissatisfaction

The differences in patterns of dissatisfaction based on rank in the party are shown in Table 2. Conflicts and career dis-

TABLE 2

Types of Dissatisfaction with the Party by Echelon*
(in per cent)

	Rank and file	Low echelon	High echelon	All respondents
Disruption of party career	13	25	35	22
Disruption of non-party career	18	14	4	13
Party associates and atmosphere	53	47	35	47
Personal relations	29	34	20	29
Party vs. intellectual values	34	30	18	29
Party vs. aesthetic values	6	10	2	6
Party as power-oriented	12	21	31	20
Means-ends conflict	23	39	33	30

* Multiple responses.

satisfactions in the party itself were most characteristic of the high-echelon respondents, and least frequent among the rank and file. In contrast, disruption of careers outside the party were most frequent among the rank and file. Since the high-echelon respondents had made their lives in the party and had most of their relationships within it, dissatisfaction with party associates and atmosphere and pressure on personal relations occurred less frequently among them than among the lower-echelon and rank-and-file respondents. Intellectual and aesthetic value conflicts were more characteristic of the low echelon and rank and file. On the other hand, the high-echelon respondents, who were in the inner party, and hence more exposed to its esoteric patterns, were more often aware of the power-orientation of the party and of the sacrifices in values and interests that it demanded.

The "transmission belt" principle of Communist Party organization is based on the assumption that a relatively small group of fully dedicated professional revolutionaries will be in a position to dominate mass organizations. The party has always operated on this dual organizational basis—a compact party at the center manipulating mass organizations at the periphery. This necessitates a dual system of leadership, with inner party functionaries controlling the central apparatus and front-organization functionaries controlling the mass organizations. The pressures and problems confronting these two groups of party leaders are different. The front-organization functionaries are caught in the conflicts of interest between the party and the particular organization which they have "colonized." The inner party functionaries are in the direct chain of command which leads ultimately to the Russian party leadership. Hence it was anticipated that the problems of assimilation and the causes of defection would differ for the two leadership groups.

The respondents included 53 inner party functionaries, 72 functionaries in front organizations (primarily trade unions), and 96 respondents who had held no paid employment at all. Table 3 shows the differences in pattern for these three groups. Both groups of functionaries were about equally repelled by the party because of some disruption of their party or front-organization career. The front-organization functionaries more often resented the party's interference in their personal relations. This suggests that leaders of front organizations are more likely to retain commitments and involvements outside the party. In other words, they are less fully assimilated into the party and hence more vulnerable to

TABLE 3

*Types of Dissatisfaction with Party by Functionary Status**
(in per cent)

	Internal party functionary	Front-organization functionary	Non-functionary	All respondents
Number of cases	53	72	96	221
Disruption of party career	30	26	15	22
Pressure on personal relations	19	29	34	29
Trade union— party conflict	17	49	23	29
Russian domination of party	36	26	19	24
Other group— party conflict	—	4	12	6
Party as power-oriented	23	26	13	20
Deviation from doctrine	19	8	9	11

* Multiple responses.

group-related conflicts than the inner party leadership. Almost half of the front-organization functionaries were caught in conflicts between trade union and party interests, as compared with 17 per cent of the inner party leaders. On the other hand, the central party functionaries were more often repelled by the Russian influence over their national parties. This would result from the fact that the central party leadership is in the international chain of command of the movement, and hence more frequently exposed to Russian pressure.

In an earlier chapter, the point was made that the high-echelon respondents had more frequently been indoctrinated in Marxism-Leninism than the lower-echelon respondents.

As heads of the party in their own countries, they were more often called upon to expound party doctrine. Because of this greater familiarity with doctrine, and because of their knowledge of high-level party policy, their opportunities to compare party policy with the basic doctrine would be greater. This is reflected in the fact that the high-echelon respondents and the inner party functionaries far more often than the other respondents disagreed with party policies because they felt that they deviated from Marxist-Leninist doctrine. The point ought also to be made that criticism of the party because of doctrinal deviation was more characteristic of the earlier high-echelon defectors than of the later. This confirms other findings as to the declining influence of formal doctrine in the party—as an attraction and as a cause of defection.

Neurotic Needs and Dissatisfaction with the Party

Thus the kinds of dissatisfaction experienced in the party are related to social and occupational characteristics, and position in the organizational structure of the party. They are also related to the kinds of needs which individuals seek to serve by joining the party. The respondents were classified into two groups from this point of view: those who had manifested emotional difficulties and maladjustments prior to joining, and those who had not. Our expectation was that persons who had had difficulties in personal relations before joining would continue to have such difficulties while in the party.

This hypothesis is supported by evidence from Table 4. Thus 29 per cent of the emotionally maladjusted respondents got into conflicts and difficulties relating to their careers in the party, as compared with 17 per cent for the non-neurotic; and 63 per cent of the neurotic were repelled by their party associates and the atmosphere of the party, as compared with 35 per cent of the non-neurotic. In contrast, the "normal" respondents far more frequently became dissatisfied because of conflicts between the requirements of the party and outside interests and loyalties. Thus the "normal" respondents resented interference in their non-party careers and experienced

TABLE 4

The Incidence of Types of Dissatisfaction among Neurotic and Non-neurotic Respondents*
(in per cent)

	Neurotic	Non-neurotic	All respondents
Number of cases	94	127	221
Disruption of party career	29	17	22
Disruption of non-party career	9	16	13
Party associates and atmosphere	63	35	47
Trade union—party conflict	16	39	29
Russian domination of party	18	27	24

* Multiple responses.

group-related conflicts more often than the neurotic ones. In particular, the "normal" respondents manifested a comparatively higher incidence of conflict between patriotic and trade union loyalties than did the emotionally maladjusted respondents. This may be explained by the fact that the neurotic respondents were more self-involved and lacking in stable loyalties, while the "normal" respondents continued to maintain their outside occupational interests and extra-party loyalties even while in the party.

The preceding analysis has described the aspects of party action which create dissatisfaction and contribute to defection. It has also indicated the particular problems of assimilation and patterns of dissatisfaction of different types of party members. The point has already been made that defection can be best understood as a process extending over time and involving a whole sequence of decisions. The process of defection is affected by the characteristics and expectations of the individual, the aspects of the party to which he has been exposed, the degree of his commitment and involvement in the party, and the opportunities available to him in the outside world. Just as there are patterns of susceptibility and dissatisfaction, so also are there patterns of defection and readjustment after leaving the party. These patterns of defection and readjustment are the themes of the chapter which follows.

CHAPTER 12

DEFECTION AND READJUSTMENT

MOVEMENT INTO and movement out of the various Communist parties increases or decreases with each great change in the party line, each "zig" or "zag," to use the Communist expression. Major changes in party tactics which bring the party to the support of the nation and the society—i.e., so-called "popular front" or "national front" tactics—increase movement into the party. In recent history, the Popular Front in 1935 and the World War II coalition after the Nazi attack on the Soviet Union are instances in which movement into the party took on massive proportions. Changes in party tactics which involve disruptive and revolutionary actions, which isolate the party within the nation and the society, greatly increase movement out of the party. In recent history, the Nazi-Soviet Pact in 1939 and the establishment of the Cominform in 1947 were dramatic instances of changes in line which produced defection on a very large scale.[1]

While movement out of the Communist Party is characterized by the sudden flows which are the consequences of changes in line, there is an unfortunate tendency to equate dissatisfaction with and defection from Communism with changes in line. It would be more accurate to conceive of these changes in line as the opening of the floodgates, permitting the already disenchanted and the dissatisfied to move out in the comparative safety and anonymity of a general party crisis.

In addition to general party crises, two other types of situations tend to result in large-scale defections. Thus party policies which affect the interests of specific party strata are likely to produce special party crises. The calling of political

[1] In selecting the respondents for this study, an effort was made to select defectors from the various periods of party history. At the same time, because of our interest in the problems of assimilation and defection in the contemporary situation, the selection was heavily weighted for recent defectors. Thus, of the total of 221 defectors, 91 left the party in 1947 or later, and 152 left in 1939 and later. Only 67 were defectors of the 1920's and 1930's.

strikes, for example, may produce defection among workers, while a cultural purge is likely to result in defection among intellectuals. Secondly, any action which has the effect of moving people out of their accustomed milieu, such as a military mobilization, facilitates defection, since party members are withdrawn from the controls of Communist organization and communication. In the first type of situation, the action of the party impinges on strongly held interests of its members, and presses group loyalty conflicts or value conflicts to the breaking point. In the second type of situation, the action of the outside society breaks party members loose from the powerful controls of the party and permits dissatisfactions and doubts which have been suppressed to come to the surface.

The members of any organization are always repelled by or opposed to certain of its aspects or activities. High morale never means unqualified approval of a group's activities, but only a substantial outweighing of the unfavorable reactions by the favorable. This problem of the balance of favorable and unfavorable reactions is of a special character in the Communist movement, for two reasons. In the first place, the party makes enormous demands upon its members. Ultimately, it asks the individual literally to give himself up and become a simple party instrumentality. This may conflict with all of the interests a man can have, may require that they be subordinated and made instrumental to the party's purposes. Hence the pressure of the party on the individual is far greater in the Communist movement than in most other organizations. Secondly, the party does not tolerate discussion and criticism. On the contrary, the strongest of sanctions are imposed upon those who protest and disagree. Thus negative reactions, dissatisfactions, repulsions from party decisions and the tone of party life must be held in suppression. They may hardly be articulated even to oneself, since some of one's capacity for unequivocal obedience is lost the moment one begins to think critically of the party. And the party quickly senses this potential disaffection, particularly in those who are in leading posts. It brings pressure to bear on them, and either forces them to suppress their dissatisfactions more effectively, or brings their disaffection into the open and forces them out of the movement.

The build-up of negative pressure in the party leadership and membership owing to the extraordinary risks and demands of party life and the elimination of opportunities to drain the pressure off through a loose and permissive internal organization may account for certain Communist phenomena which have sometimes mystified the observer. Many of the respondents remarked that immediately upon leaving the party they found it difficult to understand how it had been possible for them to have remained in it so long. Once out of the party, they found themselves with anti-Communist views and with negative feelings about the party, the content and strength of which they had hardly realized. This may be accounted for by the fact that the grave risks of defection forced them to suppress their critical reactions and the feelings associated with them. Once they are out of the party, this pressure is released. The critical thoughts can come to the surface, the hostile feelings be discharged.

The party seeks to prevent defection by portraying the world outside as unambiguously evil. One cannot leave the party and achieve a safe neutrality. We have already seen that the party hates its "renegades" more than any of its antagonists. Where it is in power, it destroys its defectors morally and often physically. Where it is not in power, it attempts to destroy their character and thereby render them politically useless.

It may very well be that the dreadful crimes attributed to defectors, the swiftness with which a party paragon may be transformed into the most detestable party object, the gross and transparent misrepresentations in the trials of Communist leaders, can be interpreted in terms of the problem of maintaining solidarity under the special conditions of tension which exist in the party. We have already seen that the pattern of intra-party personal relations tends to be full of distrust and suspicion. The party keeps a dossier on each of its members, and mutual surveillance is encouraged. Under these circumstances, and particularly among the leadership, massive anxieties build up and a silent and dreadful struggle for power and safety is inescapable.

In this kind of atmosphere, the trials and expulsions of "party traitors" take on the proportions of an ever-repeated morality play, with different characters, but with the same themes of full and integral treason, espionage, sabotage, identification as agents of foreign capital. Thus the loyal party leadership and membership is told again and again in the simplest and most compelling way that there is no middle ground between integral loyalty and integral disloyalty, that the disloyal impulses within themselves can have only one denouement, the fullest complicity in the gravest crimes and most mortal of sins. The trials, vilifications, and punishments of defectors make it easier for the loyal to keep their negative impulses in suppression by dramatizing the consequences of failure to do so. These ceremonies may be interpreted in part as ritual sacrifices that protect the solidarity and cohesion of a movement which might otherwise explode from inner hostile tension.

Among the factors which affect the ease or difficulty with which an individual leaves the party three appear to be of special significance. The first of these is the degree of commitment to and involvement in the party. The simple rank and filer who joins the party with the expectation that it will provide effective trade union leadership, who makes his living outside the movement, who has retained his ties with non-party people and organizations, and who can continue his trade union activity after leaving the party, has a minimum of difficulty in leaving and readjusting. On the other hand, the high-echelon Communist who has committed his whole future to the party, who makes his living from it, who has no ties with people outside the movement, and who must face the bitter antagonism of the party and an inhospitable world outside, may experience the most painful suffering in leaving it.

Secondly, the prospects confronting the individual on leaving are of importance in affecting the rate of flow from the party. The outside situation may affect the process of defection in two ways: through the kinds of political alternatives to Communist affiliation which are available; and through the severity of the sanctions imposed upon former party members. In a situation in which there is a broad, effective, moderate left political party, the process of defection may be facilitated. Similarly, in a situation in which the sanctions imposed on those leaving the party are relatively mild, the rate of defection may be favorably affected and the difficulties and conflicts experienced may be minimized.

A third factor affecting the ease or difficulty of leaving the party are the kinds of needs being served by party membership and the prospects for satisfying these needs as adequately elsewhere. A person joining the party because of some situational or objective damage may leave it with a minimum of difficulty as soon as he discovers that the party is not a satisfactory way of dealing with his problem. On the other hand, the person who has joined the party because he is basically antagonistic and hostile may suffer the most severe conflicts in leaving the party, since he will have great difficulty in finding another setting in which he can express his hostility under what appear to him to be morally and intellectually satisfying auspices.

Length of Time Spent in Doubt

Most defectors go through a period of doubt and conflict some time before leaving the party. Thus 10 per cent of our respondents reported having spent their entire membership in doubt as to the wisdom of their decision, 10 per cent reported more than half their membership, and 36 per cent reported somewhere between one-fourth to one-half of it as having been spent in a state of indecision. Some of the respondents remained in the party after doubts began, primarily because they were not quite sure of themselves, others because they felt it would be cowardly to leave the party in a period of difficulty, still others because they could not bring themselves to admit that they had made so serious a mistake. There were also those who were mainly afraid of what the party might do if they withdrew, and, finally, those who were especially afraid of the sanctions which the outside society might impose on them.

Almost two-thirds of the respondents had doubts about remaining in the party for more than a year before the final break (see Table 1). The number of years spent in doubt varies with rank and tenure in the party. Thus 35 per cent of the high-echelon respondents (who also had the longest tenure) were in doubt for three years or more, as compared with 21 per cent for the low-echelon respondents and 17 per cent for the rank and file. At the other extreme, 32 per cent of the rank and filers had doubts for less than one year, as compared with 12 per cent for the high-echelon respondents.

TABLE I

Length of Time from First Doubts to Defection by Echelon
(in per cent)

	Rank and file	Low echelon	High echelon	All respondents
7 years and over	7	9	14	9
3-7 years	10	12	21	14
2-3 years	15	20	26	19
1-2 years	26	25	17	23
Under 1 year	32	25	12	25
Unknown or no doubt	10	9	10	10
Total	100	100	100	100

Difficulty of Break from the Party

Just under half of the respondents (47 per cent) described their withdrawal from the party as a difficult period. Some of them were so disturbed as to be close to suicide. An American respondent said, ". . . for me, life was ended. No one would talk to me. I lost my job. I had no training for anything else. In school I had always taken courses from left-wing teachers, since they would pass me even if I didn't do any work. I had no friends. I was panicked, completely terrified. I was really close to suicide. Fortunately for me, my father was in one of his rich periods and I retired to his country place and had a nervous breakdown. I couldn't sleep or associate with people. I cried every night."

Another American respondent reported getting ulcers three months after leaving the party. A British Communist couple recalled, "It was a terrible time for us. We had cut ourselves off from all the people we knew. . . . When we left for the Continent two people saw us off, the only two friends we had left. My husband had no job. I was recovering from a long illness. We had no reason to live except for each other and the children. We felt absolutely naked."

A French defector commented, "In the old days you could leave the party on grounds of disagreement. You had the right to leave. You became an enemy, but you were not a total outlaw. But today if you leave you are treated as a political suicide; you are destroyed; none of your friends will ever speak to you again. That is how the party holds people. It is a rule that no party member may speak to an expelled member. The latter is excommunicated. I assure you, for many people it is a real drama. . . . It takes courage to break out of such a situation." An Italian respondent reported, "I cried, I'm not ashamed to admit it. I understood at last that each one of us must carry on his struggle singlehanded, that it had been useless to disown my family, to have fought, to have passed my best years in prison or in the mountains like a wolf, to have been beaten and insulted; in brief, to have lost my youth for a party, for an idea which we believed perfect and sacred."

Some of the respondents reported that for years after leaving they suffered torments of indecision as to whether or not they had made the right choice. An Italian described his state of mind after his defection in the following terms: "Thousands of times I feared I'd made a terrible mistake in abandoning a struggle which in reality was just. And the accusation of being a traitor was no small torment. Did I have the right to abandon the cause simply because I, an individual, thought the party had fallen into error? It seemed to me that my whole life was changed. For almost thirty years I had thought, talked, and acted only in the ambit of the party;

only in its ambit had I eaten and breathed. . . ." Or another Italian: "The Communist idea had been the ideal of my life. I had given myself to it body and soul, for it I'd done lawful and unlawful acts. The aims of the party had been my law, my only law."

The French and Italian respondents reported difficulties in leaving the party somewhat more than the American and British (see Table 2). A number of factors may account for this. First, the French and Italian defectors are leaving powerful movements with some prospects for ultimate success. Second, the French and Italian parties because of their power and size can threaten defectors in many more ways and with greater effect than can either the British or American parties. Finally, the moderate left parties in France and Italy are relatively weak and ineffective, and hence do not offer attractive alternatives.

TABLE 2

Difficulty of Break from the Party by Country
(in per cent)

	U.S.	England	France	Italy	All respondents
Severe difficulties	6	14	13	21	13
Difficult period	36	30	34	37	34
Difficulties not serious	19	12	19	16	17
No problems at all	33	44	25	22	31
Unknown	6	—	9	4	5
Total	100	100	100	100	100

The British respondents included the largest proportion for whom leaving the party was no problem at all. Typical of these was an intellectual who commented, "There are quite a number of people in the party whom I still know and with whom I am on reasonable terms. I didn't have the problem of making new friends. I had no problems of readjustment at all."

The most striking differences in this connection were related to rank in the party (see Table 3). Thus 30 per cent of the high-echelon respondents reported severe difficulties, as compared with only 9 per cent who reported no difficulties at all. In contrast, none of the rank and filers reported severe difficulties, and 46 per cent reported that they had no problems whatever on leaving.

TABLE 3

Difficulty of Break from Party by Echelon
(in per cent)

	Rank and file	Low echelon	High echelon	All respondents
Severe difficulties	—	19	30	13
Difficult period	29	40	37	34
Difficulties not serious	20	12	18	17
No problems at all	46	25	9	31
Unknown	5	4	6	5
Total	100	100	100	100

A special analysis was made of the problems of defection for the two types of party functionaries. The results are of interest and suggest that front-organization functionaries suffer conflicts and difficulties in withdrawing from the party far less frequently than the internal party functionaries (see Table 4). Thus 72 per cent of the latter group reported difficulties in breaking, as compared with 47 per cent among the front-organization functionaries. Those who had no paid employment either with the party or with front organizations reported no problems in leaving with the greatest frequency of all.

The reasons for the greater difficulties experienced by the internal party functionaries would appear to be clear. The inner party functionary (unless he is a member of an underground party apparatus) is prominently identified with the party. He cannot escape into political anonymity. Furthermore, the party reserves a special form of contumely for those who have been closest to it. In addition, the inner party leader has made the fullest psychological commitment to the party, and is more likely to have all his personal relations within it. In contrast, the front-organization functionary is often publicly identified with the front organization rather than with the party. In many cases, his party membership is not publicly known. If he has been a conscientious and effective trade union leader, he may command the loyalty of the trade union members regardless of his political affiliation. In other words,

TABLE 4

Difficulty of Break from the Party for Types of Functionaries
(in per cent)

	Internal party functionaries	Front-organization functionaries	Non-functionaries	All respondents
Severe difficulties	30	15	2	13
Difficult period	42	32	32	34
Difficulties not serious	11	24	15	17
No problems at all	13	21	48	31
Unknown	4	8	3	5
Total	100	100	100	100

he often has a power base independent of the party and can combat it if it attempts to destroy his position. His commitment has never been as extreme as that of the inner party leader, and his personal relations are not fully identified with the movement.

It was suggested at an earlier point that persons seeking to solve emotional problems by joining the party would have greater difficulties in breaking away from it than those whose affiliation was attributable to situational problems or pressures. This hypothesis receives some support in Table 5, which shows that 55 per cent of the emotionally maladjusted had difficulties in leaving the party, as compared with 42 per cent of the "normal" respondents. But to classify all the respondents in one group obscures the importance of the political and social setting in determining who has difficulties and who does not. It has already become clear that the Communist movements in France and Italy have quite a different social function from those in England and the United States. In France and Italy, the Communist parties are the largest and most powerful left organizations. They have successfully seized the revolutionary traditions in these countries, and the main working-class organizations. In England and the United States, on the other hand, the Communist parties have no such mass base, and they are definitely in conflict with the dominant political tendencies. The Communist movements in England and the United States provide an outlet

TABLE 5
Relationship between Types of Needs Served by Joining the Party and Difficulty of Break
(in per cent)

	Neurotic	Non-neurotic	All respondents
Severe difficulties	14	12	13
Difficult period	41	30	34
Difficulties not serious	12	20	17
No problems at all	30	32	31
Unknown	3	6	5
Total	100	100	100

for persons who are maladjusted in the general society, and who find in the party a setting in which they can express their destructive and alienative inclinations with a minimum of conflict and guilt. Thus one might anticipate that the neurotic respondents of these two countries would have especial difficulty in leaving the Communist movement, since it would be hard for them to find equally satisfying ways of solving these problems outside the movement. On the other hand, the "normal" respondents in England and the United States, other things being equal, would find it easier to recognize their error in joining the movement and to discover satisfactory alternatives for their political or other needs outside the party.

In the French and Italian cases, it might be anticipated that both the normal and the neurotic respondents would experience difficulties in withdrawing. The neurotics would have difficulties for the reasons already cited, the non-neurotics because they are leaving powerful mass-based movements and there are no broad, moderate left movements for them to turn to in these countries.

These general points are supported in Table 6, which separates out the British-American and the French-Italian cases. The proportion of neurotics having difficulties in leaving the party is just about the same for both the British-American and French-Italian, but the difference between the two groups of non-neurotics is striking. Only 29 per cent of the British-American "normal" respondents had difficulties in leaving, as compared with 50 per cent for the French and Italian. The distribution of those having no problems at all in leaving is even greater. Thus, for 51 per cent of the British-

TABLE 6

Relationship between Types of Needs Served by Joining the Party and Difficulty of Break for British-American and French-Italian Respondents
(in per cent)

| | NEUROTIC | | NON-NEUROTIC | | |
	British-American	French-Italian	British-American	French-Italian	All respondents
Number of cases	60	32	54	75	221
Severe difficulties	10	23	9	14	13
Difficult period	44	33	20	36	34
Difficulties not serious	15	7	17	22	17
No problems at all	28	33	51	19	31
Unknown	3	4	3	9	5
Total	100	100	100	100	100

American "normals," defection presented no problems at all, as compared with 19 per cent for the French and Italian.

An illustration or two may help to clarify this relationship between types of needs and the process of defection. An English case serves to illustrate how a person whose affiliation with the party was motivated by emotional needs may experience great difficulties in breaking away. Joan Murphy was born of an immigrant Irish father and an English mother. By marrying an Irishman, Joan's mother was cut off from her family, partly because the Irish were at the bottom of the working-class scale, and partly because the father was Catholic and the mother's family strict Methodists. The father died when Joan was quite young and the family lived in poverty during her childhood. In school she was persecuted by the other children because of her Irish father. Her mother joined the Independent Labor Party in the early 1920's and Joan was exposed to left-wing politics and oratory at an early age. She joined the Young Communist League during the General Strike in 1926. She described her feelings in joining the party in these terms: "I felt less lonely and unimportant. I gained a strong sense of identification with the working class and felt myself suddenly as one of the leaders, though a lesser one, of the working-class movement. I was a party member learning a great many things, not the least being the obligations of a member toward the all-supreme party. . . . My life had achieved a purpose and an end to which one dedicated one's life, and a means—a sole, inevitable, if bloody, means—by which this glorious, sanctified end could be achieved. I had been, as it were, chosen, and my life suddenly began to have some sense. . . . I had the feeling of belonging to a world movement and marching forward with history."

Joan's early career in the party was full of excitement, but she soon ran into difficulties. She was sent to Russia for a year's training to serve in the headquarters of the Red Trade Union International. While in Moscow, she fell in love with a young Rumanian Communist who was under suspicion of deviationist inclinations. The party refused her permission to be near her lover.

She returned to England in bad health and soon afterward had a nervous breakdown. After her recovery, she sought to forget her problems by working hard for the party. But the British party had been informed of her behavior in Moscow and she gradually found herself frozen out of all responsible positions. She finally broke with the party on a relatively minor matter; describing her feelings on leaving, she said, "I felt utterly alone, out in the unknown. Party life was over and I knew no other. The party would go on, but I would no longer be a part of it. There was an unending vista of lonely and empty days and evenings before me. I even contemplated suicide."

An Italian case may illustrate how an apparently well-adjusted person may experience difficulties in breaking from the party largely because of disillusionment and the lack of anything better to turn to in the political situation. Ernesto Rocco, the son of a railway official, grew up in Florence in comfort and in indulgent family surroundings. His father was not a Fascist even though a state employee, but he was quite cautious in expressing political opinions. Ernesto was attracted to the party while attending the university during the period of partisan activity. He joined one of the Garibaldi brigades in 1944. The brigade was almost completely officered by Communists. While fighting with the partisans, he read Marxist and Communist literature, and became convinced of the correctness of the Communist position.

After the liberation of Italy, Ernesto decided to give up his studies and become a party functionary. Because of his education he was made a member of the staff of one of the Communist training schools. As he participated in the activities of the school, he became increasingly disillusioned by the dogmatism and authoritarianism of the party. By 1947 he knew that he wanted to resign, but delayed doing so for another two years. He explained this delay as follows: "Already in '47 the situation in the Communist Party was clear to me, but for a long time I could not decide to make a clear cut, and I too struggled in the uncertainty of many Communists who, while they despise the methods and heads of the party, must keep silent and swallow it all, victims of a kind of spell. Once fallen into this state of apathy, it is particularly difficult to free oneself from the party. Often it seems impossible . . . that one could exist outside of the party, that one could make another life and form a new conception of the world. This happens because the party burns out the inner vitality of the individual."

Despite these doubts and fears Ernesto decided to leave

in 1949. "After this, I went through a very bad period. I had broken off every relation with the sphere which had been the central part of my life for years. I felt free, but at the same time without any moral support. Sometimes I was tempted to go back on my decisions, but I was able to resist by thinking of the double-dealing in which I would find myself. Later I found the strength of mind to snap out of my depression by thinking of the necessity of providing for my family. I was able to find work, and now I have taken up my studies at the university and will soon have completed them.

"From the time of my expulsion I have always kept out of politics. This is a condition which one easily encounters in the ex-Communists, this sense of the impossibility of again interesting oneself in politics, after such a disillusionment. I still hope, however, for a socialist party which can one day re-establish the equilibrium of the life of the nation, by meeting the social requirements which the right-wing parties cannot or will not recognize fully, and which the Communist Party exploits for its demagogic ends."

Types of Problems of Adjustment

The types of adjustment problems reported by our respondents fell into four categories. First, there were problems of self-consistency, of overcoming the unwillingness of admitting to error in having joined the party. Second, there were problems of career and professional adjustment for those who left employment in the party and its front organizations, or for those who had to change their social milieu in order to leave the party. Third, there were problems of social adjustment, of finding new friends or, in some instances, new wives or husbands. Finally, there were problems of ideological and philosophical adjustment, problems of rethinking one's values.

Sometimes a potential defector cannot face the problem of confronting his comrades and telling them that he no longer shares their faith. Thus a French respondent recalled, "I have seen several party members who would like to get out. One of them told me that he has been in the party for twenty-five years and couldn't remain any longer with that gang. But he was afraid. It was a matter of temperament. He wouldn't know how to justify himself in the eyes of his comrades." More often the respondents spoke of not being able to admit to themselves that they had spent their lives "fighting for a lie." In the words of an American, "The longer you're in, the harder it is to get out. You can't afford to admit that you've thrown so many years of your life away. It takes a lot of courage." Or another American, "You have to say good-bye twenty times."

Perhaps the classic case of having to turn away from his past was that of the Italian writer Ignazio Silone. After the events in the Communist International during 1927-1928 which led to his disillusionment, Silone made up his mind to leave the party. The story may best be told in his own words: ". . . my younger brother, the last one left to me, was in an Italian prison, accused of belonging to the illegal Communist Party. At the time of his arrest he had been so severely tortured that he suffered from internal lesions which led to his death in 1932 in the penitentiary at Procida. . . . The worst of this tragedy was that up to the time of his arrest my brother had never been a member of the Communist Party, had never sought to enter it and had never been admitted, nor had he ever taken part in any of its meetings or activities. He knew neither the statutes nor the program. He was a young man, vaguely anti-Fascist, a Catholic by education and sentiments. Sports appealed to him more than politics. Why did he confess to being a Communist? Why did he confirm his statement before the Special Court which condemned him to twelve years in prison because of this admission? He wrote me in a letter, 'I have tried to act as I imagined you would have acted in my place.' Consequently, it was not easy for me to leave the party if my remaining in it might serve as a justification of my brother's voluntary sacrifice."[2]

The career problems confronting defectors are not simply

---

[2] The quotation from Silone is taken from a lengthy interview which supplemented and elaborated his contribution to Richard Crossman, ed., *The God That Failed* (New York: Harper & Brothers, 1949), pp. 76 ff.

matters of making a living. An American who had spent his adult life as a trade union official was thrown out of his union job after leaving the party. Subsequently he did quite well and became much better off financially than he had been before. But he was now working for management, and remarked, "Here I am working for a couple of chiseling manufacturers! What a situation! Me with twenty years of union work. Nobody could be more miserable than I am." In other cases, the problem was simply one of gaining a livelihood. Thus another American reported, "I have been kept out of some jobs because the Communist-dominated union found out I was applying and told the company they would have trouble if they hired me. I had to drive a cab for a year. I was lucky to get the job I have now. It was through a friend."

With the exception of the British, each of the national groups of respondents reported instances in which the party used threats of various kinds to discourage defection. In Italy and France these often took the form of threats of physical violence. A number of American respondents reported that the party informs on defectors. One American said, ". . . they'll keep you from earning a living, tell your boss you have been a party member, or destroy your reputation so that no one else will use you. If you had something wrong on your entry papers to the United States, they'll send the information to the Immigration Bureau."

The problem of reconstructing one's social life is also difficult for many of those who leave the party. A Frenchman commented, "I had no contacts, no relations at all with anyone outside the party. I knew nobody in any other milieu. For two years I lived in a haphazard kind of way, in a void." Even more strong is the testimony of another Frenchman who had held a high party post: "When someone leaves the party there is a terrific isolation. He is like a leper. He can no longer live. In critical moments, up to half of the party members may be opposed to the party decisions, but they do not dare to leave and thus be excommunicated, without a right to a community." An American reflected a somewhat different problem, a loss of confidence in oneself and in people: "It's hard to put into words. You come out of it pretty shattered—and very reluctant to enter into any kind of association. You're completely disillusioned and don't trust your judgment. You steer clear of close relations." And another American said, in similar vein, "Since then, I have had many acquaintances and very few friends."

Finally, there is the intellectual and moral problem of deciding what it is that is wrong about the party, how one made such a serious mistake, what goals and methods are right. A Frenchman observed, "It takes a long time to re-establish contact with the rest of the world, to get rid of certain reflexes. I was obliged to remain alone for a long time and to try to find a new equilibrium. I spent much time meditating. I lost faith in science and technique and came back to religion. I also rejoined the Freemasons. I realized that Communism would lead us toward slavery, worse than in the Middle Ages. I am also against Americanism and its vicious greediness. One cannot change society by changing living conditions alone." Another Frenchman sought for a new ideology, ". . . a new theory that accorded with my conscience. I fumbled around a good deal."

An American intellectual described a painful process of intellectual self-examination: "I had the lonely job of re-reading and examining all the classics—and it took years. You start by believing in something and end by not knowing what to believe in. Most of those who leave the party prepare their new beliefs while still in the movement. Some leave without new beliefs and avoid new ones for fear of being burnt again. Some who have lost their faith never get out, but remain on the fringe because they face an emptiness."

The problems of adjustment appear to be more difficult for former party members in France and Italy than in the United States and England. Thus only 16 per cent of the Americans and 10 per cent of the English, as compared with 34 per cent of the French and 33 per cent of the Italians, had serious career problems after leaving the party. The problem of finding new friends was equally distributed among the national groups.

While problems of adjustment after leaving the party were reported more frequently by those who had joined before 1935, and by the middle-class respondents, the differences were far less striking than those related to rank in the party (see Table 7). Thus 68 per cent of the rank and file specified

TABLE 7

Types of Problems in Breaking from Party by Echelon*
(in per cent)

	Rank and file	Low echelon	High echelon	All respondents
Serious career problems	9	25	27	23
Had to find new friends	21	40	41	32
Had to rethink values	22	32	41	29
No problems reported	68	30	28	46

* Multiple responses.

no problems in leaving the party, as compared with 28 per cent for the high-echelon and 30 per cent for the low-echelon respondents. With regard to career, friendship, and value problems, those holding office in the party (and particularly high office) reported difficulties with far greater frequency than the rank and file.

A comparison of inner party functionaries with front-organization functionaries shows a similar pattern (see Table 8). Thus 45 per cent of the central party leaders had

TABLE 8

Types of Problems in Breaking from Party for Functionaries and Non-functionaries*
(in per cent)

	Internal party functionaries	Front-organization functionaries	Non-functionaries	All respondents
Serious career problems	45	29	5	23
Had to find new friends	47	32	23	32
Had to rethink values	47	29	21	29
No problems reported	23	42	61	46

* Multiple responses.

serious career problems, as compared with 29 per cent of the front-organization functionaries and only 5 per cent for non-functionaries. The central party leaders also more frequently reported difficulties in acquiring new friends and in making ideological adjustments.

The types of problems confronting the respondents on leaving the party were also related to the kinds of needs which had been served originally by joining the party. Thus Table 9 shows that twice as many neurotic respondents as "normal"

TABLE 9

Relationship between Types of Needs Served by Joining the Party and Types of Problems in Breaking from the Party* (in per cent)

	Neurotic	Non-neurotic	All respondents
Serious career problems	25	22	23
Had to find new friends	47	22	32
Had to rethink values	33	27	29
No problems reported	42	51	46

* Multiple responses.

had difficulties in making new friends on leaving the party.

If we separate out the British-American and French-Italian cases, a number of other significant differences are brought to light (see Table 10). Thus, for the French-Italian cases, neurotics and non-neurotics appear to suffer equally from problems of career adjustment and problems of rethinking value positions. The French-Italian neurotics, however, have difficulties in reestablishing their personal relations far more frequently than the non-neurotics (41 per cent to 24 per cent). In contrast, the British-American neurotics reported difficulties in every sphere far more frequently than the non-neurotics. These findings are in general consistent with those reported in Tables 5 and 6 and tend to support the interpretation offered at that point.

Phases in the Process of Disenchantment

Leaving the party involves the rejection in whole or in part of Communist beliefs, and the adoption of other political

TABLE 10

Relationship between Types of Needs Served by Joining the Party and Types of Problems in Breaking from the Party for British-American and French-Italian Respondents*
(in per cent)

| | NEUROTIC | | NON-NEUROTIC | | |
	British-American	French-Italian	British-American	French-Italian	All respondents
Serious career problems	18	38	7	32	23
Had to find new friends	48	41	19	24	32
Had to rethink values	33	31	17	35	29
No problems reported	45	38	61	40	46

* Multiple responses.

attitudes. With regard to the first process, it would appear that a substantial proportion of persons leaving the party do not reject Communist ideology (as they perceive and understand it) in its entirety at the time of defection. These individuals go through a process of ideological disenchantment which in the extreme case may take years to complete. The respondents were asked to describe their attitudes at the point of leaving the party as well as at the time of the interview. These comparisons for the respondents as a group are reported in Table 11. A small number (7 per cent) described themselves as being still loyal to the Communist movement and doctrine at the point of leaving the party. These were mainly persons who had been expelled or resigned for some immediate or specific reason not related to loyalty to the party. Another small group (9 per cent) described themselves as loyal to the international Communist movement or the Soviet Union, but as dissatisfied with the policy and leadership of their national party. A third and larger group (24 per cent) rejected Stalinism but still professed faith in Marxism-Leninism. Many of these became Trotskyites after leaving the party. A fourth group (9 per cent) retained their Marxist faith but rejected both Leninism and Stalinism.

The largest group of all (but still less than half) rejected Marxism and revolutionary socialism at the time of leaving the party. The point ought to be made that these distinctions were not necessarily based on an explicit perception and understanding of Communist ideology and of its development from Marx through Lenin. Often the continued expression

TABLE 11

Phases in the Rejection of Communist Loyalties for All Respondents
(in per cent)

	At time of defection	At time of interview
Expelled or resigned, but still loyal	7	3
Rejection of national party, but not Soviet Union	9	3
Rejection of Stalinism, but not Marxism-Leninism	24	10
Rejection of Leninism, but not Marxism	9	10
Rejection of Marxism and revolutionary socialism	46	66
Unknown	5	8
Total	100	100

of belief in Marxism appeared to represent little more than an effort to retain something positive from what had turned out to be a costly experience.

The most typical responses involved a rejection of Stalinism, but a continued loyalty to the earlier and "purer" Communist trend, or a rejection of the ideology as a whole. Table 11 also shows that the trend among former party members after defection is to reject the ideological vestiges which they carried with them out of the party. Thus, at the time of the interview, two-thirds of the respondents had rejected the Communist ideology as a whole. Since many of these defectors were fresh out of the party, so to speak, it may very well be that the percentage of those still retaining some loyalty to Communist doctrine will continue to decline through time.

For persons whose affiliation with the party was based on a thoroughgoing indoctrination, the process of disenchantment may take a long time indeed. They may "peel off" Stalinism, Leninism, and Marxism in layers and sublayers and the whole process may involve serious study and painful analysis. This, however, is not the typical pattern. Individuals either break away from the ideology in a single jump, or experience one or two fairly brief stopovers along the line.

It is of interest that proportionately more of the French and Italian respondents still retained some vestiges of their prior indoctrination at the time they were interviewed (see Table 12). This may simply reflect the process of reassimila-

TABLE 12

*Degree of Rejection of Communist Ideology
at Time of Interview by Country*
(in per cent)

	U.S.	England	France	Italy	All respondents
Expelled or resigned, but still loyal	—	4	—	8	3
Rejection of national party, but not Soviet Union	2	6	2	2	3
Rejection of Stalinism, but not Marxism-Leninism	2	6	18	14	10
Rejection of Leninism, but not Marxism	8	8	13	14	10
Rejection of Marxism and revolutionary socialism	75	76	47	62	66
Unknown	13	—	20	—	8
Total	100	100	100	100	100

tion in the various countries. In the United States and England, Marxist socialism and non-Communist Leninism are quite minor ideological currents. On the other hand, Marxism and Leninism in a variety of forms have considerable influence outside of the Communist movements in countries such as France and Italy.

Those who joined the party in the pre-1935 period have already been described as having more frequently been indoctrinated in Marxism-Leninism-Stalinism. It also appears that the early recruits more frequently retained vestiges of their indoctrination both at the time of defection and at the time of the interview (see Table 13). Thus only 33 per cent

TABLE 13

Phases in the Rejection of Communist Loyalties by Period of Joining
(in per cent)

	EARLY JOINERS		LATE JOINERS	
	Defection	*Interview*	*Defection*	*Interview*
Expelled or resigned, but still loyal	10	3	4	2
Rejection of national party, but not Soviet Union	7	3	11	2
Rejection of Stalinism, but not Marxism-Leninism	35	15	13	3
Rejection of Leninism, but not Marxism	10	14	8	6
Rejection of Marxism and revolutionary socialism	33	55	59	78
Unknown	5	10	5	9
Total	100	100	100	100

of the early recruits rejected the entire doctrine at the time of their defection, as compared with 59 per cent among the post-1935 recruits. And at the time of their interviews only 55 per cent of the early recruits had rejected the doctrine entirely, as compared with 78 per cent for the later recruits.

The most striking findings are those related to rank in the party. The trend seems to be clear. The higher the rank, the more likely it is, in the first place, that the individual will have been exposed to the party doctrine, and that, in the second, he will retain his belief in some part or aspect of it after his defection (see Table 14). Thus, at the time of defection, 64 per cent of the high-echelon respondents still retained some degree of loyalty to the doctrine or the party, as compared with 56 per cent for the low-echelon respondents and 37 per cent for the rank and file. At the time of the interview, only 14 per cent of the rank and file continued to adhere to some aspect of their prior loyalty, as compared with 32 per cent for the low echelon and 38 per cent for the high echelon.

TABLE 14

Phases in the Rejection of Communist Loyalties by Echelon
(in per cent)

	RANK AND FILE		LOW ECHELON		HIGH ECHELON	
	Defection	*Interview*	*Defection*	*Interview*	*Defection*	*Interview*
Expelled or resigned, but still loyal	6	2	6	3	12	4
Rejection of national party, but not Soviet Union	6	—	15	7	6	2
Rejection of Stalinism not Marxism-Leninism	17	6	28	12	32	12
Rejection of Leninism, but not Marxism	8	6	7	10	14	20
Rejection of Marxism and revolutionary socialism	61	77	38	57	28	56
Unknown	2	9	6	11	8	6
Total	100	100	100	100	100	100

Political Attitudes after Defection

Because of the great publicity attending their actions, those former party members who have gone to the opposite ideological extreme have created the impression that this is a typical pattern among defectors. Actually, only a small percentage of the former party members interviewed in this study manifested this instability and extremism. For most of the respondents, membership in the party represented a learning experience. They had gone into the party with certain personal, group-related, or ideological expectations.

When they found that these expectations were not being realized, or that the costs which the party demanded were too exorbitant to accept, they left the party, but they did not radically change their goals or expectations. Most of them turned to other left-wing parties or to the trade union movement (see Table 15). Thus only 6 per cent of the defectors were either converted to or returned to religion, and most of these were "returnees" rather than converts. Only 1 per cent turned to the extreme right, and another 1 per cent turned conservative. At the time of defection, the most common political attitudes were moderate left, extreme non-Communist left (Trotskyism and the like), non-political trade unionism, and political indifference. At the time of the

TABLE 15

Phases in Political Attitudes after Leaving Party for
All Respondents
(in per cent)

	At time of defection	At time of interview
Convert or return to religion	6	6
Extreme right	1	2
Conservative	1	2
Moderate left	32	41
Extreme left	18	6
Trade union activity	12	12
Indifferent	17	18
Other	4	4
Unknown	9	9
Total	100	100

interviews, most of those who had adhered to other extreme left movements had gravitated to the moderate left. Thus, at the time of the interviews, 53 per cent of the respondents had become moderate socialists or trade unionists, 6 per cent were on the extreme left, and 18 per cent were indifferent.

It would be inaccurate to describe these defectors as in the majority contented members of the moderate left and trade union movements. Most of them expressed dissatisfaction but were unable to find anything better. Thus an American remarked, "I belong to the Liberal Party [in New York] today —with great reservations. I believe in the necessity of trade unions to develop political activity and a party, but I don't think the Liberal Party will ever come up with any great solutions. At the moment, it's the place where the unions are best represented." A Frenchman reported, "I came back to the Socialist Party, where I was received with a certain coolness. The SFIO lacked dynamism, but there was no alternative. What I am looking for now is still a synthesis of Marx and Proudhon, a policy of administrative and economic decentralization, the unity of the working class in a large trade union movement, and the idea of a federated Europe."

A comparison of the post-defection political patterns for the various countries suggests that the losses from the point of view of the democratic ideal of political participation are smallest where there is a powerful, moderate left movement, and where there is a general attitude of tolerance toward former party members. Thus the percentage of British respondents who withdrew into political apathy or non-political trade union activity was strikingly small (see Table 16). At the time of defection, more than half of the British respond-

TABLE 16

*Phases in Political Attitudes after Leaving Party
for British Respondents*
(in per cent)

	At time of defection	At time of interview
Convert or return to religion	6	8
Extreme right	—	2
Conservative	2	2
Moderate left	58	78
Extreme left	8	—
Trade union activity	6	4
Indifferent	14	4
Other	2	2
Unknown	4	—
Total	100	100

ents immediately turned to the Labor Party. Only 8 per cent turned to the extreme left, 6 per cent to a non-political trade unionism, and 14 per cent described themselves as having been indifferent. By the time of the interview, the proportion of Labor Party adherents had risen to 78 per cent, there were no adherents of extreme left movements, and the proportion of politically indifferent defectors had declined to 4 per cent. In other words, in a society in which there is a large, moderate movement representing the interests of the lower income groups, and where no extreme sanctions are imposed on former members of the Communist Party, the process of defection appears to be constructive. Such individuals are reassimilated into political society with a minimum of loss both to the individuals involved and to the society at large.

Comparisons of the patterns in the other countries are instructive. Thus, in the American case (see Table 17), at the time they were interviewed, 13 per cent of the respond-

TABLE 17

Phases in Political Attitudes after Leaving Party
for American Respondents
(in per cent)

	At time of defection	At time of interview
Convert or return to religion	3	5
Extreme right	—	5
Conservative	—	3
Moderate left	23	39
Extreme left	25	—
Trade union activity	19	15
Indifferent	11	17
Other	—	2
Unknown	19	14
Total	100	100

ents had returned to religion, turned conservative, or to the extreme right, while 32 per cent had withdrawn into simple trade union activity or complete political indifference. In view of the continuous pressure on former members of the American Communist Party and the sanctions imposed on them by the society, it is perhaps worthy of comment that relatively few of them have accepted the opportunities for a safe haven offered by the Catholic Church or anti-Communist extremism. While the cases of those who have made a profession out of their former party membership are quite prominent, our data suggest that this pattern is not by any means the typical one for former American party members. Almost all of the American respondents were "anti-Communist" at the time they were interviewed. There was a small group which described itself as "non-Communist" but not anti-Communist. Anti-Communist activity for most of the American respondents involved fighting the party in the trade unions, or taking an anti-Communist position in connection with their journalistic or other professional activities, or being opposed to Communism as private citizens.

A comparison of the political attitudes of the American respondents at the time of their defection and at the time of their interviews shows a small increase in those turning to the right-wing, and in those becoming politically apathetic. But again the proportion of those turning to the right is far smaller than might be anticipated. Adhering to the moderate left for the American cases meant joining such an organization as the Liberal Party, supporting the "New Deal" or the "Fair Deal," or participating in and supporting trade union activity.

The problem for defectors in France and Italy results not so much from the kinds of sanctions and pressures imposed upon them outside the party, as it does from the absence of an alternative to the Communist movement which is satisfactory to them. In France, the Socialist movement has been declining in strength and has not provided a militant and effective alternative to Communism. In Italy, the non-Communist Socialist movement is not only small, but splintered into several different groups. In the last election the non-Communist Socialists received under 5 per cent of the votes. At the same time, in both of these countries the very power of the Communist parties and their strong support among the working classes create anxieties and moral conflicts among defectors which often lead to political apathy (see Table 18).

TABLE 18

*Phases in Political Attitudes after Leaving Party
for French and Italian Respondents*
(in per cent)

| | FRANCE | | ITALY | |
	Defection	Interview	Defection	Interview
Convert or return to religion	6	6	8	8
Extreme right	5	5	—	—
Conservative	—	—	—	—
Moderate left	25	20	28	29
Extreme left	19	2	17	22
Trade union activity	23	24	—	2
Indifferent	4	18	41	33
Other	11	9	4	4
Unknown	7	16	2	2
Total	100	100	100	100

What is particularly striking about the French pattern is the decline in the percentage of those adhering to other extreme left movements, and the increase in those who have become politically indifferent. Some 19 per cent of the French defectors joined the Trotskyites or other extreme left-wing groups immediately after leaving the party, while at the time of their interviews only 2 per cent still remained in such organizations. On the other hand, only 4 per cent were politically indifferent immediately after leaving the party, as compared with 18 per cent at the time of their interviews.

There are two significant findings for the Italian respondents. First, a large percentage still adhere to extreme left currents—in practically all cases, the national Communist movement of Magnani and Cucchi. Second, the proportion of the politically indifferent is extraordinarily high—41 per cent at the time of defection and 33 per cent at the time of their interviews. This reflects the dilemma of the left-wing adherent in Italy who can find no effective, moderate left movement to which he can turn.

There were a number of interesting differences in post-defection political attitudes related to period of joining and social class. The percentage of early recruits who turned to other extreme left movements after leaving the party was twice as large as that of the later recruits. A larger proportion of the later recruits became politically indifferent after leaving the party. This is consistent with the pattern already established of the greater degree of political indoctrination among those who joined the party in the period before the Popular Front.

Table 19 compares the post-defection patterns for the

TABLE 19

Phases in Political Attitudes after Leaving the Party
by Social Class
(in per cent)

	MIDDLE CLASS		WORKING CLASS	
	Defection	*Interview*	*Defection*	*Interview*
Convert or return to religion	3	6	9	9
Extreme right	1	2	2	3
Conservative	1	2	—	—
Moderate left	37	43	28	39
Extreme left	22	7	14	4
Trade union activity	3	6	22	18
Indifferent	21	22	12	14
Other	—	2	8	6
Unknown	12	10	5	7
Total	100	100	100	100

middle-class and working-class respondents. A number of points call for comment. The middle-class respondents included a larger percentage of persons who turned extreme left at the time of defection, although by the time of the interview most of them had withdrawn from these movements. They also included a larger proportion of persons who became politically indifferent. The two largest categories for middle-class respondents at the time of the interview were "moderate left" and "indifferent"; for working-class respondents, "moderate left" and "trade union activity."

The post-defection political history for the three party ranks is reported in Tables 20 and 21. At the time of defec-

TABLE 20

Political Attitudes at Time of Defection by Rank
(in per cent)

	Rank and file	Low echelon	High echelon
Convert or return to religion	7	4	4
Extreme right	—	—	6
Conservative	—	1	—
Moderate left	34	33	29
Extreme left	10	26	22
Trade union activity	16	8	13
Indifferent	21	19	6
Other	2	3	10
Unknown	10	6	10
Total	100	100	100

tion extremism either of the right or the left was more characteristic of the upper-echelon respondents than of the rank and file. Thus 6 per cent of the high echelon turned to the extreme right and 22 per cent to the extreme left, as compared with none for the extreme right and 10 per cent for the extreme left for the rank and filers. Very few of the high-echelon respondents (6 per cent) became indifferent, as compared with the low echelon (19 per cent) and the rank and file (21 per cent). These data suggest that the high-echelon defector at the point of defection strives to find an alternative which will provide him with the satisfactions he had formerly received in the party. This is, of course, consistent with the findings which described the high-echelon defector as striving to preserve some part of his earlier ideological position, and as going through an extremely difficult time in breaking from the party.

At the time of the interviewing, however, most of these differences had disappeared (see Table 21). Thus the percentage of the various ranks adhering to the moderate left was roughly equal; the differences in the percentages of those adhering to the extreme left were hardly significant; and the percentages of those who were indifferent were approximately the same. In other words, the process of political readjustment begins differently for the different ranks, but appears to terminate in roughly the same way.

TABLE 21

Political Attitudes at Time of Interview by Rank
(in per cent)

	Rank and file	Low echelon	High echelon
Convert or return to religion	10	3	4
Extreme right	2	1	4
Conservative	3	—	—
Moderate left	42	41	39
Extreme left	2	10	6
Trade union activity	9	17	12
Indifferent	17	21	17
Other	4	3	6
Unknown	11	4	12
Total	100	100	100

Those who joined the party to satisfy alienative emotional needs might be expected to move to the extremes after leaving the party more frequently than the other respondents. Table 22 in general supports this hypothesis. At the time they were interviewed, 12 per cent of the emotionally maladjusted British and American respondents had either turned to religion or joined the extreme right, as compared with 8 per cent of the "normal" respondents. The comparable figures for the French and Italian respondents were 15 per cent to 5 per cent. Apathy and political indifference also represent extreme reactions away from the exceptional emphasis on politics characteristic of the Communist movement. We therefore expected a greater incidence of withdrawal from politics among the neurotic respondents. On the whole, this hypothesis is confirmed in Table 22. At the same time, a number of points may be made with regard to differences in the subsequent political behavior of the French-Italian respondents as compared with the British-American. Proportionally more of the "normal" respondents in France and Italy remained on the extreme left although out of the Communist Party, and proportionately more had withdrawn into political indifference. These contrasts are probably due to the

TABLE 22

*Political Attitudes at Time of Interview Related to
Types of Needs Served by Joining the Party*
(in per cent)

	BRITISH-AMERICAN		FRENCH-ITALIAN	
	Neurotic	*Non-neurotic*	*Neurotic*	*Non-neurotic*
Convert or return to religion	8	6	9	5
Extreme right	4	2	6	0
Conservative	2	4	0	0
Moderate left	49	65	24	26
Extreme left	0	0	3	15
Trade union activity	8	13	12	15
Indifferent	17	4	31	23
Other	1	2	9	5
Unknown	11	4	6	11
Total	100	100	100	100

political situations obtaining in France and Italy, which seem to render extremist or indifferentist reactions more understandable responses. In the absence of an effective moderate left movement, emotionally normal persons may affiliate with extreme left movements such as that of Magnani and Cucchi, or give up politics entirely as offering no satisfactory outlet for their needs.

Political Activity after Defection

In analyzing the subsequent political careers of Communist defectors we are concerned not only with their ideological transformations, but with the extent to which they have continued to be politically active. Here again, two hypotheses may be proposed: first, that the degree of political activity will be affected by the availability of satisfactory alternatives to the party; and, second, that it will be affected by the sanctions and disabilities imposed on former party members.

Table 23 describes the post-defection political activity of

TABLE 23

Degree of Present Organizational Activity by Country
(in per cent)

	U.S.	England	France	Italy	All respondents
Leader	20	22	30	15	22
Rank and file	17	68	14	28	30
Inactive	52	10	27	51	36
Unknown	11	—	29	6	12
Total	100	100	100	100	100

the various groups of national respondents. Withdrawal into political inactivity was highest among the American and Italian respondents (just as ideological indifference was most characteristic of these two groups). However, the reasons for the extremely high percentage of inactive respondents in these two countries appeared to be different. In the American cases two factors seem to have been involved. First, the high proportion of emotionally maladjusted persons among the American respondents led to a high incidence of withdrawal from politics. Second, the severe sanctions imposed on former party members in the United States led to a high rate of withdrawal in the interest of safety. Among the Italian respondents, on the other hand, and to a lesser extent among the French, the main cause of withdrawal from politics appeared to be the absence of a satisfactory political alternative. Thus an Italian respondent commented, "So far, there is no political organization now existing which satisfies me." And another Italian, "There is no reliable party in Italy. The Christian Democratic Party is ruined by the interference of the church. The Socialist Party in its three divisions represents an injurious dispersion of forces. The Republican Party and the Social Democratic Party are too divided and given to rhetoric. For men like me, the only thing to do is to keep to myself in the hope that one day a party may rise which works for the interests of Italians and not for foreigners, and which may draw real profit from the tragic experience of the last thirty years of Italian history."

The effect of outside pressure on the political activity of former party members in the United States is illustrated by the comment of a former trade union leader: "At the present time I am applying for a good job in a non-union plant. The local people want to hire me, but the home office is against me because I was once the business agent of a Communist-dominated union. I've told them I would even fight attempts to unionize the company, but they are not sure about trusting me." Other American respondents reported that they dreaded any publicity, since their employment was dependent on keeping their former affiliations quiet. Thus one American said, "People still have me pegged as a Communist. They don't remember my later history. I only have a job now because my boss is a liberal. If I got any publicity he'd have to drop me."

A comparison of the degree of present organizational activity characteristic of the various ranks among the respondents shows that a high-echelon defector is more likely to move into a position of organizational leadership than are the other ranks. The type of leadership involved in most cases is in trade unions and other movements of the moderate or extreme left.

The proportion of middle-class defectors who became politically inactive was higher (41 per cent) than that of the working class (30 per cent). This difference was especially marked among the American respondents. Thus, of the 34 American middle-class and intellectual respondents, 22 were politically inactive after leaving the party, as compared with 11 out of 30 for the American working-class respondents. This higher incidence of political withdrawal among the middle-class and intellectual respondents, and the especially high incidence among the Americans, is probably due to the fact that a substantial proportion of this group joined the party as a means of coping with emotional maladjustments. Their disillusionment with the party was often associated with a general disillusionment with politics. At the same time, it is probably true that the sanctions which have been imposed on American intellectuals for having been party members, or the sanctions which threaten them should their former affiliation became public knowledge, are greater for them than for the working-class group. Former party membership may result in disqualification from public employment. It also tends to reduce the potential employment market in journalism, the entertainment professions, and academic life. Hence, the inescapable publicity associated with political activity may be particularly avoided by former Communist intellectuals in the United States.

This analysis of the process of defection provides us with a number of clues to the kinds of motives and needs which are characteristic of those who still remain in the Communist movement. We may suggest by way of hypothesis that those who have difficulties in leaving the party, those who go through long and painful periods of readjustment, are more like those who remain in the party than are the ones for whom exit is easy.

The foregoing analysis has shown a clear relationship between degree of commitment to the party and difficulties in defection. Hence we may propose the rather obvious hypothesis that the most deeply committed Communists—those who have had long tenure, those who have become functionaries (particularly those who hold high rank in the inner party apparatus), and those who have all their personal relationships in the party—are the most loyal party adherents. Those who are less committed in these senses are more susceptible to defection.

This factor affecting loyalty to the party cuts across national and class lines. It is as much true for the American and British parties as it is for the French and Italian. In other respects, the bases of loyalty to the British-American and French-Italian parties differ. Among the British-American respondents, persons who were satisfying neurotic needs had difficulties in leaving the party far more frequently than those who were not. Hence we may propose the hypothesis that neurotics are more likely to remain in the British and American parties than are the non-neurotics. In the American case, the heavy sanctions imposed on former party members are a factor creating difficulties in defection. This suggests the general hypothesis that those who remain in the British and American parties are the deeply committed, in the sense of career, personal relations, and ideological interests; those whose neurotic needs cannot be satisfied as adequately elsewhere; and, in the American case, those fearful of punishment for former party membership. Needless to say, these categories overlap.

In the French and Italian cases, one would also expect to find a connection between depth of commitment and degree of loyalty to the party, as well as a connection between neurotic needs and loyalty, although the proportion of emotionally disturbed persons in the French and Italian parties is far smaller than in the British and American. What is distinctive in the French and Italian parties, and not present in the British and American, is a large stratum, the loyalty of which is based on what appear to be realistic appraisals of the political situation.

Thus, while Communism in the United States and England may be viewed as an aberration, in France and Italy it takes on the proportions of a sub-culture. The Communist movement has adapted its appeals to the aspirations of those strata which have been historically alienated from French and Italian society, and has gained control over their communications and organizations. In this way, it controls the picture of reality to which the working class and other elements are exposed, and manipulates this picture in such a manner as to deepen their sense of alienation and destroy all hopes for constructive change within the framework of the existing political and social systems.

CHAPTER 13

CONCLUSIONS AND IMPLICATIONS

THE FINDINGS of this study may perhaps be most appropriately drawn together and summarized around two organizing themes: first, how shall we appraise the ethical significance of the Communist movement? and, second, what kinds of policies and actions are likely to be effective in dealing with it?

It is one of the obligations of the scientific calling that, while ethical impulses may affect the selection of a problem and the purposes for which the findings are used, they may not enter into the scientific process—that is, affect the methods of research or the findings themselves. Persons who are unfamiliar with the scientific discipline or who find its requirements uncongenial often assume that this ethical neutrality of the scientific process reflects a general ethical neutrality in those who carry on the work of science. Certainly, for the social sciences nothing could be further from the truth. Indeed, a kind of moral fatigue results from the sustained investigation of a problem such as the present one, which is full of human meaning and significance, and in which ethical and political digressions have, so to speak, been prohibited. Hence we turn to these aspects of the appeals of Communism with feelings of grateful release.

An Ethical Appreciation

It is one of the uglier ironies of history that the Communist movement, which first took fire as a protest against the evils of the nineteenth century, should have itself become the greatest evil of the twentieth. The history of Communism may be told in terms of the degeneration of its political ethics. In Marx the ethical good was reduced to conformity to the historical process. The Marxist vision of the historical process was one in which the good triumphed at the culmination of a great conflict involving heavy but unavoidable costs. The problem of ethical conduct was reduced to divining the stage of historical development at any given period and acting accordingly.

Nevertheless, in the original prophecy of Marxism human action was placed in an historical-ethical structure, so that costs appeared to bear some proportionate relationship to the end to be attained. The ultimate good was the classless society, a state of man in which all evil had finally been brought to bay. Intermediate to this ultimate end was the dictatorship of the proletariat, a condition in which the mature and organized working class seized political power and destroyed the repressive and inhibiting institutions of the era of capitalism. The concept of the "party" as an instrumentality in this ethical system was barely differentiated from the more general concept of the proletariat. It was that part of the proletariat which brought the mass to the stage of understanding its appropriate role in the historical process. It consisted of the guiders and clarifiers, who took specific grievances and dissatisfactions and placed them in the setting of historical development, gave them their "true" significance, and thereby made it possible to lay out the appropriate course of action which simultaneously fulfilled the requirements of expediency and of ethical propriety.

In Marxism the conception of the means to be employed in attaining these intermediate and ultimate ends was, compared to the later transformations, proportionate. In the phase before the dictatorship of the proletariat, education and organization were to produce the mature working class capable of seizing power. The actual seizure of power was to occur only when the full obsolescence of the capitalist class had become manifest, and when the proletariat had become fully conscious of its destiny. The decision to employ violent means was to be that of a great majority whose action would be proportionate to its own suffering, to the oppressive aims and practices of its antagonists, and to the awesome ethical promise of the future.

This was the ideological mixture which confronted Lenin and his associates in the early days of Russian social democracy. The Western European socialists concentrated their efforts on education and organization, and awaited the imminent collapse of capitalism by virtue of its "inherent contradictions" and the maturation of the working class before proceeding to the dangerous and ethically problematic employment of revolutionary measures. In Czarist Russia a gradual maturation of the working class through trade union and political organization and peaceful persuasion seemed to be precluded. The leaders of Russian social democracy were therefore confronted by the dilemma of employing ethically and ideologically questionable means which might create the basis for a seizure of power, or of avoiding such means and postponing effective political competition until conditions were more suitable. As a result, two versions of Marxism embodying these alternatives—Leninism and moderate social democracy—emerged in Russia. Animated by the spirit of Russian "nihilism," the Leninists selected the more extreme alternative, and proceeded to adapt Marxist doctrine to the consequences of this decision. The moderate group took the line of the Western European Social Democrats, entered into alliances with middle-class liberals and constitutionalists, and concentrated on the prior establishment of parliamentary institutions in Russia.

What emerged from the development of Leninism was a politico-ethical system vastly different from that of Marx. If in Marx there was some distribution of emphasis on ultimate ends, intermediate ends, and means, and an insistence on a measure of ethical proportionality and interdependence, all of Lenin's efforts were focused at the point of means and intermediate ends. The conception of the party as a guider and clarifier of the proletariat became in Lenin a closed movement of revolutionary conspirators "agitating" among and manipulating the proletariat or any other group which it could control. Instead of a relatively open association of activists, it became a highly centralized apparatus with a general staff enjoying imperative powers. While in the social democratic movements of Western Europe there was a greater opportunity for the individual parties, and even in considerable measure for the individual members, to make an independent reading of the doctrine and to form their own interpretations of the stage of historical development, in Leninism the party, and ultimately the Russian party, emerged as the ethical center and set itself up as "history's church" with a monopoly of interpretation.

Similarly, in Marx there was much emphasis on the phasing of revolutionary development. The working class had to become politically mature and conscious before it was to seize power. The capitalist system was to reach its end point of development, in which the middle class had become "proletarianized" and the instruments of production monopolized by a few, before the oppressive institutions of the bourgeois state were to be supplanted by the proletarian dictatorship. This emphasis on the appropriateness of action to the phases of the process set up ethical restrictions on the employment of dangerous and costly means. In Lenin this ethical phasing of the revolutionary process was for all practical purposes eliminated, and in its place he developed the doctrine of the "objective and subjective revolutionary situation." In simple summary, this doctrine meant that it was proper to employ violent means once the party had reached a high state of effectiveness on the one hand, and when the objective situation was ripe for revolution on the other. Ethically dangerous means could be employed whenever they had a good prospect of being effective. Indeed, in Lenin this readiness to employ dangerous means took the form of an explicit doctrine that heavy costs, and specifically heavy moral costs, were to be freely incurred without question-begging scruples. It was conscience, rather, that was the evil force that stood in the way of full commitment to the party and its ultimate ethical mission.

In Stalinism these tendencies were brought to their full fruition. The ultimate ends of Marxism—the final emancipation of the human race—fully emerged with all the characteristics of an eschatology, a doctrine of final things which would appear at the end of history. The doctrines of the dictatorship of the proletariat and of the guiding and clarifying party of the working class became verbal rituals, sacred words and phrases, which could be invoked to grant the color of legitimacy and a spurious moral order to the sordid work of conspirators and specialists in human manipulation. Stalin perfected the party as a weapon first by establishing complete domination over the Russian apparatus, and then by establishing control over the international Communist movement. Espionage, terror, propaganda, organization, and diplomacy reached a high level of virtuosity, and were carried on with a keen sense of their properties and interdependence, with the massive and unrelenting purpose of maximizing power and destroying alternatives. Even Lenin's signal for the seizure of power—the existence of objective and subjective revolutionary situations—was set aside, once the movement had acquired sufficient military power to bid for control through direct military action or its threat.

Today, with Communism in control of almost half the world, the lofty aspirations of Marxism are more remote than they have ever been. Instead of making dignified and free men out of the humiliated and the degraded, Communism has devised and developed into high arts many new and more crushing modes of humiliation. The vision of the final release of human spontaneity has been supplanted by the reality of apathy and automatism.

This is not the first occasion in history in which a movement purporting to seek the highest humane ends has in fact achieved their obverse. As Max Weber pointed out many years ago in his classic analysis of the relationships between politics and ethics, any advocate of fundamental human and social reconstruction must make a hard choice if he is to avoid the most serious distortion of his purposes. If he operates outside the framework of politics and influences his fellow men through sermons and exemplary behavior, he limits his effectiveness but he keeps his ethical mission pure. This is true, for example, of integral pacifists, who despite their ineffectiveness are often impressive because of the dignity and genuineness of their faith. Once involved in the struggle for political power, the ethical absolutist is confronted by the most serious temptation. Here in politics he has an instrumentality of enormous and problematic force. Is it not possible that by striking one blow, so to speak, he can hit an ethical jackpot which will in retrospect make these costs seem trivial and bring the worlds of aspiration and reality once and for all together? The socialists confronted this temptation and indefinitely postponed their decision. They could not avoid the anguish and guilt which always arises when there are serious discrepancies between an absolute calling and the mixed choices of the market place. But if they did not save the world, they at least saved their souls. The Leninists seized this temptation and let loose forces which swept them beyond humane anchorage.

It is certainly plausible to argue that the Communist movement will not survive the patient erosion of history in its present form. No movement ever has, and we have already seen how Marxism has been twisted out of all recognition in the course of a few generations. But there are several reasons why the counsel of historical analogy may be seriously misleading. In the first place, it is impossible to determine through historical comparison in what stage of its development a contemporary movement may happen to be. Has it reached its extreme limit of expansion, and is it about to recede? Or is it still in the stage of expansion? The philosopher of history can only say that it is in the nature of movements to expand and recede, to concentrate and to disintegrate; but it is precisely at those points at which historical analogy fails to guide us that all significant policy problems have to be solved. It is the extent of the expansion, the degree of concentration, the timing of the recession and disintegration, and what happens to mankind and its institutions in the course of these processes, that is humanly important and that sets the problem for policy decisions. Secondly, while all revolutionary movements have common elements and patterns, they differ from one another in their purposes, in the means which they have at their disposal, and in the spirit in which they employ these means to accomplish their purposes. While there have been other movements which have sought world dominion, Communism poses a danger which is perhaps unique in its gravity if its entire means-ends system is viewed as a whole. It seeks universal power unequivocally, it possesses an arsenal of means perhaps without parallel in history for its coerciveness and capacity to penetrate and mobilize, its versatility in the employment of means is of a very high order, and it is unencumbered by hampering moral inhibitions and conflicts.

Such a pure and unequivocal power orientation leaves most of us with feelings of disbelief and wonder. How do Communists themselves mitigate their ethical position? What ingredients are added to make lives of dedicated ruthlessness bearable? For it is quite apparent that, far from admitting to purposeless power-striving, Communists portray themselves as being animated by the highest ethical mission.

The ethical mitigation and rationalization of Communism has a number of distinct components which are distributed differently among the various party strata and, for that matter, within each individual member. If we take the great majority of the party rank and file and the larger number of party sympathizers—the exoteric Communists, in other words—it is quite evident that the party has a far different meaning for them than it has for the full initiates. For the simple peasant or workman who belongs to a party cell, the party signifies a purposeful community devoted to combating the many grievances of his difficult life. The party supplies him with a system of political perception and a closed system of communication which on the one hand constantly enforces an ethical interpretation on the actions of the Communist movement, and on the other constantly magnifies the evils of the world outside. Thus, for him, membership in the party has an ethical appropriateness at a rather simple level. He is employing effective means in the struggle against immediate evil which he knows from intimate experience. Since his capacity for understanding causation is most limited, he is quite free to attribute those evils which he knows to forces which he does not know, such as "capitalism," "American imperialism," and the like.

For the esoteric party member the problem of ethical mitigation is far more complex. He is a Communist "actor." If he is an intellectual, he often lies grossly and cannot escape knowing it because of the magnitude of the distortions he is required to produce. If he participates in a political trial, he manufactures evidence and bears false witness. If he is a party functionary, he must instigate, engage in, or condone, acts of brutality. He is initiated into the Communist system of action and it is more difficult for him to evade feelings of wickedness and fears of retribution. Although the doses vary from case to case, the ingredients from which he fashions his system of ethical mitigation would appear to be the following.

Even though the ultimate ends of Marxism-Leninism have lost all real connection with Communist practice, the Communist eschatology plays a role of considerable importance in this process of ethical mitigation. There is of course much controversy as to whether the fully initiated Communist really believes in his own ideology. Perhaps the problem has been put incorrectly. We do not have to choose between full and implicit ideological faith on the one hand and complete cynicism on the other. In this regard Communists may not be significantly different from the members of religious communities. A Communist may be the simple and pious believer who in anticipation of the imminent "coming" withdraws from the world and prepares his soul for the next. Certainly there are Communists for whom the Marxist-Leninist vision of the blessed promise of the future has more reality than the world in which they live. Or he may be the cynic for whom the eschatology performs a purely instrumental function in moments of great trial, when a reading of the "book," or a repetition of sacred formulae, provides something akin to the consolations of the host, the lighting of a sacred candle, the making of familiar and comforting signs. For it has to be remembered that the Communist has systematically destroyed for himself all other guides to conduct and to the future. And if he fully roots out his belief in his ideology, he is left with no ethics at all, haunted by the purposeless suffering of his victims and the meaningless distortion of his own character.

Actually, the Communist eschatology is a somewhat complex system and certain protections have been built in to safe-guard initiates from the dangers of disbelief. The ultimate end of Communism—the classless society—has always been vague and remote. Belief in "the party," belief in its un-ambiguous goodness and wisdom, and particularly belief in the leadership of the Russian party and in the legitimacy of the Marx-Engels-Lenin-Stalin succession is the core of the Communist faith. The "goodness" of the party results from the fact that it is the sole avenue to the ultimate good society. And the faithful party member never makes independent appraisals of the conduct of the party, since he possesses no definite criteria as to the content of the ultimate society or directions as to how to get there. What sustains the fully initiated Communist, then, is his abiding faith in the party, which in principle is incapable of evil.

This leads to the second component in the ethical mitiga-tion of Communist action, the cultivation of what we may call the tactical virtues. Since the party is the sole vehicle of the good, fulfillment of its directives is the path of virtue. For a fully committed Communist, lying, misrepresentation, and brutal actions, if done in the service of the party, are the ful-fillment of ethical obligation, mere incidents on the road to salvation. In principle, the Communist gives up his claim to judgment of the ways in which the party seeks the good. Rather, it is his task to carry forward soberly, cultivate the virtues of loyalty and obedience, and be tireless in the conduct of the party's work. In organizing his life routine around this pattern the Communist may enjoy the satisfactions of success and virtuosity which rest on the proper fulfillment of party directives. Recruiting a new member, organizing a new cell, leading a demonstration, selling a Communist periodical, or even turning in a bit of useful military information, effec-tively carrying off an act of sabotage, reporting on the devia-tions of a wayward member, or confessing one's own sinful doubts—all are acts of piety to be laid before the source of all good.

If it is still difficult to conceive how the initiated Com-munist is able to dedicate himself to the destruction of hu-

mane culture and at the same time sustain a sense of right-
eousness, then perhaps the remaining elements in this ethical
mitigation may make it plausible. The fully committed Communist lives in a closed world of perception and communication. He is meaningfully exposed only to the "good word"
emanating from party sources. So deep has been his indoctrination that even when in service on a foreign mission, he
carries a screening system with him which protects him from
effective exposure to outside influence. One of the most characteristic features of this system of communication is the
massive portrayal of the world outside as unambiguously
evil. It is a world which exploits, crushes, deceives, and
oppresses. It is a world of evil which never sleeps. This vision
of the unrelieved wickedness of the world outside justifies
ruthlessness and legitimates costly sacrifices, just as ruses
and deceptions, executions and decimation, are justified in
the awful rigors of war.

The final component in this ethical rationalization is the
dreadful consequences of disbelief. The dedicated Communist
has made his life in the party. To be cut off from the party
is to lose all contact with meaning and purpose. Even if he no
longer believes in the party, how can he believe in a world
which he has dishonored and defamed? Certainly, a powerful
mechanism protects him as whispers of doubt trouble his sleep
or as his hand falters in the conduct of his work. If he falls
from grace, he may prefer to offer up his life in penitence,
like the dishonored officer who asks to be sent to the front
lines rather than face a life outside without uniform and without the solidarity of his comrades-in-arms. Because of the
dangers of disbelief, the fully initiated Communist clings to
the party even though he is deeply troubled by its actions. He
escapes from these risks by taking cover within the party's
system of ethical and political perception, rejoices in the
enormity of the evils in the world outside since it renders
more bearable the evils of his own, fingers his ideological
beads, and walks forward soberly cultivating the tactical
virtues.

Types of Communist Movements

The foregoing is a crudely sketched ethical portrait of the esoteric, the inner Communist, who is to be found in the upper echelons of the various Communist parties. Our findings have shown that there are other types of Communists than this, and that there are different types of Communist parties. A policy which fails to take these peculiarities and differences into account, which approaches all Communist movements and all Communists as though they were identical, is bound to make serious mistakes.

Thus it is clear that the British and American Communist parties stand in the sharpest contrast to those of France and Italy. The British and American parties are "deviational." They may be understood in part as movements into which some of the disruptive tendencies of the larger society drain off. They do not touch the real fiber of the British and American societies. Communists may infiltrate other movements such as trade unions, or "capture key points" by such means as placing agents in sensitive jobs, but there is no mass susceptibility to Communism in Britain and the United States. The Communist parties of France and Italy, on the other hand, fulfill political needs, needs for protest against an inequitable distribution of values and stalemated societies which offer no promise of future improvement, needs which are not embraced by any other powerful and militant political movement. For the French and Italian working class and for considerable elements among the peasantry, the exoteric appeals of Communism are bound to have continued resonance.

The "People's Liberation" movements of the underdeveloped areas represent a third type of Communist Party which is even more threatening than the continental European variety. For here the Communist movements can not only draw upon social and economic grievances of a serious order, but can appeal to feelings of patriotism and nationalism, and to deep-seated and bitter anti-white, anti-"Western imperialism" feelings among all elements in the population. Here class, national, and ethnic protest meet in a situation which is peculiarly susceptible to violence and to civil war.

Thus we may describe the various types of Communist parties in terms of the kinds of alienations which have contributed to them, and appraise their potentialities according to the extent to which these alienations are distributed throughout the society. In England and the United States, the kinds of alienations which appear to have fed the Communist movements were those incidental to the acculturation of certain ethnic groups, the essentially private alienations of broken families and unhappy childhoods, or the temporary alienations of economic and political crisis. In France and Italy, we are dealing with societies which have failed to relate large elements of the population to dignity and meaning, and where the Communist parties draw upon historically endemic feelings of estrangement and hopelessness among certain social groupings. In Southeast Asia, and potentially in the Middle East, in addition to the estrangements of class and status, there are the alienations of race, of ethnic and cultural discrimination, which build up a potential that is frightening in its scope and intensity. The Communist movement draws the destructive energies and the desperate impatience from all of these varieties of protest and resentment and harnesses them in the service of a controlled and comprehensive destructiveness. Thus there are met in this movement all the alienations of man, rushing from many and unlike tributaries into a torrent of wrath without end.

Policy in England and the United States

While the problem of Communism in the United States is hardly more serious than it is in England, the policy approaches of the two countries radically differ. In both countries the threat is of espionage, sabotage, and infiltration and not of a mass electoral appeal. Furthermore, while the threat of espionage and sabotage is still significant, the threat of infiltration has substantially subsided. This is not to say that there are no Communist-controlled unions in England and the United States. But the number of unions under such control has declined, and the Communist "colonists" in those that remain under party control have to operate under considerable publicity, which limits their freedom of action.

The main defense against espionage and sabotage is vigilant and effective police action. Certainly a general public awareness of the nature and threat of Communism is essential as well, and there can be little question that it is a responsibility of the political organs of the State to alert the public to the danger. What is involved in the activities of the various Congressional investigating committees in the United States can hardly be confused with responsible political leadership in regard to this problem. To spread the impression that Communism has made substantial inroads into American society is to create a massive diversion from the real issues and problems of our time. For the Communist threat is only a very minor one in the United States. It is a genuine threat outside this country and particularly in the "uncommitted" areas of the Middle and Far East. Furthermore, the task of combating Communism is a slow, risky, and costly one. The activities of these Congressional investigating committees have the effect of locating the threat incorrectly and oversimplifying its nature.

The harm to American interests resulting from this approach to policy consists not only in this diversion of attention, but in the impairment of trust and confidence among the American people, to say nothing of the serious impairment of American prestige abroad. It undermines the foreign policy consensus which has united the major elements of both the Democratic and Republican parties and which have made possible the many successes of American foreign policy in the postwar period. In fact, this particular brand of anti-Communism appears to be little more than a new face for the older pattern of nationalism and isolationism. What makes it a grave threat is that this form of nationalism has access to some of the powers of the Congress, and is pressing the executive to follow a similar course.

But the danger is perhaps more significant in its moral than in its political aspects. What we are defending against the nihilistic threat of Communism is the humane and libertarian tradition of the West. There is nothing more precious or more central to this tradition than the attitude toward the individual implied in Christianity and the protections to human dignity in the common law and in the practices of democracy. If we turn against these, we have literally nothing left save wealth and power; and, left with these, the nightmares of our friends abroad that there may be no choice between West and East will have come close to reality.

In a number of respects, American policies and actions toward domestic Communism in the last few years represent flagrant violations of this tradition. Treating the former party member as though he could never purge himself of his former associations, or setting up as a condition of becoming purged acceptance of the status of a fully compliant committee witness, is one such violation. Denying the privilege of government employment to former party members, or to persons who have been members of "front" organizations, is another illustration of a violation of both our legal and religious tradition. To view all party members as equal participants in the Communist conspiracy is to fly in the face of fact. It has generally been the case that only a minority of the party membership is fully aware of the integral power orientation of the party and of its relation to the Soviet Union. The rest of the party are dupes or half dupes. Finally, the penalties imposed for error and self-deception ought not to be the same as the penalties imposed for disloyalty and treason. Our traditions require far greater discrimination in the attribution of guilt and far greater readiness for forgiveness than our actions have reflected.

The approach to the Communist problem in England is quite different. The internal threat of Communism has not been magnified, nor have heavy sanctions been imposed on persons who are or have been party members. Despite this moderation in British policy toward Communism, it does not appear that the British security record is any worse than that of the United States, nor does it appear that the British Communist Party has been more successful than the American in holding its members and infiltrating trade unions. We may therefore legitimately ask whether the moral and political costs which have attended many of the actions taken against Communists and former Communists in the United States in the last few years have been incurred without any significant gains in internal security.

These differences in policy approach in England and in the United States appear to be due to a number of factors. The entire Communist experience in England seems to be a milder, less malignant phenomenon than is true of the United States. Joining the British party does not ordinarily involve as grave an act of deviation as is the case in this country. The British party has been far less Bolshevik than the American. In general, the "moderateness" of the British party as well as of British policy toward the party reflects a general society confident of its solidarity, ready to tolerate deviance because it is basically secure. The American party and American policy toward Communism, on the other hand, reflect a society in which fundamental trust is still lacking, a society in which deviation is feared because the general social consensus itself is insecure. One of the consequences of a "melting pot" society is that it takes generations before the various ingredients are assimilated to one another. Until the time that a stable amalgam is reached, uneasiness and distrust are inescapable. In the American system of decentralized politics and mass communication these divisive potentialities can be readily played upon and given proportions far more frightening than the actual situation would warrant.

Policy toward French and Italian Communism

It was our expectation in the early years of the Truman Doctrine and the Marshall Plan that if economic conditions in such countries as France and Italy were to improve, the appeal of Communism would subside and the threat of subversion be averted. But as Communist policy in Europe grew more aggressive, it became obvious that a general political stabilization in this area required not only economic security, but military security as well. Thus the United States backed the North Atlantic Treaty, the military aid program, and measures of economic, military, and political integration in Western Europe, all designed to increase the real security in the area and to provide the kind of psychological security which might abate the Communist pressure in France and Italy.

All of these policies have been of some effect, but they have not seriously weakened the positions of the French and Italian Communist parties. They still can mount serious electoral threats, and are in actual political control on a local scale in certain areas. They constitute the strongest and most effectively organized political movements in these countries, and they are in full control of the most powerful trade unions and trade union confederations. They have a large press and periodical literature of their own, and are able to blanket their members and sympathizers within their own communications system. In effect, the Communist parties of France and Italy hold these two countries in a state of political siege. By dominating on the left and forcing governments to operate on the basis of heterogeneous and unstable coalitions, they prevent the development of an effective and dynamic policy. The Communist parties of France and Italy do not have to seize power in order to be successful. Simply by preventing the development of economic and political stability they have been enormously useful to Russian foreign policy. American efforts in these areas have merely contributed to holding the line, preventing a more serious deterioration than would otherwise have occurred.

On the whole, this must be counted as a serious failure of American foreign policy. Western Europe is not only an area of the greatest strategic importance, but also the arena in which a significant victory may be won against Communism without threatening the peace. If the position of the Communist parties in the electoral process and in the trade union movements of France and Italy were to be destroyed, a "roll-back" of Communist power would have begun which might have repercussions elsewhere. One might say that while the liberation of Eastern Europe is both risky and highly doubtful, liberation of Western Europe from Communist infiltration is both possible and less attended by risk.

One of the mistakes of American policy in Western Europe was the expectation that economic aid would by itself lessen the appeal of Communism. What we neglected to consider was the fact that the appeal of Communism in France and Italy is based not so much on the absolute standard of living of the working classes and peasantry, but on the great discrepancies between the share of income going to these groups as compared with that going to other groups in the population. Thus the problem in these countries results at least as much from the way rewards are distributed as from the absolute amounts available for distribution.

Even the language used in official statements about the Communist threat in Western Europe reflects this misconception of the factors responsible for the success of Communism. The Communism of these areas has often been referred to as "stomach" Communism. If one has to locate it in an organ of the body, it would be more appropriate to call it "heart" Communism, since what is involved in most cases is not so much hunger, as feelings of rejection and neglect at the hands of a society which gives everything to some and very little to the rest.

The working classes of France and Italy have not been well served historically by political and social movements capable of waging an effective fight in their interests. Both the trade unions and the left political parties have tended to assert general revolutionary objectives rather than bargain for the immediate interests of their clienteles. The Communist parties of France and Italy have moved into these situations and occupied the commanding positions on the left. They have no intention of using these positions as a means of improving the condition of the working class, or of the poor peasantry, but merely wish to deny them to other leaderships and organizations and prevent the effective integration of these groupings into the general society.

Thus the problem of combating Communism in France and Italy is in large part a problem of political organization and tactics. While this is not the place for a detailed elaboration of tactics, the findings of this study suggest some of the specifications for an alternative to Communism in these countries. What most of the French and Italian respondents wanted when they withdrew from the party was a militant left movement. They rejected the authoritarianism of the Communist Party, its rigid discipline, its manipulative features, its control by the Soviet Union. But they still wanted a militant party which would fight effectively for the interests of the working class and of the poorer classes generally. In both France and Italy, the Socialist movements were viewed as too weak, ineffective, and splintered to provide such an alternative. Despite this dissatisfaction, however, the parties to which the largest proportion of defectors turned were these Socialist movements.

They did not turn to the church or to church-related movements in any significant numbers. This is a point of considerable importance, since there has been much emphasis on the role of the church as a means of combating Communism on the European continent. There can be no doubt that in a crisis the church can be a most effective mobilizer of non-Communist and anti-Communist feeling. There can also be little question that the church can regain some of the ground which it has lost among the working classes and peasantries in France and Italy, but its success is largely dependent on the responsiveness of the church and of church-influenced movements to the real distress and needs of these groups. However, the church and the political movements associated with it do not appear to provide an alternative for the great bulk of the party members and sympathizers in France and Italy. They are deeply anticlerical and rationalistic in their orientation. When they leave the party, they seek not only for a militant, left movement, but for an anticlerical movement as well.

Indeed, a good case may be made for the position that the church would be far more effective as an anti-Communist force by withdrawing from politics and from government protection and subsidy. In both France and Italy there are left Catholic tendencies organized in Catholic labor groups and in the Christian parties. On all issues save those relating to the position of the church, these groups have more in common with the Socialists than they have with the right wings of the Christian parties. If the church were to follow the injunction of Lammenais and give up its privileges and protected position and really rest itself on the voluntary and spontaneous support of the people, the ugly issues of clericalism and anticlericalism might be removed from politics, and a healthy coalescence of like-minded political groups take place. This might mean the emergence of a broad non-Communist movement on the left capable of exercising a gravitational influence and pulling from the Communist parties and the Communist-dominated trade unions the many disillusioned workers and intellectuals who are loyal to the party only because of the absence of an effective alternative.

In considering the tactics of developing such a militant left movement one has to be aware of the kinds of needs and interests which the Communist Party satisfies at the grass-roots level, for it is through these needs and interests that a sound anti-Communist tactic may be devised. At the local level, the Communist Party appears to the rank-and-file members in the form of a "cell" and a local trade union headquarters. Both of these provide not only a sense of political significance and dignity at a very decentralized level, but combine these interests with convivial and recreational possibilities. Any effort to weaken the Communist movements in France and Italy will have to approach the working class and the poor peasantry on the same kind of basis. It will have to appeal to their real grievances, provide effective organization and militance, and in addition offer the attractions of conviviality and comradely association to groups of the population which ordinarily lack these opportunities. A campaign of organization at the grass-roots level in France and Italy, adequately financed and courageously and intelligently directed, may succeed in shaking the hold of the Communist movement in these areas.

For obvious reasons, this is not a campaign for the United

States government to undertake. To inspire confidence the main leadership must come from the peoples of these countries themselves. However, such a movement can be sparked, and financed, and advised by the powerful free trade union movements of the United States, England, and the European continent. Such a campaign would constitute political warfare properly conducted in an area where the gains might be great and the risks relatively low. It is not a campaign likely to produce immediate large-scale results. In its beginning phases it would have to select favorable situations and plan careful local campaigns. With time and success, the scope of the campaign might broaden and acquire an increasing momentum.

Echelon and Reliability

The findings of this study have provided us with a set of hypotheses as to the reliability of different types of party members, and the conditions which are likely to put their loyalty to the party under strain. Thus we have observed significant differences between the higher and lower ranks, and the inner and "front organization" functionaries. Most reliable of all are the high-echelon, inner party functionaries, the "upper inside" of the party leadership. The career profiles of these respondents suggest that the high-echelon Communist is a conformist and not a deviant. More often than not, he comes from a left-wing family or community in which socialism and Marxism were taken for granted. He also is likely to have come from a non-religious or anticlerical background, which simplifies his problem of assimilating to the party. More often than not, he comes from a family which has suffered some social damage. His father may have been killed or wounded in war; the family may have suffered seriously as a consequence of a depression or a labor dispute. Thus, more frequently than the other ranks, the high-echelon functionary has a sense of objective grievance. He joins the party young, before he has assumed any other commitments, comes in with positive momentum, commits himself deeply, makes his living in the party, marries and has his children in it, has no friends outside of it. In short, he makes his life in the party.

The high-echelon functionary rarely leaves the party; he is expelled. He may be expelled because he is on the losing side of a dispute, or because at the time of a change in party line he jumped the wrong way. Or he may have begun to have difficulty in carrying out party orders and to show signs of dragging his feet. Once expelled, the high-echelon functionary appears to go one of three ways. He may join or form a dissident Communist movement. He may go through a slow and painful process of disenchantment and end up in the trade union movement, or become politically indifferent. Or (and this is a rare eventuality) he may join the extreme right, or become a Catholic, or both.

In general, the rate of attrition of high-echelon party leaders is high at times of changes in the party line, when party leaders may make wrong guesses and pick the wrong side. Hence any actions which force the party to shift its position, particularly if the circumstances are unfavorable and the party is on the defensive, may have the effect of producing conflicts and expulsions among the top party leadership.

The party leadership which controls the trade unions and other front organizations has a kind of dual position and dual loyalty, and hence is inherently less reliable than the upper inside leadership. But much will depend on the extent of infiltration of the front organization by the party—for example, on the extent to which the party controls the trade union apparatus, and hence can determine the choice of the top trade union leaders. To the extent that there are other power groups in the trade union, the party trade union leader may be in a position to bargain with the party, and in the event of a showdown to fight the party and continue in control of the union. The consequences of his defection from the party are likely to be less severe than in the case of the inner party functionary. He need not feel that he is turning against his only loyalty. He chooses between loyalties and can satisfy his conscience that his action has an ethical justification. Thus there may be in his case a congenial confluence of interest, power, and ethical justification which facilitates a smooth exit from the party.

But this should not lead us into a false optimism as to the vulnerability of the party at this point of juncture with its front and mass organizations. If one compares the combat effectiveness of the party organization with that of the mass organizations which it controls, it is quite evident that only an extraordinary effort can dislodge the control of the party over a mass organization, once it has succeeded in infiltrating it. American trade union experience in the last decade shows that only a well-organized, tactically skilled, and thoroughly dedicated group can compete successfully against a Communist trade union fraction. When such a group has been formed and actually appears to be winning the battle, some of the Communist trade union leaders seem to be ready to leave the party. Or, to put it in another way, when it appears probable that the union is to be withdrawn from party control, certain of the Communist union leaders will follow the union rather than the party. Thus, once a Communist fraction in a union or other front organization is effectively engaged in battle, one can legitimately anticipate a measure of attrition among the front organization functionaries. Indeed, it may be possible to increase the rate of attrition through offers of refuge and "safe conduct."

So much for the reliability of the "commissioned officers" of the party, those who command the party itself, as well as those who command the auxiliary formations. If we follow the Stalinist military language, what of the reliability of the cadres, of the non-commissioned officers, the cell, branch, and section leaders which we have described as the low-echelon party leadership? To the extent that one can generalize from the data reported in this study, we would have to conclude that the cadres of the party in the areas studied are a mixed lot. They are not the "hard core" which Communist organizational theory requires at this level. In countries such as the United States and England, the shortage of party activists makes it possible for almost anyone to move into a low-ranking party position. In countries such as France and Italy, the enormous expansion of the party in the last decade has moved into these low-ranking positions thousands and tens of thousands of unindoctrinated and untrained persons who have been recruited to the party for many different kinds of reasons. Some of these will undoubtedly manifest the qualities of obedience, militance, and that limited tactical imagination which makes for successful assimilation into the party leadership. But many, perhaps most, will continue to maintain a measure of autonomy and extra-party commitment and loyalty which will prevent full assimilation. These half-assimilated and only half-assimilable cadres, along with the rank and file, which manifests these problems to an even greater extent, will always set limits on the freedom of maneuver of the party. A mass party necessarily results in a dilution of the quality of the great bulk of the party membership and low-ranking leadership. The mass of the party thus is available primarily for exoteric goals and tactics; it fulfills the esoteric aims of the party only in the sense that a mass base is denied to any other left-wing movement, and thus the basis for a stable government and politics is undermined.

These unassimilated and half-assimilated elements among the rank and file and the low echelons of the French and Italian parties are in a sense refugees from a society which does not offer them a sense of full membership, and a politics which does not offer them an instrument capable of fighting effectively to attain such a membership. If they are in the Communist Party rather than in a loyal left-wing political movement, it is not because they have positively chosen or are even aware of the esoteric properties of Communism, but simply through the lack of a more satisfactory alternative.

Class and Reliability

If we examine the party from the point of view of the social classes which were represented among our respondents, a number of general points are suggested. The working-class respondents were rarely indoctrinated Communists; and when they were, they were generally party functionaries. The general run of working-class respondents viewed the party in terms of working-class interests, rather than in terms of the party's aims. Thus it is that in situations in which the party goes against working-class interests, as it does in political strikes, the party uses up its credit among the working classes. Contrariwise, so long as the party can represent itself as the most effective vehicle for realizing working-class objectives, it will retain its support among these elements.

While it is probably true that the working-class contingents of the Communist movement are not to be viewed as "hard core" Communists ready for any action ordered by the party, this should not suggest a degree of vulnerability which can be exploited without great effort and resources. When a group is effectively infiltrated by the Communist movement, a serious impairment of communication with the outside world results. For it is the first objective of the party to destroy the organizational and communication network in a target group, and to replace it by its own organizational and communications system. Into this communications system the movement pumps a constant stream of vilification and diabolization of all other authorities, organizations, and channels of communication in its effort to impair and destroy all confidence in the outside.

Thus once a target group has been successfully infiltrated, as is the case with the major part of the French and Italian working classes, effective tactics require first reestablishing trusted channels of communication. It may very well be that the face-to-face agitational form of communication, to borrow from the Communist book, is the only type which can effectively reach the working classes, once they have been effectively enclosed in Communist communication. Communication through the "bourgeois-controlled" mass media or emanating from the church will hardly have any impact among a working class which has viewed capitalism and the church as its enemy for decades. The difficulties involved in breaking through the Communist communications and organizational network are formidable. In the case of many of our respondents, they first became capable of entertaining the idea of defection only after they had been physically removed from the pressures and associations of the party. So long as they had been under these pressures, no oppositional communication could effectively get through. A communications and organizational network must therefore be constructed at the very base by a militant working-class elite, anti-Communist, but dedicated to working-class interests. And such an elite will have to fight innumerable pitched battles against a clever and tenacious enemy, and by virtue of inexhaustible patience and effort unlock the fingers of Communist control one by one and bring the working classes of France and Italy back to the West.

In considering the reliability of the middle-class intellectuals in the party, one has to distinguish clearly between the British-American and French-Italian pattern. In the normal processes of acculturation and socialization in any society there is an inescapable incidence of damage, the consequence of "social friction," so to speak. A large proportion of those who have joined the Communist parties in England and the United States have been "casualties" of these acculturative and socialization processes. No society can completely eliminate these frictions and conflict situations. Hence the Communist movements in England and the United States will always find some individuals whose emotional condition and social situation will render them susceptible. In the United States, with the decline in the rate of immigration and the rapid assimilation of the newer ethnic stocks, and with the wider awareness of emotional illness and the variety of symptoms through which it can manifest itself, the scope of the problem has greatly decreased. Indeed, this decrease in susceptibility may have resulted not only, and not even primarily, from a decline in the incidence of emotional problems of the types described, but rather from the learning process itself. For the periods during which the greatest extent of susceptibility to Communism existed in both England and the United States, even among the emotionally disturbed, were the Popular Front era of the 1930's and the World War II coalition period of the 1940's. In both these periods the destructive and revolutionary character of the party was concealed. Now, with the experience of the Nazi-Soviet Pact, the Cominform, and the Korean War, it is far more difficult even for a neurotic to view the Communist movement as the defender of peace and social justice. Most of the middle-class intellectual neurotics who joined the party did so because it provided them with an opportunity to express destructive and negative impulses in an intellectually and morally satisfying setting. As the movement has been stripped bare of its moral trappings, it no longer satisfies this peculiar combination of needs.

The Communist intellectuals in France and Italy are in most cases solving political rather than emotional problems in the party. They find themselves in societies which are basically fragmented and are caught in the dilemma of whether to identify themselves with the political systems which are unable to solve pressing social problems, or to identify themselves with a movement which is resolved to destroy these systems regardless of means. Since the Communists in France and Italy have become the self-chosen protectors of the poor and the downtrodden, many intellectuals have followed them into the party and into the ranks of the sympathizers. It is on the whole likely that these intellectuals will continue to be attracted to Communism so long as the Communist movement is the most powerful movement on the left. If the Communist hold on the working class and the poor peasantry were broken, the intellectuals would in all likelihood follow them out of the party. This should not be construed as meaning that any special tactics designed to reach the Communist intellectuals in such countries as France and Italy are pointless and unnecessary. Intellectuals who are party members or sympathizers are open to communication from outside the party, and they would appear to be especially vulnerable to information demonstrating the conflict between Communism and intellectual and aesthetic values. However, it would be a mistake to anticipate from such a tactic anything more than the exacerbation of conflicts already present among these intellectuals. They can always escape from these conflicts by stressing the local evils in their own countries, and by closing their eyes to the power orientation of the party and to the purely tactical advocacy by the party of working-class or peasant interests.

The Decline of Ideology

Perhaps the most striking finding as to the differences between the earlier and later generations among our respondents was the decline in the importance of Communist ideology in the processes of recruitment and assimilation. Thus our evidence showed that in the last fifteen or twenty years persons joining the Communist movement have rarely been indoctrinated before joining the party. And, once in the party, the new members are exposed to the ideology under carefully controlled conditions. It comes to them largely in the form of slogans which have to be memorized. Furthermore, the manuals used in this internal party indoctrination are heavily tactical in their emphasis, stressing the central importance of discipline, militance, and activism, rather than of ideals and non-power goals and objectives. Persons leaving the party in this recent period tended to be disillusioned with ideology in general. They tended to become very pragmatic, or completely indifferent, in their political views.

In the first fifteen years of the Communist movement, the pattern was quite different. More of the new recruits to the party had been exposed to the classical Communist writings. Once in the party, the member had substantial freedom in reading and discussing the party literature, as well as non-party materials. The atmosphere of the party was heavily intellectual and ideological, a kind of heady mixture of seminar and prayer. The literature was rich, including the writings of Marx and Engels, non-party philosophical and literary works, and all the writings of Lenin and Stalin and other party theorists. People leaving the party did so more often on an explicit ideological basis. That is, they viewed the party as having deviated from Marxist-Leninist doctrine and, after leaving, formed or joined oppositional movements, based upon what they alleged to be a correct reading of the doctrine.

Thus there appears to have been a decline in the importance of ideology in the Communist movement. The esoteric doctrine has been divided into a part which is eschatological, and a part which is a kind of operating tactical code strictly oriented around party-power considerations. And, in addition, the exoteric mass appeals of the party are essentially negative, and they have in all probability become increasingly so. They derive their strength from a widespread readiness on the part of large numbers of people in certain areas to accept the integral debunking of the established order of things which is characteristic of Communist mass communication. There is very little "idealism" in Communist mass communication; and there is only an "eschatological idealism" in Communist esoteric communication.

It is perhaps not an exaggeration to say that the Communist movement has largely lost its capacity, at least in the West, to inspire and to appeal to idealism. But in this respect it is confronted by the problem which faces all political movements today, a kind of basic ideological sales resistance. In the West the day appears to be past when movements promising emancipation and justice can lift men above their everyday routines into visions of hope and expectations of final solutions. The peoples of Western Europe in particular have been played false too often by ideologies—by liberalism, by nationalism, by socialism, and by Fascism—until now there has developed on a substantial scale a kind of integral disbelief in all ideologies. Given such widespread attitudes of bitterness and disenchantment, particularly among the working classes in such countries as France and Italy, Communist propaganda has a special advantage. For the mass propaganda of Communism plays upon this basic distrust and suspicion, this fundamental impatience with and disbelief in words and political promises. Its mood is that of "Let's have done with all this sham and nonsense." What the Communist movement has to offer in a positive sense is not quite clear, but, given the mood, it does not have to be. There is a stage of bitterness and desperation which seeks for some definitive, some uncompromising, some integral solution without regard to costs. And this stage has been reached on a large scale in France and Italy.

Thus we can by no means conclude from the fact of the

decline of ideology as an appeal of Communism that an ideological vacuum has been created into which the Voice of America or inspirational talks by American leaders can now move with great effect. On the contrary, this spiritual vacuum plays into the hands of Communism, since the only propaganda which it will admit is that which plays upon negativism and cynicism. This widespread mood can be affected only by action, and specifically by action which results in changes in the immediate setting. In other words, there is little value in telling the French workman that the American workman is a free man and in addition has a car and a television set, while the Russian workman is a slave and has neither. He is interested in what the French workman has, and only beneficial changes in his own situation and opportunities will influence his basic political attitudes and loyalties.

This suggests the obvious point that an effective anti-Communist policy will facilitate economic and political changes abroad that will meet the grievances of groups which are now disaffected and susceptible to Communism. To this end, the United States will not only have to export some of its welfare, but must also concern itself with the development of those political and organizational skills which make possible a more equitable distribution of welfare.

If one examines recent trends in American foreign policy in the light of these requirements for an effective anti-Communist policy, there appears to be good cause for uneasiness. There has been a notable decline in imaginativeness and in willingness to experiment and take risks. From brave beginnings in the European Recovery Program, in efforts to stimulate European integration, and in technical assistance programs, we appear to have moved into an era characterized by self-doubt, confusion, impatience, and arrogance. There has been no withdrawal from commitments, but there has been a significant loss of momentum. This is particularly the case in the field of political warfare, where Western resources have never been adequately engaged, and which is one of the few fields of action available to us in which the risks are acceptable.

One may put the problem in these terms: for almost a decade the West has tolerated a situation in which two major members—France and Italy—have been held in a state of political siege by the Communist movement. These two nations are allied with the United States, England, the Scandinavian and the Low Countries, all of which are vivid examples of how pressing and dangerous social problems have been solved within a liberal democratic framework. Surely there is a fund of knowledge and experience here, as well as resources of skill and dedication, which can lift this siege and safeguard the Western tradition in two of its places of origin.

THE SAMPLE OF EX-COMMUNISTS

A. *American Cases*

Social class		Period of joining	
Middle class	34	Before 1935	31
Working class	30	After 1935	33
	—		—
Total	64	*Total*	64

Sex		Period of defection	
Male	53	Before 1935	14
Female	11	1935-1940	19
	—	1941-1946	17
Total	64	1947-	14
			—

Rank			
High echelon	8	*Total*	64
Low echelon	20		
Rank and file	36		
	—		
Total	64		

B. *British Cases*

Social class		Period of joining	
Middle class	23	Before 1935	25
Working class	27	After 1935	25
	—		—
Total	50	*Total*	50

Sex		Period of defection	
Male	42	Before 1935	7
Female	8	1935-1940	13
	—	1941-1946	9
Total	50	1947-	21
			—

Rank			
High echelon	11	*Total*	50
Low echelon	15		
Rank and file	24		
	—		
Total	50		

C. *French Cases*

Social class		Period of joining	
Middle class	24	Before 1935	43
Working class	32	After 1935	13
Total	56	*Total*	56

Sex		Period of defection	
Male	54	Before 1935	23
Female	2	1935-1940	17
		1941-1946	4
Total	56	1947-	12
		Total	56

Rank	
High echelon	23
Low echelon	15
Rank and file	18
Total	56

D. *Italian Cases*

Social class		Period of joining	
Middle class	30	Before 1943	16
Working class	21	After 1943	35
Total	51	*Total*	51

Sex		Period of defection	
Male	48	Before 1935	3
Female	3	1935-1940	1
		1941-1946	3
Total	51	1947-	44
		Total	51

Rank	
High echelon	9
Low echelon	23
Rank and file	19
Total	51

APPENDIX 2

INTERVIEWING GUIDES

A. *Interviewing Guide for Use with Ex-Communists*

This is the version that was used in interviewing the American respondents. It differs only in minor respects from the guide used in the other countries.

1. Would you tell me something about your family? Where did they live when you were a child (city population, type of neighborhood)? Father's occupations, ethnic background, etc.?

2. When (how) did you first develop an interest in political affairs?

3. What were your first (specific) political opinions? About which did you feel strongly? Which did you speak up for? To whom?

4. What was the first political group or action in which you took part?

5. What was your life like just before you became a Communist? How did you feel about it? What was your position in the community?

6. How (specifically) did you happen to join? When?

7. What were the main attractions at the time? Repulsions?

8. How big a step did joining the CP seem to be at the time? How big a step did it seem after you had been a member for a short while?

9. When did you feel that you were pulling your weight in the party?

10. What duties did you have as a new member? Were your special skills used? What kind of training did you receive?

11. Did you know any party leaders?

12. What were the people like, those with whom you had to work? What did you like about them? Dislike? How much awareness did you have of other people?

13. What kind of people were the most popular (respected) among other members?

14. Did people at the top think of rank-and-file members in terms of different types (based on why they joined; i.e., personality types)? What designating words or phrases were used? How did this affect recruitment and assignment policy?

15. Which leaders did you admire? Which dislike?
    (a) What kind of members were chosen to be leaders? What gets people ahead in the movement?

(b) What are the ideal characteristics of the top leaders supposed to be?

16. What changes take place in people as they move up the ladder?

17. Were any special preparations made for visiting officials?

18. Did leaders "pull their rank"? Did they ever try to be "one of the boys"?

19. How easy was it to talk informally to someone one or two ranks above you?

20. Was there any rivalry between cells or other kinds of units? What was the feeling tone at meetings?

21. To what extent do rank-and-file members think of the upper crust (regional) as being essentially very different from themselves? What kinds of differences (e.g., exclusive skills)?

22. Did personal problems of the rank and file attract the help of the leaders, of fellow members?

23. Were there any lonely people in the party? Before, during, and after membership?

24. What was the attitude (or attitudes) of the party or different party members toward your relations (responsibilities, sympathetic ties, etc.) with your family? How did you react to those attitudes?

25. What was the attitude (or attitudes) of the party or different party members toward your (outside) job? How did you feel about those attitudes?

26. Were the sexes more or less equal than in daily American life? In what situations?

27. How was age taken into consideration in terms of status, promotion, special assignments, etc.?

28. What kinds of jobs and skills had the most prestige?

29. What kinds of personal friendships were most common in the party? What was the attitude toward "pals," "social cliques," etc., inside the party?

30. (a) Did you have any special or particular friend in the party? What did you usually talk about? Do together (exchange confidences, have common interests, share in non-party activities)? How did you express your friendship for each other (presents, greeting cards, etc.)? Was there an effort to break up pals and cliques?

(b) How much trust and confidence was there generally among party members?

31. How did being a Communist affect your relations with non-Communists?

32. What was the party attitude toward rest and relaxation, entertainment and recreation?

33. Take a winter week: can you recall what you did for the party . . . how much time was spent, how many events participated in (different types)?
34. What were the direct means of reward for good work in the party? Indirect means?
35. What were the direct means of punishment for poor work? Indirect means?
36. What kinds of decisions were the hardest to accept? To carry out?
37. Was there a "grapevine," a "rumor route"? Did you sometimes know about decisions before you were officially notified? If so, how did it happen?
38. How did the party react to failure of some enterprise? To success?
39. What kinds of events made party members happiest? Saddest?
40. To what extent is hatred of the enemy necessary to maintain devotion?
41. Are certain attitudes toward danger encouraged by top members and certain attitudes frowned upon?
42. Did you take part in bull sessions in the party? How common were they? Among whom? What did you talk about? How often about politics? How often about the ills of capitalism or the USA, the virtues of Communism or the USSR? In what proportion?
43. While you were in the party, what were the kinds of things that made you feel that the party "couldn't miss" in the long run?
44. Why did you leave the party? How did you feel about leaving? Which loyalties went first, last? What changes were there in your broad ideals?
45. Did you have to make new friends, regain old ones, or what, after leaving?
46. What did you feel you gained by leaving the party? Lost?
47. Did you tell your friends you had left?
48. How long before leaving did you have doubts?
49. How did you break the news to the party?
50. Any circumstances of rejoining?
51. Have you taken any part in politics since leaving the CP?
52. Which party do you support now?
53. Which party do you oppose now?
54. What types of people are most likely to join the CP?
55. What are the main reasons for people leaving the CP?
56. How do you think human nature can be changed on the mass level?
57. Any visits to Russia?

58. Did you use a party name?
59. What kind of person would you like to be now?

B. *Interviewing Guide for Use with Psychoanalysts*

1. General Data
   a. Age
   b. Sex
   c. Ethnic origin
   d. Dates of treatment and duration
   e. Symptoms present at beginning of treatment

2. Life History
   a. Family structure
      (1) siblings—age and sex
      (2) family relationship: mother-father, sibling-parents, father-patient, mother-patient, siblings-patient
      (3) data on father—age at patient's birth, occupational status, social status, religious affiliation and activity, political ideology
      (4) data on mother (same as for father)
      (5) other primary relationships (nurse, grandparents, etc.)
   b. Infancy and adolescence
      (1) early disciplines (nursing, weaning, toilet training, infantile masturbation)
      (2) early extra-family adjustments—friendships, schooling, religious experience
   c. Adulthood
      (1) Later educational and religious experience—occupational history
      (2) Sexual and marital experience. Pre-marital sexuality. Marital adjustment, relations to children, if any
      (3) Group affiliations, social, civic, and recreational activities. Quality of friendships
   d. Significant experiences or trauma not previously mentioned

3. Patient's Self-picture
   a. Variety of "roles" played
   b. Goals, aspirations, ideals; values (group-linked?)

    c. Feelings of control over environment; areas of restriction; areas of effectiveness (areas of maximum security and insecurity)

4. Analyst's Picture of Patient's Character
    a. Against what was the patient defending himself?
    b. Characteristic defenses, escapes, psychological mechanisms
    c. Characteristic drives, i.e., emotional parasitism, domination, withdrawal—sado-masochistic trends, etc. (optional)
    d. Attitudes toward obligations, authority, conventionality

5. Political Attitudes and Behavior of Patient
    a. Political background
        (1) time and occasion of admission to party
        (2) nature of participation—kinds of activities, etc.
        (3) significant changes in living habits, social relationships, self-picture
        (4) if withdrawn from party—occasion and `causes of withdrawal
    b. Political attention
        (1) relative attention to evils of status quo vs. virtues of utopia
        (2) relative emphasis on impersonal ideological analysis vs. individual role pressures
        (3) relative emphasis on "I" vs. "we" references

6. Psychological function of Communist affiliation and attitudes

What is the function of CP membership for the personality structure of the patient?

7. Alternatives

Is there any reason why the same function could not have been satisfied in a different group affiliation or in an entirely different manner?

8. If you were describing this patient, what would you say was the unique characteristic or set of characteristics in his psychological structure? What is the essence? the crux? What makes him tick?

9. Analyst's Data
    a. Per cent of (long-term) patients whose political attitudes were known

b. Per cent of (a) who had stable loyalties (in analysis)
c. Per cent of (a, b) conservative, liberal, radical (right, left)
d. Estimated number of patients
e. Analytic group identification

10. Have you noticed anything uniform about your "political" patients?

11. What is unique or different about this case (if anything) in comparison with your other cases?

INDEX

Abrams, Mark, 277
Abyssinian War, 241, 262
American Communist Party, *see* Communist parties, American
American politics, models, 3-4; types of politicians, 15-17. *See also* democratic political models
anti-Fascism (anti-Fascists), 102, 103, 107, 123, 127, 197-201, 215, 226, 240, 241, 244, 262-63, 347; as propaganda version of Communism, 70, 71, 77. *See also* Fascism
Aragon, Louis, 323
assimilation into Communist movement, 67, 73-74, 93-94, 108-9, 141-42, 232, 242, 260, 308-9; three stages, 297-98
Atlantic Pact, 309

Bakunin, Mikhail, 12; *The Revolutionist*, 12
Berdyaev, Nicolas, 184
Bernal, J. D., 315, 316, 318
Bettelheim, Bruno, 194
Blanquist movement, 11
Blumenstock, Dorothy, 183, 184
bohemianism, 156, 291-92, 307, 325
Bolshevik Party, *see* Bolshevism
Bolshevik Revolution, *see* Russian Revolution of 1917
Bolshevism (Bolsheviks), 22-24, 29ff., 65, 104, 110, 133, 313, 384. *See also* Russian Revolution of 1917
Bolshevization of party, *see* Stalinization of party
Borkenau, Franz, 174, 183, 184
Brest-Litovsk, 30
Britain, *see* Communist parties, British; Communists, characteristics of, ethnic; Labor Party; moderate left movements, British; trade unions, in Britain
British Communist Party, *see* Communist parties, British
Browder, Earl, 122, 125, 140, 144
Bruner, Jerome, 204
Bukharin, Nicolai I., 31, 102

Burns, Emile, 316

Cacchione, Peter V., 125
Cahiers du Bolshèvisme, 14
Cahiers du Communisme, 14
Campbell, Johnny, 145
Capital, Das, see Marx
Catholic Church (Catholicism), 3-4, 131, 133, 155, 264, 301, 308, 344, 347, 360, 387-88, 390; anti-Communist action in Italy, 311-13
Centers, Richard, 326
Central Committee members, France, Italy, US, study of, 190 ff., 220-21, 228
Child, Irvin L., 204
Chinese Communist Party, *see* Communist parties, Chinese
Christian Church in Western Europe, 387-88. *See also* Catholic Church
Christian Democratic Party (Italy), 131, 366
Clark, Thomas C., 201-2
Cominform, 67, 133, 226, 227, 234, 309, 318, 332, 394
Cominform periodical, *see For a Lasting Peace, For a People's Democracy*
Comintern, 110, 133
Communist, The, 14, 29, 42, 55
Communist communication system, exoteric (mass) and esoteric (inner) media, 65-68, 99-104, 177, 232, 369, 379, 385, 393-94, 397; general characteristics, 68-74; style, 74-76; properties of self, 76-81; thesaurus, 81-84; properties of antagonist, 84-88; thesaurus, 88-93
Communist front organizations, 224-25, 301, 390-91
Communist International, 174, 347; *Blueprint for World Conquest,* 46
Communist militant, exoteric (outer party) model, 5; esoteric (inner party) model, 5-6, 13-14, 272; explicitness, 14-15; exclusiveness, 15; ends and means, 15, 17-20,